HEALTH INSURANCE

HEALTH INSURANCE

Michael A. Morrisey, Ph.D.

Health Administration Press, Chicago, Illinois
AUPHA Press, Washington, DC

AUPHA
HAP

Your board, staff, or clients may also benefit from this book's insight. For more information on quantity discounts, contact the Health Administration Press Marketing Manager at (312) 424-9470.

This publication is intended to provide accurate and authoritative information in regard to the subject matter covered. It is sold, or otherwise provided, with the understanding that the publisher is not engaged in rendering professional services. If professional advice or other expert assistance is required, the services of a competent professional should be sought.

The statements and opinions contained in this book are strictly those of the author(s) and do not represent the official positions of the American College of Healthcare Executives, of the Foundation of the American College of Healthcare Executives, or of the Association of University Programs in Health Administration.

Library of Congress Cataloging-in-Publication Data

Morrisey, Michael A.
  Health insurance / Michael A. Morrisey.
     p. ; cm.
  Includes bibliographical references and index.
  ISBN 978-1-56793-282-9 (alk. paper)
  1. Insurance, Health—United States. I. Title.
  [DNLM: 1. Insurance, Health—economics—United States. W 275 AA1 M8645h
     2007]
  HG9396.M6686 2007
  368.38'200973—dc22

                              2007021732

The paper used in this publication meets the minimum requirements of American National Standard for Information Sciences-Permanence of Paper for Printed Library Materials, ANSI Z39.48-1984.™

Project manager: Putman Productions, LLC; Cover design: Chris Underdown

Health Administration Press
A division of the Foundation
   of the American College of
   Healthcare Executives
One North Franklin Street
Suite 1700
Chicago, IL 60606-3529
(312) 424-2800

Association of University Programs
   in Health Administration
2000 14th Street North
Suite 780
Arlington, VA 22201
(703) 894-0940

To Elaine

BRIEF CONTENTS

CONTENTS

PREFACE

This text is the result of 18 years of teaching a course in health insurance and managed care to both master's and doctoral students. The course has been presented in a variety of formats: large lectures of 50 to 70 students, small discussion sections of 10 to 15 students, weekend programs for middle managers, and executive education programs for more senior health professionals. In every case, the principal complaint has been the lack of a textbook.

No textbook existed—perhaps, for good reason. Throughout these years of teaching, the course syllabus consisted of readings from the broad health economics, health services, and clinical research literatures. While the key concepts remained constant, the empirical literature advanced at an impressive pace. Easily 20 percent of the readings on the rather extensive syllabus changed each year. No one wants to write a textbook when the state of empirical knowledge is in such a state of flux. However, in the last few years, much of the research, while methodologically more sophisticated, has confirmed, refined, and amplified earlier work, at least in several important areas. So, it is time for a textbook.

This book is designed for master's students in health administration and health policy programs. It is also useful as a foundation text in doctoral health services research and health economics programs. Courses in those programs, of course, would supplement this text with original research material. The book should also be of use to researchers in the field inasmuch as it takes a state-of-the-research approach to describing what is known about health insurance in the United States.

The programs in which I teach have always regarded this course as essentially a second course in health economics. A first health economics course is a prerequisite, as is a biostatistics or quantitative methods course that covers regression analysis. However, you will find no comparative statistics in the text, and I resort to graphical presentations of economic concepts less than a half-dozen times. Similarly, there are no direct discussions of econometric techniques. What discussion there is of statistical methods is made in passing as I present the findings of particular studies. The underlying economics and statistics are tools used here to organize thinking and to appreciate the difficulties of obtaining estimates of the magnitudes of the effects of managerial and policy decisions.

This text presents a rigorous but intuitive examination of the issues raised by insurance and how the market and the government have dealt with these issues. The emphasis is on understanding the underlying problems from an economics perspective and then applying the empirical literature to provide insight into the impact and effectiveness of the solutions. When the evidence is equivocal, that is made clear in the text. As a result, this is not a text for those interested in the day-to-day operations of insurers. Rather, the perspective is that of one looking in from the outside, trying to understand the role that private health insurance plays in the United States.

This emphasis on intuitive understanding is important to success. The vast majority of students will not go on to be researchers, actuaries, or even insurance executives. They will buy insurance for their families and worry about coverage for their employees. Most will work as healthcare providers or in organizations that provide healthcare; they will be concerned about how they are paid by private and public insurers. As citizens, policymakers, and those in a position to influence policymakers, they will want to understand how innovations in insurance delivery, in government policy, and in healthcare reform will affect them. An intuitive understanding of the problems and solutions and a general appreciation for what we know empirically will allow them to make more-informed decisions and to cast a much more critical eye on proposed solutions.

The text begins with a history of the development of health insurance in the United States and the theory of demand of insurance. It then works through the classic insurance problems of adverse selection and moral hazard. It examines managed care and the purchasing of health services, as well as the large role played by employer-sponsored health insurance, and then moves on to insurance regulation and the Medicare and Medicaid programs. The early chapters identify why somewhat abstract concepts are important to current events by referencing discussions in later chapters. The later chapters then provide cross-references back to the discussion of the underlying insurance concepts.

In all instances, the emphasis is on private insurance and insurance markets. Medicare and Medicaid are described in some detail, but this is primarily for setting the stage for discussions of private supplemental coverage in the case of Medicare and crowd-out and long-term care insurance in the case of Medicaid. Many detailed references on these major government programs are available to the interested reader; there is little systematic material on the private insurance industry.

Pedagogically, most chapters can be presented in a single 75-minute class period. Chapters 9 and 11 are probable exceptions, since they introduce issues of competition, antitrust, and related materials that typically are new to most students. Chapter 1 usually takes two periods as well, given the administrative issues that take up part of the first class period.

Each chapter ends with a series of questions for class discussion. These questions could easily be used as take-home assignments, but it is important that they also be discussed or debated in class because there are no necessarily right or wrong answers. The questions serve three purposes: (1) they may call for the application of the concepts developed in the chapter; (2) they may introduce the next chapter; and/or (3) they may require students to recall key concepts from earlier chapters that have a clear application to the current material.

PowerPoint® slides to assist in teaching the course are located in a secure area on the Health Administration Press (HAP) web site and are available to adopters of this book. For access information, e-mail hap1@ache.org.

Throughout the book, I have avoided including discussions or analyses of current state or federal reform initiatives. The proposals change rapidly and are likely to be out of date by the time the text is used in the classroom. However, if the material in the text has been mastered, students will be in a position to knowledgeably discuss whatever proposals are currently being proposed.

I typically invite one guest speaker each term, usually a local health insurance executive, a health benefits consultant, or a corporate benefits manager. With this text, I hope to be able to bring in more guest speakers, such as representatives from the state insurance commissioner's office and the Medicaid agency, as well as benefits managers from major employers.

Acknowledgments

This effort owes a debt of thanks to many people. First are the students over the last 18 years who raised provocative questions and alternative explanations and who offered suggestions for improvement each term. I am particularly grateful to my fall 2006 class, who pilot-tested the various chapters and offered written critiques of each. My department chair, Peter Ginter, provided enormous support and advice on textbook writing. He and my dean, Max Michael, were gracious in allowing me a sabbatical to pursue much of the writing. Stephen Mennemeyer foolishly agreed to teach this course while I was away and has my undying thanks. The folks in Wallingford, UK, are also owed thanks. While I was on sabbatical, they took me in, made me truly feel part of the community, and prompted many discussions of the U.S. and British healthcare systems from which this text has benefited.

Janet Davis, the acquisitions editor at Health Administration Press, made the editing and production process transparent and much easier than I had any right to expect. I have had considerable experience with copy editors at academic journals, not all of it pleasant! In contrast, Mary Monner is an exceptional copy editor. Her light hand significantly improved the text, and her concern over inadvertently changing the meaning of the discussion was greatly appreciated. Victoria Putman and her team did a superb job of rendering the tables and the graphs, often from rough, hand-drawn figures, and of preparing the page layout.

Finally, thanks are due to my wife Elaine, who has been ever encouraging of this project and who read and commented on every chapter. As was said in the dedication of a dissertation long ago, may profits always be hers.

AN INTRODUCTION

HISTORY OF HEALTH INSURANCE IN THE UNITED STATES

Health insurance as we generally think of it in the United States began with the Great Depression in the 1930s. In this chapter, we review the history of health insurance and demonstrate how that history is linked to current health insurance developments. Predating private health insurance were efforts at government-sponsored coverage for workplace injury. The Great Depression led hospitals and then physicians to implement forms of insurance as means to assure payment for services. Ironically, conventional insurance and managed care were developed at this same time. The advent of World War II, the growth of the labor movement, and the federal tax code all fostered the growth of employer-sponsored coverage. Medicare was introduced in 1965 to provide coverage to older citizens; it mimicked the private coverage common at the time. Commercial insurers aggressively competed with others by offering lower premiums to larger employers, based on their lower claims experience. Government preemption of state insurance laws led to dramatic growth in self-insured employer plans. The 1980s saw the development of managed care, prompted by rapidly increasing healthcare costs and the emergence of self-insured employer plans. Managed care's ability to selectively contract revolutionized healthcare markets by introducing price competition and led to a backlash against managed care. Currently, healthcare costs are again rising rapidly, and efforts are underway to encourage insured individuals to pay more out-of-pocket in an effort to contain costs.

Prehistory: Workers' Compensation

At the turn of the century in 1900, Teddy Roosevelt was president, and the United States was entering what came to be known as the Progressive Era. Roosevelt championed a series of antitrust enforcement efforts designed to reduce the influence of manufacturing, transportation, and oil firms that had grown large during the Industrial Revolution. Women's suffrage was seriously debated. At the state level, there were efforts to shorten the workweek, limit child labor, and deal with workplace injury.

Under common law, employers were liable for injuries that occurred at their facilities if the employer was negligent. Employers had three defenses against negligence claims. First, they could argue that the worker had assumed the risk as part of the employment contract. Second, they could argue that the injury was caused by the negligent acts of a coworker rather than those of the employer. Third, they could argue that the worker was at least partially at fault. Injuries were common, and court cases seeking to determine negligence and obtain awards for damages were common. Fishback and Kantor (2000) argued that state workers' compensation laws arose because workers' rights advocates saw such reforms as a means of shifting the costs of workplace injury to the employer. Employers saw the reforms as a way to reduce the legal costs associated with negligence claims and to increase the payments to injured workers while at the same time reducing overall costs.

Between 1910 and 1915, some 32 states enacted workers' compensation insurance. Under these programs, employers accepted full liability for workplace injuries and could buy insurance coverage through their state. If employers purchased workers' compensation insurance, they retained all three legal defenses against negligence. However, if they did not buy coverage, they were denied these defenses.

Organized medicine supported the workers' compensation legislation apparently under the view that injured workers would go to their family doctor for care and the doctor would be paid by the workers' compensation fund. Instead, however, employers began to directly retain and sometimes employ physicians to provide care. This followed the model of some firm-specific clinics in the mining and lumber industries, notably in the states of Minnesota and Washington, respectively (Starr 1982). As a result, the majority of local physicians saw a reduction in the demand for their services. Those who had employer contracts did better, of course.

All of this is relevant because it affected the design of subsequent health insurance plans. Numbers (1979) and Starr (1982) described the political dynamics. In the period leading up to and following World War I, there were a number of state initiatives for compulsory health insurance based on the workers' compensation model. One plan, promoted by the American Association of Labor Legislation, called for coverage of all manual laborers with income of less than $100 per month for medical bills and lost income. There were to be compulsory contributions from the employee, the employer, and the state government. Those who were not in a covered group could join voluntarily.

> *Compulsory health insurance is . . . "Un-American, unsafe, uneconomic, unscientific, unfair, unscrupulous legislation supported by paid professional philanthropists, busybody social workers, misguided clergymen, and hysterical women."*
>
> *—Brooklyn physician in 1919 symposium on compulsory health insurance (Numbers 1979, p. 181)*

Between 1916 and 1919, 16 states considered such legislation; none adopted it. Employers tended to oppose this legislation because, unlike workers' compensation, it didn't have any offsetting reduction in costs. Labor unions had mixed views. Samuel Gompers, the founder of the American Federation of Labor (AFL), was opposed. He believed that workers knew how to spend their money and that it was the role of the union to get them more money to spend. The American Medical Association (AMA) officially favored this legislation in 1915 but opposed it by 1920, arguing that the insurance interfered with the doctor-patient relationship. Indeed, the experience with workers' compensation suggested as much. Physician opposition could be intense.

The Great Depression

Blue Cross

The Great Depression began in October 1929 and as fans of the movie *Ferris Bueller's Day Off* well know, was caused by escalating international rounds of tariff increases that reduced worldwide demand for goods and services. In the United States, the Hawley-Smoot Tariff raised import taxes on agricultural commodities to 49 percent. Students of Friedman and Schwartz (1963) will also know that an extraordinarily tight money supply leading to the collapse of the banking sector was the other major cause.

Local hospitals were affected by the Depression like other firms. Ronald Numbers (1979) reported that between 1929 and 1930 Baylor University Hospital, then in Dallas Texas, saw its receipts drop from $236 to $59 per patient. Occupancy rates dropped from 71.3 to 64.1 percent, and contributions were down by two-thirds. Charity care, in contrast, was up 400 percent.

Justin Kimble, the administrator of Baylor University Hospital, devised a means for people to pay for hospital care. He enrolled 1,250 Dallas public schoolteachers into the Baylor Plan. For 50 cents a month, he promised to provide 21 days of care in his hospital. Because of AMA opposition to insurance plans, the plan only covered the hospital, not physicians' services.

The model spread to other hospitals. In 1932 a plan was established in Sacramento, California. However, unlike the Baylor plan, which covered services at only a single hospital, the Sacramento plan covered services at any hospital in the community. By 1933, 26 such "hospital service plans" were in operation.

Local hospitals turned to their trade association to provide guidance in establishing hospital service plans. They were called such because the participating hospitals agreed to provide the services regardless of reimbursement from the plan. The American Hospital Association (AHA) established its Committee on Hospital Service in 1933 and began approving plans. This committee became the AHA Hospital Service Plan Commission in 1936 and the AHA Blue Cross Commission in 1946. The criteria for approval included that the plans were nonprofit, were designed to improve public welfare, had dignified promotion, covered hospital charges only, and allowed for a free choice of physicians (MacIntyre 1962). In 1937 the AHA added an additional criterion—no competition among plans. This meant that the Blue Cross Commission granted exclusive geographic market areas to each approved plan. Even today, each Blue Cross plan has an exclusive market area.

In today's terms, we might think of the original Baylor single-hospital plan as a preferred provider organization. Subscribers had hospital coverage but only if they used the single hospital in the network. This gave consumers a financial incentive to choose one hospital over another. In fact, other hospitals in the Dallas area soon developed their own hospital service benefit plans (Starr 1982). In contrast, the all-hospital plans did not pit one local hospital against another, which meant that patients benefited little financially from shopping for inpatient services among hospitals.

> Single-hospital plans resulted in: ". . . competition among hospitals and interference with the subscriber's freedom of choice and physician's prerogatives in the care of patients."
>
> —Rufus Rorem, director of the AHA Blue Cross Commission (Starr 1982, p. 297)

> As the Depression continued, physicians became more tolerant of hospital insurance: "Hospital services plans reduce for the patient any financial worry which so frequently retards recovery. Nor is it too crass to take cognizance of the fact that the patient without a hospital bill to pay can more readily meet the expense of medical fees."
>
> —Carl Vohs, physician at AMA convention in 1937 (Cunningham and Cunningham 1997, p. 34)

Most states viewed the new hospital service plans as the prepayment of hospital services, rather than as insurance. In 1933, however, the New York state insurance commissioner determined that they should be viewed as insurance. The logic was clear. The plans collected payments in advance and promised to provide care at some future date, not unlike life or casualty insurance. The upshot of this was that the new health plans were required to comply with existing insurance laws; particularly, they had to have reserves to meet future claims. The service benefit plans argued that their "reserves" were their ability to provide care, that it was the bricks and mortar and staff, not money in the bank, that was the assurance that care would be available when needed. The state legislature was called on to resolve the dispute, and it created special enabling legislation that specified that these service benefit plans—that is, these Blue Cross plans—would be nonprofit, and exempt from reserve requirements and state premium taxes. The insurance commissioner would review their rates, and because the reserves were the hospitals themselves, the majority of the board would be comprised of the directors of the participating hospitals. By 1939, 25 states had such enabling legislation.

Today Blue Cross (and Blue Shield) plans exist in most states under enabling legislation. This is why they sometimes must go to the state legislature to add a line of business, such as life insurance, or to convert from a nonprofit to a for-profit status.

Blue Shield

The development of Blue Shield plans mirrors that of Blue Cross. The first medical service plan, the California Physicians' Service, was established in 1939. The plans had two key features. First, they required free choice of physician, and second, they were indemnity rather than service benefit plans. This meant that the plans paid the patient a dollar amount for each covered event; the patient, in turn, was responsible for paying the physician. This is much like the AFLAC® plans of today. The AMA began approving plans in 1939 and followed the model established by the hospitals with Blue Cross.

Commercial Insurance

Commercial life, casualty, and maritime insurance had long existed. However, health was regarded as uninsurable because hazards had to be both definite and measurable. Health was neither. The problem with offering a policy that paid when one was "sick" was that everyone had an incentive to declare themselves sick once they had coverage. When the hospital service plans became popular, the commercial insurers found a way to resolve the problem. They didn't offer "health" insurance; they offered hospitalization coverage. An admission to a hospital was a definite event, determined by a physician. In 1934 commercial carriers began offering hospital coverage. Initially, they did not cover physician coverage, but they did offer *surgical* coverage, beginning in 1938. They did so because surgeries were definite events. Both types of plans provided indemnity coverage. This made the loss in a covered event measurable, based on the schedule of agreed payments per event. The indemnity coverage also avoided provider concerns that the insurer would contract directly with selected hospitals and physicians.

Prepaid Group Practice

Prepaid group practice was the forerunner of managed care. Like Blue Cross, the plans began in 1929 in response to the Great Depression. Kessel (1959) provided a vivid discussion of the early history. The Ross-Loos Clinic in Los Angeles was among the first prepaid group practices, although there were some earlier plans in Virginia, Minnesota, and Tacoma, Washington, and as early as 1905 and 1909, respectively (MacIntyre 1962, pp. 117–18). The clinic provided prepaid care to the two thousand workers and their families of the Los Angeles Department of Water and Power. The department contracted with the clinic to provide employees with comprehensive care. In response to this action, the founders of the Ross-Loos Clinic were expelled from the county medical society. This was a serious penalty because hospital bylaws required medical staff members to be members in good standing of the local medical society. Lack of medical society membership meant that hospital access was denied.

Such physician opposition to prepaid group practice was common. Dr. Michael Shadid and the Elk Grove, Oklahoma, Farmers Union created a prepaid health plan enrolling six thousand residents of Elk Grove for $50 per year. The state medical society opposed the plan, attempted to deprive Shadid of his license to practice, expelled him from the medical society, and kept other physicians who were willing to practice with him out of Oklahoma through licensure denials.

In 1933 Dr. Sidney Garfield established the Kaiser Foundation Health Plan in California. He was charged with unprofessional conduct, and the state board of medical examiners suspended his license to practice. This ruling was overturned by the courts. Similar actions were directed against group practice plans in Milwaukee, Chicago, and Seattle. Plan physicians were denied membership in their local medical societies and denied access to hospitals.

As a result of being denied access to hospitals, the early prepaid plans were forced to build and use their own hospitals. Today's health maintenance organizations (HMOs) that own their own hospitals, plans such as Kaiser-Permanente and Group Health Cooperative of Puget Sound, may continue to operate their own facilities for reasons of control and efficiency, but originally, they did so because it was the only means of obtaining ongoing access to hospitals.

In 1937 Group Health in Washington, D.C. was a nonprofit cooperative of Federal Home Loan Bank employees. It had salaried physicians. The AMA and the local medical society engaged in reprisals against participating physicians, prevented consultations and referrals, and persuaded all hospitals to refuse privileges. In 1938 the Justice Department charged the AMA under the Sherman Antitrust Act. The Supreme Court held against the AMA in 1943. Opposition continued, however (see Box 1-1). Group Health Cooperative filed an antitrust suit against the King County (Washington) medical society and won a state supreme court decision in 1951 (McCaffree and McCaffree 2001). As late as 1959, Kaiser physicians were still excluded from the San Francisco Medical Society (Kessel 1959).

BOX 1-1

Why Was Medicine So Opposed to Prepaid Group Practice?

Reuben Kessel (1959) argued that the opposition to prepaid group practice stemmed from the threat that such plans posed to physicians' incomes. At that time, physicians used a "sliding fee schedule" to charge patients. Patients with a greater ability to pay were charged a higher price, and those with fewer resources paid less. Physicians argued that this was a mechanism to provide care to those who couldn't afford to pay. While this may have been true, Kessel argues that it was simple price discrimination designed to maximize profits. Prepaid practice posed a threat because it could undercut the price paid by higher-income patients, thereby taking away substantial profits.

More formally, see Figure A. This is a Janus diagram with two back-to-back physician service market diagrams. To keep the graphics simple, assume the marginal cost (MC) of physician services is constant and identical in each market—thus, the horizontal MC curve. Panel A is the more affluent market, characterized by a greater willingness to pay and a more inelastic demand curve D_A. The marginal revenue associated with these patients is MR_A. The profit-maximizing price charged to them is P_A. Panel B reflects a less-affluent market. Here, too, profit maximization requires setting marginal revenue (MR_B in this case) equal to MC and selling that

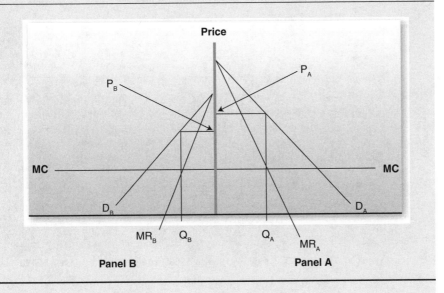

FIGURE A
Economics of Price Discrimination

Continued

Box 1-1
Continued

quantity in the less-affluent market at price P_B. The advent of a prepaid group practice would disproportionately attract people from Panel A, who have more to save financially by leaving their current doctor and joining the new group practice plan. Physicians might argue (and did) that they had patients who couldn't even afford to pay a price equal to MC and that the physicians, nonetheless, provided the patients with care, incurring a loss on each. Regardless of the veracity of these claims, the people in Panel A (as well as those in Panel B, as drawn here) were paying more than the cost of care, and these are the people who were most likely to abandon their physicians for the prepaid plan. Thus, regardless of whether the physicians spent their profits on themselves or on the poor, prepaid group practice posed a serious threat.

Early Growth of Health Insurance: The 1940s and 1950s

Private health insurance grew rapidly during the 1940s and 1950s, and obtaining accurate measures of the extent of coverage is difficult. Figure 1-1 shows the percentage of the U.S. population with some sort of health insurance coverage from 1940 through 1985. Only 9 percent of the population had insurance on the eve of World War II. That percentage had more than doubled to nearly 23 percent by the end of the war. It more than doubled again by 1950 and was close to 70 percent by 1960.

FIGURE 1-1

Percentage of U.S. Population with Some Form of Private Health Insurance, 1940–1985

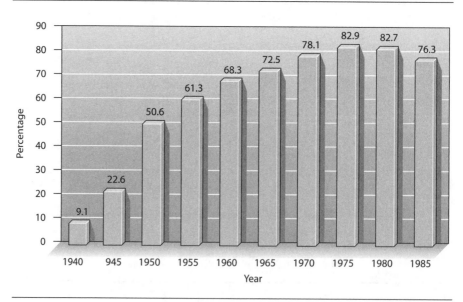

SOURCE: Data from Health Insurance Association of America (1990).

Three reasons are usually given for this rapid growth. The first is the imposition of wage and price controls during World War II. The United States entered the war in December 1941. As men volunteered and were drafted into the armed forces, the domestic economy was stressed by increased demand for war material. Through its National War Labor Board, the Franklin Roosevelt administration set wages in each industry, beginning in 1942. Firms, competing for labor, attracted many women into the labor market for the first time. In addition, the Labor Board determined that health insurance was not to be considered a wage. This meant that one way firms could complete for scarce labor was to offer health insurance to their employees.

A second reason for the rapid growth in health insurance was the expansion of organized labor over this period. Union influence on health insurance stemmed in part from the 1947 Taft-Hartley Act, which defined health insurance as a condition of employment and, therefore, a subject for collective bargaining.

The third reason for the rapid growth in health insurance was the treatment of health insurance in the federal tax code. The tax code was actually silent on whether employer-sponsored health insurance was to be considered income subject to federal income taxation. As Thomasson (2003) noted, in 1943 the Internal Revenue Service issued a private ruling holding that employer-provided health insurance benefits were not subject to federal income taxation. Contradictory private rulings emerged over the 1940s and early 1950s, prompting Congress to enact legislation in 1954 that exempted employer-sponsored health insurance from federal income taxation. As we will discuss in later chapters, this tax exclusion is a key reason why the U.S. health insurance market looks the way it does. The tax code effectively encourages employees and their employers to shift compensation toward untaxed health insurance and away from taxed money income. This tax subsidy is a big deal. Tom Seldon and Brad Gray (2006) estimated that the value of the federal and state tax-subsidy was $208.6 billion in 2006. To put this in context, total Medicare expenditures in 2005 were $330 billion (Boards of Trustees, Federal Hospital and Insurance and Federal Supplementary Medical Insurance Trust Funds 2006), so the tax subsidy for private health insurance approaches two-thirds of current federal spending on the Medicare program.

In the insurance industry, the 1940s and 1950s saw the AHA's Blue Cross Commission spun off from the AHA and the creation of the Blue Cross Association in 1960; it merged with Blue Shield in 1977 to form the Blue Cross and Blue Shield Association (Cunningham and Cunningham 1997). Heretofore, Blue Cross and Blue Shield plans had dominated the health insurance markets; however, in the 1950s, commercial insurers became much more formidable players and consistently had more total subscribers than did the

Blue Cross and Blue Shield plans after 1954 (Health Insurance Association of America 1990).

> *We fought tooth and nail. To the last gasp. But then you get to the point where unions are pulling out because they know damn well their experience is better. We would have lost the telephone company. We would have lost the gas company. We would have lost—we did lose—the state employees, 30,000 of them, because we were not experience rating.*
>
> —*William McNary, CEO, Blue Cross of Michigan (Cunningham and Cunningham 1997, p. 100)*

Experience Rating, Medicare, Medicaid, and ERISA: The 1960s and 1970s

The insurance functions of Blue Cross and Blue Shield plans were pretty simple in their early years. The plans engaged in community rating. This simply meant that all of the subscribers of a plan were in one large risk pool. Premiums were determined essentially by projecting the growth of claims and dividing by the number of subscribers. Commercial insurers began to challenge this in the 1950s through experience rating, and by the 1960s, experience rating had driven out community rating.

Suppose an insurer is able to identify a group of people who are reasonably healthy and, therefore, low utilizers of care, relative to others. Teachers or bank employees may be good examples. The insurer could approach these groups and promise them an insurance premium that reflected their likely lower claims experience. This is experience rating. While community-rated plans, such as Blue Cross, include low-, medium-, and high-cost subscribers, the experience-rated plan disproportionately includes low-cost subscribers. As a result, it can provide the same coverage at a lower premium and still make money. Moreover, the community-rated plan will experience cost increases simply because it loses its low-cost subscribers.

This was the commercial insurers' approach. They offered lower premiums to groups with low claims experience. Blue Cross and Blue Shield were forced to switch from community rating or face a future in which they were the insurer of only the highest-cost subscribers. In the 1960s, the last Blue Cross plan gave up community rating.

The 1960s saw the enactment of the Medicare and Medicaid programs, during the Lyndon Johnson administration. Medicare provided coverage for hospital and physician services to those over age 65 who were covered by Social Security. With the lens of today's private health insurance plans, Medicare looks strange. This is because, as Congress cast about for an insurance model to follow, it focused on the Blue Cross and Blue Shield models of the time. It created separate hospital (Part A) and physician (Part B) coverage that reflected the nature of the coverage under each type of plan. It also followed Blue Cross and Blue Shield in paying hospitals based on costs and physicians based on their allowable charges.

Medicaid is a joint federal-state program designed to provide coverage to the poor. It was essentially an expansion of the 1960 Kerr-Mills Act. The federal government specified the nature of coverage and eligibility across broad parameters, but allowed the states considerable flexibility in deciding how much of each type of service was to be covered and what income threshold was to be used for eligibility. The federal contribution was pegged to the relative poverty in a state and ranged from 50 percent in the most affluent states to 83 percent in the poorest.

The key event in the 1970s with respect to private health insurance actually was triggered in December 1963, when the Studebaker Corporation closed its U.S. automobile plant in South Bend, Indiana, and left an underfunded pension plan. Congress responded to this and other pension concerns in 1974 with the Employee Retirement Income Security Act (ERISA). This large piece of legislation was designed to protect defined benefit pension plans. It did this largely by providing tax incentives to encourage employers to prefund their pension plans and by requiring participating pension plans to contribute to a government-affiliated reinsurance fund to bail out future pension plan defaults. The legislation also included a relative handful of provisions dealing with "welfare plans"—that is, health insurance plans.

Employer health insurance plans that were self-insured under the terms of ERISA were subject to the federal ERISA statute and not subject to state insurance regulation. Large employers had argued that they often had plants in several states and that trying to provide consistent and uniform coverage was made difficult by the differing insurance regulations that the states imposed. Moreover, efforts to self-insure their workers were hampered by state insurance regulations that were not designed for such efforts. Under ERISA, self-insured plans were not subject to state insurance regulations dealing with reserves or coverage requirements, and they were not subject to state premium taxes.

ERISA resulted in a quiet revolution in the health insurance industry. Heretofore, large firms were usually experience-rated through an insurer. This meant, in essence, that a firm was responsible for its own claims experience and paid the insurer to administer the plan. If such a plan was "fully credible," meaning that its premiums were based solely on its own claims experience, the move to self-insurance was a no-brainer. The firm bore the same claims risk, but now it could shop for a less costly claims administrator, or it could undertake those activities itself and, in the process, avoid state premium taxes of 2 to 4 percent. Moreover, somewhat smaller firms could incur the claims risk over some range of losses and buy stoploss coverage for big individual claims or for aggregate claims that exceeded some threshold. Medium- and even small-sized firms could be self-insured.

These events happened at the same time that mainframe computer processing was rapidly dropping in price. In the 1960s, large conventional insurers had comparative advantages in both bearing claims risk and in claims processing. They lost both in the 1970s. ERISA meant that there was potential entry into the risk-bearing segment of the business. Efforts to extract more than competitive returns from this segment would lead to the entry of many self-insured employers providing their own coverage. The advent of low-cost mainframe computing meant that the claims-processing segment was also competitive. If the large insurers attempted to charge more than competitive processing fees, new providers would appear and undercut them. Indeed, a new industry emerged—third-party administrators (TPAs) that handled the claims processing of self-insured firms. Insurers opened new lines of business as well, such as ASOs (administrative services only). Through these lines, they also provided claims-processing services to self-insured firms. By 2001, 50 percent of insured workers were in a self-insured plan (Gabel, Jensen, and Hawkins 2003).

Ironically, ERISA also spurred more state insurance regulation. Prior to 1974, there were virtually no state insurance coverage mandates (Jensen and Morrisey 1999a). However, by the close of 2005, there were over 1,800 individual insurance mandates (Council for Affordable Health Insurance 2006). Providers and concerned citizens often ask the state legislature to require insurance companies operating in the state to include specific coverage. They may, for example, demand that *in vitro* fertilization be covered like other procedures. In the period prior to ERISA, proponents of such legislation faced opposition, typically from large employers. However, after ERISA, larger employers were unaffected by such laws, and the legislative scale tipped toward the proponents.

Managed Care and Beyond: The 1980s, 1990s, and 2000s

The 1980s saw rapid increases in health insurance premiums, driven by new medical technology and cost-based reimbursement systems used by insurers and the Medicare program. In 1983 Congress changed the system Medicare used to pay hospitals. Rather than paying based on allowable costs, it introduced the prospective payment system, in which hospitals were paid a fixed price based on the diagnosis of admitted patients.

At about the same time, and for the same reasons, the private health insurance industry was changing as well. Prepaid group practice plans, now called health maintenance organizations (HMOs), were beginning to enroll more subscribers, and new forms of managed care, preferred provider organizations, and point-of-service plans were developing.

There are three general forms of managed care plans. The first are HMOs. These are insurance companies, meaning that they bear claims or "underwriting" risk. Like a conventional insurance plan, they are responsible for the cost of covered medical care provided to a subscriber. If these costs exceed the premium collected, they are still obligated to provide the care. A conventional insurance plan typically allows the policyholder to receive care from any licensed provider. In contrast, an HMO has a panel of providers, and the HMO is only responsible for the cost of the care from these providers.

Traditionally, there have been four HMO models. Staff model HMOs hire their physicians and usually own their own hospitals. The original Group Health Cooperative in Seattle is an example of a staff model HMO. Such models are rare. Group models are somewhat more common. In this form, the HMO-insurer contracts with a single physician group that provides all the clinical services rendered to the HMO subscribers and typically provides care only to the HMO's subscribers. Kaiser-Permanente is the classic example. Kaiser is the health insurer. It contracts exclusively with the Permanente medical group. Third is the network model HMO. In this case, the HMO-insurer contracts with several physician groups in the local market. Each physician group sees a significant number of the HMO's subscribers, but the group also sees patients from other insurers. Network model HMOs are the most common. The fourth HMO model is the independent practice association (IPA). This model emerged as a response by local medical societies to the growth of HMOs. Under this model, the HMO-insurer provides services through a large panel of physicians throughout the community. These community physicians typically only see a small number of the HMO's subscribers.

Note that none of this discussion has focused on the form of physician payment. At one time, it was argued that physicians in HMOs were salaried employees or that they were "capitated"—that is, paid a monthly fee per patient. In fact, the payment arrangements between the HMO-insurer and the participating physicians vary enormously.

Preferred provider organizations (PPOs) developed in the 1980s, partly in response to ERISA and the shift to self-insured employer-sponsored health plans. PPOs are often not health insurers because they frequently do not bear underwriting risk. Instead, they are coordinators of contracts. In principle, a PPO is easy to establish. One approaches a local hospital and negotiates a price below hospital billed charges in exchange for encouraging (future) subscribers to use this hospital. One similarly obtains agreements from physicians who have privileges at this hospital. These are "preferred providers." One then goes to self-insured employers and asks them if they would like to pay less for hospital and physician services. They, of course, would like to do so. The employers agree to allow their employees to use the preferred providers for a smaller out-of-pocket payment per visit than is required for other providers. One then executes a contract between the employer and the participating providers and manages the set of contracts for a per-member-per-month fee. This is a stereotypic PPO.

Many insurers, of course, also offer a PPO product. In some cases, these are simply contracting vehicles, and the insurers bear no underwriting risk. In other cases, the PPO may bear such risk as it contracts with networks of providers and sells coverage to employer groups and individuals.

Point-of-service (POS) plans are hybrids of HMOs and PPOs. HMOs observed that people seem to prefer choice, and PPOs allow their members a wider choice of providers. HMOs responded by creating new plans that allow their members to use nonpanel providers if the members are willing to pay more out-of-pocket per visit. The members can decide at each "point-of-service" whether they wish to use a panel provider or nonpanel provider. PPOs observed that HMOs tended to assign each member to a primary care provider, who provided continuity of care and who had to approve referrals to specialists. They responded to HMOs by establishing plans in which their members had assigned primary care gatekeepers. These, too, are called POS plans. Today, many insurers offer conventional coverage, as well as all three forms of managed care plans.

Table 1-1 shows the growth in managed care and the commensurate shrinkage of conventional insurers. As recently as 1988, conventional insurers held a commanding share of these workers—73 percent. By 2005, conventional plans only enrolled 3 percent of insured workers. PPOs enrolled only 11 percent of insured workers in 1988 and had over 60 percent by 2005. HMO and POS enrollment peaked in about 2000 and has declined since. As discussed later in the chapter, high-deductible health plans (HDHPs) emerged in the mid-2000s. These consumer-driven health plans

TABLE 1-1

Percentage of Insured Workers by Type of Plan

Type of Insurance Plan	1988	1995	2000	2005	2006
Conventional insurance	73%	27%	8%	3%	3%
Health maintenance organization (HMO)	16%	28%	29%	21%	20%
Preferred provider organization (PPO)	11%	25%	42%	61%	60%
Point-of-service (POS) plan	—	20%	21%	15%	13%
High-deductible health plan (HDHP)	—	—	—	—	4%

SOURCE: Data from Claxton et al. (2006).

combine a high-deductible insurance plan with a tax-sheltered health savings account. By 2006, some 4 percent of insured workers were covered by such arrangements.

> *In the past year, the Commission has reached settlement with five groups of physicians for allegedly colluding to raise consumers' costs. . . . The alleged conduct I have described is naked price fixing, plain and simple.*
>
> *—Timothy J. Muris, Chairman, Federal Trade Commission, Chicago, November 7, 2002*

The 1980s through the mid-2000s has been a roller coaster of successes and failures for managed care and private health insurance more generally. Much of this can be summarized by examining the trends in health insurance premiums over the period. Figure 1-2 tells the story. In the late 1980s, premiums for employer-sponsored health insurance were increasing at 18 percent per year, much faster than general inflation. The rates of increase declined precipitously over the first half of the 1990s. So much so that, by 1996, premium increases were virtually nonexistent and well below inflation. In real terms, health insurance premiums had declined! Premiums began to increase again in the latter half of the 1990s, peaked in 2003, but were still increasing at about 7.7 percent in 2006, more than twice the rate of inflation.

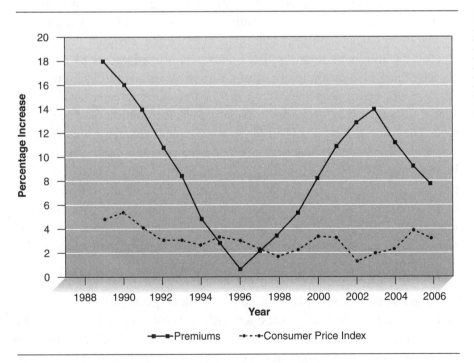

FIGURE 1-2

Percentage Increase in Health Insurance Premiums

SOURCE: Data from Jensen et al. (1997), Gabel et al. (2005), and Fronstin (2006).

What happened? As we will discuss in considerable depth later in the book, the first half of the 1990s can be characterized as the success of selective contracting by managed care plans. By entering into contracts with only some providers in a local market, the plans were able to negotiate lower prices. When there were more hospitals, for example, HMOs and PPOs were able to get lower prices. Two things happened subsequently, and their relative importance has yet to be fully identified.

First, providers began to consolidate. A handful of hospitals closed; many more joined hospital systems. Physicians joined somewhat larger medical groups but also entered into joint marketing arrangements. These actions arguably had the effect of reducing competition in local provider markets and reducing the ability of managed care plans to negotiate lower prices. Indeed, the federal government has obtained court decisions breaking up some physician marketing arrangements and has continued to challenge hospital mergers. In 2004 the Federal Trade Commission and the Department of Justice jointly issued a report *Improving Healthcare: A Dose of Competition.*

Second, there was a backlash against managed care plans precipitated by providers and consumers. In addition to selective contracting, managed care plans have used a variety of utilization management techniques to try to control utilization. These include preadmission certification and concurrent review of hospital admissions, and "gatekeeper" primary care providers who limit access to specialists. Managed care plans were also accused of preventing physicians from discussing more costly treatment alternatives and forcing new mothers and other patients to leave the hospital before it was medically prudent.

The upshot of this was that consumers wanted access to a greater choice of providers as a way of assuring themselves of better care, if needed. As a result, narrow-panel HMOs expanded to allow greater choice, and PPOs, with their much broader provider panels, became the preferred plan type. The irony in this, as we will see in a subsequent chapter, is that remarkably little evidence indicates that utilization management has been effective in reducing utilization. However, it is abundantly clear that the broader provider panels meant that managed care plans could not take full advantage of selective contracting. We cannot trade a high volume of patients for a lower price if we can't channel patients toward a limited number of selected providers. Thus, managed care plans appear to have shot themselves in the foot through their efforts at utilization management.

Currently, attention in the health insurance industry is focused on consumer-driven health plans (CDHPs). These plans combine a high-deductible health insurance product with a tax-sheltered health savings account (HSA) The intent is to encourage individual healthcare consumers to become more prudent purchasers of healthcare by making them see a bigger share of the cost of routine health services. As we saw in Table 1-1, 4 percent of insured workers were in such plans in 2006.

The future will likely see the emergence of "new managed care." New managed care will look a lot like old managed care except that utilization management will be gone. Utilization management often did not work, and it alienated consumers. Instead, new managed care will return to its roots of aggressive selective contracting. Some merger of the CDHP concept and new managed care is also expected because managed care plans are in a better position to negotiate lower provider prices than are individual consumers. But more on all of this after we discuss the current state of the industry and understand the demand for insurance and the challenges insurers face.

Chapter Summary

- Private health insurance in the United States began as efforts by hospital and physician providers to deal with the revenue consequences of the Great Depression.
- The forerunners of managed care plans emerged at the same time as conventional insurance but were subject to serious challenge by physicians, who were concerned about the potential loss of income from the inability to price-discriminate among patients with different demands for care.
- The growth of health insurance over the middle of the 20th century was spurred primarily by the tax-exempt status of employer-sponsored health insurance. Wage and price controls during World War II, the rise of labor unions, and the declaration of health insurance as a proper focus of collective bargaining were other key factors.
- Commercial insurers were successful in the insurance market because they introduced experience rating, which allowed them to offer lower-priced coverage to groups with lower expected claims experience. The rest of the industry followed suit.
- The enactment of Medicare in 1965 expanded insurance coverage to older Americans. The current Medicare program reflects the nature of private health insurance in the 1960s. The allowable cost reimbursement system, largely borrowed from the provider-designed Blue Cross and Blue Shield plans, entrenched cost-based reimbursement for 20 years.
- The passage of the Employee Retirement Income Security Act (ERISA) in 1974 led to the growth of self-insured employer health plans and all but assured competition in the risk-bearing segment of the conventional insurance market.
- The growth of managed care in the 1980s and 1990s was the result of the introduction of selective contracting as a response to growing healthcare costs. Selective contracting introduced price competition into healthcare markets.

- The 1990s and 2000s saw consolidation among healthcare providers and a backlash against the utilization management of managed care plans. Both actions undercut the ability of managed care plans to selectively contract.
- Consumer-driven health plans offering a high-deductible insurance plan and a tax-sheltered health spending account were emerging in the mid-2000s.

Discussion Questions

1. How might the history of U.S. healthcare been different if single-hospital plans rather than all-hospital plans had been the model Blue Cross adopted?
2. In what ways did insurance undercut physician income opportunities? Overall, how has health insurance affected the demand for physician and hospital services?
3. How might tax policy toward employer-sponsored health insurance affect the extent of coverage employers offer?
4. What features of a PPO have contributed to its rise as the predominant form of managed care for insured workers?

A SUMMARY OF INSURANCE COVERAGE

This chapter briefly summarizes the nature of health insurance in the United States. The focus is on the extent and sources of coverage, including employer-sponsored and individually purchased coverage, as well as the public programs of Medicare and Medicaid. We also look at the number and characteristics of the uninsured.

The Extent of Coverage

At the end of 2006, the resident population of the United States was approximately 300 million. Roughly 250 million people had some form of health insurance. The operative word is *roughly*. People obtain health insurance from a variety of sources. Many of them have access to and sometimes coverage from more than one source. Moreover, they may not have coverage for the entire year, and there is no single repository of data on who has what sort of coverage over what period of time. Thus, a person living in a two-earner household may have coverage from both workers, from only one, or from neither. A retiree may have Medicare coverage and a private supplemental policy. An early retiree may not yet be eligible for Medicare but may have coverage through a former employer or may have purchased individual coverage. A college student may have coverage through her parents as long as she is a full-time student, but if she drops a class tomorrow, the coverage may lapse.

The most commonly used data source on overall health insurance coverage is the March Supplement of the Current Population Survey (CPS). This large, nationally representative survey is largely conducted by telephone but uses household visits for those without phones. Members of approximately 50,000 households are interviewed each month, using a somewhat complex set of rules for when respondents answer particular questions. The insurance questions are about coverage in the preceding calendar year, and in principle, the responses relate to the entire year. The Employee Benefit Research Institute (EBRI) releases an easily accessible summary of these data each year and provides a summary of the survey methods (see Fronstin 2006).

Because virtually all persons age 65 and older have Medicare coverage, most discussion of the nature of coverage focuses on the nonelderly—those under age 65. Table 2-1 shows the number and proportion of the nonelderly population that had health insurance in 1994 and in 2005. Note that in each

TABLE 2-1

Number and Percentage of Americans under Age 65 by Source of Insurance, 1994 and 2005

	1994		2005	
	Millions	*Percentage*	*Millions*	*Percentage*
Employer-sponsored	148.1	64.4	159.5	62.0
Individual	17.3	7.5	17.8	6.9
Medicare	3.7	1.6	6.5	2.5
Medicaid	29.1	12.7	34.7	13.5
Military	8.7	3.8	7.7	3.0
Uninsured	36.5	15.9	46.1	17.9
Total	229.9	104.9	257.4	105.3

SOURCE: Data from Fronstin (2006), Figure 1.

year more than 100 percent of persons surveyed either had coverage or were uninsured. This is because some people have multiple sources of insurance coverage. Note, too, that the sum of the details of the number of people covered by each insurance category is greater than the reported total. The total reflects the unduplicated count.

Approximately 62 percent of the nonelderly had coverage through an employer in 2005 (Fronstin 2006). Just over half (52 percent) of these had coverage through their own employment; the rest had coverage as a dependent. While the total number of people with employer-sponsored coverage has increased by 11.4 million since 1994, the percentage of nonelderly persons with employer-sponsored coverage has declined from 64.4 to 62.0 percent.

The age distribution of those with employer-sponsored health insurance is generally U-shaped. Nearly 60 percent of children under age 18 have such coverage (Fronstin 2005). The percentage drops to a low of 43.7 percent from ages 21–24, largely because children end their schooling, are dropped from their parents' coverage, and either do not have a job that offers coverage or decline coverage that is offered. The percentage then rises through ages 45–54, at which point 71.7 percent have coverage, but declines among older workers. Those in the 55–64 age group are somewhat less likely to report having employer-sponsored coverage (67.3 percent), in part because of early retirement and in part because of health problems that have led them to stop working.

Employer-sponsored coverage differs widely by industry. Slightly more than one-half of workers in the agricultural, forestry, fishing, mining, and construction industries had coverage in 2005 (see Figure 2-1). In contrast, public-sector workers are most likely to be covered, with nearly 90 percent of them having employer-sponsored health insurance in 2005.

FIGURE 2-1

Percentage of Workers with Employer-Sponsored Insurance Coverage, by Industry, 2005

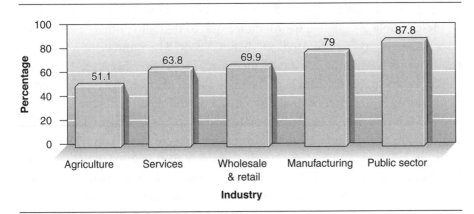

SOURCE: Date from Fronstin (2006), Figure 10.

FIGURE 2-2

Percentage of Nonelderly Americans with Individual Coverage, by Age, 2004

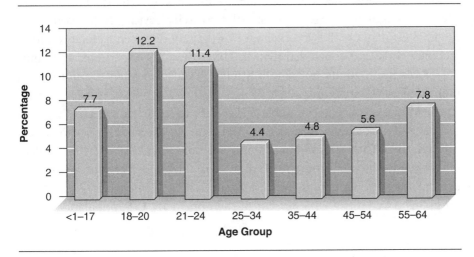

SOURCE: Data from Fronstin (2005), Figures 21 and 22.

Individual coverage is private insurance that is not purchased through a group. Some 6.8 percent of the nonelderly had such coverage in 2005 (Fronstin 2006). The individual market is of considerable interest to policymakers. Some would use tax credits to encourage the uninsured to buy individual coverage. Others would change the current tax incentives that favor employer-sponsored coverage to ones that encourage individual coverage. As Figure 2-2 shows, young adults ages 18–24 had the largest probability of buying such coverage in 2004. This is undoubtedly a reaction by many to the lack of employer-sponsored coverage. Approximately 7.8 percent of older workers ages 55–64 had individual coverage in 2004. Many of these individuals had retired from an employer, some starting another career, and were not yet eligible for Medicare.

Medicare covered some 2.5 percent of the nonelderly in 2005. Many of these people are eligible for Medicare due to disability; others are covered dependents or spouses of Medicare beneficiaries. The number of nonelderly residents with Medicare coverage increased 75 percent between 1994 and 2005 (Fronstin 2006). Much of this increase stems from Medicare's more-generous interpretation of disability (Autor and Duggan 2003).

Medicaid is a joint federal-state insurance program for low-income individuals. The number of Medicaid recipients increased by over 19 percent between 1994 and 2005. The CPS data indicate that, in 2005, Medicaid provided coverage to some 13.5 percent of nonelderly U.S. residents. This percentage is an understatement of Medicaid coverage for two important reasons. First, as noted later in the chapter, Medicaid is the primary source of nursing home coverage in the United States. The vast majority of persons in nursing homes are over age 65 and not included in Table 2-1. Second, there is some suspicion that the CPS methodology inadvertently undercounts Medicaid eligibles. The Congressional Research Service (2005) compared the CPS estimates with two other surveys that are designed to focus on low-income people and concluded that, in 2004, the CPS understated the number of Medicaid adults by some 5.8 million and overstated the number of uninsured by 3.7 million.

Military coverage in Table 2-1 refers to coverage of U.S. military retirees and dependents of active-duty, retired, and deceased service members through the Tricare Program. It also includes CHAMPVA, the Civilian Health and Medical Program of the Department of Veterans Affairs for dependents with disabilities and certain survivors of veterans. In 2005, these programs covered almost 3 percent of the nonelderly U.S. population.

The Uninsured

Table 2-1 reports the CPS estimate of 46.1 million uninsured in 2005, 17.9 percent of the population. Figure 2-3 shows the 2004 distribution of the nonelderly uninsured by age group. As would be expected from our earlier discussion, individuals in the 21–24 age group are the most likely to lack coverage; by the CPS estimate, more than one-third lack insurance coverage. Figure 2-4 reports the percentage of uninsured by race/ethnicity. Over one-third of Hispanics, 21.2 percent of African Americans, and 13.2 percent of whites lacked coverage in 2004. Given the relatively large numbers of young people, Hispanics, and African Americans who live in the Southwest, it is no surprise that the West South Central region (Arkansas, Louisiana, Oklahoma, and Texas), along with the Mountain and Pacific regions, have a larger proportion of their populations uninsured.

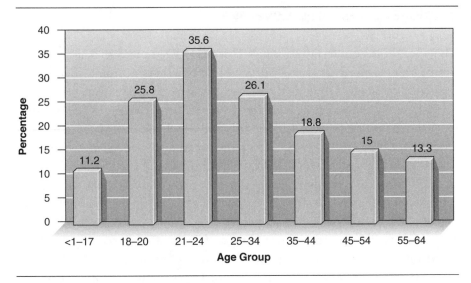

FIGURE 2-3

Percentage of
Nonelderly
Americans
Without Health
Insurance, by
Age, 2004

SOURCE: Data from Fronstin (2005), Figures 21 and 22.

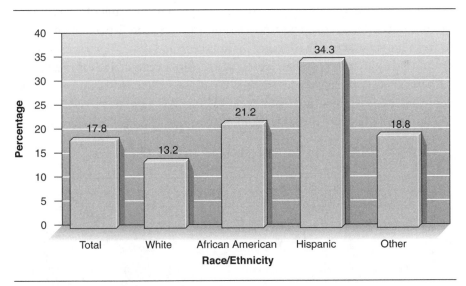

FIGURE 2-4

Percentage of
Nonelderly
Americans
Without Health
Insurance, by
Race/Ethnicity,
2004

SOURCE: Data from Fronstin (2005), Figure 14.

Employer-Sponsored Coverage

The Health Research Educational Trust (HRET) and the Kaiser Family Foundation conduct an annual survey of employers concerning their health insurance coverage. A summary of the findings is readily available on the Kaiser Family Foundation website (www.kff.org/insurance/7031/index.cfm) and in annual summary articles by Jon Gabel and colleagues in a fall or winter issue of *Health Affairs*. The survey is nationally representative of public and private employers, and is drawn from the Dunn and Bradstreet listing of U.S. firms. Responding establishments are resurveyed in subsequent years. Approximately 1,400 firms respond each year, and the overall annual response rate is approximately 50 percent.

Figure 2-5 reports the percentage of firms offering coverage in 2006 based on the HRET/Kaiser employer survey (Claxton et al. 2006b). As is clear from the figure, the vast majority of larger employers offer coverage. Indeed, it is only the smallest of the small employers that do not. Among employers with 3–9 workers, only 48 percent offered health insurance coverage in 2006. This estimate is down from the 2000 to 2001 estimates of 58 percent.

Employers typically offer coverage to full-time workers. The HRET/Kaiser survey also reported that 31 percent of firms offering coverage in 2006 offered coverage to part-time workers, and 3 percent offered it to temporary workers. On average, the survey found that 78 percent of workers in a firm offering coverage were eligible for coverage, and of these, only 82 percent took the coverage offered. We discuss these issues in much more depth in later chapters, but employees decline coverage for several reasons. These include having coverage available through a spouse or believing that the employee's out-of-pocket premium contribution is too large.

FIGURE 2-5

Percentage of Firms Offering Health Insurance, by Number of Employees, 2006

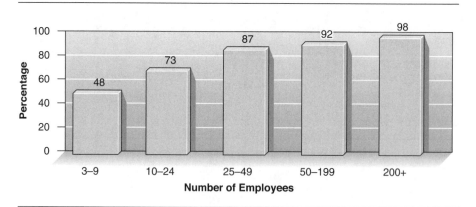

SOURCE: Data from Claxton et al. (2006b), Exhibit 2.2.

Many employers offer a choice of health plans, but the extent of choice varies significantly over the size of the firm. In 2006, for example, among firms with five thousand or more workers, 29 percent of the firms offered three or more plans, while another 42 percent offered two. In contrast, only 10 percent of firms with fewer than two hundred workers offered more than one plan. Much of this has to do with the administrative costs of offering multiple plans and fears that multiple plans offered in small groups will encourage adverse selection (see Chapter 4).

As noted in Chapter 1, employers today almost always offer one or more managed care plans, typically a preferred provider organization (PPO). Smaller employers are the most likely to continue to offer a conventional plan. Morrisey (2003) reported that, in a survey of small employers, 24 percent of those with fewer than 250 employees offer only a conventional plan.

Health insurance premiums have been rising at a rate faster than general inflation. In 2006, the HRET/Kaiser data indicate that the average premium for single coverage across all firms offering coverage was $354 per month. Family coverage, on average, cost $957 per month. Historically, health maintenance organization (HMO) premiums have been lower than those of other plans, while conventional plans have been the most expensive. More recently, however, PPO plans have had by far the highest premiums. It is dangerous to make too much of these differences at this point. Raw premium differences reflect differences in covered services, copayments, deductibles, and the expected claims experience of those who enroll.

Nominal and inflation-adjusted premiums have been increasing since 1996, and employers have increased the premium contribution that employees must make for single and family coverage. In 2006, the average monthly premium contribution for single coverage was $52 and $248 for family coverage. It is important to note, however, that while the amount of the employee premium contribution has been increasing, the share of the full premium paid through a premium contribution has remained remarkably stable over the last decade (Gabel et al. 2005). Workers tend to pay out-of-pocket 16 percent of the single premium and 26 percent of the family premium at the average firm.

Virtually all employer plans cover hospitalizations, physician visits, prescription drugs, and outpatient and inpatient mental health services, among many other health services. The extent of coverage may differ, however, and the amount of copayments and deductibles may vary substantially across firms and across plans within firms. In 2006, for example, 13 percent of covered workers had unlimited covered outpatient mental health visits, while 65 percent were limited to 30 or fewer covered visits. Some 37 percent of those workers with HMO coverage faced $15 copays per physician visit, while 25 percent had $20 copays. About 70 percent of covered workers in a

TABLE 2-2
Percentage of
Insured
Workers in
Larger Firms
Enrolled in
Plans Using
Utilization
Management
Techniques

	1997	2005
Hospital preadmission certification	92%	80%
Ambulatory surgery precertification	52%	52%
High-cost case management	81%	91%
Disease management	—	67%

SOURCE: Data from Gabel et al. (2005).

PPO paid an annual deductible for care in 2006. Among single workers with a deductible, the average PPO deductible associated with using in-plan services was $473; it was $1,034 for family coverage. Most plans (90 percent in 2006) also use multitiered copays for prescription drugs. For example, workers may pay $11 per prescription for generic drugs, $24 for preferred brand-name drugs, and $38 for nonpreferred brand-name prescriptions (Claxton et al. 2006b).

Plans also tend to use a variety of utilization management techniques. Table 2-2 reports the 1997 and 2005 HRET/Kaiser employer survey results for specific techniques. Hospital preadmission certification is the requirement that a physician receive prior approval to admit a covered patient to a hospital. Use of this technique declined markedly between 1997 and 2005. Ambulatory surgery precertification requires that a physician obtain plan approval before performing an outpatient surgical procedure. About 50 percent of covered workers had this requirement in both 1997 and 2005. High-cost case management and disease management refer to plan efforts to assign a nurse case manager to specific types of cases to ensure that the patient receives care according to clinical guidelines. These efforts have not been rigorously evaluated, but their intent appears to be as much to help patients maintain a regimen of care as much as to control costs.

Consumer-driven health plans (CDHPs) provide a reasonably generous health insurance plan, once a high deductible is satisfied. In addition, these plans provide a tax-sheltered Health Savings Account (HSA) from which people can pay for uncovered expenses. We discuss these new models in considerable depth in Chapter 16. Here we note that the HRET/Kaiser survey reported that 4 percent of employers offered one of these arrangements. The average single-coverage deductible was $1,715 ($3,511 for families), and the employer, on average, made a contribution of $689 to the HSA (Claxton et al. 2006b).

Medicare

Medicare generally provides health insurance coverage to those over age 65. The Medicare Trustees (2006) reported that Medicare covered 42.5 million individuals in 2005, 35.8 million of whom were over age 65. The elderly Medicare program has four "parts." Part A essentially covers hospital, skilled nursing facility, and home health services, which are paid for by the payroll taxes earmarked for the Medicare program. Part B essentially covers physician services and durable medical equipment. Three-quarters of its cost is paid from general tax revenues of the federal government. The other quarter is paid by a monthly beneficiary premium. In 2007, this premium was $93.50 for most people.

Some seniors prefer to enroll in a Medicare managed care plan. Approximately 15 percent of Medicare beneficiaries are in such plans. The Medicare managed care program is officially called "Medicare Advantage" or Part C. Seniors enroll with an approved plan and receive all of their Part A and Part B services and often additional benefits, including annual physicals and prescription drugs. They sometimes have to pay an additional monthly premium in a Medicare Advantage plan, however.

Medicare Part D became available in 2006. This voluntary program, enacted in late 2003, provides prescription drug coverage in exchange for a monthly additional premium in the $25 range. The coverage is purchased through one of many approved private insurers in the community. The coverage itself is unusual. Beneficiaries in 2006 had a $250 deductible; then Medicare covered 75 percent of the next $2,000 in expenses. No coverage is available for the next $2,850, but after that, Medicare will pay 95 percent of drug expenses above $5,100. We discuss this so-called "donut-hole" coverage in the Chapter 21.

Of particular importance for our current purposes is the knowledge that most Medicare beneficiaries have some form of additional coverage. As Figure 2-6 shows, all but 7 percent of Medicare beneficiaries had some form of supplemental coverage in 2003. Over one-third (39 percent) had coverage through an employer. These are people with employer-sponsored retiree coverage. Also included in this group are those over age 65 who are still employees and have active worker coverage through their employer.

Another 27 percent of Medicare beneficiaries have what are called "Medigap" plans. Traditional Medicare requires a $992 (in 2007) deductible for each spell of illness and copays of $248 for each hospital day in excess of 60 for each spell of illness. Among other cost-sharing arrangements, there are annual deductibles for Part B services, and the beneficiary is expected to pay

FIGURE 2-6
Percentage of
Medicare
Beneficiaries
with
Supplemental
Insurance
Coverage, 2003

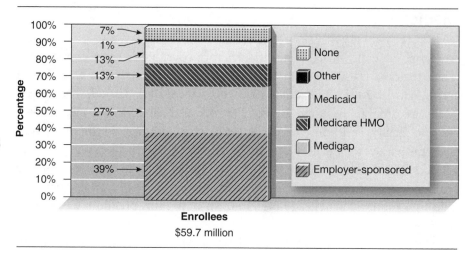

SOURCE: American Association of Retired Persons (2005), Figure 2.

20 percent of the physician's allowable charge. Many seniors purchase a Medigap policy that is designed to cover some or all of these out-of-pocket expenses. Occasionally, Medigap plans will also cover benefits not handled by Medicare. Prior to 2006, prescription drug benefits were the most common additional benefits that Medigap plans might offer, but their ability to provide drug coverage was eliminated with the launch of Part D.

Medicaid

Medicaid is a joint federal-state program providing medical care services to low-income individuals. Eligibility is established through the categorically needy and medically needy programs, or as a result of membership in a few special groups recognized by federal law. Categorical eligibility includes families covered by the state welfare program, pregnant women and children under age 6 with family income up to 133 percent of the federal poverty line, children ages 7–19 with family income up to 100 percent of the federal poverty line, and those covered by the federal Supplemental Security Income program, among others. Medically needy programs exist in 34 states and generally cover those whose medical expenses reduce their income sufficiently to make them eligible under the categorical program. Special program eligibility includes low-income Medicare beneficiaries and the working disabled.

While the federal government specifies broad rules with respect to both eligibility and covered services, the states have considerable flexibility in deciding where eligibility thresholds are established and how generous the benefit provisions will be. Thus, each state Medicaid program is different. See

FIGURE 2-7
Distribution of
Medicaid
Enrollees and
Payments,
2006

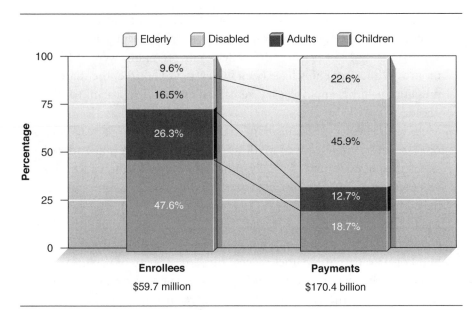

SOURCE: Data from Congressional Budget Office (2006), Table 1.

Centers for Medicare and Medicaid Services (CMS, 2005) for an overview of the program and a brief description of the eligibility and coverage differences across states. The program is paid for by a matching program tied to the relative per capita income in the state, with the federal government providing 50–83 percent of the program costs from general tax revenues.

For all of its complexity, the Medicaid program essentially provides care to four low-income groups of people: children, adults, individuals with disabilities, and the elderly. While children are by far the largest group of care recipients and individuals with disabilities are the most costly, the greatest expenditure per recipient is spent on behalf of the elderly because Medicaid is the principal source of coverage for nursing home care (see Figure 2-7).

Chapter Summary

- Health insurance in the United States is provided through a variety of sources, including employer-sponsored coverage, individually purchased coverage, and Medicare and Medicaid.
- In 2005, approximately 62 percent of the nonelderly obtained health insurance through an employer, 6.9 percent bought individual coverage, and 17.9 percent were uninsured.
- The smallest of small employers are the least likely to offer coverage. Part-time and temporary workers seldom have employer-sponsored coverage, and some workers decline coverage that is offered.

- Small employers tend to offer only a single plan; larger firms may offer several. Single premiums for employer-sponsored coverage in 2006 were approximately $354 per month, while family premiums were $957 per month. While premiums have been increasing over time, the share of the premium paid by employees has remained essentially constant for the last decade.
- Medicare provides health insurance for some 36 million persons over age 65. However, 93 percent of Medicare beneficiaries have some sort of supplemental coverage—typically, retiree coverage through a former employer or an individually purchased Medigap policy—although many have Medicaid.
- Medicaid provided services to some 59.7 million persons in 2006. While children are the largest group receiving services, individuals who are blind or who have disabilities receive the largest share of payments. However, the elderly, because of Medicaid's payment for nursing home services, receive the greatest payments per recipient.

Discussion Questions

1. Why would employers choose to provide health insurance to their employees?
2. What factors do you think a two-earner couple should take into consideration when they choose jobs and health insurance coverage?
3. Why do you think so many Medicare beneficiaries obtain some supplemental form of coverage?
4. Suppose the Medicaid program were to be expanded. What effects would this have on the number of uninsured? On the number with employer-sponsored coverage?

THE DEMAND FOR HEALTH INSURANCE

Life is a gamble. Suppose we were to flip a coin. If it comes up "heads," you lead a healthy, normal life. If it comes up "tails," you become seriously ill. Medical science can return you to the healthy state, but medical science is not cheap. Treatment will cost you $20,000, plus some associated pain and suffering. Are you willing to buy a health insurance policy to attenuate the financial consequences of your potential bad luck?

The correct response is "maybe." It depends on the price of the policy and the nature of the coverage. In this chapter, we present the theory of insurance and develop four hypotheses about the conditions under which we would be willing to buy coverage. We also use these hypotheses to begin to explain some of the data on health insurance coverage that we examined in Chapter 2. At first blush, the theory of insurance appears inconsistent with real-world experience. This is largely because the simple theory abstracts from real-world complexities. In particular, it ignores adverse selection, employer-sponsored health insurance, and the special tax treatment of health insurance. We will anticipate future chapters by introducing these topics and the roles they play in the demand for health insurance.

The Theory of Insurance

Friedman and Savage (1948) and Ehrlich and Becker (1972) viewed the demand for insurance as reflecting the maximum we would pay, over and above the expected loss, to avoid the consequences of the loss. The expected loss is the amount we would expect to pay, on average, if the event occurred many times. Thus, if we would have to pay $20,000 every time we flip a coin and "heads" occurs and pay $0 whenever "tails" appears, then the expected loss for 100 flips of our coin is $10,000 on each flip. Sometimes, we will have to pay nothing; we win. Sometimes, we will have to pay $20,000; we lose. On average, we will pay $10,000 per flip.

Again, consider the question of insurance against the financial consequences of the coin flip. Are you willing to pay *more* than $10,000 to avoid the coin flip? If so, you are like most of us and are risk averse. You are willing to pay more than the expected loss to avoid the consequences of the loss. Stated somewhat differently, you are willing to pay some "loading fee" over and above the actuarially fair premium to avoid the consequences.

Insurance exists because there are enough of us who feel that way. The extra amount we are willing to pay, often called a "risk premium," means that there is the potential for someone to come in and get a hundred or more of us to buy an insurance policy from her. Her "claims costs" will be $10,000 on each policy, on average. The risk premiums we are willing to pay will compensate her for running the program.

Our simple insurance model suggests that many of us would pay a risk premium (plus the expected loss) to avoid the consequences of the coin flip. What is the maximum amount you would be willing to pay? It depends on three factors: how "chicken" you are, how much you would lose if the bad outcome occurred, and how great the chances are that the bad outcome will actually occur. How chicken you are is merely a reflection of your unwillingness to bear risk. The more chicken—that is, the more risk averse you are—the larger will be the risk premium and the more you are willing to pay to get coverage. This raises an important point. Everyone does not have the same demand for insurance. Some will prefer broader and/or deeper coverage. Others will prefer to buy much less. Some may prefer to buy none at all.

We need to formalize this discussion a bit. When we say that someone is risk averse, what we mean is that the loss of $1 reduces their well-being by more than the gain of $1 increases it. This is just another way of saying that risk-averse individuals have diminishing marginal utility of wealth. Each dollar of wealth makes them better off, but each additional dollar is not as satisfying as the one before. This idea is no different than the discussion you undoubtedly had in an introductory economics class, except there the discussion revolved around the diminishing marginal utility of beer, or pizza, or ice cream cones consumed at a single sitting.

Figure 3-1 shows this. The curve depicts total utility of wealth. The individual whose utility of wealth is graphed here receives 4,727 units of utility from $20,000 and 8,000 units of utility from $40,000. Each additional dollar increases total utility, so the curve is upward sloping. However, each additional dollar gives less additional utility than the previous dollar, so the curve increases at a decreasing rate.

Now consider the coin-flip problem. If it comes up "heads," the person represented in Figure 3-1 with an initial wealth position of $40,000 will have to pay $20,000. If it comes up "tails," he pays nothing. The endpoints of the straight line in Figure 3-1 reflect these outcomes. He could end up with $40,000 or $20,000. The midpoint of the line reflects the expected loss of many coin flips. The expected loss is $10,000, so he would move from a wealth position of $40,000 to one of $30,000. How much does he value the $30,000 wealth position? If he had $30,000, it would give him 7,090 units of utility. However, he doesn't have $30,000; he has $40,000 and a 50/50 chance of losing $20,000. How much utility does that provide? The answer is 6,364 units of utility. According to Figure 3-1, the individual gets just as much utility from a 50/50 chance of losing $20,000 as he does from having a

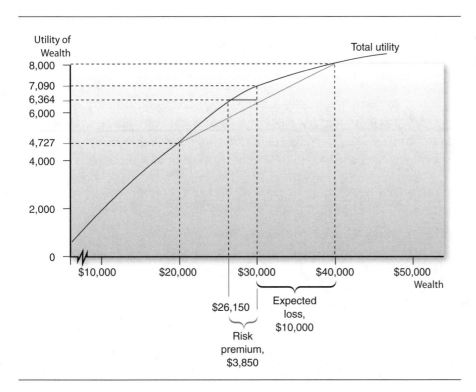

FIGURE 3-1

The Risk
Premium

certain $26,150. This individual is willing to pay *up to* $13,850 to avoid the coin flip: $10,000 reflects the expected loss, and $3,850 is the "risk premium."

Two points are important here. First, the risk premium is the measure of our willingness to pay for insurance. It is the amount over and above the expected loss that we are willing to pay to avoid the consequences of the loss. This is the reason why insurance can exist. Insurers must pay to settle claims; claims are the expected losses. If insurers are to cover administrative and marketing costs, and make at least a normal profit, they have to collect something over and above the expected loss. The presence of a (big enough) risk premium allows this to occur.

Second, the risk premium reflects *the most* that we are willing to pay. If the insurance market is competitive, we may end up paying much less than what we are willing to pay for coverage, just as we often pay much less than what we are willing to pay for a cold beer.

Not everyone has the same degree of risk aversion. Most of us are at least somewhat uncomfortable dealing with risk, others are very uncomfortable, and some love it. Thus, in principle, each of us has our own unique total utility curve like that shown in Figure 3-1. Box 3-1 gives you an opportunity to determine your personal degree of risk aversion. Answer enough of the questions to allow you to plot four or five points on your own total utility curve, and see how much you would be willing to pay to avoid this gamble. But be forewarned: while the questions themselves are not hard, coming up with honest answers is!

BOX 3-1

How Risk Averse Are You?

To determine how risk averse you are, consider the following exercise. First, choose two dollar amounts—say, $40,000 and $20,000, as we did in Figure 3-1. Next, assign arbitrary utility values to each. The only requirement is that the utility of $40,000 be greater than that of $20,000. In Figure 3-1, we chose the utility of $40,000 to be 8,000 [U($40,000) = 8,000] and the utility of $20,000 to be 4,727 [U($20,000) = 4,727]. You choose whatever you like, and plot the two points on a graph like Figure 3-1.

Now you are faced with a series of coin flips. Here is the first: If the coin comes up "heads," you win $40,000. If it comes up "tails," you win $20,000. What is the *minimum amount* you would accept to sell your right to this single flip of the coin? Your answer is $X. We now need to know the utility value associated with your answer. To do this, we compute the expected utility (EU):

$$EU = .5[U(\$40,000)] + .5[U(\$20,000)] = U(\$X)$$

That's simply the probability of getting "heads" (.5) times the utility if "heads" occurs U($40,000) plus the probability of "tails" (.5) times the utility if "tails" occurs U($20,000). Substituting what we already know (from the example in the text):

$$EU = .5[8,000] + .5[4,727] = U(\$X)$$

$$EU = 4,000 + 2,364 = U(\$X)$$

$$EU = 6,364 = U(\$X)$$

If you said that the minimum you would accept was $26,150 (as we did in Figure 3-1), then X = $26,150, and the U($26,150) is 6,364. Plot the point that emerged from your answer on your graph.

Now consider a second gamble. If "heads" occurs on your single coin flip, you get the value you chose for $X ($26,150 was our choice in Figure 3-1), and if "tails" occurs, you get $40,000. What is the minimum amount you would accept to sell your right to this coin flip? Choose your answer and redo the math:

$$EU = .5[U(\$X)] + .5[U(\$40,000)] = U(\$Y)$$

$$EU = .5[U(\$26,150)] + .5[U(40,000)] = U(\$Y) \text{ (in the case in Figure 3-1)}$$

$$EU = .5[6,364] + .5[8,000] = U(\$Y)$$

$$EU = 7,182 = U(\$Y)$$

If your answer is $30,770 (as was ours in Figure 3-1), then the utility of $30,770 is 7,182. Plot the utility associated with your answer for $Y.

From here on, simply set up similar gambles of two known dollar amounts, identify your minimum acceptance price, and then compute the utility value and plot it. Once your individual curve has been plotted out, you can consider losses as we did in the text and determine your risk premium for a relevant potential loss.

Note, however, that your answers may differ greatly from those in the example. You have different tastes for risk than we do. As a consequence, your graph may look very different from the one in Figure 3-1. In fact, if you are a risk lover, your curve will be convex from below rather than concave. If so, the model predicts that you will not be buying any insurance!

Hypothesis I: The Degree of Risk Aversion

Your mother is likely to have a different tolerance for risk than you do. You know how she worries! Suppose your utility curve was shown in Figure 3-1. Because your mother is less willing to take chances than you are, she is more risk averse. Her total utility will lie above yours over the relevant range shown in Figure 3-2. When we again play out the 50/50 chance of losing $20,000, we see that her risk premium is $5,380. She is willing to pay $5,380 to avoid the consequences of the coin toss. This reflects the first hypothesis that emerges from the theory: **As the degree of risk aversion increases, the size**

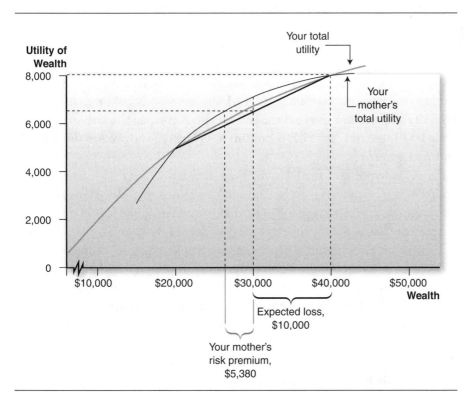

FIGURE 3-2

Effect of Change in Risk Aversion

of the risk premium increases, and the probability that we will buy insurance increases. Because your mother is more risk averse than you are, she is more likely to buy insurance than you are, other things being equal. The other "equal things" are the conditions of the coin toss: the fair coin, the same possible outcomes, and the same initial wealth positions.

This rather obvious hypothesis begins to give us some insight into the mix of people who do and do not have health insurance. In the context of auto safety, the National Highway Traffic Safety Administration (2003) said ". . . the apparent disregard for one's own personal safety appears to be a defining element of youth." If this is true, it suggests that young people are less risk averse than older folks. As such, they are willing to pay smaller risk premiums and, therefore, are less likely to buy insurance. This could begin to explain why over 35 percent of those in the 21–24 age group do not have health insurance (see Chapter 2).

Hypothesis II: The Size of the Potential Loss

The size of the possible loss is also relevant. If "heads" in the coin toss only implied a $200 loss, you might be willing to pay only $10, plus the $100 expected loss to avoid the consequences. At $20,000, you might be willing to pay $3,850, plus the $10,000 expected loss, and at $200,000, you might be willing to pay $10,000, plus the expected loss of $100,000 to avoid the consequences. As the size of the possible loss increases, the risk premium we are willing to pay increases. This is demonstrated in Figure 3-3. It reproduces Figure 3-1 but includes the circumstance where "heads" on the coin flip yields a $30,000 loss instead of just $20,000. A very risk-averse individual is willing to pay a risk premium of $4,614 to avoid this risk, rather than the $3,850 risk premium to avoid the smaller risk. **Thus, as the size of the possible loss increases, the risk premium gets larger, and we are more likely to buy insurance.**

This hypothesis predicts, for example, that other things being equal, people will be more likely to buy hospital insurance than dental insurance. It also suggests that coverage for big-ticket, or catastrophic, loss is more valuable to consumers than is coverage for first-dollar losses. Thus, if health insurance were to become more expensive, we would expect consumers to shift away from coverage for physician office visits or prescription drug coverage, but retain coverage for hospital care. They may do this by switching to a policy that has a higher deductible or one with larger copays associated with ambulatory service use. Finally, notice that this hypothesis provides some of the rationale for catastrophic health insurance plans and Health Savings Accounts (HSAs). A catastrophic plan only provides coverage after a relatively large deductible, perhaps $3,000 or $4,000, has been met. An HSA is

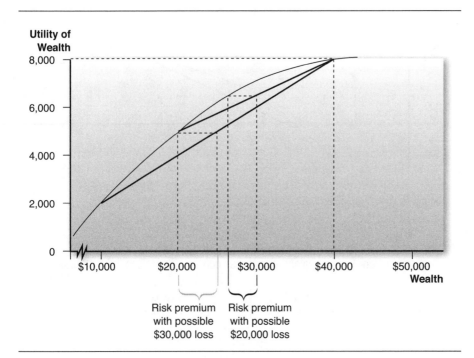

FIGURE 3-3

Effect of
Change in the
Magnitude of
Possible Loss

a new form of health insurance that ties a catastrophic health insurance plan to a tax-sheltered bank account from which you can spend to satisfy the deductible. We discuss these plans in Chapter 16.

Hypothesis III: The Probability of Loss

The size of the risk premium also depends on the probability of the loss occurring. If instead of a 1 in 2 chance of a bad outcome, suppose the chance were only 1 in 10. Then we would be willing to pay only a very small risk premium, perhaps only $400 in addition to the $2,000 expected loss (0.1 × $20,000 + 0.9 × $0 = $2,000) to avoid the gamble. Surprisingly, the model also suggests that we would not pay much above the expected loss for a policy that insured against an event that was virtually certain to occur. This is demonstrated in Figure 3-4. Here, we again reproduce Figure 3-1, but now we shift the probability of loss. A 50/50 chance of a loss was characterized in the original figure as bisecting the straight line between the two possible outcomes. If the chance of a loss is only 1 in 10, however, then the expected loss appears one-tenth of the way from our initial wealth position, and the risk premium in Figure 3-4 is only a few hundred dollars. As the probability of a loss increases, the expected loss line in the figure shifts further to the left. As it does so, the risk premium continues to increase in size, reaches some maximum, and then starts to decrease. This is the third hypothesis. **As the**

FIGURE 3-4

Effect of
Change in the
Probability of
Loss

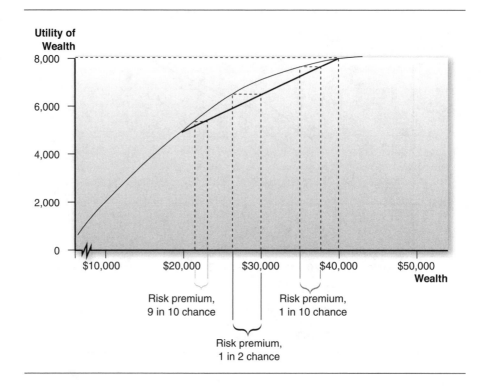

probability of the loss increases, the size of the risk premium initially
increases but then declines, and the probability of buying insurance initially increases but then declines.

This is the least intuitive of the hypotheses, but it is clear with a little
thought. We do not buy insurance for very small probability losses because the
expected loss is very small and the risk premium associated with a small
expected loss is even smaller. But as the probability of loss increases, coverage
is more attractive. However, we also do not buy coverage for very likely
events. If you knew that the cost of some medical procedure was $20,000 and
that you had a 95 percent chance of needing this procedure, then the expected
loss would be $19,000. How much more than $19,000 would you pay to
avoid the consequences of paying $20,000? The answer is "not much." Thus,
the theory says we do not buy coverage for virtually certain events.

But you say, "Suppose I know that my probability of loss is 95 percent,
but the insurer doesn't know this. Surely, I would buy coverage under this
circumstance." The answer, of course, is yes you would. The problem you
raise is called "adverse selection." You know more about your likely use of
health services than does the insurer, and you use this knowledge to your best
advantage when buying insurance. This is a fundamental issue for insurers,
and we will spend the next three chapters dealing with it. The insurer tries to
reduce this problem by putting you in a "risk class" that reflects your

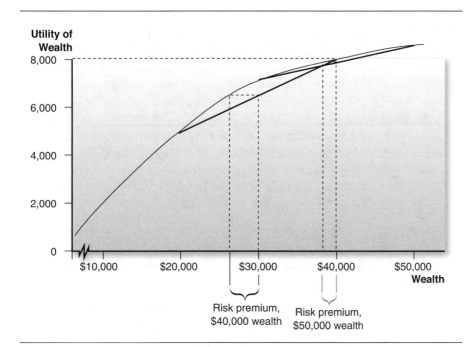

FIGURE 3-5
Effect of
Change in
Wealth

expected claims experience. In our simple insurance model, you and the insurer have the same (complete) information. So, you might like to buy the coverage designed for others, but no insurer would sell it to you.

Hypothesis IV: The Wealth Effect

Finally, the maximum amount we are willing to pay depends on our wealth position. People with higher wealth are able in some sense to "self-insure" against losses that the rest of us might buy insurance to protect against. Figure 3-5 shows the effect of higher wealth. It takes the individual in Figure 3-1 with the same 50/50 chance of losing $20,000. However, here he has an initial wealth position of $50,000 instead of $40,000. The risk premium associated with the expected loss of $10,000 is $2,307, less than the risk premium of $3,850 in Figure 3-1. **As wealth increases, the risk premium declines, and we are less likely to buy insurance.**

This could also be called the "Best Buy Hypothesis." Whenever you purchase an electronic device or electrical appliance from Best Buy, the clerks ask if you wish to buy the extended warranty. They are asking if you want to buy insurance. We could test the wealth hypothesis by simply knowing the zip codes in which customers reside and whether or not they purchased the extended warranty. From the zip codes, we could go to recent census data and determine the average household income in the zip code; this serves as

BOX 3-2

Health Insurance: The Access Hypothesis

In addition to the four classic rationales for the purchase of health insurance presented here, Nyman (1999) argued for a fifth consideration: the access motive. The argument is straightforward. Some health conditions, should they occur, are so expensive that they exhaust your wealth. Since you could not pay for such treatment in the first place, under the traditional rationales, you would not buy insurance to avoid the consequences of the event occurring. Nyman argued that health insurance may be the only mechanism whereby you *could* obtain such treatment and that people do buy coverage to have such treatments available to them, should they need them.

a proxy for wealth. Insurance theory predicts that those in the more-affluent zip codes will be less likely to buy the extended warranty.

Your reaction to this hypothesis is likely to be simple disbelief because all of the data suggest that more-affluent people are more likely, not less likely, to have health insurance. The reason for this discrepancy between the theory and our real-world observations has to do with the complexity of the real world. Recall from Chapter 1 that one of the key reasons for the growth of health insurance in the mid-twentieth century is the tax-exempt status of employer-sponsored health insurance. Factors such as this are excluded in our simple model.

To summarize: This simple model is the basis of the demand for health insurance. In the absence of employers, tax subsidies, and the like, we expect to see four sorts of behavior (see also Box 3-2):

- People who are more risk averse will buy more health insurance.
- People will be more likely to buy insurance for events that have large financial consequences.
- People will be less likely to buy insurance for events that are very unlikely or very likely to occur.
- People will be less likely to buy insurance as their wealth position increases.

Taxes and Employer-Sponsored Health Insurance

Analysis of the demand for health insurance is complicated by the fact that most people in the United States get their insurance through their workplace.

The reason for this is twofold. Workers value health insurance, and it is less costly when purchased through an employer. Both points are important.

Workers *do* value health insurance. A 1991 Gallup poll indicated that health insurance was the single most valued employment fringe benefit for 64 percent of respondents (*Wall Street Journal* 1991). In 2004, MetLife reported that 81 percent of full-time employees ranked medical benefits as most important. Vacations ranked second with 57 percent (Medical Benefits 2005b). Because many people value health insurance, they are willing to trade some of their compensation for health benefits. (This willingness to trade wages for benefits is key to understanding employer-sponsored health insurance; we will consider it in Chapter 13.)

Health insurance also tends to be less expensive when purchased through an employer. There are three reasons for this. The first has to do with "favorable selection," the flip side of adverse selection. Employed people tend to be healthier, on average, than those who are unemployed. Employment serves as a good signal of lower expected claims costs, and consequently, an employer group can usually purchase coverage at a lower price than can an individual. The second reason for lower costs has to do with the nature of the existing tax laws. Health insurance is not taxed as federal or state income, nor is it subject to Social Security and Medicare payroll taxes. Thus, if an employee values a dollar of health insurance as equivalent to a dollar of take-home pay, an employer need only spend a dollar on health insurance rather than a dollar plus tax on money compensation. Third, there are economies in the marketing and administration of employer group plans, relative to individually purchased insurance.

Tax advantages have provided a significant incentive for employer provision of health insurance. As discussed in Chapter 1, employer contributions to group health insurance are exempt from federal and state personal income taxes. They are also exempt from federal payroll taxes for Social Security and Medicare. This tax treatment can be viewed as a subsidy for the provision of health insurance (Feldstein and Allison 1974; Miller 2003). Workers in the 27 percent federal income tax bracket, paying 5 percent state income tax and 7.65 percent in Social Security and Medicare taxes, would find that an extra dollar of employer-sponsored health insurance effectively cost them less than 61 cents. If workers are in a higher tax bracket, the tax subsidy for employer-sponsored health insurance is even greater.

This is likely to explain why we observe that more-affluent people have more health insurance. With a progressive tax system as in the United States, higher incomes imply higher tax rates. Higher tax rates reduce the effective price of employer-sponsored health insurance, and at these lower effective prices, people buy more coverage. Thus, the tax subsidy provides an incentive for broader and deeper coverage.

In the simple insurance market discussed earlier, someone may not purchase dental coverage because the size of the potential loss is relatively low. The tax subsidy reduces the effective price, encouraging workers to press their employers to include dental coverage in the benefit package. Similarly, the tax subsidy encourages the coverage of events with low expected losses, such as well-baby care.

The purchase of health insurance through the employer is a complex issue. It involves not only the premium charged but also the tax rates of workers and the relative costs across firms. (We will examine the empirical literature on the effects of tax law changes in Chapter 14.)

The tax incentives also complicate the business decision to change the coverage of health benefit plans. Suppose, for example, that a benefits manager discovers the cost-saving implications of implementing greater cost sharing in the form of larger out-of-pocket payments for health services. The firm implements this in a new health insurance plan. As expected, claims costs decline. However, workers correctly view this change in benefits as a diminution of their compensation. To keep the best workers from leaving for other firms, the employer decides to raise wages. Indeed, if full-coverage insurance caused workers to consume units of healthcare that were only of minimal extra value to them, the cost savings from reduced claims should be enough to make the workers whole and have something left to enhance firm profits. That is, the employer has to add something to the compensation basket to make up for the reduced health insurance coverage, thus "making the worker whole." As a result, benefits changes have to not only save money, but save enough money to make workers whole—after tax considerations. This is a rather high hurdle to cross.

Chapter Summary

- Insurance exists because enough people are willing to pay something over and above the expected loss to avoid the consequences of the loss. This willingness to pay is called the "risk premium."
- The greater the risk premium, the more likely we are to buy insurance.
- The greater the extent of risk aversion—that is, the greater the level of discomfort with uncertain outcomes—the larger the risk premium.
- The greater the size of the potential loss, the larger the risk premium.
- The risk premium increases with the probability of a loss, reaches some maximum, and then declines with higher probabilities of loss.
- The risk premium declines with greater wealth.
- The tax treatment of employer-sponsored health insurance serves to reduce the price of health insurance and may outweigh the effects described by the pure theory of insurance.

Discussion Questions

1. Suppose that health insurance premiums have increased substantially in the past year. You are a member of your firm's fringe benefits committee and have been charged with reducing the cost of health insurance. Based on the analysis in this chapter, what sort of changes to the benefits package would you recommend? Why?

2. Suppose that Congress is successful in reducing the marginal income tax rates on money wages. What effect would you expect this to have on the nature of health insurance benefits offered by employers? Why?

3. One of your high school buddies has just graduated from college and accepted a great job in a small consulting firm. However, the firm does not offer health insurance. Over dinner one night, he asks you whether he should buy some health insurance, and if so, what kind. What do you say? Why?

4. The *Wall Street Journal* (2006) reports that "mini-medical plans" have come onto the market. These plans cover routine services, provide little hospital coverage, often cap payouts at $10,000 or less, and can cost as little as $40 per month. Is an insurance plan of this sort consistent with the hypotheses developed in this chapter? Why? What might people be buying with a mini-medical plan if they are not buying insurance?

ISSUES OF ADVERSE SELECTION

ADVERSE SELECTION

4

You know more about your likely use of health services than does your typical insurance company. As a result, you have an incentive to use this information to your best advantage. In particular, if you have some health problem—say, heart disease—you might try to find an insurance plan that is designed for healthier people. If you were successful, you would pay a premium that was less than your expected claims experience. The insurer, on the other hand, would probably lose money on you. As you might imagine, insurers worry a good deal about this.

Adverse selection in health insurance exists when you know more about your likely use of health services than does the insurer. Insurers deal with the problem by trying to design risk classes that group similar risks together. They then charge premiums that reflect this differential risk. The same information that goes into defining risk classes can be used to identify potential marketing opportunities for insurers. If one insurer can identify an employer group that has lower claims experience, for example, it might be able to quote a premium that will attract the group away from another insurer.

In this chapter, we explore some of the implications of adverse selection in the context of the reported differences in the utilization experience of people enrolled in managed care plans (e.g., HMOs) and people enrolled in

---

BOX 4-1

Adverse Selection in Pension Plans

Adverse selection arises in a number of insurance markets. In the pension world, for example, you can purchase an annuity that pays out monthly until you die, or alternatively, you can buy an annuity that pays out monthly for a fixed number of years, thereby leaving money to your heirs if you die early. In a fascinating study of a large pension plan in the United Kingdom, Finkelstein and Poterba (2000) found that those people who ultimately lived longer disproportionately purchased pension plans that paid out until they died. Those who died early disproportionately purchased fixed-term annuities. The implication is that adverse selection is present in the pension markets, and people appear to know more about their likely remaining length of life than does the annuity seller.

conventional insurance plans. We discuss mechanisms whereby the differences could reflect efforts by the managed care plan to reduce utilization and efforts it might make to attract lower utilizers. This leads to a discussion of the insurance cost implications for employers who might begin to offer the HMO. Finally, we review the literature on the extent that adverse selection and changes in use patterns explain actual differences in HMO and conventional utilization.

"HMO Effect" vs. Favorable Selection

Much of the empirical research on adverse selection in healthcare was done in the 1980s, as employers began to offer HMOs and other managed care plans. The issue arose because of substantial differences in the utilization experience of those enrolled in HMOs and those in conventional insurance plans. Robert Miller and Hal Luft (1994) reviewed much of the literature on the differences in utilization, and Box 4-2 presents a summary of their findings. Essentially, Miller and Luft found that people enrolled in an HMO use considerably less hospital care. The question is why.

One explanation is that HMOs do something to keep people out of hospitals. This is the so-called "HMO effect." It might be the result of a number of strategies. For example, HMOs could substitute ambulatory services for inpatient services at a much more aggressive rate than do conventional insurers. HMOs could employ effective utilization management techniques that are designed to limit hospital use to only those most likely to benefit for it. HMOs may only affiliate with physicians who are very conservative in their use of hospital services and/or they may provide financial incentives to physicians that lead the physicians to admit fewer patients. HMOs may provide preventive services that identify harmful conditions at an early stage and reduce hospitalizations.

BOX 4-2

HMO Performance

Compared to indemnity insurance, HMOs had:

- Admission rates: 26–37 percent lower
- Length of stays: 1–20 percent lower
- Hospital days: 18–29 percent lower
- Office visits: Higher or equal
- Expensive services: Used less

SOURCE: Data from Miller and Luft (1994).

Alternatively, HMOs may do nothing at all to lower the hospital utilization experience of its members. Instead, they may attract members who are low utilizers to begin with ("favorable selection"). They could accomplish this in many ways. HMOs could target their enrollment efforts at younger and/or healthier groups by, for example, marketing to schoolteachers rather than construction workers on the theory that schoolteachers, on average, are less likely to take risks in their daily lives. HMOs might contract with physician groups and hospitals that are located in suburbs populated by young, upwardly mobile professionals, believing that such proximity will disproportionately attract the residents. HMOs could offer excellent maternity and well baby care in the hopes of attracting otherwise healthy young families into their plans. Similarly, they could offer abundant preventive services, expecting that those who value such services prefer to keep themselves healthy and out of the hospital. HMOs might offer a tie-in sale with their health insurance plan—for example, enroll in the HMO and receive a substantial discount at a local gym. Indeed, recently, some HMOs have begun giving "health credits" to members who undertake healthy activities. While these could be efforts to keep people out of the hospital, they could also be efforts to attract people with healthy lifestyles. Perhaps those who are less prone to exercise will see these offers as wastes and not join the plan. HMOs may choose their panel of providers such that there are an abundance of primary care physicians but very few specialists. The theory may be that an individual with chronic health problems probably has an ongoing relationship with a specialist, and if that specialist is not in the HMO's panel of providers, the consumer is less likely to join.

Alternatively, HMOs may do none of these things. It may simply be that the philosophy of "health maintenance" attracts people who do not like to interact with the healthcare system. If so, even though HMOs may reach out to *all* members of the community, they may still attract a favorable draw of the population.[1]

Obviously, HMOs could seek to attract low utilizers and also to limit their use of hospitals once they join the plan. To an employer considering offering an HMO in addition to a conventional plan, however, it is critical to appreciate which effect dominates. If the difference in utilization is largely attributable to the HMO effect, then the plan can do something that will lower healthcare costs for the employer and employees. There are potential savings to be had. On the other hand, if the difference in utilization is largely attributable to favorable selection, then there are no savings. The best the employer could hope for is writing two checks, one to the traditional plan

---

1. Given the somewhat unseemly assertions about HMO behavior in this section, the author is compelled to report that he has been a member by choice of one or another HMO for virtually all of the past 30 years.

and one to the HMO.[2] Moreover, the employer may conceivably be even worse off as a result of adding the HMO to the employee benefits.

Consider an employer that has long offered a conventional insurance plan. It now adds an HMO that achieves its lower utilization by means of favorable selection and attracts a disproportionate share of the employer's healthy workers. As Feldman and Dowd (1982) noted, it is not at all obvious that the lower claims experience will be passed on to the employer and employees in the form of lower premiums. The HMO may try to set the premium just a shadow below the competitively priced conventional plan's premium. If so, the employer and employees will effectively pay a higher premium for the healthy employees than they were when only the conventional plan was offered. To make matters worse, the conventional plan may find that its claims experience now has increased and the plan will have to raise its premiums! Thus, in the face of both favorable selection and "shadow-pricing," the employer finds that its efforts to reduce insurance costs resulted in higher costs. A solution to the shadow-pricing problem, as we will discuss in later chapters, is competition in the HMO segment of the market.

Evidence of an HMO Effect

The best evidence supporting the HMO effect is the RAND Health Insurance Experiment (Manning et al. 1987). This study was designed to estimate consumers' price responsiveness to alternative coinsurance rates for the use of clinical services. We will discuss this study at considerable length in Chapter 7. For current purposes, however, it is enough to know that the experiment randomly assigned families to alternative health insurance plans. This has the advantage of largely overcoming the adverse selection problem.

In one part of the experiment, people in Seattle, Washington, were alternatively assigned to Group Health Cooperative of Puget Sound, a large, well-run staff model HMO, or to a conventional health insurance plan that, like Group Health at the time, had no out-of-pocket charges associated with the use of covered services (a fee-for-service plan that had no cost sharing—Free FFS). Thus, both plans covered an extremely wide range of health services, and both required no copays or coinsurance for the use of the covered services. Since people were randomly assigned to one plan or the other, any difference in utilization should arise from an HMO effect of keeping people out of the hospital.

---

2. This abstracts from the case where some or all of the employees prefer the HMO. If that is the case, the employer may be able to give employees the HMO and somewhat lower wages than they would have had, had the employer offered the traditional health plan. We defer the discussion of "compensating differentials" in employer-sponsored health insurance until Chapter 13.

	Likelihood of Any Use	One or More Admissions
HMO assigned	87%	7%
HMO control	91%	6%
Free FFS	85%	11%

TABLE 4-1
HMO Effect

SOURCE: Data from Manning et al. (1987).

NOTES: HMO = Health maintenance organization; FFS = Fee-for-service plan.

The results are summarized in Table 4-1. Those in the Free FFS plan had an 85 percent chance of interacting with the healthcare system. Those assigned to Group Health (HMO-assigned) had an 87 percent likelihood of any use. The results are virtually identical. In contrast, the probability of one or more hospital admissions was lower for the HMO-assigned group. They had a 7 percent chance of being hospitalized, while the Free FFS group had an 11 percent chance. This statistically significant difference suggests that the HMO did something to keep people out of the hospital.

The row in Table 4-1 entitled "HMO control" reflects the experience of a group of long-time Group Health Cooperative members with characteristics similar to those in each of the randomly assigned groups. It allows a comparison of whether the newly assigned individuals have a different experience than long-time enrollees. The answer is that the long-time enrollees have an even lower probability of using hospital care (although the difference is not statistically significant), and they are more likely to interact with the healthcare system. This suggests that the long-term enrollees may see more substitution of ambulatory for inpatient services.

While this study is the best evidence of an HMO effect, like all studies it is not without limitations. The key question in this case is the extent to which differential participation rates introduced some selection bias into the study. The participation rate for those Seattle residents participating in the Free FFS plan was 93 percent, while the participation rate in the HMO-assigned plan was only 75 percent (Davies et al. 1986).

Evidence of Favorable Selection

The evidence for favorable selection into HMOs comes from a series of natural experiments that have the following framework: Suppose everyone in an employer group is enrolled in a conventional health plan that collects detailed information on employees' use of covered health services. Then, at some open-enrollment period, employees can choose to take a newly offered

HMO or to remain in the existing plan. Once people have made their choices, the researcher goes back into the preceding year's claims data and compares the health services use of those ultimately choosing the HMO with those ultimately choosing to stay in the conventional plan. If favorable selection into the HMO is present, we should see that, prior to having a choice, those who ultimately chose the HMO had lower claims experience. In contrast, if the conventional plan retained the low utilizers, the prior claims experience of its ultimate enrollees should be lower. If there is no favorable selection, then there should be no difference in the reported levels of prior utilization.

Table 4-2 reports the results of one of the first of these sorts of studies. Jackson-Beeck and Kleinman (1983) reported on the experience of 11 employers who first offered an HMO in the early 1980s. They found that those ultimately enrolling in a newly offered HMO had much lower claims experience in the year prior to the choice than did those who remained in the conventional plan. The difference was $23.14 per member per month. This difference was largely attributable to institutional (i.e., inpatient) services, but professional services (i.e., ambulatory services) were also lower.

Wilensky and Rossiter (1986) reviewed the findings of a score of studies that examined the issue of patient favorable selection into HMOs published between 1974 and 1986. Of the dozen most recent studies, beginning with the Jackson-Beeck and Kleinman study in 1983, eight found evidence of favorable selection into HMOs, three were inconclusive, and only one found no evidence of biased selection.

While the RAND study does offer some strong evidence of an HMO effect, at least in one large, well-run staff model HMO, the research literature suggests that there is typically substantial favorable selection into HMOs. The evidence with respect to other forms of managed care plans is less definitive. However, there is limited but strong evidence to suggest that preferred provider organizations (PPOs) get a less-favorable draw of the population and, in fact, may have become the conventional plan of the 2000s, at least with respect to selection bias (see Morrisey, Jensen, and Gabel 2003).

TABLE 4-2
Favorable
Selection

	Total Expense	Institutional Expense	Professional Expense
FFS	$57.35	$40.45	$16.45
HMO	$34.17	$22.23	$11.45
Difference	$23.14*	$18.22*	$ 5.00*

SOURCE: Data from Jackson-Beeck and Kleinman (1983).

NOTES: *Significant at the 99% confidence level. FFS = Fee-for-service plan; HMO = Health maintenance organization.

Favorable Selection in the Medicare Program

Adverse and favorable selection are not just concerns of private insurers; they are also significant issues for the federal Medicare program for the elderly. Since the 1970s, the Medicare program has allowed beneficiaries to be in traditional Medicare or to join a Medicare HMO. (See Chapter 21 for a more complete discussion of the Medicare program and of Medicare managed care options, currently called Medicare Advantage.)

Until 2006, the program allowed Medicare beneficiaries to transfer to or from traditional Medicare each month. As with most HMOs, Medicare HMOs provide a limited panel of physicians and hospitals. Traditional Medicare covers virtually all providers. However, many Medicare HMOs offer broader coverage, including prescription drug coverage and annual physicals, which were particular advantages in the days prior to Medicare Part D prescription drug coverage. The Medicare program paid its participating HMOs on a capitated basis for each covered beneficiary. The payment was essentially 95 percent of the average Medicare cost of care in the local community. Medicare HMOs are required to accept all beneficiaries who choose to enroll, but if a Medicare HMO is able to somehow attract sufficiently low utilizers of care, it could reap substantial profits.

Box 4-3 reports the findings of a congressional advisory commission on the costs to Medicare of those who choose Medicare HMOs, relative to those in traditional Medicare. The commission used the same methodology as did the Jackson-Beeck and Kleinman study discussed earlier to look at 1989 to 1994 Medicare claims data. It identified those who newly enrolled in a Medicare HMO and then examined their Medicare claims experience in the six months prior to switching to the HMO and compared it to the average claims experience of all those in traditional Medicare in those months. As is clear in Box 4-3, those who ultimately switched to a Medicare HMO had total covered claims experience that was only 63 percent of average. This suggests substantial favorable selection, to say the least!

BOX 4-3

Total Medicare Expenditures of HMO Enrollees Relative to Traditional Medicare Enrollees

- Six months prior to enrollment: 63 percent
- Six months after disenrollment: 160 percent

SOURCE: Data from Prospective Payment Assessment Commission (1996).

The study also examined the claims experience of those Medicare HMO enrollees who switched back to traditional Medicare. In the six months following their switchback, they had claims experience that was 160 percent of the average. It is easy to speculate that the HMOs sought out low utilizers, encouraged them to join the plan, and if they had health problems, somehow pushed them out of the plan.

However, much less pernicious scenarios also are consistent with these data. Consider a reasonably healthy, elderly, Medicare-eligible woman. She joins a Medicare HMO perhaps because of its coverage of an annual physical or its encouragement of preventive services. Unfortunately, her hip has deteriorated, and she discovers that she needs a hip replacement. Her primary care doctor refers her to the plan's orthopedic surgeon, but her children want her to see the "orthopod" they consider the best in town. That surgeon is not in the HMO's panel. Under the terms of the Medicare program, the woman can disenroll from the HMO, be immediately covered by traditional Medicare, and have her surgery. Once she has recovered, she may even switch back to the HMO. If stories of this sort are common, they could explain the lower claims experience prior to joining the HMO and the higher experience after disenrollment. Other scenarios, such as the urban legend in Box 4-4, are also possible, but unethical at best.

In more recent work, Batata (2004) used county Medicare enrollment over the 1990 to 1994 period to estimate the effect on one-year change in traditional Medicare's share of seniors to estimate the marginal cost of Medicare HMO enrollees. She found that a 1 percent reduction in the traditional share was associated with an increase in average county Medicare expenditures of $1,033, almost all of this coming from Medicare Part A hospital services. This is consistent with favorable selection. It says that when Medicare HMOs had a somewhat larger enrollment, those people who remained in traditional Medicare had higher average costs; that is, the lower utilizers disproportionately moved out. Batata concluded that, in their first year of enrollment, Medicare HMO enrollees had costs that were 20 to 30 percent lower than the average 1994 costs of $3,932.

BOX 4-4

An Urban Legend

Medicare HMOs must enroll any Medicare-eligible person who wants to enroll. The legend, alternatively described as occurring in Florida or New York, has it that the Medicare HMO sets up its enrollment office in a third-floor walkup. Any senior who can walk up three flights of stairs is enthusiastically enrolled!

Persistence of Favorable Selection over Time

The research strongly suggests that HMOs attract a healthier draw of the population. This raises the important managerial and policy question of whether favorable selection continues over time. If the experience persists over time, then all an HMO has to do to remain successful is attract some low utilizers and keep them happy enough to stay in the plan (and work to prevent entry into its market). On the other hand, if low utilizers quickly become average utilizers or worse, this suggests that the plan must continually turn over its enrollment or do something to keep the enrollees healthy. From a policy perspective, if favorable selection is enduring, we might consider efforts to promote competition or regulate insurer practices. If the selection bias is fleeting, we might worry more about plan turnover and the quality of care provided.

Obviously, the foregoing discussion of using prior utilization as an indicator of favorable selection rests on a presumption of some persistence of behavior. In the absence of changes in incentives, two factors are likely to influence the persistence of healthcare usage. The first has to do with the chronic versus random nature of personal health status. If a person's illnesses or injuries are largely random, that would suggest that particularly high or low utilization in any one year is an unusual event and that the individual would quickly revert to the average level of utilization. If the conditions are chronic, it suggests that utilization will continue at an elevated level for some time. The second factor is behavioral. For a given health condition and set of prices, one individual may seek care, and another may not. The former will be a persistent higher utilizer; the latter will be a persistent lower utilizer.

Only a handful of studies have examined healthcare utilization over more than two years. One of the problems with undertaking such an analysis is finding several years' worth of data on a large, identifiable cohort of people who have unchanged health insurance coverage over the period. Garber, McCurdy, and McClellan (1999) undertook such a study using Medicare beneficiary data over the 1987 to 1991 and 1992 to 1995 periods. While the study focused only on those who had traditional Medicare over the period, it was not able to control for differences in supplemental coverage that the beneficiaries may have obtained, dropped, or changed over the years. Figure 4-1 summarizes the findings for the more-recent cohort.

Garber and colleagues had Medicare claims data on a cohort of 37,000 Medicare beneficiaries who were alive in 1989. They divided this group into three subgroups based on their 1993 Medicare spending. The low utilizers were those in the 0 to 50th percentiles. Their average Medicare expenditure in 1993 was $211. The middle subgroup was composed of those in the 51st to 95th percentiles; they had average expenditures of $5,758. The high utilizers were those in the 96th+ percentiles; they had average expenditures of $41,921, which is off the scale. (This is the typical health insurance experience. A very

FIGURE 4-1

Persistence of
Expenditures
for Surviving
Medicare
Beneficiaries

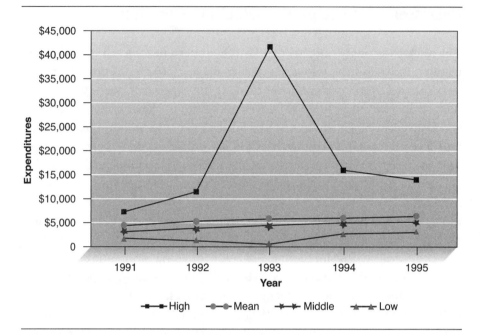

SOURCE: Data from Garber, McCurdy, and McClellan (1999).

small proportion of the covered individuals incur the vast majority of the expenditures.)

The pattern of results was clear. First, those with low expenditures in the base year (1993) had unusually low expenditures for that year; however, in the two prior years and two subsequent years, they had much higher expenditures. Analogously, those who were high utilizers in the base year had unusually high expenditures that year. Their experience was much lower in the prior and subsequent years. Second, even though their respective claims experience did "revert toward the mean," low utilizers continued to be low utilizers, and high utilizers continued to be high utilizers. In short, while there is a large random component to healthcare utilization, there is sizable persistence in use. Selection bias tends to be enduring.

We should note that this pattern of results was observed in the 1989 to 1991 cohort as well. The study also noted the effects of deaths among the sample in the two latter years (1994 to 1995 and 1990 to 1991, respectively). Figure 4-1 only includes survivors in the last two years; however, the same pattern of results occurs if we include the decedents in the analysis.

Selection Bias in Non-HMO Settings

This chapter has focused on evidence on adverse selection in the HMO vs. conventional coverage decision because that is where most of the empirical research has been conducted. The extent of any selection bias is always an empirical question and is not limited to the managed care setting. In some early work, Randy Ellis (1985) examined the extent of selection bias in an employer group that offered a single conventional plan in 1982 but three conventional plans with differing deductibles and stoploss features in 1983. Ellis concluded:

> The results presented here suggest that the self-selection effects in these settings may be enormous, with high-coverage plans attracting enrollees who are as much as four times as expensive as enrollees choosing the low-coverage option. (p. 167)

Similarly, it is not at all unheard of for families and individuals to "save up" their use of dental services and obtain dental coverage only when they expect to use the services. Such actions constitute adverse selection. Currently, a number of reformers are encouraging the use of "consumer-driven health plans." These products encompass a high-deductible health plan and a tax-sheltered Health Savings Account (HSA). Proponents argue that such plans give consumers strong incentives to be value-conscious purchasers of health services because they must spend their own, albeit tax-sheltered, dollars on the first $1,000 or $2,000 of services used. Consumers are expected to forego services that are not viewed as worth the cost and to shop around for providers who will give them good quality at a lower price. Opponents argue that such plans will be riddled with favorable selection. As always, the extent of adverse or favorable selection is an empirical question. However, its potential is always present in voluntary insurance markets.

Chapter Summary

- Adverse selection arises when there is asymmetric information. One party, usually the consumer, knows more about his or her likely use of health services than does the other.
- Enrollees in HMOs have substantially lower utilization experience than do enrollees in traditional plans. The difference is largely attributable to differences in the use of hospitals.
- The difference in utilization can be attributable to favorable selection into HMOs, an HMO effect (whereby HMOs do something to keep people out of the hospital), or both. While there is evidence on both sides of the debate, the preponderance of evidence supports the favorable selection argument.
- The available evidence also suggests that the propensity to be a high or low utilizer of services regresses toward the mean over time, but nonetheless, persists.

Discussion Questions

1. Suppose that the difference in utilization experience between conventional insurance and managed care is attributable to favorable selection. If so, would a state Medicaid program save any money if it required all of its recipients to join a Medicaid managed care plan?
2. A common experience of employers that began offering multiple health plans instead of a single plan was that their total health insurance costs increased. How could this occur?
3. If insurers of dental services understand that high utilizers are disproportionately likely to join their plan, what actions would you expect them to take to deal with this condition when they design their insurance plan?

UNDERWRITING AND RATE MAKING

Adverse selection is a potentially fatal problem for insurers. If they combine dissimilar risks in the same pool, those with lower expected utilization will see premiums that are too high. These individuals or groups will tend to decline coverage or will be attracted by other insurers with policies designed for low risks. To make matters worse, high utilizers will see premiums that are too low. They will be attracted to the plan, raising average claims well above the plan's expectations and generating losses for the insurer.

Insurers deal with adverse selection through the underwriting and rate-making process. They seek to identify the determinants of claims experience and use this knowledge to put individuals and groups into risk pools that reflect their expected utilization. The nature and extent of this underwriting process depends in large part on the rating techniques employed. Community rating, in which everyone is in the same risk pool, requires little formal underwriting. Similarly, retrospective experience rating requires little underwriting; each employer group constitutes its own risk class.

In this chapter, we paint a broad-brush picture of objective risk and use this to discuss the nature of underwriting. We describe community, manual, and experience rating. This leads naturally into a discussion of self-insured groups. The final section of the chapter examines the effects of ignoring meaningful differences across groups. We investigate the effects of state laws that mandate unisex insurance rates and of other laws that prohibit the use of medical underwriting in the nongroup market.

Premium Computations

When calculating premiums, insurers begin with the "pure premium" or "actuarially fair premium" and adjust it for the costs of running the insurance plan as in the following equation:

Gross premium = Pure premium / (1 – Loading percentage)

The pure premium is simply the expected claims experience we discussed in Chapters 3 and 4. It is defined as the probability of loss times the magnitude of the loss. The loading percentage is the markup the insurer applies to cover its objective risk, profit, and costs of marketing, adjudicating and processing claims, coordinating benefits, and providing access to its network. These costs also would be reduced by any investment earnings the insurer obtains on the premiums and reserves it holds. Obviously, the size of the loading percentage is going to depend not only on the actual marginal costs of running the insurance plan but also on the nature of the competition the insurer faces.

The size of the loading percentage varies between group and non-group markets. Pauly and Percy (2000), for example, reported that, in 1995, the loading percentage was in the neighborhood of 10 percent for group coverage and 50 percent for individual coverage.

Objective Risk

Objective risk is the relative variation in actual claims experience from what was expected. The key point of this definition is to distinguish objective risk from subjective risk. We dealt with subjective risk in Chapter 3 when we examined an individual's degree of risk aversion. We concluded that those with a greater degree of risk aversion are more likely to buy insurance coverage at any level of the probability of loss or the size of the potential loss. The concept of objective risk focuses only on the underlying possible losses and their distribution.

In some sense, it is tempting to think of subjective risk as characterizing the demand side of the insurance market and objective risk as characterizing the supply side. This is somewhat misleading, however, for two reasons. First, as consumers of insurance, we do take objective risk into consideration. We just don't have the same number of covered lives to work with as do those selling coverage. Second, suppliers of insurance will apply their own (corporate) degree of risk aversion to a given objective risk. Insurers will exhibit different degrees of subjective risk tolerance when they evaluate a given objective risk. One insurance company may enter a market, while another may judge it too risky.

A useful way of thinking about objective risk is the following simple formula:

$$\text{Objective risk} = \sigma \,/\, (\mu\sqrt{N}),$$

where σ is some measure of the dispersion in the average claims of the group, μ is a measure of the expected loss, and $\sqrt{N}$ is the square root of the number of covered lives. It should come as no surprise that objective risk increases with the dispersion of the possible losses. It is much riskier if losses can range from $0 to $1,000,000 than if the range is only $0 to $10,000. Formal definitions of statistical variance, standard deviation, and range are common measures of the dispersion of claims.

The larger is the expected loss, other things equal, the smaller is the objective risk. This is counterintuitive; the objective risk declines with μ, the size of the expected loss. This conundrum, however, is easily understood when we remember that the dispersion is held constant. Suppose the possible loss can range from \$0 to \$10,000. If the expected loss is \$1,000, this is a relatively large risk. On the other hand, if the expected loss is \$8,000, the risk is much smaller.

Finally, objective risk declines with the number of covered lives ($\sqrt{N}$). This is essentially, the law of large numbers. With a given expected loss and a given dispersion of losses, we have more confidence that the actual loss will be the expected loss if we have many more people in the risk pool (see Box 5-1). Suppose we were to flip a coin, losing \$1,000 on each "heads" and

BOX 5-1

Example of Differing Objective Risks

Table A gives some sense of the objective risk associated with employer groups of different sizes in communities with differing rates of hospital days per 1,000 people. The hospital day rates in this context can be thought of as a measure of expected claims. The employer group sizes are alternative measures of the number of covered lives. The 95 percent confidence interval used to generate the table is based on an assumption that the constant standard deviation of hospital days per 1,000 people is 200. Standard deviation is a traditional measure of dispersion. Thus, the numbers in the table are one approach to measuring objective risk.

TABLE A
Expected Deviation in Hospital Days per 1,000 as a Percentage of the Expected Utilization

	Employee Group Size				
Hospital Days per 1,000	20	50	100	1,000	10,000
300	±1,460%	±369%	±131%	±4.1%	±0.13%
400	±1,096%	±277%	±98%	±3.1%	±0.10%
500	±877%	±222%	±78%	±2.5%	±0.08%
600	±730%	±185%	±65%	±2.0%	±0.07%

NOTE: Computed under the assumptions of a standard deviation of 200 days per 1,000 and a 95 percent confidence interval.

Continued

Box 5-1
Continued

It is immediately clear, as we move from left to right along any row in Table A, that as the size of the group increases, the hospital day risk associated with the group declines. With a 400 hospital day rate, for example, a group of 100 covered lives would have an expected deviation of +/–98 percent. That means, at the 95 percent confidence interval, we could not reject the conclusion that any hospital utilization for this group between 8 and 792 days was just random fluctuation around a stable mean of 400 days per 1,000. In contrast, a group of 10,000 has an expected deviation of only +/– 0.08 percent. Clearly, when insurers see a group of 10,000 covered lives with a 425 hospital day rate in a community with a day rate of 500, they likely conclude that the group has lower claims experience.

Now consider any column. For a given group size of 100 members, as the expected loss increases, moving down the column, the objective risk declines. At 300 days, the risk is +/–131 percent of the community day rate. At 500 days, it is only +/–78 percent.

As a consequence, insurers may want to combine reasonably similar small groups to reduce objective risk. They may even want to combine reasonably similar small groups across communities with different day rates for the same reason.

losing nothing on each "tails." We would expect to lose $500 on each flip. But a long run of "heads" or "tails" can occur, meaning that the actual outcome can vary significantly from the expected loss. With 50 or 100 or 10,000 flips, we have increasing confidence that the actual loss is the expected loss.

Nature of Underwriting

Given this definition of objective risk, the underwriting task is straightforward. All we do is create a number of risk pools or risk classes. Each one has an expected loss that is meaningfully different from the others. Each has a very small dispersion of possible outcomes, and each has a large number of covered lives!

We might start by establishing differences based on gender and age on the theory that older people have higher claims experience, perhaps due to the prevalence of chronic conditions. Women have higher claims experience in their younger years, based on childbearing, but have lower experience later. We might want to establish different risk classes based on occupation or industry. Those who choose more-dangerous occupations may also engage in more-risky activities outside the job setting. We could also create different risk pools based on geography, given different disease patterns across areas; for example, the southeastern United States is commonly known as the "stroke belt." Moreover, providers may charge different prices based on local market forces, and regulatory constraints may influence the nature of coverage that is offered across regions. Finally, we may wish to establish different risk pools based on health status.

The problem for insurers is that, while the differences in expected claims across these groups may be meaningful, there is also dispersion around each of the expected claims estimates. In addition, some potential risk classes may be too small to provide much assurance that the expected claims and dispersion measures are reliable. There may be only a few 26- to 30-year-old female miners in Kentucky, for example. As a consequence, insurers may combine somewhat dissimilar groups, such as female miners and construction workers, trading off somewhat dissimilar expected losses to get substantial reductions in dispersion and greater confidence resulting from more covered lives.

In addition to establishing reliable risk pools, insurers have to be concerned with the cost of acquiring data on potential members of the health plan. Such data are used to place an applicant in the proper risk class. In the nongroup market, it may be simple to use a driver's license to establish age, gender, and place of residence. Obtaining information on health status or family medical history, however, may be much more problematic. Insurers could insist that the applicant go to his or her physician and have a physical and medical history completed. Alternatively, they might request that the applicant make an appointment with the health plan's physician. Both of these are very expensive means of collecting data. In the former case, the consumer incurs the cost of the doctor visit, raising the full price of the coverage. In the latter case, the insurer incurs the cost, again raising the cost of the coverage.

Alternatively, insurers can simply ask applicants to identify any health problems—for example, "Do you smoke?" "Do you have heart disease?" The problem is that applicants have an obvious incentive to portray themselves as being in perfect health. One way insurers can deal with this is to ask those questions but reserve the right to deny coverage if it is subsequently discovered that the applicant has lied. Thus, the insurer would take the application, but if the subscriber subsequently submits a claim related to chronic obstructive pulmonary disease (COPD), the insurer will investigate, and if it discovers that the applicant was a smoker, it would deny payment of the claim based on a fraudulent application.

In general, we expect insurers to collect data for underwriting only to the extent that the information is relevant to meaningful differences in expected claims experience and sufficiently inexpensive to collect so that the collection costs are less than the savings from knowing the information.

Approaches to Rating

There are essentially three approaches to determining the rate or premium to charge an individual or group: community rating, manual rating, and experience rating. The industry and public policy uses of these terms, however, are not standardized. Federally qualified health maintenance organizations (HMOs), for example, are required to use "adjusted community rating" or "community rating by class," both of which are closer to manual rating than community rating. State legislatures may often mandate that an insurer must "community rate" and then define that to permit differences by age, gender, and location, but not health status. This, too, is closer to manual rating than community rating.

Community Rating

Community rating is eminently straightforward. All individuals and/or all groups are put in a single risk pool. This is the approach to rate making that the Blue Cross and Blue Shield plans used in their first 30 years and that HMOs and other managed care plans used well into the 1970s. It is also an approach that proponents of universal health insurance plans sometimes advocate.

The rate-setting framework is simple. Insurers compute the actual claims experience per covered life for the recent past and project that value forward to account for general inflation and anticipated changes in real medical care costs and patterns of utilization. They then add the costs of running the plan, a normal profit, and a contribution to reserves in case the utilization experience is worse than anticipated. They subtract the investment earnings on premiums and reserves held. Unlike life insurance, where loses are incurred over many years, often decades, in healthcare, reserves are a relatively minor factor because the claims tail is relatively short.

This process establishes the cost basis of the premium that will be charged. The actual premium will also reflect the nature of competition in the local health insurance market.

Manual Rating

Manual rating reflects the traditional role of underwriting in the insurance industry. Insurers seek to identify characteristics of individuals or groups that are associated with higher or lower claims experience. In the individual market, such factors as age, gender, location, occupation, and health status may be used. In the group market, the mix of employees and dependents with those characteristics may be used, as well as firm-specific factors, such as industry. The term *manual rating* is derived from the practice of insurers in precomputer days of constructing rate manuals that contained pages for specific risk characteristics. For example, one page may have focused on the Cleveland, Ohio, market area and listed rates for men and women of specific age groups with various health conditions in that area.

Manual rating is used extensively in the individual nongroup market and to some extent in the small-group market. You can go to the eHealthInsurance website (www.ehealthinsurance.com) and provide your zip code, age, gender, and whether or not you smoke, and get a preliminary rate quote for several policies with varying degrees of coverage. This is a manual rating system. The Medicare system also uses an increasingly sophisticated manual rating system when it determines how much it will pay Medicare HMOs. We will examine that system in some detail in the next chapter.

Experience Rating

Experience rating bases the premium on the prior or current claims of a group. There are two generic forms: prospective and retrospective experience rating.

Prospective Experience Rating

Prospective experience rating occurs when insurers examine the past claims experience of a group and develop a premium on that basis. Consider an employer group that has been with an insurer for some 10 years and has 1,000 workers and a comparable number of dependents. The group has past claims experience that is only 80 percent as high as the insurer's overall book of business. Consider a second employer group that has been with the insurer for 2 years and has 100 employees plus dependents. The group has past claims experience that is 90 percent as high as the insurer's overall book of business. Both ask for a premium that reflects their lower claims experience.

Given our earlier discussion of objective risk, the first firm clearly has a stronger case. The insurer has some 20,000 life-years of data on the firm, and the utilization experience is substantially lower than the overall average. In this circumstance, the insurer is likely to develop a premium that is based entirely on the prior claims experience of the first firm, rolled forward to reflect higher anticipated provider prices and utilization trends. This is prospective experience rating. The insurer quotes a future or prospective premium based on the firm's prior claims experience. It is important to note that the insurer is bearing the underwriting risk. It quotes a premium and incurs any losses that occur if the rate is too low.

The insurer may also quote a prospective experience-rated premium to the second firm. However, the insurer obviously is much less confident that this firm's experience reflects any true lower utilization. In the terms of the industry, this firm's experience lacks "credibility." In general, an insurer will create a blended premium that reflects both the firm's own experience and the experience of the insurer's overall book of business. The weights that are applied to the firm's own experience and to the overall book of business are determined by the "credibility factor" that the insurer has developed. Each insurer has its own approach to developing this formula, but it obviously is going to depend on the same factors that make up objective risk: the number of covered lives, the size of the expected losses, and their associated variances. In addition, the insurer may weight the firm's experience with other firms in its industry, state, or size, as well as with the entire book of business.

Retrospective Experience Rating   Retrospective experience rating is a much simpler approach than prospective experience rating and is more commonly used with larger firms. Essentially, the insurer has the firm open a checking account from which the insurer writes checks to pay the claims of the firm's employees and their dependents as those claims arrive. In addition, the insurer charges the firm a fee to administer the plan and adjudicate the claims.

In fact, however, the process is a bit more complex. The firm makes monthly or quarterly payments to the insurer that reflect both the administrative costs and the prepayment of claims. The insurer draws from the prepayment account as claims are processed. At the end of the year, the firm and the insurer settle-up accounts. Typically, the firm will make a "retro payment" at the end of the year to reconcile the quarterly payments with the actual experience. Note that, in retrospective experience rating, it is the firm, not the insurer, that bears the underwriting risk. If the prepayments are insufficient to cover claims, the firm pays.

Of course, a firm may not be willing to bear all of that underwriting risk. Retrospective experience rating can accommodate this easily. The firm can essentially buy stoploss coverage from the insurer. In such a circumstance, the firm's "premium" to the insurer includes three components: the administrative fee, the prepayment of claims, and the payment for stoploss coverage.

Stoploss coverage can take two forms. The firm can buy aggregate stoploss. In this case, once the annual claims expenditures reach some predetermined level—say, $2,000,000—the firm is not liable for any additional claims for the remainder of the year. In addition, or alternatively, the firm can buy specific stoploss. This coverage limits the amount that the firm would have to pay on any single claim or individual—say, $40,000. Once an employee has a health event that results in claims exceeding the threshold, the firm is no longer responsible for additional claims from that individual; the remaining claims are paid by the stoploss policy.

Self-Insured Plans

With retrospective experience rating, the immediate reaction is to say that these firms are really self-insured. Substantively, this is exactly correct. The firms buying such coverage are bearing some or all of the underwriting risk. As a matter of law, however, this is not correct. As discussed in Chapter 1, when the forerunners of Blue Cross attempted to create a new health insurance plan, they were confronted by insurance commissioners who required that the plans conform to the state laws regulating insurance. Any retrospectively experience-rated firm that was literally self-insured prior to 1974 ran the risk of a similar fate.

However, as we also discussed in Chapter 1, the 1974 ERISA (Employee Retirement Income Security Act) legislation allowed plans that were self-insured under the terms of the legislation to be exempt from state insurance regulation. The number of self-insured plans grew rapidly after the enactment of ERISA. The explanation for this is now clear. Many large employers were "essentially" self-insured prior to ERISA. With the enactment of the law, they could easily switch to being really self-insured, and in doing so, they could avoid the premium taxes and other insurance regulations that the states could impose. Today, an employer group can bear the underwriting risk itself and buy administrative services from an established insurer through an administrative services only (ASO) contract or from a third-party administrator (TPA), or provide the services itself in-house.

It is not at all clear how common the various approaches to underwriting are. One of the difficulties is that a firm may offer several health insurance plans, some of which are self-insured and some of which are purchased. Figure 5-1 provides one set of estimates for conventional health insurance plans offered by larger employers, but the data are over 15 years old. In 1991, 46 percent of conventional plans were self-insured without a stoploss, and 19 percent were self-insured with a stoploss feature. However, another 14 percent were "minimum premium plans." Insurance terminology varies

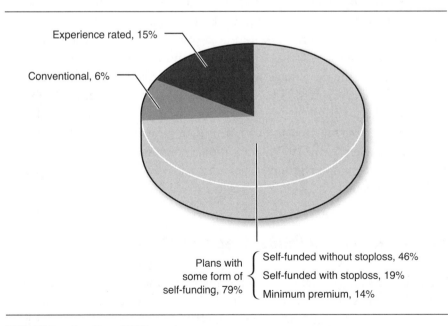

FIGURE 5-1
Underwriting Methods Used for Traditional Health Plans by Larger Employers, 1991

Experience rated, 15%

Conventional, 6%

Plans with some form of self-funding, 79%
{ Self-funded without stoploss, 46%
Self-funded with stoploss, 19%
Minimum premium, 14%

SOURCE: Data from Humo (2003).

TABLE 5-1

Percentage of Insured Workers in Partially or Fully Self-Insured Plans

	1993	1996	1999
Conventional	74%	74%	62%
HMO	5%	20%	19%
PPO	74%	70%	67%
POS	22%	81%	47%
All	55%	57%	53%

SOURCE: Data from Jensen and Morrisey (2003).

NOTES: HMO = Health maintenance organization; PPO = Preferred provider organization; POS = Point-of-service plan.

across carriers and states, but minimum premium plans are simply self-insured plans with a stoploss in which the plan administrator is also the stop-loss insurer. Thus, according to Figure 5-1, some 79 percent of conventional plans in larger firms were self-insured in some fashion in 1991. Fifteen percent of those reporting indicated that they had experience-rated conventional coverage, but the type of experience rating is undisclosed. The remaining 6 percent were presumably in a manually rated plan.

Another way of examining the prevalence of underwriting techniques is to examine methods by plan type. This is done to some extent in Table 5-1, which reports the percentage of covered employees across all firm sizes that are in self-insured plans by type of coverage. By 1999, just over one-half of covered workers were in some form of self-insured plan. Workers in conventional and PPO plans were most likely to be self-insured; those in HMOs were least likely. Note, too, that the percentage in conventional self-insured plans in 1993 is close to the value reported in Figure 5-1 but also that it has declined substantially since then. This decline is almost certainly attributable to the decline in conventional coverage (and the commensurate growth in managed care) discussed in Chapter 2. By 1999, conventional coverage was disproportionately found in small employer groups. These firms are the least likely to self-insure, and as a consequence, the percentages in Table 5-1 decline over time.

Manual Rating Methods Used by HMOs

While HMOs are generally free to use any rating method, federally qualified HMOs are allowed to use only adjusted community rating or community rating by class if they do not use community rating. In addition, HMOs have traditionally not had the claims or patient encounter data that would allow them to experience-rate the way commercial insurers or Blue Cross/Blue Shield plans can.

Perhaps the best way to appreciate these methods is to understand the market forces that brought them about. By the late 1960s and early 1970s, larger employers had moved to experience rating when they realized that their employees and dependents had lower claims experience than average. As they began to offer HMOs in addition to conventional plans, they discovered that their costs often increased. They also found that the HMOs quoted premiums based on a community rate.

Large employers noted the inconsistency that their conventionally insured workers were said to have lower claims experience, but those employees who choose to join the HMOs were combined with presumably higher-cost people from elsewhere in the community. The employers insisted that HMO premiums also reflect the claims experience of their workers. The HMOs responded that one of the advantages of managed care was that workers and their dependents were not burdened with the paperwork associated with conventional coverage. The downside of this convenience was that HMOs did not have a paper trail of claims tied to individuals that would allow the experience-rated methods that other insurers used. The employers were not dissuaded. So, the managed care plans tried to be responsive, given the limitations of their data.

Adjusted Community Rating

Adjusted community rating uses the HMO's entire pool of utilization experience and applies specific characteristics of a firm to weight these data to better reflect the characteristics of the employer's workforce. The plan uses the firm's own "contract mix" and "contract size" applied to the "charging ratios" to weight the poolwide data. *Contract mix* refers to the proportion of single, two-party, and family contracts within the firm; *contract size* relates to the average number of people in a family; and *charging ratios* refer to the difference in claims cost between two-party and family coverage, relative to single coverage.

Suppose that an HMO's entire pool has one-third single, one-third two-party, and one-third family contracts and that the poolwide family contract has 3.5 people. Suppose, too, that two-party contracts use twice the medical care as singles and that family contracts use four times as much as singles. The community rate that the HMO charges will reflect this mix. If an employer has many more single and two-party workers and very little family coverage, its premium will be lower with adjusted community rating. Similarly, if the firm's average family contract only has 3.2 members, its quoted premium will also be lower. With adjusted community rating, the firm's own contract mix and family size are multiplied by the average charging ratios to produce an adjusted rate. Lippe (1996) provided a detailed discussion with numeric examples of adjusted community rating and community rating by class.

Community Rating by Class

Community rating by class uses the same adjusted community rating factors but adds analogous adjustments for the industry and for the age and gender mix of the group. Figure 5-2 provides insight into the potential magnitude of such adjustments. The figure presents HMO data from the mid-1980s on the relative costs of coverage in its poolwide data. Single contract costs are always lower than two-party and family costs, but the costs increase with age. In contrast, two-party costs are U-shaped and are lowest in the age 40–44 cohort. Family contract costs are also U-shaped but are only slightly more expensive than two-party contracts at age 60 and above. Notice that if a firm had a relatively large number of young single workers and middle-aged two-party workers, its quoted premiums would be substantially lower with community rating by class.

Finally, neither the adjusted community rating nor the community rating by class is in any way based on the firm's past or current claims experience. So, they are not experience-rated methods. Instead, the HMO is forced to assume that the claims experience of a firm with a given contract and age and gender mix is in fact comparable to the experience of the overall risk pool members with those characteristics. It seems plausible that they are comparable, but it is the

FIGURE 5-2
Relative Subscriber Cost (mean cost = 1.0)

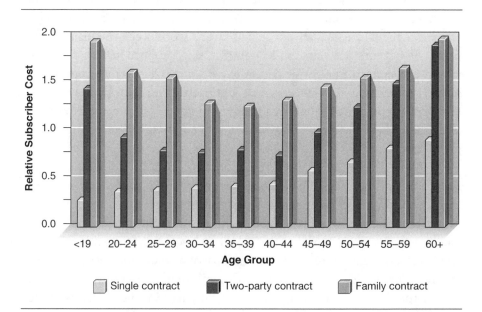

SOURCE: Anderson (1986), "Presentation to Business Coalition on Health, Hartford, CT" presented in the session The Purchases' Perspective: What Employers Want—Data and Rates, Group Health Association annual meeting, Minneapolis, MN, June 2, 1986, overhead 1. Reprinted with permission.

HMO's money that is at risk. The HMO is presumably willing to bear this risk rather than potentially losing the business to another HMO.

The Consequences of Combining Dissimilar Groups

Underwriting may appear to be a rather prosaic endeavor, but getting it wrong can have dramatic effects. Montana enacted "unisex" insurance rates in 1983. Under the provisions of the act, an insurer may not use gender for underwriting purposes. This has the effect of lumping men and women into the same risk pool. This is innocuous if men and women have the same expected utilization but can have dramatic effects if they do not.

Suppose young women have lower automobile crash rates than young men. If young men and women are combined into a single risk pool, we would expect the premiums for young women to increase because they are now averaged in with higher-risk young men. Premiums for young men fall. As a result of these premium changes, we should also expect to see changes in enrollment. Young women will disproportionately disenroll from auto insurance plans because of the higher premiums. Conversely, young men will be more likely to buy the lower-priced auto insurance. Table 5-2 reports estimates of the change in premiums for various types of insurance that were prepared by the Montana Insurance Department at the time. The Montana legislature considered repealing the unisex insurance rates as recently as 2005, but at last check, the law remains in force (*Helena Independent Record* 2005). The European Union considered a plan to introduce unisex insurance rates as well, but the plan was dropped when 17 of the 25 member states opposed it (Excite 2005). None of this is to imply that governments should or should not implement such policies. The point is only that if groups with significantly different claims experience are combined in the same pool, one group will see lower rates and the other higher rates with commensurate increases and decreases in the quantity of coverage purchased.

TABLE 5-2 Consequences of Underwriting Limitations: Effects of Unisex Insurance Rates

Percentage Change in Premiums		
	Women	*Men*
Whole life insurance (age 30)	+15%	−3%
Health insurance (age 40)	−13%	+28%
Auto insurance (age 20)	+49%	−16%

SOURCE: Data from *Wall Street Journal* (1987).

More typical are state efforts to limit the use of medical underwriting in the individual or small-group markets. Medical underwriting is simply the use of health status or medical history in establishing risk pools.

LoSasso and Lurie (2003) analyzed the effects of prohibitions on medical underwriting in eight states between 1993 and 1996. The state legislatures differed in the extent to which they would allow other characteristics to be used. New Jersey required pure community rating. New York allowed geographic differentials. Vermont allowed rates to vary by plus or minus 20 percent, based on demographic factors (except for HMOs and Blue Cross plans). New Hampshire allowed rates to differ by a factor of three for age. Kentucky, Massachusetts, Maine, and Washington State allowed some combination of age, geography, family composition, and gender.

The objectives of the study were twofold: first, to estimate the laws' effect on the probability that someone had individual nongroup coverage, and second, to estimate the laws' effect on the probability of being uninsured. The data for the study came from the 1990 through 2000 Survey of Income and Program Participation (SIPP), a nationally representative panel survey of individuals ages 18–64 from 41 identifiable states, yielding approximately 35,750 observations per year.

Our discussion of underwriting suggests that everyone in these states should not be affected equally. In particular, healthy people should find that they are lumped together with unhealthy people; as a consequence, their premiums should increase. They should be less likely to have nongroup coverage after the enactment of the law and perhaps more likely to be uninsured. In contrast, unhealthy people should find that their premiums drop. They should be more likely to buy nongroup coverage and perhaps less likely to be uninsured. (The effects on being uninsured are unclear because some may take up [or drop] employer-sponsored group coverage or public coverage as a result of the change in the law.)

In this study, LoSasso and Lurie defined "healthy" people as men ages 22–35 with self-reported health status of "very good" or "excellent." "Unhealthy" individuals were defined as those ages 40–64 of both sexes who reported health status of "poor." Women ages 22–35 were excluded from the "healthy" definition because pregnancy or potential pregnancy decisions may influence their decisions about coverage. The model used probit regression techniques and included state and year fixed effects.

The results are summarized in Table 5-3. After their states adopted prohibitions on medical underwriting, healthy individuals experienced a 2.0 percent decline in the probability of nongroup coverage. Since only 5.4 percent of this cohort had nongroup coverage, this implied a 37 percent decline relative to the mean. The healthy cohort also experienced a 3.9 percent increase in the probability of being uninsured. This was a 13 percent increase relative to the mean. In contrast, the unhealthy cohort saw a 4.5 percent

	Healthy	Unhealthy
Probability of having nongroup coverage	2.0% decline	4.5% increase
Probability of being uninsured	3.9% increase	7.4% decline

SOURCE: Data from LoSasso and Lurie (2003).

TABLE 5-3
Effects of Prohibiting Medical Underwriting on Coverage

increase in their probability of nongroup coverage (50 percent relative to their initial mean) and a 7.4 percent decline in the probability of being uninsured (50 percent relative to that mean.) Thus, the limited empirical research available supports the contention that combining dissimilar risks yields lower premiums and more coverage for high-risk groups but higher premiums and less coverage for low-risk groups.

From a public policy perspective, these results suggest that tinkering with allowable underwriting provisions is not without some costs. It may well be socially desirable to limit the use of medical underwriting provisions in the nongroup market, for example. However, doing so makes those low-risk people who buy nongroup coverage worse off. The broader question is whether there are alternative ways to achieve the same ends. From a management perspective, these results can be seen as a warning about the consequences of underwriting decisions that are inconsistent with the underlying claims experience. In this case, if a private insurer chooses to combine healthy and unhealthy groups, it should expect that competing insurers will arise to offer medically underwritten policies that will attract the healthy segment of the market.

Chapter Summary

- Underwriting is the process of identifying the characteristics of individuals or groups that reflect differences in expected claims, using that information to establish insurance pools with common risk, and matching new applicants to the appropriate risk.
- Underwriting focuses on objective risk and depends on the expected loss, the dispersion of possible losses, and the number of covered lives.
- Community rating essentially puts all members of the community in a single risk pool.
- Manual rating establishes rates based on characteristics of the individual or group. Adjusted community rating and community rating by class are examples of manual rating approaches that HMOs use.
- Experience rating bases the premium on the prior or current claims experience of a group. With prospective experience rating, the insurer

continues to bear the underwriting risk. With retrospective experience rating, the group itself bears some or all of the risk.

- Self-insured groups are conceptually no different than retrospectively experience-rated groups but have the advantage of not being subject to state insurance laws due to ERISA preemption.
- If an insurer combines dissimilar risk groups or if it is forced to do so by state or federal law, the effect is to raise the premium on the low-risk group and lower the premium on the high-risk group. Those facing now higher prices are likely to disproportionately drop out of the plan, and those facing now lower prices are likely to join.

Discussion Questions

1. Suppose your insurance competitor begins to use information from genetic testing to set insurance rates in the nongroup market. Suppose further that these tests do identify meaningful differences in claims experience. You choose not to implement such a model. Discuss what is likely to happen to your enrollee mix and to the premiums you charge.

2. Suppose your small, general medicine physician group is offered a capitated managed care contract. Through this contract, the group will be paid on a capitated basis. This means that the medical group will be paid a fixed amount per month for each patient and will be responsible for all of the costs of each patient's care. What does the concept of objective risk tell you about the desirability of this contract?

3. The *Wall Street Journal* (2002) described "reunderwriting" in the nongroup market. In this process, individuals are reclassified into a higher-risk group once they have a significant illness or claim. Discuss the effects of such a model on premiums and enrollment. If healthcare claims were essentially random over time in each of an insurer's established risk pools, how would this affect your conclusions?

4. Given the discussion of self-insured health insurance plans, under what conditions would you expect a small employer to become self-insured?

5. The available data suggest that experience rating (together with self-insurance) is by far the most common underwriting method used for larger employers. The avoidance of state insurance regulations and premium taxes may explain why firms tend to self-insure, but why do you think experience-rated approaches are more common than manual rating?

RISK ADJUSTMENT

In Chapter 5, we considered a variety of measures that insurers conceptually could use to place people into risk classes that reflected their likely claims experience. In this chapter, we look at some empirical evidence about the predictive power of alternative measures. In particular, we examine the extent to which demographic, health status, and prior utilization measures predict individual use of health services.

Two key points emerge from this discussion. First, even the most complete set of measures explains only a small proportion of the variance in an individual's use of health services. If utilization was wholly predictable based on readily available measures, there would be no role for insurance. Instead, we would borrow and lend to even out the peaks and troughs of our spending patterns. It should not be surprising that models have limited predictive power. If our health status has a large random component to it, then by definition, it is not predictable.

The second key point to emerge is that some sets of measures are better predictors than others of use of health services. Demographic characteristics perform surprisingly poorly. Prior utilization is the best predictor, and various measures of health status fall somewhere in between. It would be a mistake, however, to dismiss the predictive abilities of these measures. The ability to predict even a couple of percentage points better than others can yield a substantial competitive advantage, provided it can be done at relatively low cost.

In this chapter, we consider risk adjustment measures in the context of the payment system that Medicare uses to pay the health maintenance organizations (HMOs) that provide care to covered Medicare beneficiaries. While this is a risk adjustment system used by a payer rather than an insurer, it has the very great advantage of being publicly available. It also highlights the key issues.

Medicare Adjusted Average Per Capita Costs (AAPCC)

Since HMOs do not have a claims database, they were at a disadvantage in participating in Medicare when it was introduced in 1965. After a number of largely unsuccessful efforts, Medicare implemented in 1985 the Adjusted Average Per Capita Costs (AAPCC) payment methodology under authorization from Congress in the Tax Equity and Fiscal Responsibility Act of 1982 (TEFRA). See Zarabozo (2000) for a history of Medicare's approaches to paying managed care plans in its first 35 years.

Under TEFRA, Medicare essentially paid participating HMOs a fixed dollar amount for each beneficiary that chose to join the plan. Because HMOs were thought to be more efficient than traditional care providers, the legislation prescribed that the capitated rate should be 95 percent of the average Medicare Part A (i.e., hospital) plus Part B (i.e., ambulatory) expenditures per beneficiary. As we speculated in Chapter 5, claims experience likely varies by location. Congress appreciated this as well and ordered that the average expenditures be computed and applied for each county. These rates were then adjusted by the mix of beneficiaries the plan enrolled, taking into account their age, gender, Medicaid status, whether or not they were in a nursing home, and whether the beneficiary was an active worker with coverage through an employer. Thus, the AAPCC paid 95 percent of the county average Medicare Part A and Part B expenditures adjusted for age, gender, Medicaid, institutional, and active worker status. This is analogous to a simple manual rating system.

As we saw in Chapter 4, the Medicare payment system appears to provide HMOs with substantial incentives for enrolling people with lower-than-average expected claims and avoiding people with above-average claims. One government study found that Medicare HMO enrollees had expenditures that were only 63 percent of the average of all beneficiaries in the six months prior to joining the HMO (Prospective Payment Assessment Commission 1996). If this is so, Medicare is consistently overpaying for the services provided by Medicare HMOs, and higher-cost beneficiaries may be effectively denied access to a form of healthcare delivery that they may prefer.

Improving the AAPCC

Almost immediately, Medicare funded research to try to improve its payment system. Such research requires data on the demographic, health status, and healthcare utilization characteristics of a relatively large number of heterogeneous people over time. Moreover, these people should face the same financial incentives for the use of health services; otherwise, as we will see in Chapter 7, their use of services will be distorted.

The RAND Health Insurance Experiment provided a data set that approximately satisfied these conditions. We discuss this experiment in some detail in Chapter 7, but for current purposes, it is enough to know that the study randomly assigned people from six sites across the country into different health plans and monitored their use of health services over the four to five years of the experiment during the 1970s. It also recorded demographic and health status characteristics of the participants at baseline. In fact, much of the current knowledge about the measurement of health status had its genesis with this study. Thus, the study is well suited to examine alternative predictive models of utilization based on demographic characteristics, subjective and physiological measures of health status, and prior utilization (Newhouse et al. 1989). Box 6-1 summarizes the measures available for consideration.

BOX 6-1

Measures of Potential Risk Factors Used in the RAND Study

Demographic Measures (AAPCC Variables)

- Age
- Gender
- Location (indicator for each of the six sites in the study)
- Eligible for welfare at baseline

Subjective Health Status Measures

- *Physical health* (based on self-reported measures of role and personal limitations)
- *Mental health* (based on self-reported measures of psychological distress, behavioral/emotional control, and positive affect)
- *General health* (based on self-reported measures of general well-being)
- *Disease count* (based on the presence of any of 32 chronic conditions)

Physiological Health Status Measures

- Dichotomous measures
- Continuous measures
    (based on 27 measures, including such items as elevated cholesterol, hypertension, diabetes, electrocardiogram abnormalities, active ulcer, anemia, dyspepsia, abnormal thyroid function, etc.)

Prior Utilization

- Outpatient expense in prior year
- Inpatient expense in prior year

SOURCES: Data from Newhouse et al. (1989) and Newhouse and the Insurance Experiment Group (1993).

While the analysis was somewhat more complicated than this, the study team essentially ran a series of regressions in which total inpatient and outpatient expenditures of each individual in year t were the dependent variables and were explained by alternative sets of potential risk characteristics. When prior-year utilization measures were included, these were expenditures in year $t - 1$. Because the overall RAND study was concerned with the effects of insurance copayment arrangements on expenditures, the regressions also controlled for the health plan in which the person was enrolled.

Table 6-1 reports the "R^2" or percentage of explained variation for many of the regressions the study team ran. Because their interest was in improving the AAPCC model Medicare used, all of the models include the demographic or AAPCC factors. The AAPCC variables by themselves explain 1.6 percent of total expenditures, 0.7 percent of inpatient expenditures, and 7.2 percent of outpatient variation. Notice that, in general, outpatient expenditures were more predictable than inpatient spending. This probably reflects the greater extent to which behavioral and chronic factors influence ambulatory use. Notice, too, that the percentage of explained variation is quite small. Age, gender, location, and welfare status explained less than 2 percent of total expenditures.

Medicare, or any insurer, can ask its subscribers to report their health status and use the responses to assign the subscribers to appropriate risk classes. This study had rather extensive measures of subjective health. When these were added to the AAPCC measures, the model explained 2.8 percent of total expenditures—a 75 percent improvement! Operationally, however, self-reported health status is likely to be problematic for Medicare. Beneficiaries (and the health plans that they wish to join) may have an incentive to

TABLE 6-1

Percentage of Explained Variation in Healthcare Expenditures Yielded by Alternative Specifications

	Total	Inpatient	Outpatient
AAPCC	1.6%	0.7%	7.2%
AAPCC + Subjective health status	2.8%	1.2%	11.1%
AAPCC + Dichotomous physiological health status	3.8%	2.0%	13.5%
AAPCC + Continuous physiological health status	4.2%	2.6%	13.0%
AAPCC + Prior utilization	6.4%	2.8%	21.2%
All	9.0%	5.0%	25.1%

SOURCE: Data from Newhouse et al. (1989).

report poorer health status in the hope that a higher capitation payment will be forthcoming. Confirming that the information that beneficiaries provide is truthful could become a serious and costly challenge.

Alternatively, Medicare could obtain relatively simple dichotomous physiological measures of health status, such as measures from a clinical record that indicate whether the beneficiary has hypertension, diabetes, etc. These measures were added to the AAPCC measures and are reported in the third row of Table 6-1. Together with the demographic factors, they explained 3.8 percent of total expenditures. This is a substantial improvement over simply using the demographic measures, but obtaining even simple clinical data is expensive both for Medicare and for the beneficiary.

We could go further and use even more-detailed clinical information. For example, we could collect and use data on actual blood pressure, instead of a simple measure of whether or not the beneficiary has hypertension. And we could use a measure of elevated glucose, rather than a simple measure of whether the beneficiary has diabetes. Such continuous measures of physiological health are reported in the fourth row of Table 6-1. Together with the AAPCC measures, they explained 4.2 percent of variation in total expenditures. Thus, more-detailed clinical measures do provide more predictive power, but the costs of collecting such detailed data are probably prohibitive.

Alternatively, Medicare (or another insurer) could use prior utilization data. These measures were added to the AAPCC demographic factors and are reported in the fifth row of Table 6-1. This approach explained 6.4 percent of total expenditures, 2.8 percent of inpatient claims, and 21.2 percent of outpatient expenditures. Relative to the other approaches, prior utilization has substantially greater explanatory power. This result probably explains why health insurers tend to focus on prior claims experience when setting insurance premiums. The data exhibit relatively strong predictive power. Moreover, once insurers have a set of subscribers and their claims experience, using those data to predict future use is relatively inexpensive.

We could go further and combine various sets of health status measures. The final row of Table 6-1 presents the percentages of explained variation when all of the measures of subjective and physiological health and prior utilization were included with the AAPCC measures. The model explained 9.0 percent of variation in total expenditures. Thus, using all of these data does improve ability to predict expenditures, but routinely collecting such information is very expensive.

Implications of Better Risk Adjustment

The final exercise the RAND study team undertook was to estimate the potential profit that an HMO could achieve if it could somehow better predict future

TABLE 6-2

Profits from Better Prediction of HMO Medical Expenditures

Additional Variance Explained by HMO	Profit per Enrollee, 1988 Dollars	Profit per Enrollee, 2006 Dollars
0 percentage points	$0	$0
1 percentage point	$630	$1,102
5.5 percentage points	$1,170	$2,046
7.5 percentage points	$1,320	$2,308
13 percentage points	$1,530	$2,675
18.5 percentage points	$1,650	$2,886

SOURCE: Adapted from data in Newhouse et al. (1989).

Medicare expenditures of potential enrollees than the existing AAPCC formula. The admittedly unrealistic assumption is that the HMO could do this costlessly and would use the information to enroll only profitable beneficiaries. The results are presented in Table 6-2, inflated to 2006 dollars using the Consumer Price Index, all items.

Obviously, if HMOs cannot predict expenditures any better than can Medicare's AAPCC formula, there is no extra profit. However, if they could predict 1 percentage point better and use this information to enroll only healthier people, they would gain profits of $1,102 per enrollee because their costs would be lower than the Medicare payment rate. If HMOs could do 5.5 percentage points better, the profit per enrollee would be $2,046. Notice in Table 6-2 that, as we move to greater and greater additional explanatory power, higher profits are garnered. But notice, too, that the extra profit gets smaller with each increment. One additional point yields $1,102 in profit, but the next 4.5 percentage points only result in an additional $944 ($2,046 – $1,102). Two additional percentage points beyond that yield only an extra $262. The modeling reported in Table 6-1 makes it clear how difficult it would be to get an additional 4.5 percentage points of explanatory power. Using all the information available to the study, the RAND team could only get 7.4 percentage points greater predictive power than the AAPCC.

This had important implications for Medicare. If it could improve its AAPCC model enough to predict just a few percentage points better than it currently did, it could remove the easy opportunities for favorable selection that the HMOs seemed to enjoy. To do better than, say, the AAPCC plus prior utilization, would likely require HMOs to incur considerable costs of improved predicting for rather modest increases in profits. Even HMOs bent on taking full advantage of favorable selection would find that their efforts were likely to be unremunerative.

Generalizing the RAND Findings

Your first reaction to the RAND findings might be to say: "Surely, one can do better than predicting only 6.4 or 9.0 percent of total expenditures!" Van de Ven and Ellis (2000) provided a detailed summary of the research on risk adjustment in their chapter in *Handbook of Health Economics*. Table 6-3 (on page 84) reproduces a table from their work that summarizes six major studies of risk adjustment, beginning with the RAND study that we just discussed. With the exception of the study of U.S. HMO enrollees (column 3), all of the results are remarkably similar, with age/sex variables explaining 0.7 to 3.8 percent of variation, and all variables explaining 7 to 9 percent.

Medicare's Current AAPCC Approach to Risk Adjustment

The Balanced Budget Act of 1997 (BBA) required Medicare to phase in a new AAPCC methodology, beginning in 2000 (Ingber 2000). The new methodology was to better incorporate health status into the capitation rates. Medicare implemented a transitional risk adjustment system based only on inpatient data in 2000 and a full model based on both inpatient and ambulatory data in 2004. It is also worth noting that because a risk-adjusted payment system is based on patient health status measures, then the BBA requires Medicare HMOs and other providers to provide encounter data to the Centers for Medicare and Medicaid Services (CMS). For a detailed discussion of what is now called the CMS Hierarchical Condition Categories (CMS-HCC) model, see Pope et al. (2004).

The CMS and its contractors developed the payment system by running a series of regression models not unlike those used in the earlier RAND study. In essence they ran a model something like the following:

$$\text{Expenditures}_{it} = a1 * \text{Age } (65–69) + a2 * \text{Age } (70–74) +$$
$$a3 * \text{Age } (75–79) + \ldots + a6 * \text{Male} + a7 * \text{Medicaid eligible} +$$
$$a8 * \text{Condition1} + a9 * \text{Condition2} +$$
$$a10 * \text{Condition3} + \ldots + a60 * \text{Condition52} + \varepsilon_{it}$$

The estimated coefficients—the *a*'s in the equation—tell the CMS how much the associated variable contributed to Medicare expenditures, on average. The CMS experimented with how age, sex, and other demographic factors were specified and with how alternative measures of the clinical conditions explained contemporaneous expenditures and subsequent expenditures. This experimentation continued until the CMS was satisfied that its final model reflected an acceptable compromise across the ten principles summarized in Box 6-2 (on page 85). As a reading of the principles makes clear, there is considerable experimentation and judgment required to develop such a risk-adjusted payment system.

TABLE 6-3

Comparison of R^2 from Various Risk Adjustment Models from Six Papers

Study	Newhouse et al. (1989)	Van Vliet and Van de Ven (1992)	Fowles Weiner et al. (1996)[†]	Physician Payment Review Commission (1994)	Pope et al. (1998)*	Lamers (1999)
Sample population	U.S. privately insured	Netherlands	U.S. HMO enrollees	U.S. Medicare	U.S. Medicare	Netherlands sickness fund
Sample period	1974–1979	1981–1982	1991–1993	1991–1992	1991–1993	1991–1994
Sample size	N = 7,690	N = 20,000	N = 5,780		N = 10,893	N = 10,570
Age/sex	0.016	0.028	0.058	0.016	0.007	0.038
All socioeconomic*		0.037				
Functional status*					0.252	
Self-reported chronic conditions*		0.071	0.111	0.032	0.0274	
Self-reported health*	0.028			0.03	0.0311	
Short-form 36 like*			0.111	0.033	0.0405	
Prior year spending*	0.64				0.0413	
Comprehensive survey*		0.114		0.062	0.0418	0.060
Diagnosis based*	0.045		.124[‡]		0.0727[§]	0.080[‖]
All variables*	0.09			0.07	0.0785	0.086

SOURCE: This table was published in *Handbook of Health Economics,* Culyer and Newhouse, eds. Van de Ven and Ellis, "Risk Adjustment in Competitive Health Plan Markets," pp. 755–845, table 3, Copyright Elsevier 2000. Reprinted with permission.

NOTES: * All models include age and sex as well as variables shown. [†] Dependent variable was truncated at $25,000, which inflates R^2. [‡] ACG/ADG model. [§] DCG/HCC model. [‖] Three-year DCG-model.

BOX 6-2

Guiding Principles in Medicare's Risk Adjustment Approach

The new risk adjustment system was designed to meet ten guiding principles (Pope et al. 2004). These principles relate to insurance underwriting issues, understanding and acceptance by users, and minimization of opportunities to "game the system." Briefly, the ten principles are:

1. The health-status–related measures should be clinically meaningful. This means that they should have face validity and be sufficiently clinically specific to make it difficult for plans to assign a beneficiary with a vaguely defined condition into a higher payment group.

2. The measures should predict both current and future medical expenditures. Thus, a transitory condition such as an ankle sprain would not be a useful measure.

3. The measures should be based on large enough sample sizes that they yield accurate and stable predictions. Thus, as we saw in Chapter 5, Medicare as with any insurer may have to sacrifice some risk categories to gain reduction in variance.

4. Related clinical conditions should be treated hierarchically, while unrelated conditions should increase the level of payment. Thus, someone identified as having had a recent acute myocardial infarction (i.e., a heart attack) and having unstable angina would only be counted as having the more-severe condition rather than both. However, someone with unstable angina and lung cancer would be counted as having both.

5. Vague measures should be grouped with low-paying diagnoses to encourage specific coding of health conditions.

6. The measures should not encourage multiple reporting of the same or closely related diagnoses. Thus, the hierarchy of related conditions should be used and only the most severe condition coded.

7. Providers should not be penalized for reporting many conditions. Thus, no condition should have a negative payment associated with it, and a more-severe condition must pay at least as much as a less-severe manifestation.

8. Transitivity must hold. If condition A results in a greater payment than condition B and if B is paid more than C, then A should be paid more than C.

9. All of the diagnoses that clinicians use have to map into the payment system.

10. Discretionary diagnostic codes should be excluded to prevent intentional or unintentional gaming of the system.

The chosen model would be used to determine the annual payment that an HMO would be paid on behalf of a Medicare beneficiary living in a particular county. For example, the base payment for a woman, age 75–79, living in the community might be $2,475. If in the last year she had diabetes without complications, that might add $1,024. If she also had unstable angina, that might add $1,785. In this case, the Medicare HMO would be paid $5,284 on her behalf.

The model that Medicare ultimately adopted contains 12 age times 2 sex times 2 site (community vs. institution) categories for a total of 48, plus 6 Medicaid categories, plus 70 Hierarchical Condition Categories (i.e., the condition codes), plus another 6 condition code interactions. In some instances, the costs associated with having two conditions are greater than simply the sum of the costs of each; diabetes together with cerebrovascular disease is an example. The interactions allow Medicare to pay an HMO more for the care of such patients. There are also categories that relate to the Medicare disabled.

Age and sex explain approximately 1.0 percent of the variation in Medicare expenses. The new CMS-HCC model explains 11.2 percent. Table 6-4 compares the predictive ratio of the age/sex model and the CMS-HCC model for the quintiles of Medicare expenditures. The predictive ratio is just the predicted costs of a group divided by the actual cost. If the value is greater than 1, it means that Medicare would be overpaying for the care of people in that group. If the value is less than 1, Medicare would be underpaying.

The first quintile of expenditures (i.e., the least expensive one-fifth of Medicare beneficiaries) is shown in the first row. On average, just using age and sex as adjusters (the first column) leads to an overpayment of 266 percent of actual costs. In contrast, an HMO caring for Medicare beneficiaries

TABLE 6-4
Predictive Ratios for Alternative Risk Adjustments

Quintiles of Expenditures	Age/Sex	CMS-HCC Model
First	2.66	1.23
Second	1.93	1.23
Third	1.37	1.14
Fourth	0.95	1.02
Fifth	0.44	0.86
Top 5%	0.28	0.77
Top 1%	0.17	0.69

SOURCE: Data from Pope et al. (2004).

in the most expensive one-fifth of the distribution would be paid only 44 percent of what their care would cost, on average.

Clearly, the CMS-HCC model is an improvement. While it still overpays for the less costly quintiles, the overpayments are drastically reduced. Similarly, while it underpays for the most expensive fifth quintile, the payment is much closer to actual costs. These findings have led some researchers to suggest that future risk adjustment models should continue to employ a CMS-HCC–like model but incorporate a mechanism to directly pay some share of costs for particularly high-cost beneficiaries (Newhouse 1996; Ellis and McGuire 1993).

The CMS began phasing in risk-adjusted payments to Medicare HMOs beginning in 2000. In 2006, Medicare Advantage plans (the new name for Medicare managed care plans) received 75 percent of their payment based on the CMS-HCC formula and 25 percent on the old AAPCC. In 2007, payment rates were based entirely on the CMS-HCC methodology. As with the original AAPCC formula, it continues to establish the basic payment level based on Medicare's expenditures in geographic regions, usually counties. However, instead of being simple averages as in the AAPCC, the payments are now based on the risk-adjusted mix of beneficiaries in the county. Box 6-3 presents the payment that a Medicare HMO in Lake County Illinois, just north of Chicago, would receive for a 72-year-old woman who is on Medicaid and who has diabetes and unstable angina. The base rate for her county of residence is $691.50 per month. The factors for her gender, Medicaid status, and health conditions are added and then multiplied by the base rate to determine the payment to be made to the HMO each month on her behalf.

While this format is less intuitive than the dollar-based formats discussed earlier in the chapter, it has the administrative advantage that the CMS need not recompute each value every year. New data on average risk-adjusted

---

BOX 6-3

Sample Medicare Advantage Payment under the CMS-HCC Model, Lake County, Illinois, 2006

Basic Lake County, Illinois, rate:	$691.50
Female, age 70–74:	.384
Medicaid female, age 70–74:	.183
HCC19 diabetes without complications:	.200
HCC82 unstable angina:	.348

Total payment is: $691.50 (.384 + .183 + .200 + .348) = $771.02

Current Medicare Advantage Payment Plans Include a Bidding Mechanism

As discussed in more detail in Chapter 21, the Medicare Modernization Act of 2004, which provided for prescription drug coverage for Medicare beneficiaries, also modified the way Medicare Advantage plans are paid. The managed care plans proffer a bid per enrollee per month to Medicare to provide a basic set of benefits consistent with traditional Medicare. If this bid is below the CMS established "benchmark" for the county (or region, if applicable), the managed care plan keeps 75 percent of the difference to apply to reduced cost sharing or expanded benefits for enrolled beneficiaries. If it is above the benchmark, the plan charges enrollees an additional premium. However, the CMS-HCC model is used in all cases to adjust the payments for beneficiaries actually enrolled by the plan to reflect their demographics and health status.

expenditures and any congressionally mandated across-the-board increases or decreases can simply be applied to the base rates. The relative values of the person-specific components are unaffected.

Other Uses of Risk Adjustment

The extended example discussed in this chapter focuses exclusively on the Medicare AAPCC and its replacement—the risk-adjusted CMS-HCC model. When private insurers use manual rating with medical underwriting or prospective experience rating for smaller employer groups, they increasingly make use of risk adjustment methods, albeit the methods seldom are as sophisticated as those discussed here. Similarly, when insurers seek to identify high-cost enrollees who may benefit from case management or disease management, they employ versions of risk adjustment methods to accomplish this.

Florida enacted reforms to its Medicaid program for the poor in 2005. That program calls for providing Medicaid-eligible people with the equivalent of a voucher to purchase private insurance. The size of the voucher is to be risk-adjusted based initially on ambulatory data but eventually on both ambulatory and inpatient data (State of Florida 2005).

Finally, there have been several proposals to replace or supplement the current employer-sponsored health insurance system with one that provides a tax credit for the purchase of private insurance. Some tax credit proponents argue for risk adjustments to scale the size of the tax credit to the health status of the recipient.

Chapter Summary

- In general, risk adjustment models have been able to predict about 12 percent of total claims. Ambulatory use is easier to predict than inpatient use, perhaps because there is a larger behavioral component to it.
- Demographic characteristics such as age and gender are only modestly predictive of future claims experience. While subjective and physiological measures of health status are more predictive, prior utilization provides the most predictive power.
- The Medicare Adjusted Average per Capita Cost (AAPCC) is a manual rating program by which Medicare paid Medicare HMOs based on the average costs in the county, adjusted for the age, gender, and Medicaid, institutional, and active-worker status of the beneficiary.
- Medicare currently pays Medicare Advantage plans on the basis of the CMS-HCC (Hierarchical Condition Categories) model. This manual rating program uses some 70 clinical conditions, in addition to demographic and location factors, to determine the amount Medicare will pay HMOs for the care of its beneficiaries.
- Risk adjustment methods of the types described in this chapter have been proposed to determine the amount of payment to be given to state Medicaid recipients in voucher-based programs, and in health-status–adjusted health insurance tax credits. In addition to underwriting, health insurers use these methods to identify likely candidates for case management and disease management utilization programs.

Discussion Questions

1. How would you describe the CMS-HCC risk adjustment system? Does it use prior utilization, physiological, and demographic information to determine payment rates? How?
2. Suppose a Medicare HMO had been aggressively using some method to attract low utilizers into its plan. In what ways would you expect it to change its behavior, if at all, as a result of the implementation of the new CMS-HCC model?
3. How would a CMS-HCC type model apply to people newly eligible for Medicare?
4. If Medicare HMOs must now provide Medicare with encounter data on the healthcare utilization of their subscribers, what would you predict about the nature of the underwriting that managed care plans will use when negotiating future contracts with private employers?

ISSUES OF MORAL HAZARD

7

MORAL HAZARD AND PRICES

The first major challenge for insurers was adverse selection; the second is called "moral hazard."[1] The term comes from the casualty insurance market. A house may face a variety of fire hazards: it may be struck by lightning, it may burn because of faulty wiring, or it may be destroyed because the owner set it on fire to collect the insurance. This last hazard is referred to as moral hazard. The terminology has carried over to health insurance in that it is assumed that individuals with a health insurance policy use more health services. Of course, unlike the casualty market, there is nothing immoral about using more health insurance when you have coverage. It is simply an application of the law of demand. The issues for insurers are how much people are going to increase their use of various health services when they pay less out-of-pocket and whether there are cost-effective strategies that can minimize the extra utilization.

In this chapter, we develop the concept of moral hazard in healthcare and examine the empirical evidence on the extent to which higher coinsurance, copays, and deductibles are successful in reducing use. In Chapter 8, we explore the effectiveness of utilization management techniques, such as preadmission certification and gatekeeping, as mechanisms to control moral hazard.

Price elasticity is the economist's rigorous way of quantifying the effect of a change in price on the change in quantity demanded. It is simply the percentage change in quantity divided by the percentage change in price. It has the advantage of being independent of the units in which the price or the quantity is measured. Health services generally have a price elasticity of about –0.2. This means that a 10 percent increase in the out-of-pocket price reduces the use of services by about 2 percent. However, the effects of changes in price differ rather substantially across types of health services. Ambulatory mental health visits, for example, are much more price sensitive than are physician visits. Dental care exhibits a large transitory effect not seen with other services, and hospital care is much less price responsive than physician services. Moreover, people with different opportunity costs of time have different responses to changes in out-of-pocket charges. These differences in elasticities explain much of the difference in the structure of health benefits.

---

1. This chapter draws heavily on Chapter 3 of Michael A. Morrisey, *Price Sensitivity in Health Care: Implications for Policy*, 2nd edition. Washington, D.C.: NFIB Research Foundation, 2005. Used with permission.

The Nature of Moral Hazard

Moral hazard is nothing more than the law of demand. Consider Figure 7-1, which shows a downward-sloping demand curve for physician visits. At $60, individuals might purchase X1 visits. At $20, they would buy more—X2. This is the law of demand: at a lower price, people buy more of a good.

Now suppose that the market price of physician office visits is $60 and that people buy a health insurance policy that covers such physician visits. Under the contract, subscribers only have to pay a small copay of $20 for each physician visit used. A copay is the amount the insurance contract may require the insured to pay for each unit of a covered service, regardless of either the actual price the provider charges or the actual amount the insurer pays. Copays may differ by type of service and by which provider the subscriber uses. In Figure 7-1, individuals purchased X1 physician visits when they had to pay the full $60 price, but now, since they only have to pay the $20 copay, they purchase X2 physician visits. This sliding down the health services demand curve in response to the lower out-of-pocket payment is precisely what is meant by moral hazard. It is also precisely what is meant by the law of demand.

The nature of demand is that each additional unit of service is worth less to consumers than the preceding one. Our consumers in Figure 7-1 stop buying at X1 because an additional physician visit is not worth the cost. Suppose they are not feeling well. At $60 a visit, they will wait and see if they feel better tomorrow. At $20 a visit, they may try to get a physician visit later this afternoon. Thus, they stop consuming when the price of the service is greater than what they perceive that unit to be worth.

FIGURE 7-1
Moral Hazard
in Healthcare

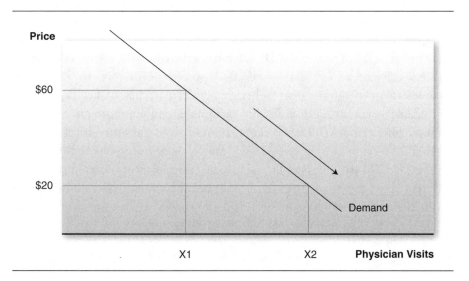

The problem with moral hazard is that the extra units of health services subscribers consume as a result of having insurance coverage are worth less to them than the price of care the insurer pays on their behalf. Consider Figure 7-2. Again, the market price of a physician visit is $60, and the copay required of the insured is $20. For every visit between X1 and X2, the physician is paid more for the visit than the consumer's demand curve says it is worth. Yet, subscribers rationally consume up to X2. The triangle marked "Z" is the loss associated with this extra consumption. It reflects the expenditure made on behalf of the insured over and above the value of the service.

If the insurer could find a low-cost way of "pushing" subscribers back up the demand curve, it could save $40 ($60 – $20) on each visit averted and easily compensate subscribers for giving up some low-valued physician visits. One way to achieve this is to raise the copay by $10 or $20 and lower the insurance premium. Another way is to establish a utilization management program designed to identify and eliminate low-value visits. The utilization management program, of course, would have to cost less than the visits averted. This chapter and Chapter 8 examine the extent to which health services uses responds to price and utilization management techniques to push subscribers back up the demand curve.

Early Efforts to Estimate the Extent of Moral Hazard

One approach to estimating the magnitude of the moral hazard effect is to identify two groups of people—one with health insurance and one without—and then compare their use of health services. Eichhorn and Aday (1972) and Donabedian (1976) provide excellent reviews of these types of studies. The

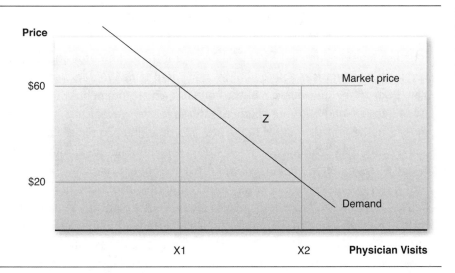

FIGURE 7-2

Loss Associated with Moral Hazard

problem with this approach is that adverse selection is likely to confound the comparison. The group with coverage is likely to have acquired insurance because group members were more likely to use health services. Simply comparing use rates will overstate the effect of differences in the out-of-pocket price. If insurers followed this route, they would find that utilization was not reduced as much as they anticipated. They would have reduced their premiums too much, and they would lose money.

Scitovsky and Snyder (1972) undertook the classic early study of moral hazard. They analyzed a natural experiment in which Stanford University employees faced the introduction of a 25 percent coinsurance rate on physician services when the rate previously had been zero. (A coinsurance rate is an insurance contract provision by which the subscriber pays a fixed percentage of the price of health services.) Scitovsky and Snyder compared use by the same employees in 1966, when care was "free," with use in 1968, the year after the plan went into effect. They found that the physician office visit rate in 1966 was 33 percent higher when visits cost nothing out-of-pocket than it was in 1968. Ancillary services were 15 percent higher in the year prior to the change. Phelps and Newhouse (1972) also analyzed these data, and Scitovsky and McCall (1977) revisited the study with new data five years later. The results were confirmed.

There are problems with case studies, even one as clean as the Stanford University experience. For example, the Stanford study represents only one firm and one local area, it covers only a single small range of coinsurance, and it also attributes all of the change in use to the natural experiment. While there was no obvious reason to believe other factors were at play in the Stanford case, as Box 7-1 suggests, this is not necessarily the case in natural exper-

---

BOX 7-1

Problems with Case Studies

Scheffler (1984) examined the effects of the introduction of a 40 percent physician coinsurance requirement in the United Mine Workers healthcare plan. Prior to the introduction of the coinsurance requirement in 1977, the union had not had any cost-sharing features in the 30-year history of the benefit. In the first six months of the study, probability of a physician office visit declined by 28 percent. The study was terminated at that point because the union went out on strike over its health benefits! Unfortunately, it is not at all clear what to make of the results of Scheffler's study. Was the changed behavior reflective of the new price? Was it some mixture of price and disgruntled union effects? Follow-up work by Roddy, Wallen, and Meyers (1986) suggested that many of the effects of cost sharing in this population disappeared in the subsequent year.

iments. A number of other early studies attempted to estimate the extent of price sensitivity of health services. See Newhouse (1978) and Morrisey (2005) for reviews.

The RAND Health Insurance Experiment

While the early studies provided only limited information regarding the extent of price responsiveness, the RAND Health Insurance Experiment (RAND-HIE) provided considerable insight into the price responsiveness of consumers of health services. The study is particularly useful because it largely (but not entirely) avoided the adverse selection problem by randomly assigning families to health insurance plans. It investigated a wide range of coinsurance rates, allowing consideration of a broader set of price responses, and it was conducted over six sites chosen to be reflective of urban and rural communities in the four census regions. See Manning and colleagues (1987) for a summary of the experiment and the major findings, and Newhouse and the Insurance Experiment Group (1993) for a systematic presentation of this seminal study.

You may legitimately ask about the relevance of a 30-year-old study. Clinical practice and insurance institutions have changed dramatically in the intervening years. However, the RAND-HIE is still the gold standard for examining price sensitivity of health services for three reasons. First, its methodology was very strong. It overcame the adverse selection problem in a way that no other study ever has. Second, it examined virtually the whole range of health services provided, and it did so in a consistent framework. Third, more-recent studies have been able to look at the price sensitivity of selected health services and almost always find results consistent with the older RAND-HIE.

Between 1974 and 1977, families in Dayton, Ohio; Seattle, Washington; Fitchburg, Massachusetts; Franklin County, Massachusetts; Charleston, South Carolina; and Georgetown County, South Carolina were enrolled in a health insurance program run by RAND under a federal contract. Participating families were randomly assigned to one of 14 different fee-for-service health plans. In Seattle, some participants were enrolled in Group Health of Puget Sound, a health maintenance organization (HMO). The plans had coinsurance rates of 0, 25, 50, and 95 percent. Within each coinsurance group, families were assigned to stoploss groups of 5, 10, and 15 percent of income to a maximum of $1,000. That is, out-of-pocket expenses for covered services could not exceed the percentage of income cap or $1,000, whichever was lower. While the $1,000 stoploss feature appears low, in 2006 dollars, it would be approximately $4,160. Virtually all medical services were covered.

One final point about the design of the RAND-HIE: You might ask what happened to people who already had health insurance. The answer is that they kept it. Since the RAND-HIE only lasted four to five years, there was some concern that a health event could make participants uninsurable, or uninsurable at the same prices, if they did not continue coverage. Also, by keeping the existing policies in force and assigning the benefits to the RAND-HIE, the study was able to pass on many of the claims expenses to the participants' existing insurers.

Many participants received more-generous coverage from the RAND-HIE than from their existing plans, but some were assigned to worse plans. Why did some people give up the coverage they had to take inferior coverage through the RAND-HIE? The answer is that the RAND-HIE paid them to participate. A lump-sum payment of this sort did not affect their incentives to use services within the context of the RAND-HIE plan to which they were assigned (Newhouse and the Insurance Experiment Group 1993). The sample of families was generally representative of the under age 65, nonwealthy population. It excluded those who would be eligible for Medicare over the course of the experiment, those with incomes above $25,000 ($104,900 in 2006 dollars), as well as those in the military and veterans with service-connected disabilities. Slightly more than 5,800 people were enrolled in the various fee-for-service plans, and data on 20,190 person-years of experience were collected.

Overall RAND-HIE Findings

The major findings of the RAND-HIE with respect to the price responsiveness of ambulatory and inpatient services are summarized in Table 7-1. When faced with a zero out-of-pocket price, people had an 86.7 percent annual probability of interacting with the healthcare system. They also used 4.6 physician visits per capita per year. In contrast, those who had to pay 95 percent of the bill (up to the $4,160 stoploss in 2006 dollars) had only a 68 percent probability of using any healthcare and used only 2.7 visits per capita. Those who had to pay 25 cents on the dollar had a 78.8 percent probability of using any care and used 3.3 visits per year per capita. Relative to those who had to pay 25 percent, those with free care used nearly 37 percent more physician visits. Thus, the use of ambulatory services decreases with higher out-of-pocket prices. The difference between the free plan and any of the others is statistically significant at the 95 percent confidence level.[2] Children's care exhibited about the same price responsiveness for the use of ambulatory services as did adults.

---

2. The differences among the 25, 50, and 95 percent plans were not statistically different at this level.

Coinsurance Rate	Likelihood of Any Use (percentage)	Face-to-Face Physician Visits Per Capita	One or More Admissions (percentage)	Medical Expenses (2006 dollars)
0%	86.7 (0.67)	4.55 (0.17)	10.37 (0.42)	$3,164 (133.6)
25%	78.8 (0.99)	3.33 (0.19)	8.83 (0.38)	$2,565 (118.1)
50%	74.3 (1.86)	3.03 (0.22)	8.31 (0.40)	$2,374 (132.7)
95%	68.0 (1.48)	2.73 (0.18)	7.74 (0.35)	$2,174 (111.6)

TABLE 7-1

Various Measures of Predicted Mean Annual Use of Medical Services, by Plan

SOURCE: Adapted from data in Manning et al. (1987).

NOTE: Standard errors in parentheses.

BOX 7-2

Effects of Hospital Coinsurance on Appropriate vs. Inappropriate Admissions

Inappropriate admissions do not appear to have been disproportionately reduced as a result of the cost sharing. Siu (1986) and Lohr et al. (1986) showed that the same proportions of what they identify as appropriate and inappropriate admissions were found among those with free care and those with each of the coinsurance rates. Similarly, on examining small area use of services, Chassin and colleagues (1987) found that differences in hospital admission rates across areas were not attributable to differences in the rate of appropriate or inappropriate admissions.

The results for hospital admissions also displayed evidence of price sensitivity (see Box 7-2). Those covered under a free care plan had 128 admissions per 1,000 persons. This was 29 percent greater than those with the 95 percent coinsurance plan. Similarly, inpatient expenditures were 30 percent higher for those who had a free plan.

Unlike the ambulatory results, where reductions in use were seen across the range of coinsurance rates, with hospital use, the vast majority of the effect is found between the free and 25 percent plans. This result reflects the stoploss features of the plans. Seventy percent of those hospitalized exceeded the maximum out-of-pocket limit imposed. Once this threshold was exceeded, care became free. Thus, the lack of additional reductions in hospital use as a result of higher coinsurance rates may merely reflect the fact that prices quickly became zero. Unlike adult care, children's inpatient use showed almost no price responsiveness.

The final column of Table 7-1 is perhaps the most important. It indicates that, in 2006 dollars, those who faced no out-of-pocket costs had average annual total medical expenditures of $3,164. This was 23 percent more than those who had to pay 25 percent of the bill and nearly 46 percent more than those who had to pay 95 percent (up to the stoploss). Thus, substantially higher out-of-pocket prices result in meaningfully lower medical care expenditures.

More formally, the RAND-HIE provided elasticity estimates of the extent of price responsiveness across types of medical care services and tried to put them in the context of the earlier literature. Essentially, the RAND-HIE estimates are in the lower range of the nonexperimental estimates. These results are summarized in Table 7-2. In the free to 25 percent coinsurance range, hospital care had an elasticity of –.17, as did overall ambulatory care. In the coinsurance range of 25 to 95 percent, ambulatory care had an overall elasticity of –.31, while hospital care was estimated to be –.14. The small response for hospital care at higher levels of out-of-pocket payment reflects the stoploss in place in the insurance plans. The one-sentence summary of the RAND-HIE is that the price elasticity of health services is about –0.2. In other words, a 10 percent increase in out-of-pocket price reduces use by 2 percent.

Full Coverage vs. Inpatient-Only Coverage

One component of the RAND-HIE examined the consequences of having insurance only for hospital services, rather than for both ambulatory and hospital care. At the time of the experiment, many people had generous hospitalization coverage but only limited coverage for ambulatory services. Some said that this was "penny-wise and pound-foolish." They argued that people with only hospital coverage would forego relatively simple and inexpensive services because they had to pay the full price. The result, they said, would be that many people would be hospitalized and spend large amounts of money when timely and inexpensive ambulatory services would have avoided such costs.

TABLE 7-2

RAND-HIE
Elasticity
Estimates for
Health Services

| Coinsurance Range | Ambulatory | | | | Hospital | All Care |
	Acute	Chronic	Well	All		
0–25%	–.16	–.20	–.14	–.17	–.17	–.17
25–95%	–.32	–.23	–.43	–.31	–.14	–.22

SOURCE: Manning et al. (1987), "Health Insurance and the Demand for Medical Care: Evidence from a Randomized Experiment," *American Economic Review* 77: 251–277, Table 2. Reprinted with permission.

The RAND-HIE set up an additional arm of the study in which people were randomly assigned to an "individual deductible." In this arm, they had free care if they were treated in a hospital but paid 95 percent of their bill if they obtained ambulatory services. This arm reflected the common hospitalization coverage of the time. It was compared to the free-coverage arm, in which both inpatient and ambulatory services were free. The study found that those in the "individual deductible" arm did interact less with the healthcare system: they had a 72.6 percent chance of using any care, compared to 86.7 percent for those with free care. However, they also had fewer hospital admissions (9.52 percent compared to 10.37 percent). Overall, those with the hospital-only coverage had total medical expenditures of $2,537 (in 2006 dollars), compared to $3,164 for those with full coverage. While this difference lacks statistical significance at the conventional levels, it clearly does not support the "penny-wise pound-foolish" argument. If anything, it suggests that ambulatory and inpatient care are complements, not substitutes.

This complementary relationship was also found in a 1996 study of increased access to primary care in the U.S. Department of Veterans Affairs (VA). Weinberger, Oddone, and Henderson (1996) studied nearly 1,400 veterans who were hospitalized for diabetes, chronic obstructive pulmonary disease, or congestive heart failure in nine VA medical centers. They randomly assigned half of the veterans to an intensive intervention designed to increase access to primary care after discharge from the hospital and the other half to usual postdischarge care. They found that the group with greater access to primary care had significantly higher, not lower, readmission rates.

Findings by Income Group

The out-of-pocket money price is only one component of the full price of health services use. There is also a time component. You must go to the physician's office, wait to be seen, receive services, and return to other activities. The full price of a visit includes both the money price and this time price. If you have a high opportunity cost of time, the time component can easily be the larger portion of the full price. We should expect, therefore, that, other things being equal, those individuals with higher opportunity costs of time will be less responsive to a given change in the out-of-pocket money price of care. A given change in money price is a smaller change in the full price for these individuals than for those with lower opportunity costs of time.

The RAND-HIE looked at the effect of differing coinsurance rates across income groups. This is effectively an examination of the time-price hypothesis. Figure 7-3 shows the effect of a 25 percent coinsurance rate relative to free care across low-, medium-, and high-income groups. Low-income (i.e., low opportunity cost of time) people had twice the price

FIGURE 7-3

Reduction in the Probability of Any Health Services Use, Free Care versus 25 Percent Coinsurance Rate, by Income Class

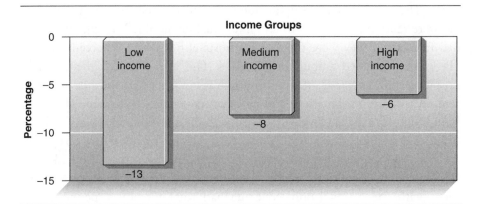

SOURCE: Data from Manning et al. (1987).

responsiveness as those with high opportunity cost of time. The implication of this is that an insurer would have to use much higher copays or coinsurance rates to get higher-income subscribers to reduce their use of health services. Analogously, a small copay on, say, emergency department visits may be enough to encourage Medicaid recipients to not use the emergency department for routine care.

Moral Hazard and Specific Types of Health Services

The RAND-HIE provided estimates of the price sensitivity for many types of health services. In addition, a number of more-recent studies have independently estimated service-specific elasticities. In this section, we review the findings for a variety of services.

Hospital Services

As noted earlier, the RAND-HIE found that free care, relative to the 95 percent plan, resulted in 29 percent more hospital admissions, as well as inpatient expenses that were 30 percent higher. Relative to the 25 percent plan, those with free care had 22 percent more admissions but only 10 percent higher expenses. These results suggest that the additional admissions in the free plan relative to the 25 percent plan were for very short stays.

Since the RAND-HIE, only a small handful of studies have examined the effects of health insurance on hospital use. Buchmueller and colleagues (2005) reviewed the studies and concluded that having private health insurance increases adult inpatient use by .17 to .24 days per year and childhood use by 3 to 4 percent. The trouble with these estimates is that they do not account for the size of out-of-pocket payments, and they often do not control for the adverse selection problem.

Hospital Emergency Department Services

The RAND-HIE results for the use of hospital emergency departments (ED) were generally similar to those for ambulatory care (O'Grady et al. 1985). Persons with free care used about 54 percent more ED visits than did persons in the 95 percent plan, and about 27 percent more than persons with 25 percent cost sharing. Comparable estimates for ED expenses were 45 and 16 percent higher, respectively. It was also the case that, within the ED, the type of services used increased differently as prices were lowered. Relative to no coverage, free care increased the use for "less-urgent" care by 90 percent and "more-urgent" care by only 30 percent. Thus, the less-serious services appeared to be the most price sensitive.

Selby, Fireman, and Swain (1996) provided a more-recent and detailed analysis of ED use in an HMO. At the request of some electronics and computer firms, Kaiser-Permanente of Northern California introduced in 1993 a $25 to $35 copay for ED use for members employed by these firms. Other Kaiser-Permanente members continued to have no copays for ED use. The study compared the change in the number of ED visits before and after the introduction of the copays for both this affected group and for two unaffected groups. There were no changes in copays for other services. This is a classic "differences-in-differences" evaluation method. Comparison group 1 consisted of a sample of members selected by age, gender, and area of residence to be similar to those facing the copay. Comparison group 2 consisted of members who were similarly selected by age, gender, and area but were also employed in the electronics and computer industries.

Table 7-3 summarizes the findings. Overall ED visits per 1,000 persons declined by 14.6 percent among those facing the new copay *relative to* the change in either control group (statistically significant at the 95 percent confidence level). The investigators went further and looked at the severity of diagnosis. They found the largest relative reductions (20.8 to 29.2 percent, depending on control group) in visits deemed "often not an emergency." Visits that were "always an emergency" showed the smallest relative change (a decline of 9.6 percent and an *increase* of 7.3 percent, depending on control group), but these differences were not statistically different from no change. Interestingly, office visits also declined as a result of the ED copays, even though there was no change in copays for such visits. This suggests that ED and office visits, on net, are complements rather than substitutes.

Physician Services

The RAND-HIE found that people with free care had nearly 37 percent more physician visits per capita than did those facing a 25 percent coinsurance rate; their use was 67 percent higher than those who essentially paid they entire bill out-of-pocket.

TABLE 7-3
Adjusted
Kaiser-
Permanente
Emergency
Department
(ED) Use

	Overall ED Visits per 1,000 Persons
Visits in 1992:	
Copayment group	162
Control group 1	206
Control group 2	173
Visits in 1993:	
Copayment group	135
Control group 1	202
Control group 2	169
Percent Change in Copayment Group:	
Relative to percent change in control group 1	−14.6 (−19.4 to −9.5)
Relative to percent change in control group 2	−14.6 (−19.9 to −8.9)

SOURCE: Data from Selby, Fireman, and Swain (1996).

NOTE: Values are adjusted for age, sex, socioeconomic status, and study group. Values in parentheses are the 95 percent confidence intervals of the change.

Cherkin, Grothaus, and Wagner (1989) examined the effects of a five-dollar copay introduced in 1985 on the use of physician office visits for Washington State government and higher-education employees enrolled in Group Health of Puget Sound, a staff model HMO. As a control group, Cherkin and colleagues used federal government enrollees who did not face the copay. In examining the utilization patterns of two-year, continuously enrolled persons, they found that office visits for primary care decreased by an estimated 10.9 percent as a result of the copay. Specialty visits declined by 3.3 percent, optometry by 10.9 percent, and all visits by 8.3 percent. However, the effect on specialty visits lacked statistical significance at the conventional levels, perhaps because specialty visits required a primary care referral.

More-recent studies have tried to examine the effects of having health insurance versus not having health insurance on physician visits. There are, of course, adverse selection issues associated with such comparisons. Buchmueller and colleagues (2005) provided a review of these studies. Overall, for adult ambulatory use, the studies found having coverage to be associated with one to two additional physician visits per year. This is a pretty narrow range around the 1.85 additional visits reported by the RAND-HIE.

Interestingly, chiropractic services appear to be more price sensitive than physician visits (Schelelle, Rogers, and Newhouse 1996). The RAND-HIE found that free care relative to the 25 percent plan increased expenditures on chiropractic care by 132 percent. There was essentially no additional effect of higher coinsurance rates.

Dental Services

The RAND-HIE randomly assigned individuals to 0 (free), 25, 50, and 95 percent coinsurance rate insurance plans. It found that, in steady state (that is, after a transition period), participants in the free plan had 34 percent more dental visits and 46 percent higher expenses than did enrollees in the 95 percent coinsurance plan (Manning et al. 1985). Again, most of the effect was observed in the difference between free care and a 25 percent coinsurance. Also, nearly two-thirds of the response was attributed to number of visits per enrollee, the remainder to expenditures per user. Thus, cost sharing tended to affect the decision to seek treatment much more than the expenditure once treatment was sought. Preventive services were about as price sensitive as general dental visits; in contrast, prosthodontics, endodontics, and periodontics were more price sensitive.

Of particular note, dental care seems to be much more sensitive to a transitory effect of cost sharing than does medical care more generally. The RAND-HIE found that, in the first year of coverage, the difference in use between the free plan and the 95 percent plan was nearly twice as large as in the second year. However, in the second year (i.e., the steady state), dental care was less price sensitive than other health services.

Conrad, Grembowski, and Milgram (1987) and Grembowski, Conrad, and Milgram (1987) have analyzed survey data on the effects of coinsurance on the use of dental services among adults and children, respectively. Their population was covered by dental insurance (Pennsylvania Blue Shield in 1980), so the issue was the effects of differences in the coinsurance rate within an insured population. They found little money price (i.e., coinsurance) sensitivity among this insured population. This result is consistent with the RAND-HIE because most of the price sensitivity was found between free care and a 25 percent coinsurance rate with little additional sensitivity at higher levels of cost sharing. These findings are also supported in work by Muller and Monheit (1987). Like the RAND-HIE, the Conrad and Grembowski studies found increased price sensitivity for more extensive (i.e., expensive) services. It also appears to be the case that children's basic dental services were less price sensitive than adult care. As with the RAND-HIE, these researchers found substantial transitory effects on dental usage. Little new work on the price effects for dental care has been done since the mid-1980s.

A particularly interesting aspect of the Conrad, Grembowski, and Milgram (1987) study was a consideration of people with dental coverage through community-rated and experience-rated group dental plans. Recall from Chapter 5 that community-rated plans are more likely to be subject to adverse selection because the single average price will overcharge low utilizers and undercharge high utilizers. The results from Conrad and his colleagues indicated that expenditures were 37 and 90 percent higher, respectively, for insured workers and spouses in community-rated plans than in experience-rated plans.

Ambulatory Mental Health Services

Ambulatory mental healthcare services are considerably more price sensitive than ambulatory medical services generally. In a natural experiment, Wallen, Roddy, and Fahs (1982) found that the introduction of a five-dollar copay per visit reduced mental health visits from 110 to 60 visits per 1,000. McGuire (1981) was the first to use econometric techniques on individual level data. He analyzed data from a survey of heavy users of psychiatric services and found a price elasticity of greater than –1.0 for actual and anticipated visits. This suggests that a 1 percent increase in price would result in a more than 1 percent reduction in the number of visits.

Horgan (1986) found that a 10 percent increase in the coinsurance rate led to a 2.7 percent reduction in the probability of any use. However, visits and expenditures, conditional on some use, were much more price responsive. A 10 percent increase in the coinsurance rate reduced visits by 4.4 percent and expenditures by 5.4 percent. These results suggest that the intensity of mental health use is more responsive to price than is simple use of services. This is in contrast to general ambulatory medical services, where the probability of use is more responsive. Taube, Kessler, and Burns (1986) found similar results. There was no significant relationship between price and the probability of using mental health services, but substantial price sensitivity, given some use. They reported a price elasticity of nearly –1.0 for those with some use. Thus, use of care, by those who used some care, would likely more than double if free care replaced full payment.

The RAND-HIE confirmed these results. It found that free care would result in a quadrupling of mental healthcare expenses, relative to no insurance. Further, the response between 50 percent and 95 percent out-of-pocket payment was about twice as price responsive as general medical care. The response between 25 percent coinsurance and free care was about equal to that of medical care (Keeler et al. 1986; Wells, Keeler, and Manning 1990).

The use of mental healthcare in the presence of expanded insurance coverage can be described as subject to a slow buildup. With dental coverage, there was an immediate burst of use, followed by a lower, sustained level. With mental healthcare, use increased over time from a relatively low initial level. Keeler and his colleagues (1986) speculated why mental healthcare is more price responsive:

The additional users may be better informed and simply want help only if the price is right. Alternatively, they may not know how mental healthcare would help them, or they may be deterred by real or imaginary stigmatization, until coverage legitimizes taking a chance on use. (p. 166)

Ultimately, the high price sensitivity of mental health services suggests why insurance coverage for these maladies tends to be different that for medical conditions. Simple application of copays reduces the use of services substantially, relative to no coverage. Similarly, limitations on the number of mental health visits and more-aggressive use of nonprice-rationing devices are common in managed care plans as a means of reducing moral hazard. See McGuire (2000) for a discussion.

Prescription Drugs

Early studies of prescription drugs found that the quantity demanded approximately doubled when drugs became free under a full-coverage plan, apparently due to an inability to control for adverse selection. The RAND-HIE data did not bear out these early studies. In general, the RAND-HIE found that prescription drugs were about as price responsive as physician services. Leibowitz, Manning, and Newhouse (1985) found that prescription drug expenses per person were 76 percent higher for those in the free plan, relative to those with 95 percent coinsurance. Relative to those in the 25 percent coinsurance plan, those in the free plan used 32 percent more. These results were largely driven by the number of prescriptions filled, rather than differential costliness of the drugs received. Those in the free plan filled 50 percent

BOX 7-3

Effects of Coinsurance on Health Outcomes

In the RAND-HIE, what was the effect of having free care on the health status of the participants? The results showed some improvement in health status, but only in three circumstances. First, poor adults with high initial blood pressure had a clinically significant reduction in blood pressure in the free plan. Second, poor adults in the free plan saw an improvement in correctable vision problems. Third, gum health showed "modest improvement" and decayed teeth were more likely to be filled for those ages 18–35 in the free plan. No other health status effects were statistically significant (Manning et al. 1987). This may understate the true effects, of course. The study only lasted four to five years, and the samples were too small to detect differences in relatively rare events.

more prescriptions than did those in the 95 percent coinsurance plan, and 23 percent more than those in the 25 percent coinsurance plan.

Pharmaceutical use is certainly one of the areas where clinical practice has changed the most since the RAND-HIE. Prescription drug coverage now often includes two-, three-, and even four-tier programs in which subscribers pay one low copay for generic drugs (perhaps $10), a higher copay (perhaps $20) for brand-name or "preferred brand-name" drugs, and a still higher copay for nonpreferred brand-name drugs. The fourth tier is reserved for very expensive biotech drugs. Several recent studies have investigated the effects of these copayment systems on prescription drug use.

Motheral and Fairman (2001) examined the effect of introducing a three-tier drug coverage program among employers who offered employees a preferred provider organization (PPO) over the 1997 through 1999 period. In a differences-in-differences model, they examined generic copay changes from $7 to $8 per prescription, $12 to $15 for preferred brands, and $12 to $25 for nonpreferred branded drug prescriptions. There was essentially no reduction in drug use in the first two tiers. In the third tier, the copay elasticity with respect to utilization was −0.21 with respect to utilization and −.24 with respect to total tier-three pharmaceutical expenditures. This is consistent with the RAND-HIE.

Joyce and colleagues (2002) also examined drug benefit copays over the 1997 to 1999 period, but used an unnamed health benefits consulting firm's data on 25 firms with over 702,000 person-years of data. The study essentially compared those with one regime of copays relative to another, controlling for sociodemographic characteristics and chronic health conditions of the subscribers. The overall findings are summarized in Table 7-4. Higher copays did reduce overall drug spending substantially. Those in a one-tier plan (i.e., one with a single copay for all covered drugs) that had a ten-dollar copay had expenditures that were 22.3 percent lower than those with only a five-dollar copay. Indeed, in every tier, for each drug type, those with higher copays had lower drug expenditures. The price elasticities ranged from −0.22 to −0.40, with the three-tier nonpreferred brand-name prescriptions being the most price sensitive. These results are nearly twice as price sensitive as those found in the RAND-HIE.

The Joyce et al. study also demonstrated expenditure reductions in moving from a one-tier to a two-tier, or from a two-tier to a three-tier drug plan. In Table 7-4, moving from a one-tier plan with a common $10 copay to a two-tier plan with $10 and $20 copays reduced average spending from $563 to $455, a 19 percent reduction. Moving from a two-tier to a three-tier plan with $10, $20, and $30 copays was estimated to reduce expenditures by an additional 4 percent.

TABLE 7-4

Predicted Average Annual Prescription Drug Spending per Member

| | One-Tier Copay | | Two-Tier Copay | | Three-Tier Copay | |
	$5	$10	$5 Generic, $10 Brand	$10 Generic, $20 Brand	$5 Generic, $10 Preferred, $15 Nonpreferred	$10 Generic, $20 Preferred, $30 Nonpreferred
All drugs	$725	$563	$678	$455	$666	$436
Generic	$ 91	$ 69	$ 71	$ 41	$ 81	$ 53
Preferred	$571	$448	$534	$367	$518	$343
Nonpreferred	$ 63	$ 46	$ 73	$ 47	$ 67	$ 40

SOURCE: Data from Joyce et al. (2002).

NOTE: All values in 1997 dollars. All horizontal comparisons within tiers are statistically significant at the 95% confidence level.

The shift from nonpreferred to preferred brands is one of the key objectives of three-tier pharmacy benefits plans. Recter and colleagues (2003) examined the use of ACE inhibitors, proton pump inhibitors, and statins in four health plans from 1998 to 1999. They found that the presence of an average $18 higher copay for nonpreferred drugs was associated with a 13.3, 8.9, and 6.0 percentage point increase, respectively, in the use of the preferred brands in each drug class.

Finally, Goldman and colleagues (2004) examined the effect of doubling the copay associated with the use of eight classes of therapeutic drugs. They examined the claims data from 30 employers with 52 health plans over the 1997 to 2000 period. Reductions in days of prescription use across the eight classes ranged from 45 percent for nonsteroidal anti-inflammatories to 25 percent for antidiabetics. They concluded that:

> The use of medications . . . which are taken intermittently to treat symptoms, was sensitive to co-payment changes. . . . The reduction in use of medications for individuals in ongoing care was more modest. Still, significant increases in co-payments raise concern about adverse health consequences because of large price effects, especially among diabetic patients. (p. 2344)

The RAND-HIE also investigated the extent to which over-the-counter (OTC) drugs were substituted for prescription drugs. Given greater cost sharing, we might expect consumers to use OTC drugs as a substitute for prescriptions or physician visits. Leibowitz (1989) found no evidence of this. Based on biweekly reports filed by the insurance experiment participants, she found that OTC drug use was relatively low and that it was complementary with prescription drug use. Those with lower out-of-pocket insurance plans used more OTC drugs than did those facing higher out-of-pocket prices, even though OTC drugs were generally not covered by the insurance experiment.

Few other studies have addressed this issue, probably because of the difficulty in getting OTC utilization data. However, as part of their study of drug copays and chronic health conditions, Goldman and colleagues (2004) found that those drugs with close OTC substitutes had larger reductions in prescription drug use than did those without close substitutes. A doubling of the prescription copay led to a 32 percent reduction in the days of drug treatment supplied for medications with close OTC substitutes, such as antihistamines, but only a 15 percent reduction for those with no close substitutes.

Nursing Home Services

There has been little analysis of the private demand for nursing home and related long-term care services. Historically, this is understandable because much of nursing home care was provided through Medicaid. While this continues to be the case today, the advent of a large number of relatively affluent baby-boomer retirees suggests that the price sensitivity of nursing home and other long-term care services will be increasingly relevant for long-term care management and policy decisions.

Early work by Scanlon (1980) and Chiswick (1976) used metropolitan- and state-level data. Only Scanlon examined private payers distinct from Medicaid-subsidized payers. However, both found substantial price sensitivity— elasticities of –1.1 and –2.3, respectively—implying that a 10 percent reduction in nursing home prices would increase volume by 11 to 23 percent. The work, however, can be criticized for its aggregated units of analysis and the potential that the results are overstated by a failure to account for spend-down conditions commonly in force during the period. In an analysis of 1983 Wisconsin facility specific data, Nyman (1989) also found substantial price sensitivity—an elasticity of –1.7.

In more-recent and sophisticated work, Reschovsky (1998) used the 1989 National Long-Term Care Survey to examine the effect of Medicaid eligibility on nursing home use among older persons with disabilities. As part of this, he estimated a series of private demand equations. Price elasticity among private payers was –0.98. The married disabled had an elasticity nearly two and one-half times higher (–2.40), presumably because married individuals have access to relatively inexpensive informal care provided by a spouse. Unmarried individuals had much lower price sensitivity (–0.53), as did those with high levels of disability. In both cases, there are fewer viable substitute sources of care and, therefore, less price responsiveness. Care must be used in employing these estimates because the estimates often lacked statistical significance at the conventional levels.

Mukamel and Spector (2002) used 1991 New York State data on for-profit nursing homes to impute a degree of price sensitivity derived from marginal cost estimates. They found firm-specific elasticities in the neighborhood of –3.46. A 10 percent decrease in price would increase demand at a given nursing home by nearly 35 percent. As with managed care plans' demand for inpatient services from a specific hospital, we would expect firm-specific demand for nursing homes to be much larger than marketwide demand.

In one of the very few efforts to look at price sensitivity for other types of long-term care services, Nyman and colleagues (1997) examined the extent to which long-term care service users substitute adult foster care for nursing home care. (Adult foster care is a program in which an older adult lives in a private home of an unrelated individual.) A simple regression of the number of foster-care residents in Oregon counties in 1989, controlling for other factors, indicated that a nursing home lost .85 residents for every additional foster-care resident. In addition, an analysis of the demand for foster care demonstrated substantial price responsiveness in the private market. A 1 percent increase in the average adult foster-care price was associated with a 5.2 percent decrease in day-care residents.

The number and rigor of the long-term care studies do not match those of other service areas, largely because of an inability to account for adverse selection and, certainly, the lack of a controlled experiment of the nature of the RAND-HIE study. Thus, these findings inevitably overstate the extent of price sensitivity. Nonetheless, by the standards of acute-care services, the private demand for long-term care services appears to be very price sensitive.

Deductibles

With the passage of the Medicare Reform Act in late 2003 and its provisions for Health Savings Accounts (HSAs), attention again turned to the effects of higher deductibles on healthcare spending. Individuals and employers are able to establish tax-sheltered spending accounts that allow unused balances to be rolled over from one year to the next if they have an eligible health insurance plan. Among other requirements, an eligible health insurance plan must include a deductible of at least $1,000 per individual. This amount is to be adjusted annually for inflation under the terms of the legislation. HSAs are discussed in detail in Chapter 16.

The effect of a deductible depends on the nature of coverage once the deductible is satisfied. Suppose you have an annual deductible of $500 and must pay an out-of-pocket copay of $20 for each physician visit once the deductible is satisfied. If you knew with certainty that you would satisfy the deductible, then you would consume as though the price of a doctor visit was $20. If you knew you would not satisfy the deductible, then you would consume as though you had to pay the full price of the visit—perhaps $60 per visit. The higher the deductible, the less likely you are to satisfy it and the more likely you are to act as though you are paying the full price for medical services.

There has been virtually no empirical research on the effects of deductibles on medical usage, at least in the United States. The RAND-HIE is, again, the exception. As part of the experiment, some participants were enrolled in the 95 percent plan. In this plan, people paid 95 percent of every medical bill until they had spend 5, 10, or 15 percent of their family income (depending on the plan) or $1,000, whichever was lower. This was essentially a plan in which participants faced a deductible of $1,000 and afterward paid nothing out-of-pocket. In 2006 dollars, this is equivalent to a deductible of $4,160.

The results of the RAND-HIE shown in Table 7-1 indicated that the presence of a $4,160 family deductible followed by free care (i.e., the 95 percent plan) resulted in over a 31 percent reduction in medical spending, relative to the plan with free care.

In recent work, Van Vliet (2004) reported the effects of alternative deductibles in private health insurance plans in the Netherlands in 1996. In the Netherlands (at least during this time period), about 32 percent of the population voluntarily bought private health insurance from a number of different firms. The benefits packages differed largely with respect to the size of the deductible. Once the deductible was satisfied, there was little if any out-of-pocket payment for the wide range of services considered in Van Vliet's analysis. Considerable care was taken in the study to account for adverse selection by using a family's prior healthcare expenditure to predict what expenditures would have been had the deductibles not been present in 1996. Table 7-5 presents the findings, converted to 2006 U.S. dollars.

The highest range of deductibles, more than 1,750 Dutch guilders, is roughly equivalent to a deductible of more than $1,280 in 2006 U.S. dollars. Those Dutch residents with this level of deductible were estimated to have reduced their medical care spending by $650, nearly 28 percent. This compares with the RAND-HIE results, which found a 31 percent reduction for a deductible of $4,160. Given the differences in the health systems and

Deductible in 1996 Dutch Guilders	Deductible in 2006 U.S. Dollars	Expected Expenses (2006 dollars)	Effect of Deductible on Expected Expenses (2006 dollars)	Effect of Deductible as Percentage of Expected Expenses
0–100	0–73	$1,949	$23	1.2%
101–350	74–256	$2,222	–182	–8.2%
351–750	257–549	$1,227	–$222	–18.1%
751–1,250	550–915	$1,408	–$171	–12.1%
1,251–1,750	916–1281	$1,814	–$276	–14.1%
›1,750	›1281	$2,333	–$650	–27.9%
Total		$1,886	–$113	

TABLE 7-5
Effects of Deductibles on Health Spending

SOURCE: Adapted from data in Van Vliet (2004).

NOTE: 12/31/1996 Exchange rate: 1NLG = .57$. 1996 to 2006 U.S. CPI–All Items inflation adjustment = 1.284.

the details of the range of the Dutch deductible, these results are remarkably consistent.

The Van Vliet study suggested that deductibles in the neighborhood of $1,000 U.S. dollars could reduce medical care expenditures by about 14 percent. Care must be taken in this generalization, of course. First, the Dutch study only applied to upper-income groups with such coverage. Second, if catastrophic coverage plans with HSAs require copays for the use of health services once the deductible is satisfied, the savings would be somewhat greater.

Chapter Summary

- The story that emerges from this chapter's rather extensive review of the literature is that there is moderate price sensitivity in the overall use of health services. Described in terms of elasticities (economists' measure of price responsiveness), health services in general have an elasticity of about –.2. That means that a 1 percent increase in the price of health services generally will result in about a two-tenths of 1 percent reduction in use. Stated differently, a 10 percent increase in price reduces use by about 2 percent. To put this in some context, gasoline has an estimated elasticity of –.5; new cars, –1.2 to –1.5; and foreign travel, –4.0 (Reynolds 1976). Thus, health services are among the consumer goods that are less price responsive.

- This is certainly not to say that prices in healthcare do not matter. Even relatively small price elasticities can have large effects on use of services when the price change is large. The growth in health insurance over the last several decades has in many cases reduced the money price by nearly 100 percent. The provision of full-coverage insurance for the currently uninsured is a large effective price reduction and should have relatively large effects on use. Similarly, doubling typical insurance copays to $30 or $50 will have more than trivial effects.

- The price responsiveness of different health services is different. The salient findings from the empirical literature follow. Our knowledge rests heavily on the methodological strength of the RAND Health Insurance Experiment (RAND-HIE):

  - *Hospital services.* Hospital care is the least responsive to price. Full coverage compared to no coverage increased admissions by about 29 percent and total inpatient expenses of by 30 percent. Almost all of this effect was found in the difference in usage between 25 percent coinsurance and free care. This is an understatement of the full effect of cost sharing on the use of hospital services, however, because the RAND-HIE experiment made hospital care free once a family had incurred out-of-pocket expenses of $4,160 dollars (in 2006 terms).

  - *Hospital emergency department services.* Full coverage relative to no coverage increased visits by 54 percent and expenses by 45 percent. A free plan resulted in 27 percent more visits and 16 percent more expenditures than a plan with 25 percent coinsurance. Free care resulted in about a 90 percent increase in less-urgent visits but only a 30 percent increase in visits for more-urgent cases. Thus, emergency department cost sharing appears to reduce less-urgent cases much more than urgent ones.

  - *Price sensitivity by income level.* In general, higher-income groups were found to be less sensitive to price changes than were lower-income groups.

  - *Children versus adults.* Children's use of ambulatory services was about as price sensitive as was adults' use. However, hospital services tended to be almost insensitive to differences in price, at least under the conditions of the RAND-HIE health insurance experiment.

  - *Physician services.* Generally, the introduction of insurance providing full coverage increased both visits and expenditures by about two-thirds, controlling for other factors. The effect of moving from a 25 percent coinsurance rate to free care accounted for about one-half of the overall change.

- *Dental services.* Dental services are subject to a large transitory effect when coverage is first introduced. The RAND-HIE found that the first year of coverage had price effects that were twice as large as subsequent use. In the steady state, full coverage increased visits by 34 percent and expenses by 46 percent. Most of this effect was seen in the differences in usage between 25 percent coinsurance and free care. Preventive services were about as price sensitive as basic care. More-expensive services were more price sensitive.

- *Mental health services.* Greatest price sensitivity was found in outpatient mental health services. Full coverage relative to no coverage increased expenditures 300 percent. The increase in expenditures between those with 25 percent coinsurance and free care was about one-third more, the same as for ambulatory medical services. There was also evidence that, unlike dental care, use of mental health services increased over time.

- *Prescription drugs.* Prescription drugs appear to be about as price sensitive as ambulatory medical services. In the RAND-HIE experiment full coverage relative to no coverage increased the number of prescriptions per person by 50 percent and increased drug expenditures by 76 percent. Prescription drugs tend to be used with physician visits and are not used as substitutes for additional visits. Further, over-the-counter drugs also appear to be economic complements to physician services. The evidence suggests that they, too, are used with physician services, not in place of those visits. More-recent research has focused on differential copayments for generic, preferred brands, and nonpreferred brands. The research demonstrates that copays at each tier reduce drug use, and higher copays for nonpreferred relative to other tiers lead to substitution away from the nonpreferred categories. The limited evidence suggests that copays have a bigger effect on drugs taken intermittently to treat symptoms than on those taken in ongoing care. There is some concern about the health consequences for these groups particularly, but little research in this area currently exists.

- *Nursing home services.* Remarkably little research has addressed the price sensitivity of nursing home use. The very limited existing research suggests that the price elasticity of demand by private payers may be −1.0 or higher, particularly for older married persons. One study suggests that there is substantial cross-price sensitivity between adult foster care and nursing home care. Unfortunately, there has been no RAND-HIE experiment equivalent in this sector and the existing estimates may be subject to substantial bias resulting from adverse selection.

- Deductibles have become a potentially more important insurance tool with the advent of consumer-driven healthcare plans and Health Savings Accounts (HSAs). The RAND-HIE experiment found that a $4,160 family deductible (in 2006 dollars) followed by free care reduced medical care expenditures by 31 percent. More-recent work from the Netherlands found reductions of 28 percent for a similar insurance program with a $1,200 or more deductible (in 2004 U.S. dollars). This study suggests that a family deductible of $1,000 U.S. dollars might reduce spending by approximately 14 percent.

Discussion Questions

1. Why do you think the moral hazard response for dental care was different than that for medical services more generally?
2. Prescription drug plans often have three tiers of increasing co-payment. Given the results noted in the chapter, do you think the third tier saves enough to justify its presence?
3. Ambulatory mental health services appear to be among the most price sensitive. Some have argued that this area of healthcare has changed dramatically since the RAND-HIE was conducted in the 1970s. If mental health services are less price sensitive now than formerly, what evidence in the current market would you look for to support or refute this argument?
4. Suppose the RAND-HIE could be redone again in 2008 for $50 to $75 million. What topics would you include that were not in the original 1974 study? What topics would you give less attention? If you were a member of Congress, would you vote to fund a new study? Why or why not?

UTILIZATION MANAGEMENT

This chapter continues our Chapter 7 discussion of moral hazard. As a result of having health insurance, people typically pay less out-of-pocket for health services than they would if they had no insurance. As a consequence, they use more health services. As we saw in Chapter 7, one way of dealing with this problem is to increase the size of the copays or coinsurance rates that consumers pay. Faced with higher prices, consumers choose to forego those visits, drugs, and services that they perceive as not being worth the out-of-pocket price. This pushes them back up the demand curve, reducing their use of health services.

Another approach to dealing with moral hazard is to use some form of clinical judgment to decide which units of health services do not do enough good to justify the expenditure. Even though consumers may be willing to pay $20 for a visit to a pulmonologist, for example, insurers will only pay their share of the price if the visit is approved in advance by a primary care physician. Before patients can be admitted to a hospital, their internists must receive prior authorization from insurers for the admission. Obviously, these sorts of utilization management techniques cost resources. The key question, as with copays and coinsurance, is: how effective are they in reducing utilization? Ultimately, can insurers reduce utilization enough to pay for the utilization management program, compensate consumers for giving up services, and add to the corporate bottom line?

In this chapter, we review the relatively modest evidence on the effectiveness of various utilization management techniques. In general, utilization management shows some effectiveness with respect to inpatient services, but little effectiveness with respect to ambulatory services. Thus, based on this chapter and Chapter 7, we should expect to see copays and coinsurance techniques for controlling moral hazard in the use of ambulatory services, and utilization management for controlling moral hazard in the use of inpatient services.

Defining Utilization Management

Utilization management (UM) refers to any clinical restriction on utilization designed to approve or disapprove care based on clinical necessity. UM techniques do not preclude patients from obtaining the service; they simply say that the insurer is not liable for the cost of the service if UM procedures are not followed. Several types of UM techniques have been used over the years, including:

- *Preadmission certification.* The insurer requires that nonemergency hospital admissions be approved by the insurer before the patient is admitted to the hospital.
- *Concurrent review.* This is typically used in conjunction with preadmission certification. It specifies the number of hospital days a patient is authorized to stay. If a physician wants a patient to stay longer, additional days have to be requested.
- *Retrospective review.* This inpatient review is undertaken after the patient has been discharged. If the insurer determines that the patient should not have been admitted or should not have stayed so long, it will advise the provider to follow the insurer's admission protocols.
- *Denial of payment.* This inpatient review is used in conjunction with retrospective review. If the patient should not have been admitted or stays too long, the insurer will not pay for the inappropriate admission or days.
- *Mandatory second surgical opinion.* This protocol requires the patient to obtain a second opinion before a nonemergency surgical procedure is undertaken. If the second opinion does not confirm the initial recommendation, it is typically left to the patient to decide whether the procedure should be done.
- *Case management.* This program identifies high-cost cases. A case coordinator has authority to approve the substitution of some otherwise-uncovered services as lower-cost or more-appropriate alternatives to covered services. Home healthcare as a substitute for additional hospital days is an example.
- *Discharge planning.* This program requires the provider to have a plan in place at the time of admission for the patient's care on discharge from the hospital.
- *Gatekeeper.* This program assigns a primary care physician to each subscriber. This physician must approve visits to a specialist, or the insurer is not obligated to pay for the specialist visit.
- *Disease management.* This program provides coordination of care across multiple providers for patients with chronic diseases for which there are well-defined practice guidelines.
- *Intensive case management.* This is an individualized program that targets patients with high-cost and multiple or complex medical conditions.

These activities are at least conceptually distinct from the claims adjudication efforts that insurers also undertake. Claims adjudication refers to determination of whether a person, provider, or service is covered under the insurance contract and whether the price and copayment are in accord with the contract. Thus, claims adjudication may conclude that a contract does not cover a motorized wheelchair, for example. It may determine that a particular condition is covered but that the physician used is not a participating provider and, therefore, the claim is rejected. It may conclude that, while the plan ordinarily does not cover dental crowns, the crowns may be covered if they are required as a result of a sports injury. In practice, the distinction between UM and claims adjudication is not always clear. Conceptually, however, the distinction is straightforward: UM is the determination of the medical necessity of otherwise covered services. Claims adjudication is the determination of whether the service is covered.

Preadmission Certification and Concurrent Review

The first rigorous work to evaluate the effects of UM programs was conducted by Tom Wickizer and his colleagues John Wheeler and Paul Feldstein (1989). They analyzed 12 quarters of utilization experience on 223 insured groups over the 1984 to 1986 period. All of these groups purchased coverage from a single unnamed insurer, and 41 percent of them purchased a UM program from that insurer. The UM program consisted of preadmission certification together with concurrent review. The analysis essentially consisted of the presence or absence of the UM program, controlling for plan, market, and worker characteristics, together with season and year effects. They found that the UM program was associated with 3.7 percent fewer admissions and 20 fewer hospital days per 1,000 subscribers, but had no effect on length of stay. Thus, the program achieved its effects by reducing admissions.

In a similarly structured study, Khandker and Manning (1992) considered the preadmission certification and concurrent review program sold by Aetna to some of its insured groups. They examined quarterly data over the 1987 to 1988 period and found that the program reduced overall medical expenses by 4.4 percent and inpatient expenses by 8.1 percent, mostly by reducing length of stay. Both of these studies may overstate the effectiveness of UM programs, however. Insured groups voluntarily purchased these plans, and presumably, those with the greater perceived utilization problems were the ones most likely to purchase the programs.

Wheeler and Wickizer (1990) revisited their data to examine whether the UM effects were influenced by the workings of the local medical care market. They argued that:

1. A UM program may be more effective if there are higher admission rates in the community. This may indicate that some admissions could be treated on an ambulatory basis.

2. A UM program may be more effective if there is more idle hospital capacity in the market. If there are more empty beds, physicians may be encouraged to unnecessarily treat more patients on an inpatient basis.
3. A UM program may be more effective if there are more surgical specialists per 1,000 population in the area. More surgeons implies more competition, and somewhat more-aggressive surgical decisions may be needlessly made.
4. A UM program may be more effective if there is less HMO penetration in the market. If the HMO effect dominates (see Chapter 4), a smaller share of the population enrolled in an HMO would imply that some avoidable admissions were occurring.

Wheeler and Wickizer found that, indeed, the UM program they studied had a larger retarding effect on admissions when these factors were present in the local market. Thus, the effectiveness of a UM program may depend significantly on the nature of the local healthcare market.

Finally, Scheffler, Sullivan, and Ko (1991) examined six UM techniques employed by Blue Cross/Blue Shield plans during the mid-1980s. They examined six UM strategies that a plan may have employed from 1980 to 1988. Like the other studies, this one also used quarterly data and controlled for demographic, plan, and market characteristics, as well as seasonal and year effects. Unlike the other studies, their unit of observation was the plan's overall utilization. The findings are summarized in Table 8-1.

TABLE 8-1

Effects of Blue Cross/Blue Shield Utilization Management Programs

Utilization Management Strategy	Admissions per 1,000 Members	Days per 1,000 Members	Average Length of Stay	Inpatient Expenditures per Member
Preadmission certification with concurrent review	−5.3 %[‡]	−4.9 %[‡]	+0.4	−2.6 %[‡]
Mandatory second surgical opinion	+0.8	+0.9	+0.0	+1.1
Retrospective utilization review	+0.5	+0.8	+0.4	+2.1
Denial of payment	−2.3[*]	−4.5[‡]	−2.1[‡]	−2.0[*]
Case management	−1.0	+0.1	+1.1	−0.6
Discharge planning	+0.7	+1.2	+0.0	−0.8

SOURCE: Data from Scheffler, Sullivan, and Ko (1991).

NOTE: *, †, ‡ indicates that the coefficient is statistically different from 0.0 at the 90, 95, or 99 percent confidence interval, respectively.

Only preadmission certification with concurrent review and denial of payment were found to be effective in reducing utilization. Preadmission certification with concurrent review reduced hospital days by 4.9 percent per 1,000 members. This was achieved by reducing admission rates; length of stay was unaffected. This had the effect of reducing hospital expenditures per member by 2.6 percent. Presumably, expenditures were reduced less than admissions because the relatively short and inexpensive admissions were the ones avoided. Denial of payment was about 80 percent as effective as preadmission certification with concurrent review in reducing inpatient expenditures. It reduced admission rates by about the same percentage as average length of stay. In contrast, none of the other UM programs reduced hospital utilization, although the case management programs were beginning to approach statistical significance in the last years of the study.[1]

These studies constitute the first generation of evaluations of the effectiveness of UM. They suggest that preadmission certification with concurrent review may be effective in reducing hospital use, although the path by which this effect is achieved differs by study. The studies examine only selected programs; we have little knowledge of the effectiveness of programs run by other organizations, and there is some suggestion that the effectiveness of programs will depend on the nature of the local healthcare market. Further, the effects of ambulatory UM programs were not evaluated.

The Second Generation of UM Studies

The second generation of UM studies attempted to look more carefully at whether the programs reduced utilization and also at whether they affected quality of care. As a result, these studies were more narrowly focused around specific diseases and conditions. However, they also continued to be studies of opportunity in the sense that the analysts had data associated with a single UM program.

Lessler and Wickizer (2000) used data from the same insurer they studied previously but focused on the period from 1989 to 1993. The UM techniques they studied continued to be preadmission certification and concurrent review. However, in this study, they only examined utilization by patients with cardiovascular disease. Unlike the older but more-general data, here there was no evidence that UM reduced the number of admissions. All but one of the 2,813 requests for a medical admission were approved, and all but four of 1,513 procedural admission requests were also approved. There are at least three interpretations of this finding. First, it may be that the UM

---

1. More recently, Hennessy et al. (2003) evaluated the Medicaid retrospective drug utilization review program and concluded that it was ineffective.

program was ineffective in reducing admissions. Second, it may suggest that cardiovascular patients are much less likely to have discretionary admissions than other patients. Finally, it may suggest that providers knew the clinical conditions that would lead to approval and did not request admissions for cases that they knew would be disapproved. Unfortunately, the study design did not allow a test of these competing hypotheses.

Instead, the focus of the study was on the number of hospital days requested and approved, and the effect of denied days on 60-day hospital readmission rates. Readmission rates are a commonly used measure of quality of hospital care for cardiovascular patients. Table 8-2 reports the median number of days requested by diagnosis or procedure and the proportion of days denied. For a heart attack (i.e., an acute myocardial infarction), the median requested length of stay was 7.0 days. The UM program reduced the approved number of days by one day in 10.5 percent of the requests and reduced it by two or more days an additional 7.7 percent of the time. Thus, the requested length of stay for myocardial infarction was reduced almost 20 percent of the time. For all medical admissions related to cardiovascular disease, the number of requested days was reduced 17.4 percent of the time. For surgical procedures, the length of stay was reduced in 19 percent of the cases.

These results clearly suggest that the UM program was effective in reducing length of stay. Given that 17 to 19 percent of the cases faced shorter lengths of stay, the findings may also suggest that the lack of reductions in admissions did not come about because of providers learning the UM algorithms.

Lessler and Wickizer then explored the consequences of the reduced lengths of stay. Their results are summarized in Figure 8-1 (on page 124). There was no statistically meaningful difference in the readmission rates for medical diagnoses; 9.5 percent of those with no days denied were readmitted within 60 days, and those denied two or more days had readmission rates of only 9 percent. A similar story can be told for one-day reductions for surgical procedures. However, the difference in readmission rates between those without a denial and those with two or more days is 2.2 percentage points and is significant at the 99 percent confidence interval, suggesting that quality of care may have been impaired for these surgical patients.

Kapur, Gresenz, and Studdert (2003) provided insight into the prevalence of denials of coverage by UM programs. In this case, they reviewed the records on all coverage requests of two large, multispecialty group practices in California in the late 1990s. Each group had several hundred physicians and contracts with scores of insurance plans. Requests related to whether a service was covered under a capitation agreement were excluded, as were all drug, vision, dental, and behavioral health services requests because these are often subject to separate "carve-out" insurance contracts. Medical Group 1 submitted nearly 147,000 coverage requests during calendar years 1997 through 1999. Medical Group 2 submitted more than 329,000 requests.

TABLE 8-2
Length of Stay (LOS) Reductions among Utilization Review Cases for Selected Diagnoses and Procedures

Diagnosis or Procedure (ICD-9 Code)	Number of Reviews	Median Total Days Requested	LOS Reduction (percentage of utilization reviews)		
			0 Days	1 Day	2+ Days
Medical Admissions					
Angina (411.1)	614	3.0	85.7%	9.9%	4.4%
Congestive heart failure (428.0–428.9)	416	7.0	81.5	9.9	8.7
Cerebral vascular accident (435.9, 436.0–436.9)	414	5.0	83.6	8.5	8.0
Arrhythmia/Conduction disturbance (426.0–427.9)	370	3.0	83.5	9.5	7.0
Myocardial infarction (410.0–410.9)	313	7.0	81.8	10.5	7.7
All Medical Admissions	2,813	5.0	82.6	10.2	7.2
Surgical Procedural Admissions					
Catheterization (37.21–37.23)	456	1.0	89.5	6.8	3.7
Coronary bypass surgery (36.10–36.16)	257	8.0	68.4	17.0	14.6
Valve replacement/ Valvuloplasty (35.00–35.28)	88	9.0	77.3	14.0	8.0
Carotid endarterectomy (38.12)	69	5.0	71.0	13.0	15.9
Head/neck vessel replacement (38.42)	47	10.0	83.0	2.1	14.9
All Procedural Admissions	1,513	4.0	81.0	11.0	8.0

SOURCE: Lessler and Wickizer (2000), "The Impact of Utilization Management on Readmissions among Patients with Cardiovascular Disease," *Health Services Research* 34(7): 1315–1329, Table 2. Reprinted with permission courtesy of Wiley–Blackwell Publishing Ltd.

Table 8-3 on page 125 reports the distribution of coverage requests by type of service. Overall, between 8 and 10 percent of requests were denied. The percentage of requests differs substantially across the two medical groups, in part because each group classified services somewhat differently. However, over half of all denials were for diagnostic testing, durable medical equipment, and emergency services.

FIGURE 8-1
60-Day
Readmission
Rates by
Reduction in
Length of Stay

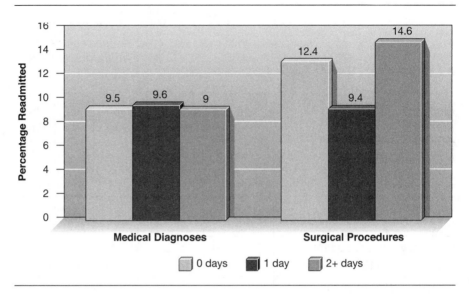

SOURCE: Data from Lessler and Wickizer (2000).

Only Medical Group 1 was able to classify the requests as prospective, meaning an inquiry regarding whether a service would be covered if provided, or retrospective, meaning that the service had been provided before the request was made. Prospective requests were much more common (81 percent), and only 6 percent of them were denied. In contrast, nearly one-fourth (23 percent) of the retrospective requests were denied. Durable medical equipment (33 percent), other care (23 percent), and diagnostic testing (14 percent) constituted most of the prospective denials. Most of the retrospective denials occurred as a result of emergency care (37 percent) and diagnostic testing (24 percent).

Finally, Kapur and colleagues reported the reasons for denial by type of service for the prospectively denied services of Medical Group 1. The results indicate that over 40 percent of the denials stem from the insurer not being contractually liable for the service. This was the case for 86 percent of the durable medical equipment requests, for example. Nearly one-fourth (22 percent) of the denials were because the proposed provider was not a participating provider under the contract. Fewer than one-third (29 percent) were denied as not medically necessary. The most commonly denied services in the prospectively denied services group were emergency care (100 percent); ancillary health services, such as physical or speech therapy (64 percent); and minor surgery (64 percent). For the retrospectively denied services (not shown):

TABLE 8-3

Distribution of Coverage Requests and Denials by Type of Service

Type of Service	Medical Group 1			Medical Group 2		
	Percentage of Requests	Percentage Denied	Percentage of All Denials	Percentage of Requests	Percentage Denied	Percentage of All Denials
All services	100%	10%	100%	100%	8%	100%
Diagnostic/Testing	22	8	19	19	8	20
Durable medical equipment	8	23	19	3	15	5
Emergency care	11	17	18	13	16	27
Inpatient care	6	3	2	9	4	5
Nonacute care	2	4	1	<1	9	<1
Obstetrical care	4	<1	<1	4	8	4
Ancillary services	14	4	5	4	6	3
Other care	17	13	23	1	14	1
Physician services	11	9	11	28	7	24
Surgery	8	4	3	16	3	5
Miscellaneous	—	—	—	2	21	5

SOURCE: Data from Kapur, Gresenz, and Studdert (2003).

NOTES: "Diagnostic/Testing" includes imaging, lab, and pathology; "durable medical equipment" includes orthotics and prosthetics; "emergency care" includes ambulance and emergency department; "nonacute care" includes home health and skilled nursing; "ancillary services" includes physical and speech therapy; "other care" includes chiropractic, infertility treatment, and sterilization. Most groups also included "other."

Almost every denial of emergency care services was that the enrollee's medical condition was not deemed an emergency according to the "prudent layperson standard." (Kapur, Gresenz, and Studdert 2003, p. 279)

For other services, virtually all denials were for failure to obtain prior approval.

While it is always dangerous to generalize from such a small sample of physician groups, the data suggest that a relatively large number of denials—over 60 percent—appear to relate to claims adjudication issues rather than utilization management, per se. That is, the issue was whether or not the service or the provider was covered under the insurance contract. UM seems to have had an impact in less than one-third of the cases, and these were disproportionately related to emergency department use, ancillary services, and minor surgery.

Effectiveness of Gatekeeping

A somewhat more-generic approach to UM is gatekeeping. The argument is that each subscriber is assigned to a primary care provider who is responsible for the care provided to that individual. There are three rationales for assigning a primary care provider to each subscriber. The first rationale is continuity of care. The argument is that a regular provider will readily appreciate changes in the patient's condition and will see the interactions across conditions that might be missed if the patient only saw a series of specialists. The second rationale is financial. The assignment of a primary care provider is sometimes a mechanism to provide financial incentives to the physician or physician group through capitation or some other mechanism. We will defer the discussion of financial incentives for physicians until Chapter 10. The third rationale is gatekeeping, per se. The argument is that the primary care physician is in a better position than the patient to evaluate the clinical value of alternative diagnostic and treatment protocols. As such, the gatekeeper serves as the patient's agent, deciding whether a referral should be made for specialist visits, diagnostic tests, physical therapy, etc. It is a short step to transform this patient-agency into a UM technique that requires patients to see their primary care physician before other services are covered.

Ferris et al. (2001) provided one of the few rigorous evaluations of whether a gatekeeper model reduced the use of subsequent specialty visits. The HMO now known as Harvard Vanguard eliminated the requirement of prior approval of specialty referrals effective April 1, 1998. This HMO had 140,000 adult subscribers, and for the 25 years prior to that time, prior approval was required for virtually all specialist appointments.

The study team undertook the evaluation by considering the 36 months prior to and the 18 months after the elimination of the prior-approval requirement. In each six-month period prior to and after the program change, they selected a random cohort of 10,000 members of the health plan and made some minor corrections for differences in age, sex, and season of the year. They then compared the average number of visits before and after the elimination of gatekeeping. Their results are summarized in Table 8-4.

As is clear, there was literally no difference in the average number of specialty visits per member before and after the elimination of gatekeeping. The number of first specialty visits per member increased slightly. The difference is the equivalent of six more visits per year for each 100 members. This was offset by four fewer primary care visits per year for every 100 members. It is difficult to justify a program that has this little impact, and indeed, Harvard Vanguard did eliminate their gatekeeping program. Work by Forrest et al. (2001), Escarce et al. (2001), and Pati et al. (2003) corroborate these findings. As Forrest and colleagues (2001) concluded,

> The potential downside of uncoordinated, self-referred service use in POS [point-of-service] health plans is limited and counterbalanced by higher patient satisfaction with specialist services. (p. 2223)

Disease Management and Intensive Case Management

The newest approaches to UM are disease management and intensive case management. The programs appear to be popular with employers and some health plans as of the early 2000s (Short, Mays, and Miller 2003). However,

Physician Visits	Gatekeeping	No Gatekeeping	Difference (p-value)
Average number of specialty visits per patient per six-month period	0.78	0.78	0.00 (0.35)
Average number of first visits to specialists per patient per six-month period	0.19	0.22	+0.03 (<0.001)
Average number of primary care visits per patient per six-month period	1.21	1.19	−0.02 (0.05)
Visits to specialists as a proportion of all primary care visits	39.1	39.5	+0.4 (0.58)
Initial visits to specialists as a proportion of all specialty visits	24.7	28.2	+3.5 (<0.001)

TABLE 8-4
Visits to Specialists and Generalists Before and after the Elimination of Gatekeeping

SOURCE: Data from Ferris et al. (2001).

there is remarkably little evidence regarding whether the programs have been effective in reducing utilization (Congressional Budget Office 2004).

Chapter Summary

- Utilization management (UM) consists of a variety of mechanisms to deal with the moral hazard problem by using clinical judgment to determine whether particular health services are worth their cost for specific patients.
- Preadmission certification used in conjunction with concurrent review appears to be successful in reducing hospital days, although the studies are not necessarily generalizable. Some evidence indicates that more-aggressive limits on surgical stays for cardiovascular disease resulted in higher 60-day readmission rates.
- There is remarkably little evidence regarding the effectiveness of ambulatory UM. While there is limited evidence that denials of coverage are relatively common, two-thirds of these denials appear to relate to claims adjudication rather than medical necessity.
- Evidence is growing that primary care gatekeeping does not reduce healthcare utilization or control costs.
- There is little convincing evidence regarding whether newer forms of UM, such as disease management and intensive case management, are effective or not.

Discussion Questions

1. Consider the evidence presented in this chapter and Chapter 7. What sort of strategies would you suggest to a managed care firm to deal with the moral hazard problem? Would your strategies differ for inpatient and ambulatory services? If so, how?
2. Chapter 1 suggested that managed care firms have suffered from a backlash against their utilization management efforts. Suppose managed care plans were to largely abandon utilization management efforts. What effects would this have on their claims experience? What effects would it have on enrollment? What decision rule would you use to determine whether a UM program should be implemented or continued?

MANAGED CARE AND SELECTIVE CONTRACTING

SELECTIVE CONTRACTING: MANAGED CARE AND HOSPITALS

Between 1988 and 2005, the proportion of insured workers enrolled in a managed care plan increased from 27 percent to 97 percent (Gabel et al. 2005). This change came about because managed care offered an advantage over other forms of health insurance. The advantage is selective contracting. Prior to the advent of managed care, insurers tended to cover a fixed percentage of the bill at any provider that the insured chose. Managed care plans were able to negotiate lower prices in exchange for some assurance of patient volume. In this chapter, we explore the nature of hospital market competition and the fundamental change that arose as a result of selective contracting by managed care plans.

The "Golden Era" of Hospitals

From the advent of private health insurance through the mid-1980s, payments to hospitals were based on cost. Blue Cross and Blue Shield, Medicare, and Medicaid paid hospitals on the basis of their allowable costs. Commercial insurers tended to pay billed charges. This process essentially meant that anything that was done for a patient in a hospital generated costs which, in turn, generated revenue. While insurers may have exerted some pressure on providers, insured patients typically paid a 20 percent coinsurance rate and often had stoploss features that limited their out-of-pocket expenditures. As a consequence, there was very little price competition among hospitals.

This is not to say that hospitals did not compete with each other. They did. However, since price did not matter much, hospitals rationally competed along dimensions that *did* matter. They attracted physicians and their patients by providing more services, amenities, and quality. This had the effect of taking the textbook theory of competition and standing it on its head. Standard economics argues that more suppliers in a market should lead to prices being driven down to marginal cost. The mechanism for this is each provider shaving its price a bit to sell more services and, ultimately, the price is driven down to the lowest price that allows an efficient provider to cover its costs of production.

FIGURE 9-1
Hospital
Average Cost
per Admission,
1982

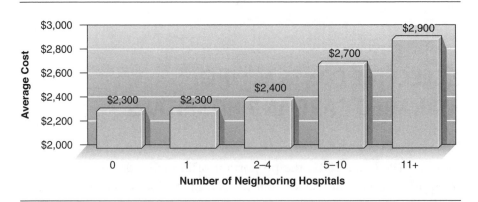

SOURCE: Robinson and Luft (1987), "Competition and the Cost of Hospital Care, 1972 to 1982," *Journal of the American Medical Association* 257(23): 3241–3245, Figure 1. Copyright © 1987 American Medical Association. All rights reserved.

When price does not affect the quantity sold, but service, quality, and amenities do, a greater number of suppliers should lead to higher quality and more services and amenities as one hospital competes with its neighbors. This has the economically counterintuitive result that more hospitals in a market leads to higher, not lower, prices. Jamie Robinson and Hal Luft (1987) provided striking evidence of this phenomenon. They estimated hospital costs per admission in 1982, controlling for a variety of appropriate market characteristics, and found that costs were higher when there were more hospitals within a 15-mile radius. Their findings are shown in Figure 9-1. Hospital costs rose rapidly with the number of neighboring, and arguably competing, hospitals. Commentators at the time referred to this as the "medical arms race." In some sense, this was the "golden era" of hospitals in that they were paid what they spent.

The Advent of Selective Contracting

Managed care introduced selective contracting into health services markets. Selective contracting is easily defined: some providers get contracts; some do not. With selective contracting, an insurer agrees to pay for only the hospital and physician services that are provided by a small panel (relative to the market) of hospitals, physicians, therapists, and drugstores. This arrangement introduces price into the decision-making calculation, since providers are included in a panel based on services, amenities, quality, *and* price. As such, the traditional economic concept of competition can lead to prices driven down to marginal cost as insurers trade assurances of patient volume for lower prices. See Dranove, Shanley, and Simon (1992), Cutler, McClellen, and Newhouse (2000), and Morrisey (2001) for detailed discussions of the incentives that selective contracting provides.

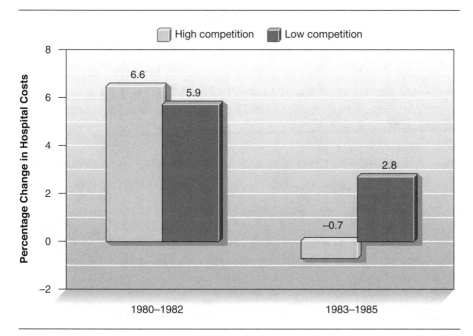

FIGURE 9-2

Effects of California Selective Contracting Laws

SOURCE: Data from Melnick and Zwanziger (1988).

Selective contracting had it origins in California in 1983. In that year, the California legislature passed two laws dealing with contracting between insurers and providers. First, the legislature allowed California's Medicaid program (called MediCal) to enter into contracts with some hospital providers, but not necessarily all. MediCal asked for proposals from hospitals. Ultimately, some hospitals got MediCal contracts; others did not. Second, the legislature made it clear that a private insurer did not have to contract with all licensed providers in a given market. The insurer could selectively contract, giving a contract to some providers but choosing not to contract with others.

Melnick and Zwanziger (1988) examined the effects of these changes on California hospital costs before and after enactment. They controlled for a variety of other factors, including the Medicare prospective payment system that was being phased in during this time. Their key finding, summarized in Figure 9-2, was that prior to the enactment of legislation, hospital costs from 1980 to 1982 rose much more rapidly (6.6 percent) in the quartile of markets with the most hospital competition, compared to the least competitive quartile, where costs rose 5.9 percent. This is wholly consistent with the medical arms race. In contrast, from 1983 to 1985, after the enactment of the legislation, costs in the most competitive quartile rose the least rapidly. In fact, they declined by 0.7 percent. Costs rose 2.8 percent in the least competitive quartile of markets. This is strong evidence that something changed in 1983.

This is only suggestive evidence of selective contracting, however. There is no actual link to selective contracting other than the story line that argues that the laws were the key feature intervening in 1983. What was needed was a study that directly showed the pathways by which differences in prices could be plausibly linked to contracting behavior by managed care plans.

Melnick and colleagues (1992) provided the best evidence of these pathways. They were able to get information on the prices actually negotiated between a large preferred provider organization (PPO) run by Blue Cross of California and 190 general hospitals with which it had entered into contracts. Market participants are often reluctant to disclose the prices to which they have agreed, and this was also the case in this study. However, the researchers were able to obtain an index of the price for inpatient general medical-surgical admissions. The index was simply the ratio of the actual negotiated price divided by the average negotiated price. Thus, a value of 1.2 for a hospital meant that it agreed to a price that was 20 percent higher than the average negotiated price. Melnick and colleagues then used regression analysis to try to explain the differences in the index of prices as a function of hospital characteristics, local hospital market conditions, and hospital and insurer bargaining power. Their findings provided key insights into the effects of competition in a selective contracting setting. The results are summarized in Box 9-1.

First, other things equal, the Blue Cross PPO was able to negotiate lower hospital prices when there were more hospitals in the local market. Envision the PPO's contracting representative meeting with the hospital chief financial officer (CFO) and suggesting that Morrisey Memorial Hospital, just down the street, is very willing to contract with the PPO at a lower price.

BOX 9-1

Effects of Competition in the Presence of Selective Contracting

The preferred provider organization (PPO) run by Blue Cross of California was able to negotiate a lower hospital price per day when:

- There were more hospitals in the local market.
- The PPO had a larger share of the hospital's book of business.
- The hospital had a smaller share of the PPO's book of business.
- Occupancy rates were lower
  —at the negotiating hospital.
  —at neighboring hospitals.

SOURCE: Abstracted from Melnick et al. 1992.

Melnick and colleagues found that actual prices were lower when there were more Morrisey Memorial equivalents in the community.

Second, the Blue Cross PPO obtained a lower price when it had a larger share of the hospital's book of business. When a PPO is providing, say, 35 percent of a hospital's volume of patients, the hospital CFO is usually much more willing to provide a lower price than if the PPO only provides a handful of patients. Empirically, the Melnick et al. (1992) study did find that the hospital agreed to lower prices under those circumstances.

Third, the Blue Cross PPO obtained a lower price when the hospital had little bargaining power. Suppose that a hospital provides, say, 25 percent of a PPO's local hospital admissions. If the PPO asks for a lower price, the hospital CFO might say: "Look, we have an excellent hospital, and your subscribers value the care they get here. You could move your business to Morrisey Memorial, but many of your subscribers will change health plans to stay with us." According to the Melnick study, when the hospital had this sort of leverage, prices stayed up; when it did not have this leverage, the PPO was able to negotiate a lower price.

Finally, controlling for all of the foregoing effects, the Blue Cross PPO was able to get a lower price when the hospital had a lower occupancy rate. Hospital marginal costs are lower than average costs. Thus, as long as a hospital is able to negotiate a price that covers its extra (i.e., marginal) costs of providing services, it should do so, even if it only makes a small contribution to fixed costs. Thus, a hospital with, say, a 60 percent occupancy rate usually is willing to offer a lower price to fill some empty beds and to make a contribution to fixed costs. The Melnick study found that hospitals with low occupancy rates did agree to lower prices.

In addition, however, the study also found that hospitals with high occupancy rates also agreed to lower prices if hospitals in their local market had lower occupancy. Idle hospital capacity meant that even a high-occupancy hospital would agree to a lower price because of the fear that other hospitals would offer lower prices to fill their beds.

If these findings can be generalized across other hospitals and other provider markets, they have enormous implications. They imply, for example, that:

- Insurers and consumers generally should encourage the entry of new and additional capacity in the local healthcare market as a means of reducing prices.
- If a managed care plan has a relatively small network of providers, it is likely to be able to negotiate lower prices in exchange for directing substantial patient volume to providers with contracts. In contrast, a managed care plan with a large network relative to its subscriber base will be less able to negotiate lower prices.

- If there is idle capacity in a local hospital market, many, if not all, of the local hospitals will financially bleed red ink until one or more of the facilities closes.
- Certificate-of-need laws have real potential to keep hospital prices high by keeping new competitors and/or additional capacity out of the market.[1]
- The merger of several pediatric groups in a market will likely result in higher prices charged to managed care plans.

The key issue is whether the findings of Melnick and colleagues can be generalized.

Generalizing the Evidence on Selective Contracting

The first issue is whether managed care plans actually do contract with only a subset of the available providers. Zwanziger and Meirowitz (1998) provided the best evidence. They examined the hospital networks of the managed care plans operating in the 13 largest metropolitan statistical areas (MSAs) in 1993. They found that across these markets the typical managed care plan had contracts with 44 percent of the hospitals. The averages ranged from 31 percent in Tampa and Houston to 60 percent in Minneapolis. In addition, the typical hospital had contracts with several managed care plans. This suggests that price may play a role across several markets in determining which hospitals get contracts.

The second issue is whether lower hospital prices result in more contracts and greater patient volume at contracted hospitals. Feldman and colleagues (1990) examined hospital contracting among six health maintenance organizations (HMOs) in four unnamed (but non-California) cities in the mid-1980s. They sought to explain which hospitals got contracts as a function of price, quality, and location. Location is easy to measure, quality is enormously difficult, and price is problematic. They used hospital characteristics like teaching status, number of services provided, and ownership as proxies for quality, and costs as a proxy for price. They found that price did not predict which hospitals got contracts; the quality proxies did. However, in a second portion of the study, they examined the patient volume of each hospital with a contract as a function of price, quality, and location. Here they had actual negotiated prices. What they found was that price mattered tremendously. For staff and network HMOs, a 1 percent higher price was

---

1. Certificate-of-need laws, applicable to hospitals, exist in 26 states. These laws require a hospital to obtain state permission to enter a market or to expand. The Federal Trade Commission and the Department of Justice (2004) have argued that certificate-of-need laws are anticompetitive.

associated with a 3 percent reduction in volume. Contracts followed "quality," but volume followed price.

Young, Burgess, and Valley (2002) examined 1992 to 1997 Florida hospital data to determine the effects of hospital price and nonprice characteristics on the share of HMO revenues and admissions that a hospital received. They, too, found a complex relationship between price and nonprice attributes. They concluded that hospitals had a larger share of HMO business when they had lower prices, but that a central location and the provision of technologically sophisticated services were more important.

Gaskin and colleagues (2002) analyzed a 1997 survey of 50 HMOs to identify which hospitals got contracts to provide coronary artery bypass graft surgery (CABG). They found that 44 percent of the relevant hospital-HMO pairs involved a contract for care. The probability of a contract increased with hospital quality, but decreased with distance and with cost. However, they had no actual price data and were unable to look at patient volume.

In contrast, Dor, Koroukian, and Grossman (2004) obtained the actual prices hospitals received for angioplasty. (Angioplasty is a treatment for blocked arteries in which a catheter is pushed through the artery to clear it.) The private database they used had claims from approximately 80 large self-insured employer plans in 1995 and 1996. Essentially, they ran a series of price regression equations in which the price the hospital received was a function of the characteristics of the angioplasty received, hospital characteristics and case mix, hospital and insurance market characteristics, and whether the insurer was an HMO, PPO, or traditional insurance plan. They found that, controlling for the other factors, prices paid by HMOs were 27 percent lower than those paid by traditional insurance plans. PPO prices were approximately 8.5 percent lower.

Gaskin and Hadley (1997) looked more generally at the role of HMO penetration on hospital cost growth in 84 MSAs from 1985 to 1993. If we accept the foregoing studies as evidence of the pathway by which managed care plans use selective contracting to achieve lower prices, then the Gaskin and Hadley study offers a broad national picture of how effective this approach has been. They found little evidence of an effect of HMO market share on hospital costs during the mid-1980s. However, after 1988, the presence of HMOs resulted in lower hospital costs. Gaskin and Hadley estimated that by 1993 HMOs reduced hospital costs by 7.8 percent. The effects were largest in markets with both a large HMO market share and more-rapid HMO growth. Figure 9-3 shows Gaskin and Hadley's key finding. The difference between the top line and the lower ones is the estimated growing effect that HMO penetration had on hospital costs—arguably, because of the ability of HMOs to selectively contract.

Bamezai and colleagues (1999) more directly tested the interplay of managed care penetration and hospital competition. They examined the

FIGURE 9-3

Effects of
HMO
Penetration on
Hospital Costs

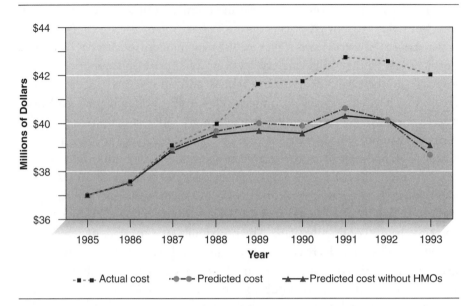

-■- -■- Actual cost   ··-●-●- Predicted cost   -▲-▲-Predicted cost without HMOs

SOURCE: Gaskin and Hadley (1997), "The Impact of HMO Penetration on the Rate of Hospital Cost Inflation, 1985–1993," *Inquiry* 34(3): 205 –216, Figure 3. Reprinted with permission.

change in hospital operating costs over the 1989 to 1994 period, using Medicare cost report data on over 3,400 hospitals reporting in both 1989 and 1994. They looked at HMO and PPO penetration separately, and found that HMO effects were larger and that the effects depended dramatically on the nature of the local hospital competition. They concluded that HMO penetration above 7 percent could reduce the increase in hospital costs by 15.3 percent if the hospital market was fully competitive. Similar PPO penetration could reduce the increase in costs by 7.7 percent under similar circumstances. From the earlier research, we can speculate that the PPO effect is smaller because PPOs tend to have larger networks of providers that limit their ability to selectively contract as effectively. Morrisey (2001) used these results to simulate the effects of having more equal-sized hospitals in a market. He concluded that nearly two-thirds of the HMO effect, but only one-quarter of the PPO effect, could be achieved in a market with four equal-sized hospitals.

More-recent work by the U.S. Government Accountability Office (GAO 2005) suggests that the role of hospital competition continues to be key in determining the prices paid by managed care firms. Federal employees obtain their employer-sponsored health insurance through the Federal Employees Health Benefit Program (FEHBP). In each market, the government offers a traditional health insurance plan and often several managed care plans. The GAO was able to get the actual prices paid by these managed care plans for hospital services in 2001. It found that hospital prices were 18 percent higher in markets with the least competition, compared to those with the most competition. Competition was defined as the proportion of hospital beds controlled by the two largest hospitals or hospital systems in the metropolitan area. When the GAO controlled for other factors, this difference in prices was reduced but still substantial.

Other Effects of Selective Contracting

To the extent that price has entered the decision-making calculation, it is likely that other elements of the hospital market have changed as a result. We briefly summarize the literature here.

First, some speculated that selective contracting would lead to an expansion of the geographic hospital market. They argued that managed care plans would enter into contracts with suburban or outlying hospitals at favorable prices and require their patients to travel further. There is no evidence to support this. White and Morrisey (1998) and Mobley and Frech (2000) each examined California hospital discharge data from the late 1980s and early 1990s. Neither found any evidence that travel distances had increased either on average or with respect to specific inpatient procedures.

Second, an argument can be made that managed care should slow the proliferation of services. The effect on service offerings is conceptually ambiguous, however. On the one hand, economies of scale suggest that if hospitals specialized in particular service niches, they could achieve cost economies and garner managed care contracts with lower prices.[2] On the other hand, if economies of scope predominate, a hospital may have lower costs in one product line because it also has other products. Morrisey (2001) reported a mixed picture. Increased managed care penetration may be reducing the availability of high-technology services, but the few studies do not agree, and there is very little evidence on the effects of new technologies.

We might expect selective contracting to result in nonprofit hospitals providing less charity care. The argument is that these hospitals may use their "profits" to do good works like providing care to those who cannot pay. Lower prices may result in lower profits and, consequently, less charity care. Gruber (1994a) examined the provision of uncompensated care by nonprofit hospitals in California between 1984 and 1988. He concluded that greater managed care resulted in a reduction in charity care in competitive hospital

---

2. Economies of scale exist when one can increase all inputs by 1 percent and output expands by more than 1 percent. Thus, a larger hospital may exhibit economies of scale compared to a small hospital. Economies of scope exist when the costs of providing two service lines together is less expensive than providing each line separately. Maternity care and pediatrics may be examples of economies of scope.

BOX 9-2

How Big Are Hospital Discounts?

How large are the price concessions that managed care plans are able to negotiate with hospitals? This question is not easily answered because hospital pricing strategies are complex and the data are not publicly available. For example, while hospitals have a nominal price list that is typically referred to as full billed charges, like new car sticker prices, virtually no one pays full billed charges.

We can go to publicly available American Hospital Association (AHA) data to get a very crude approximation of the size of hospital discounts. It is important to appreciate, however, that there may be no direct relationship between the size of a discount and the actual price of hospital services. One hospital may set very high billed charges and grant very large discounts. Another may set more-modest charges, give very small discounts, and still end up offering a lower actual price. Nonetheless, the range of discounts gives a sense of the order of magnitude in the negotiations.

Table A shows the reported 2004 community hospital "discount" by state. This discount is defined as the amount of "deductions from revenue" divided by hospital gross revenue. Note that these deductions include: (1) price reductions negotiated with private insurers; (2) price reductions implicit in the payments made by Medicare, Medicaid, the Department of Veterans Affairs (VA), and other government programs; and (3) charity care and bad debt. Thus, they are not solely a measure of negotiated price reductions.

TABLE A

The Magnitude of Hospital "Discounts," 2004

	Alabama	California	Indiana	Missouri	New Jersey	United States
Aggregate Discount	69.6%	71.8%	52.0%	59.4%	75.4%	62.0%

SOURCE: Computed from American Hospital Association (2006), Tables 3 and 6.

According to Table A, in 2004, across all short-term community hospitals, the average "discount" was on the order of 62 percent. Stated another way, hospitals received 38 cents for every dollar of "billed charges." The table also reports the statewide discounts in five states chosen to include California and some geographic representation. What is clear is that the discounts are always greater than 50 percent but vary sub-

> stantially for reasons that may have to do with systematic hospital pricing strategies, competition, and the extent of bad debt and charity care provided.

markets after the advent of selective contracting. Thorpe, Seiber, and Florence (2001) used national 1991 to 1997 data from the AHA Annual Survey of Hospitals. They concluded that a 10 percentage point increase in managed care penetration was associated with a 2 percentage point reduction in hospital total profit margin and a 0.6 percentage point decrease in the provision of uncompensated care. More recently, Currie and Fahr (2004) examined California hospital data from the 1988 to 1996. They found little evidence that nonprofit hospitals turned away uninsured or Medicaid patients. Moreover, they also found that for-profit hospitals had reduced their share of privately insured patients and increased their share of Medicare patients and Medicaid births, perhaps because these cases had become relatively more profitable.

Finally is the issue of quality of care. Here, the prevailing public view is that managed care results in lower quality (Blendon, Brodie, and Altman 1998). However, there has been surprisingly little evidence on this issue—in part because general measures of quality are difficult to obtain and apply consistently. Hellinger (1998) concluded that when quality was measured along dimensions of effectiveness, satisfaction, and access to care, there were no significant differences between managed care and indemnity plans. However, some of the studies that Hellinger reviewed do suggest that vulnerable populations may be more at risk in managed care plans. Sari (2002) used in-hospital complication rates in 16 states between 1992 and 1997 to shed additional light on the issue. He concluded that increases in managed care penetration were associated with improved quality of care when measured as inappropriate utilization, wound infections, and adverse/iatrogenic complications. For other measures, such as obstetrical complications and major surgery complications, there were no statistically significant differences.

Rogowski, Jain, and Escarce (2007) used 1994 to 1999 California data to examine 30-day mortality after hospitalization for acute myocardial infarction, hip fracture, gastrointestinal hemorrhage, congestive heart failure, and diabetes. They found that greater hospital competition was associated with lower mortality for three to five of these six conditions (depending on the competition measure used) and that greater HMO penetration was associated with lower mortality for gastrointestinal hemorrhage and congestive heart failure.

Favorable Selection versus Selective Contracting

Research has demonstrated two distinguishing characteristics of managed care plans. They have lower utilization experience, largely as a result of favorable selection, and they pay lower prices to providers as a result of selective contracting. When we look at differences in healthcare expenditures per enrollee between managed care plans and indemnity plans, it is important to know which of these effects dominates and by how much. If the difference is almost entirely attributable to favorable selection, there is little reason to recommend managed care to an employer or as an alternative to a traditional Medicare or Medicaid program. On the other hand, if the difference is largely attributable to selective contracting, then there is good reason to recommend managed care because selective contracting implies that managed care plans are able to provide the same clinical services at lower cost.

Altman, Cutler, and Zeckhauser (2003) provided the only work that disaggregates these two effects. They examined the health plans offered to state and local employees by the Group Insurance Commission of Massachusetts in 1994 and 1995. The commission offered one indemnity plan, 10 HMOs, and a PPO. However, because the PPO only had enrollment of 25,000, they excluded it from the analysis. The indemnity plan had nearly 68,000 enrollees, and the HMOS, combined, had over 122,000.

The indemnity plan had claims expenditures of $2,638 per enrollee in 1995, while the HMOs had per-enrollee claims costs of $1,226. The question is: how much of this difference reflects favorable selection, how much lower negotiated prices, and how much the substitution of less costly treatment options in the HMOs? Because Altman and colleagues had information on the types of people enrolled, the incidence of conditions and treatments, and the expenditure per condition in each plan, they were able to decompose the magnitudes of the respective effects.

The HMOs clearly received a younger draw of the population. While 30 percent of the indemnity enrollees were under age 35, just over 50 percent of the HMO enrollees were. And while over 35 percent of the indemnity plan enrollees were age 50 or older, only 14 percent of the HMO enrollees were. Thus, we would expect that the younger HMO cohort would be less likely to be diagnosed with as many of the conditions studied. Table 9-1 reports the actual incidence of the eight health conditions across the indemnity and HMO cohorts. The incidence rate for all but cervical cancer was higher in the indemnity group. The differences became much smaller when adjusted for demographics, but even then, the indemnity plan had enrollees with the higher incidence of these conditions. Clearly, much of the difference in overall claims experience comes from the favorable selection that HMOs enjoy.

Health Condition	Overall Incidence			Incidence Adjusted for Demographics		
	Indemnity Plan	HMOs	Ratio	Indemnity Plan	HMOs	Ratio
Acute myocardial infarction	0.67%	0.30%	2.23*	0.54%	0.40%	1.35*
Live birth	6.09%	5.05%	1.21*	6.80%	4.82%	1.41*
Breast cancer	1.33%	0.59%	2.25*	1.12%	0.72%	1.56*
Cervical cancer	.013%	0.13%	0.93	0.14%	0.13%	1.08
Colon cancer	0.21%	0.08%	2.62*	0.16%	0.10%	1.60*
Prostate cancer	0.75%	0.26%	2.88*	0.52%	0.38%	1.37*
Type I diabetes	1.39%	0.55%	2.53*	1.18%	0.65%	1.82*
Type II diabetes	2.33%	1.07%	2.18*	1.76%	1.36%	1.29*

TABLE 9-1
Incidence Rates of Study Conditions

SOURCE: This table was published in the *Journal of Health Economics* 22(1), Altman, Cutler, and Zeckhauser, "Enrollee Mix, Treatment Intensity, and Cost in Competing Indemnity and HMO Plans," pp. 23–45, Table 4, Copyright Elsevier 2003.

NOTES: *Denotes that the ratio of the indemnity plan rate to the HMO rate is statistically significant at the 95 percent confidence level. HMO = Health maintenance organization.

The treatment options may have differed between the indemnity plan and the HMOs as well. Table 9-2 shows the treatment shares for those patients with acute myocardial infarction (AMI). It is not at all obvious, however, that the HMO patients received less-aggressive treatment. They were slightly more likely to receive no cardiac catheterization (53.4 percent vs. 51.9 percent) and much less likely to receive cardiac catheterization only (13.5 percent vs. 22.3 percent for those in the indemnity group). However, they were more likely to receive a catheterization and a CABG (coronary artery bypass graft) and much more likely to have a catheterization and a PTCA (angioplasty).

Table 9-2 also reports the prices paid (in 1994 to 1995 dollars) by the indemnity plan and the HMOs for each of these treatment paths. Here, the HMOs clearly were able to negotiate lower prices. The HMOs paid over $2,900 less, on average, for care that included cardiac catheterization. They paid $51,885 for a bypass graft (CABG), compared to an average $64,109 paid by the indemnity plan. Together, the HMOs, on average, paid $17,000 per patient less for intensive AMI treatment.

TABLE 9-2

Treatment Path
Frequency and
Payment for
Patients with
Acute
Myocardial
Infarction

	Indemnity Plan	HMO
Two-year incidence of AMI	0.54%	0.40%*
Average cost per episode	$29,488	$19,821*
Share of Treatment Path		
Null	51.9%	53.4%
Catheterization	22.3%	13.5%
PTCA	13.0%	19.3%
CABG	12.9%	14.2%
Intense paths (PTCA + CABG)	25.7%	33.5%*
Payments, AMI Episodes		
By path: Null	$17,473	$10,573
Catheterization	$24,907	$21,939
PTCA	$37,330	$21,302
CABG	$64,109	$51,885
Intense paths (PTCA + CABG)	$50,569	$33,562*

SOURCE: This table was published in the *Journal of Health Economics* 22(1), Altman, Cutler, and Zeckhauser, "Enrollee Mix, Treatment Intensity, and Cost in Competing Indemnity and HMO Plans," pp. 23–45, Table 4, Copyright Elsevier 2003.

NOTES: *Denotes that the means are significantly different at the 95 percent confidence level. AMI = Acute myocardial infarction; CABG = Coronary artery bypass graft; HMO = Health maintenance organization; PTCA = Percutaneous transluminal coronary angioplasty.

Finally, Table 9-3 presents the difference in per capita expenditures for each of the eight conditions and decomposes those differences into selection, treatment intensity, and price effects. For acute myocardial infarction, there was a difference in expenditures of $143 per capita, of which 62.1 percent was attributed to the favorable selection into the HMOs, 1.0 percent was attributed to the slightly less intense treatment paths used by the HMOs, and 36.9 percent was attributed to the lower prices negotiated by the HMOs. Across all eight conditions, 51 percent of the difference in expenditures was attributed to selection, 5.1 percent to lower treatment intensity, and over 45 percent to lower prices. Thus, managed care plans can provide actual cost savings due to their ability to selectively contract with providers.

Health Condition	Difference in Indemnity–HMO per Person Claims Cost	Percentage Due to Mix of Enrollees	Percentage Due to Treatment Intensity	Percentage Due to Price or Unobserved Selection
Acute myocardial infarction	$143	62.1%	1.0%	36.9%
Live birth	$152	51.8%	11.3%	36.9%
Breast cancer	$273	45.2%	1.2%	53.6%
Cervical cancer	$9	13.8%	14.4%	71.8%
Colon cancer	$56	41.1%	5.3%	53.6%
Prostate cancer	$100	64.5%	−2.5%	38.0%
Type I diabetes	$53	68.4%	—	31.5%
Type II diabetes	$70	61.4%	—	38.6%
Average	$107	51.0%	5.1%	45.1%

TABLE 9-3
Decomposition of Cost Differences Across Plan Types

SOURCE: This table was published in the *Journal of Health Economics* 22(1), Altman, Cutler, and Zeckhauser, "Enrollee Mix, Treatment Intensity, and Cost in Competing Indemnity and HMO Plans," pp. 23–45, Table 7, Copyright Elsevier 2003.

NOTE: HMO = Health maintenance organization.

Chapter Summary

- Selective contracting is the process whereby managed care plans enter into contracts with some, but not all, of the providers in a market.
- Selective contracting has changed the face of competition in the hospital industry because the use of provider services now depends on price as well as on services, amenities, and quality. This increases the odds that greater provider competition will drive prices toward marginal cost.
- A managed care plan will get a lower price for health services when there are more providers in the market, when the managed care plan has a large share of the provider's book of business, when the provider has only a small share of the managed care plan's book of business, and when there is idle provider capacity in the market.
- Empirically, provider prices matter with respect to obtaining a managed care contract and the volume of patients cared for through that contract. However, the location and the availability of services also matter.

- The claims experience of managed care plans tends to be lower than that of indemnity plans. Recent empirical work suggests that perhaps half of the difference is due to favorable selection, whereby younger and healthier cohorts are attracted to managed care plans. However, perhaps 45 percent is due to selective contracting, whereby managed care plans negotiate lower prices for services. Differences in treatment intensity appear to be a minor factor.

Discussion Questions

1. A colleague has described the difference between health policy and health administration programs as: "In health policy programs, one learns to break up little monopolies. In health administration programs, one learns to create little monopolies." Evaluate the comment in light of selective contracting.
2. So-called "any willing provider laws" require a managed care plan to accept into its network any provider that is willing to abide by the terms and conditions of the contract. To what extent is a managed care plan able to assure volume under such a law? Is such a law likely to enhance or retard price competition?
3. Health Savings Accounts (HSAs) allow consumers to purchase a high-deductible health insurance plan and pay for the medical expenditures they incur prior to satisfying the deductible with tax-sheltered health savings. Advocates argue that this model gives consumers a strong incentive to shop for lower-priced, high-value medical care. Based on the analysis of selective contracting, under what conditions would consumers be successful in negotiating lower provider prices?
4. Suppose the dentists in a metropolitan area find that managed care plans have successfully negotiated substantially lower prices for dental services in their community. What does the theory of selective contracting and the empirical evidence from hospital markets say about how the dentists might respond?

MANAGED CARE AND PHYSICIANS

This chapter explores the effects that managed care has had on physician markets. The economics of these market responses are the same as those seen in hospital markets. The issues are somewhat different, of course. The biggest ones are the effects of managed care on physician incomes and location decisions, and the effects of alternative payment arrangements on physician performance. However, unlike hospitals, data on physicians are much more difficult to obtain; thus, the research on physicians is much more limited.

Managed Care and Physician Contracting

Most physicians have contracts with managed care plans. The Center for Studying Health System Change (2002) reported that 91 percent of physicians had one or more managed care contracts in 2001. On average, responding physicians had contracts with 13 managed care plans and received nearly 46 percent of their practice revenue from these plans. These reports are broadly consistent with earlier surveys conducted by the American Medical Association (AMA 1998), which reported similar proportions of physicians with managed care contracts (92 percent) and the shares of revenue from private managed care plans (32 percent) in 1997.

With regard to compensation arrangements, however, the story is a bit more complicated. Physicians or medical groups can be compensated in a variety of ways, and each provides a different set of incentives. Salary arrangements, for example, imply no direct link between the quantity or quality of physician effort and the physician's compensation. Fee-for-service means that the physician or medical group is paid directly on the basis of the volume of services provided. More office visits means greater fees and, therefore, greater revenue. Capitation means that the physician or medical group is paid on the basis of the number of covered lives for which they are responsible. Under capitation, the physician or medical group will only make money if the visits they provide and the services they order cost less than the capitated amount.

Within each of these generic models, all sorts of variations are possible. For example, the physician or medical group may be paid fee-for-service up to a "withhold." Under this sort of contract, the physician or medical group is paid, say, 80 percent of the fee-for-service amount at the time the bill is submitted. The other 20 percent is paid if the managed care plan is able to cover its overall claims costs. Within the capitation model, the physician or medical group may be responsible for all care, only ambulatory care, or only ambulatory primary care services.

A further complicating factor is that there may be substantial differences between the nature of the contracts negotiated between the managed care plan and the medical group, and the compensation arrangements between the medical group and individual physicians. Hillman, Welch, and Pauly (1992) were the first to describe these arrangements, reporting that in 1988 approximately 35 percent of health maintenance organizations (HMOs) were "three-tier" models in which the HMO paid the medical group, and the medical group, in turn, paid the physician. The remaining 65 percent were two-tier models in which the HMO paid the physician directly. However, adjusted for patient volume, the three-tier models were much more important, representing some 60 percent of enrollment. The payment system used at the medical group level is often not used to pay the participating physicians. For example, Hillman, Welch, and Pauly (1992) reported that among three-tier plans, only 27 percent of the medical groups paid under a capitation arrangement also paid their physicians on a capitated basis.

It is also the case that the use of capitation payment for physicians has been declining over time. As Figure 10-1 shows, between 1997 and 1999, the percentage of physician practice income reported to come from capitated contracts declined markedly. This should come as no surprise. Recall the Chapter 5 discussion of the nature of objective risk. If a medical group accepts a capitated contract, it has essentially become an insurance company bearing risk. Objective risk depends on the expected loss, the variance, and the number of covered lives. An individual physician may have roughly 6,500 patients. Even if all of them are members of the same managed care plan, this is a small risk pool and represents substantial objective risk. If only 20 percent of these are in a given managed care plan, the risk is even greater. Thus, as physicians became more aware of the risks associated with capitated contracts, they shied away from them. The AMA (1998) reported that 57 percent of those doctors with capitated contracts had stoploss provisions or reinsurance that limited their liability. However, the use of capitation has continued to decline. The Center for Studying Health System Change (2002) reported that the proportion of physicians with managed care contracts who derived *at least some revenue* from capitation declined from 59 percent in 1999 to 49 percent in 2001.

Managed Care and Physician Earnings

Inflation-adjusted physician incomes have been falling. The Center for Studying Health System Change (2003) reported that, between 1995 and 1999,

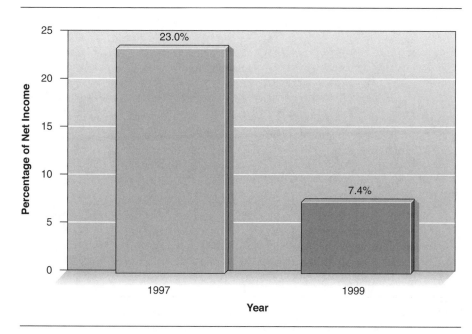

FIGURE 10-1

Percentage of Physician Net Income from Capitation

SOURCE: Data from American Medical Association (1998, Table 4; 2001).

income after expenses but before taxes declined by 5.0 percent for all physicians, 6.4 percent for primary care doctors, and 4.0 percent for specialists. Figure 10-2 presents more recent estimates that compare median incomes for self-employed physicians in selected specialties. The downward trend continues, with general internal medicine and family practice seeing real declines of about 15 percent and other specialties incurring smaller declines in inflation-adjusted net incomes.

If managed care effectively means selective contracting, as discussed in Chapter 9, then managed care plans should contract with a subset of physicians in a given specialty in a local market. The physicians who get contracts presumably have agreed to lower prices, and the managed care plans channel subscribers to them. While the overall demand for physician services is inelastic (recall Chapter 7), the demand for an individual physician or medical group is much more price sensitive. Thus, the contract is likely to result in the physician with the contract getting disproportionately more patients and earning greater practice income. In contrast, his fellow physicians without contracts find that they have fewer patients and lower earnings. Other things equal, physician earnings decline overall and on average in the community.

Hadley and Mitchell (1999) used a 1990 Robert Wood Johnson Foundation survey of young physicians (under age 45) to investigate whether greater HMO penetration was associated with changes in physician earnings. They argued that physician income was a function of physician characteristics, such as specialty and years of experience, the local demand for medical

FIGURE 10-2

Inflation-
Adjusted
Change in
Median
Physician
Income,
1998–2004

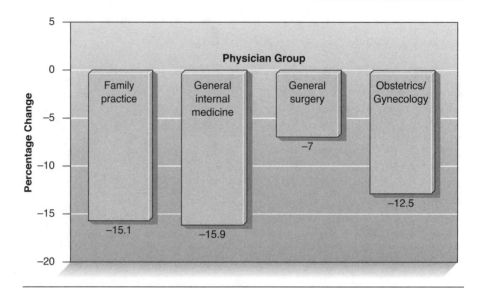

SOURCES: Data from American Medical Association (2001) and Bureau of Labor Statistics (2006).
NOTES: Incomes of self-employed physicians in 1998 imputed at 1.219 percent of overall median. (Inflation adjustment using the annual consumer price index [CPI–All Items]).

care, whether the physician was self-employed, and the proportion of the local (metropolitan) population enrolled in an HMO. HMO enrollment may be endogenous, meaning that factors that affect physician incomes may also affect HMO enrollment. Hadley and Mitchell dealt with this by using a more sophisticated regression technique. The one thing they could *not* do was identify which physicians had managed care contracts. Thus, they essentially estimated the effect on the average physician.

Hadley and Mitchell found that a doubling of the average level of HMO market share reduced the annual earnings of young physicians by 7 to 11 percent and reduced hourly earnings by 6 to 9 percent. The greater reduction in earnings than in hourly earnings suggests that there was some reduction in utilization attributable to greater HMO presence as well as to a pure price effect. They also found that the effects were greater for self-employed physicians, compared to those who were employed. This is consistent with other evidence that suggests that managed care leads to somewhat fewer self-employed physicians.

It is worth noting that this effect is not quite as large as it may appear. The average HMO market share in Hadley and Mitchell's sample was 17.8 percent. A doubling of HMO market share implies that 35.4 percent of the population was in an HMO. In 2005, HMOs enrolled approximately 21 percent of insured workers (see Chapter 1). Thus, the typical market would not have seen that large an increase in HMO market share and, therefore, the effect on physician earnings would be somewhat smaller.

In perhaps the most interesting study of physician markets to date, Jack Zwanziger (2002) examined the effects of managed care penetration, the supply of physicians, and the type of managed care plan on the fees negotiated by managed care plans with physicians. From 1990 through 1992, Zwanziger had access to the fees that HMOs, preferred provider organizations (PPOs), and other managed care plans negotiated for 41 clinical procedure codes. Through a statistical technique called hierarchical modeling, he controlled for the difficulty of the procedure, the local indemnity fee structure, and other characteristics of the service. He was then left with the average difference in fees paid by each managed care plan. Finally, he explained these average plan differences based on managed care penetration, competition among managed care plans, and the particular type of managed care plan that provided the data.

Zwanziger's results were consistent with our earlier examination of hospitals and managed care. He found that:

- The managed care plans paid lower fees for procedures when there was greater managed care penetration in the metropolitan market.
- The managed care plans paid lower fees when there were more physicians per capita in the metropolitan area.
- HMOs were able to negotiate lower fees than were PPOs, presumably because the HMOs had smaller networks of physician providers and were able to use more aggressive selective contracting to get lower fees.

Zwanziger's estimates with respect to the extent of managed care competition (as distinct from managed care market penetration) suggested, however, that this competition had no statistically significant effect on fees.

There is a major caveat with this study, however. The survey of managed care plans' negotiated fees had a response rate of only 10 percent. Thus, assigning too much significance to this study is dangerous because the results may be biased in unknown ways, due to the potentially unique nature of those plans that chose to participate.

Effects of Managed Care Payment Methods on Medical Group Practice

Kralewski and his colleagues (2000) investigated the effects of managed care payment mechanisms to medical groups and medical group payment to physicians on the cost experience of the plan. In the process, they also provided insight into the economies of group practice and the effects of gatekeeping, physician profiling, and the use of clinical guidelines on costs. The study examined a Blue Cross of Minnesota managed care product called "Blue-Plus." Eighty-six participating medical groups—mostly in Minnesota, together with others in the Dakotas, Iowa, and Wisconsin—agreed to provide survey data for 1995.

The study estimated a medical group cost function of the form:

$$\text{\$PMPY} = f \text{ (Group payment, Physician payment, Utilization}$$
$$\text{management, Group coverage, and Patient characteristics)}$$

where $PMPY is the per member per year cost of the group to the managed care plan, measured in natural logarithms.

This single managed care plan used a variety of mechanisms to pay the participating medical groups. As Table 10-1 shows, 18.2 percent of the medical groups were paid on a capitation basis. While capitation for both physician and hospital expenditures was most common, other, smaller, risk exposures were also used. Sixty-one percent of the medical groups were paid on a fee-for-service basis, but again, there was considerable variation within this category. For 27 percent of the medical groups, Blue-Plus negotiated a fee schedule that set the rates the group would be paid. In 21.6 percent of the medical groups, a "withhold model" was used. In this model, a group received a percentage of its billed charges and the remainder was held until year-end and released if the revenue associated with the patients using this medical group covered the costs incurred. Over 12 percent agreed to discounted charges. Perhaps most surprisingly, nearly 21 percent of the medical groups were paid their full billed charges.

The medical groups used a variety of methods to pay their physicians. The distribution is shown in Table 10-2. Nearly half of the groups paid physicians a guaranteed or base salary. Another 40 percent used a mechanism based on physician productivity, such as total billings or the number of visits. Surprisingly, only 10 percent of the groups paid their member physicians a share of the medical group's net revenue.

The results of the Kralewski team's analysis indicated that capitation (of any form) relative to the other forms of payment to the medical group reduced expenditures per member per year by four-tenths of 1 percent. No other payment mechanism had a statistically significant effect on the plan's costs. Some have argued that fee-for-service (FFS) used with a withhold could be as effective as capitation. The Kralewski team found that such arrangements were less effective. The small differences in effects across payment forms may explain why managed care plans continue to use a variety of methods to pay medical groups and why they have acquiesced to the movement away from capitated payments.

The results on forms of physician compensation are more interesting. Compensation based on a share of the group's net income reduced plan expenditures, presumably by giving physicians an explicit incentive to maximize the difference between the revenues received and the costs incurred. The research compared other forms of compensation to a share-of-net-

Medical Group Payment Method	Percentage
Capitation	
Physician and hospital	11.0%
Physician and some hospital risk	0.4%
Physician services	1.8%
Primary care physician services	5.0%
Fee-for-service (FFS)	
With a withhold	21.6%
Discounted or negotiated FFS	12.4%
Fee schedule	27.0%
Billed charges	20.8%

SOURCE: Data from Kralewski et al. (2000).

TABLE 10-1
Prevalence of Medical Group Payment Methods

	Percentage
Guaranteed or base salary	48.1
Individual physician productivity—billings, visits, etc.	40.4
Individual physician quality—patient satisfaction, chart review	1.2
Individual physician management of utilization—rate of referrals, lab, X-ray, etc.	0.4
Performance of the group—share of net revenue	9.9

SOURCE: Data from Kralewski et al. (2000).

TABLE 10-2
Primary Care Physician Payment Types

revenue approach. Thus, the Kralewski team found that, if physicians were paid entirely on salary, the health plan's costs were 30 percent higher than they would have been under the share-of-net-revenue approach. Basing compensation entirely on individual productivity, such as billings or the number of visits, resulted in plan costs that were 10 percent higher. Basing part of compensation on quality measures had no statistically significant effect on plan costs. Finally, basing some portion of physician compensation on the physician's own careful utilization of resources lowered plan costs. The effect was large, but in the sample, no medical group based more than 6 percent of compensation on such a measure. In the study, a 1 percentage point increase in compensation of this form reduced plan costs by 3.2 percent.

The Kralewski study also investigated the effects of using gatekeepers, clinical guidelines, and physician practice profiles. Like the direct research on gatekeeping in Chapter 8, Kralewski and colleagues found no statistically significant cost savings in groups where a primary care gatekeeper was assigned to patients. In contrast, medical groups that used clinical guidelines that provide evidence-based protocols for care *did* have lower costs. Practice profiles tell physicians how their use of tests and treatments compares to other physicians with similar patients. Physician practice profiling was also shown to reduce costs.[1]

Finally, Kralewski and colleagues (2000) examined the effects of such factors as the size of the medical group, its years of experience, and its affiliation with group practice systems. They concluded that economies of scale in medical group practice appear to be exhausted by about eight to ten members in the group. Beyond that, plan costs were higher. Medical groups with greater average years of physician experience had costs that were 1.6 percent lower for each additional year. Kralewski and colleagues also found no effects of membership in group practice systems. It is difficult to know what to make of this last result. Healthcare providers tend to argue that systems are able to provide lower costs of care because of the ability to purchase supplies in bulk and to centralize some administrative functions. Others argue that systems provide a vehicle for medical groups to combine and potentially raise the prices they are able to obtain from insurers. The Kralewski results suggest that neither effect dominated in these practices.

While the Kralewski et al. (2000) study is one of the very few to provide insights into the effects of managed care, medical group contracting practices, and medical group organizational characteristics, it is not without its limitations. The foremost limitation is that this is a relatively small sample of medical groups concentrated in the upper Midwest, and the groups were somewhat smaller than other medical groups. As such, some caution must be exercised in generalizing the study's findings.

Managed Care and Physician Location Decisions

Escarce and colleagues (1998) examined the effects of rapid HMO growth on the location decisions of young physicians. They had data on physicians who had completed their graduate medical education between 1989 and 1994 and decided to practice in a U.S. metropolitan area with a population of one-half million or more. Early in the study period, they found that new

---

1. Physician profiling consists of comparing one physician's utilization or spending performance to that of others in the group.

generalist physicians were more likely to locate in metropolitan areas with high HMO penetration, while specialists were apparently unaffected by HMO presence. This is consistent with work by Simon, Dranove, and White (1998), who found that higher managed care penetration over this period was associated with higher primary care incomes but not related to specialist incomes. By the end of the period, however, the Escarce team found that greater HMO market share was associated with a small but statistically significant reduction in the probability that a new primary care physician would locate in the metropolitan area, and also with a large and significant reduction in the probability that specialists would locate in the metropolitan area.

Escarce et al. (2000) expanded on the earlier study to examine the effects of HMO penetration across all 316 U.S. metropolitan areas. They looked at all active patient care physicians and over a longer time period, 1986 through 1996. They found that, overall, HMO penetration did not affect the number of generalist physicians or hospital-based physicians, but faster HMO growth did result in smaller increases in the number of specialists. Faster HMO growth also led to greater increases in the proportion of physicians who were generalists. Escarce and colleagues estimated that a 10 percentage point increase in the HMO market share between 1986 and 1996 reduced *the rate of increase* in specialists by over 10 percent and that of total physicians by 7.2 percent. Their study suggests that HMOs were able to reduce the demand for physician services, particularly of specialists. Thus, there is some evidence that the supply of physicians and the mix of generalists and specialists did respond to the growth of managed care.

Chapter Summary

- The vast majority of physicians have contracts with managed care plans and receive nearly half of their practice revenue from them.
- Managed care plans use a variety of mechanisms to pay physicians and medical groups. However, the use of capitation has been declining, arguably because it puts physicians and medical groups at substantial objective risk.
- Physician incomes have declined in real terms since at least the mid-1990s. Evidence suggests that the growth of managed care is responsible for at least part of this decline.
- Other evidence suggests that managed care plans are able to negotiate lower physician fees when there is a greater managed care presence in the local market and when there are more physicians per capita.
- The system that managed care plans use to pay medical groups and the method of compensation used to pay physicians in the medical group affect managed care costs. The methods that medical groups use to pay

their physicians seem to matter much more, with payment based on a share of the group's profits being the most effective in reducing costs.

- Given the effects of managed care on physician income, it is no surprise that greater managed care penetration has reduced the supply of physicians and shifted the mix away from specialists.

Discussion Questions

1. Suppose you are part of a medical group of cardiologists concerned about the effects managed care has had on your earnings. What sort of efforts would you encourage your fellow specialists to undertake to improve their well-being? Are there actions you would encourage your state medical schools and licensure agencies to consider?

2. In the mid-1990s, some academic health centers purchased local primary care practices to assure a flow of patients to their hospitals. In these acquisitions, the academic health centers allegedly bought out the physician-owners of the practices and then hired them back, on salary, to continue to provide clinical services to their patients. The health centers are said to have discovered that the primary care practices were not nearly as profitable after the acquisitions as they were before. What likely happened?

3. Suppose patients came to dislike the narrow choice of physicians and the gatekeeping models required of them by managed care plans. If they were to switch to plans that provided greater choice of providers, what effect would this have on managed care costs? What would it do to physician incomes?

MANAGED CARE BACKLASH, PROVIDER CONSOLIDATION, MONOPSONY POWER, AND MOST FAVORED NATION CLAUSES

In Chapters 9 and 10, we discussed the development of managed care and its effects on hospital and physician markets. The key point in the discussion was that managed care selectively contracted with a limited number of providers and negotiated lower prices in exchange for some assurance of patient volume. Research showed that this process of selective contracting resulted in the deceleration of healthcare costs through the first half of the 1990s. However, healthcare costs began to increase more rapidly after 1996 and reached annual rates of increase in the 8 to 14 percent range by the mid-2000s.

In this chapter, we explore several topics related to managed care markets in the 2000s. First, we discuss the increases in insurance prices and explore the available explanations for the increases. In this context, we look at the so-called managed care backlash and the concerns over increasing concentration in provider markets. Second, we investigate the assertions made by some providers that managed care plans have market power and have used that power to drive down prices to hospitals and physicians. Finally, we discuss a contracting device called the "most favored nation" (MFN) clause, which allegedly makes it more difficult for a managed care plan to compete with a dominant local insurer and/or allows providers to collude to keep prices high. Alternatively, MFN clauses are said to enhance efficiency by allowing an insurer to obtain lower prices in the face of considerable service and cost uncertainty.

Why Have Insurance Premiums Increased Since the Mid-1990s?

As Figure 11-1 demonstrates, employer-sponsored health insurance premiums increased at an ever-decreasing rate from the late 1980s through 1996. The evidence in Chapters 9 and 10 suggested that this decrease was the result of the expansion of managed care and its use of selective contracting and provider competition to lower the prices insurers paid for medical services. However, from 1996 through 2003, premiums grew at increasing rates and have grown somewhat more modestly since. These increases have also been

FIGURE 11-1

Percentage Increase in Health Insurance Premiums

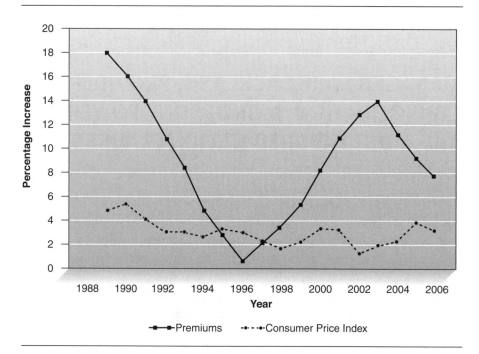

SOURCES: Data from Jensen et al. (1997), Gabel et al. (2005), and Fronstin (2006).

well in excess of general inflation, which has been in the 2 to 4 percent range over the entire period.

Two arguments have been advanced to explain the increase in premiums: the backlash against managed care and decreased competition among providers. These explanations are not mutually exclusive, and other factors undoubtedly pay a role as well.

Managed Care Backlash

The managed care backlash is said to consist of physicians and patients complaining about the nature of the restrictions that managed care plans impose. A plethora of cartoons and late-night comedy bits about managed care pinpoint the popular antagonism. This intuition is supported by consumer survey work by Blendon et al. (1998) and media criticism of managed care reported by Brodie, Brady, and Altman (1998). We should look at these concerns carefully, however.

Physician opposition is said to revolve around the difficulty in admitting patients to hospitals and keeping them there as long as physicians think prudent. There are concerns about limited drug formularies, limitations on which specialists are covered, and allegations (largely unproven) that managed care plan contracts prevent physicians from discussing some treatment options with patients. However, as we saw in Chapter 8, while utilization management techniques did reduce hospital days, there is little evidence that this had a large impact on quality of care and very little evidence that ambulatory utilization management tools had any impact on services. Quality of care has not been measured fully, however, and it may be that providers came to abide by utilization management protocols even as they objected to them. However, it is also the case, as we saw in Chapter 10, that physician incomes were reduced as a result of managed care. It is conceivable that the physician backlash against managed care arose, at least in part, because managed care plans were successful in reducing fees to providers.

Patients' concerns are similar to those of physicians with respect to perceived access. In addition, patients are worried about quality of care. Judging the quality of a physician, hospital, or other medical care provider is difficult. The concern with managed care is that the limited panel of providers that makes managed care successful on the price front locks patients into providers who may not be right for them in either a clinical or an interpersonal sense.

Marquis, Rogowsi, and Escarce (2004/05) examined the decline in private health maintenance organizations (HMO) enrollment in metropolitan areas between 1998 and 2001. In this study, they broadly defined HMO enrollment to include both HMO and point-of-service (POS) plan enrollment. They found only modest declines in HMO enrollment over this period (from 47.7 to 44.9 percent) and little association between these declines and measures that might be indicators of having a greater local choice of insurance options. They "conjecture[ed] that backlash either represented the views and perceptions of physicians and the media while consumers were generally satisfied . . . or that consumers exercised 'voice' and health plans responded very quickly to avoid losing market share" (p. 387).

However, the decline in HMO (and POS) enrollment has been more substantial since the time of the Marquis, Rogowsi, and Escarce study. Table 11-1 shows that HMO enrollment among ensured workers declined by over 30 percent (from 29 to 20 percent) and POS enrollment declined by 38 percent between 2001 and 2006. During this same period, enrollment in preferred provider organizations (PPOs) increased by 18 percentage points and did so at the expense of all other plan types. One interpretation of this shift is that employees switched to a less-restrictive form of managed care. PPOs typically allow members to pay higher copays to use a provider who is not part of the health plan network. By switching to a PPO, consumers arguably have some of the benefits of managed care selective contracting but avoid the risk of poor-quality or incompatible providers by being able to step outside the network if they deem it necessary.

TABLE 11-1

Percentage of
Insured
Workers by
Type of Plan

	1988	1995	2000	2005	2006
Conventional	73%	27%	8%	3%	3%
HMO	16%	28%	29%	21%	20%
PPO	11%	25%	42%	61%	60%
POS	—	20%	21%	15%	13%
HDHP	—	—	—	—	4%

SOURCE: Data from Claxton et al. (2006).

NOTES: HMO = Health maintenance organization; PPO = Preferred provider organization; POS = Point of service; HDHP = High-deductible health plan.

There is a cost to this switch, however. Because of the patient's freedom to step outside the network, PPOs are unsure of the volume of patients who will actually use the providers in their networks. As a consequence, PPOs are not as effective in negotiating lower prices with providers. Indeed, as we saw in Chapters 9 and 10, the limited research that examined differential effectiveness of HMOs and PPOs found that HMOs were more effective. Moreover, as Stires (2002) reported, HMOs themselves have been much more willing to pay for treatment outside their networks. From this perspective, the message is simply that greater choice costs more, and the increase in health insurance premiums over the last decade reflects, at least in part, consumers' desire for greater choice of providers.

There is some irony in this. The public's perception of managed care, and of HMOs particularly, seems to be one of denial of referrals to specialists, restrictions on hospital days, and substitution of cheaper but less-effective drugs and treatments for more-effective ones. Yet, as we saw in Chapter 8, not much of the cost difference between HMOs and indemnity plans can be attributed to differences in treatment protocols, and the management of ambulatory utilization has been far from successful. It is hard not to conclude that managed care plans have shot themselves in the foot by implementing and continuing utilization management techniques that have not saved money but have alienated consumers.

Provider Consolidation

The second explanation for the increase in insurance premiums is the assertion that provider markets, both for hospitals and physicians, have become more concentrated. Selective contracting works best when there are a large number of providers with substantial idle capacity and each with a small share of the plan's book of business. Under these circumstances, managed care plans are able to negotiate lower prices. If there is less competition among providers, health plans are less likely to be able to negotiate low prices.

Perhaps Timothy Muris (2002), then chairman of the Federal Trade Commission (FTC), made the strongest statement of this view:

> The Commission continues to see a wide variety of overt anticompetitive behavior in healthcare, along with some new variants. The Commission continues to bring cases against physicians alleging price fixing—much like those brought by the agency during the last 20 years—although several of the new cases involve an unprecedented number of doctors and consultants, who coordinated the conduct under the guise of assisting in negotiations with payers. (p. 3)

The FTC has acted on anticompetitive behavior of several physician groups. From 2001 to 2002, it reached settlements with five physician groups—three in Denver, Colorado; one in Napa, California; and one in Dallas, Texas—over "naked price fixing, plain and simple" (Muris 2002, p. 17).

More recently, as noted in Box 11-1, the FTC entered into a consent decree with San Francisco-based Brown & Toland Medical Group over alleged price fixing. The complaint alleged that Brown & Toland formed a PPO network of otherwise competing physicians in which it negotiated fee-for-service contracts under which the physicians collectively agreed on the price and other terms on which they would enter into contracts with health

---

BOX 11-1

San Francisco's Brown & Toland Medical Group Settles FTC Price Fixing Charges

San Francisco-based Brown & Toland Medical Group, which was sued by the Federal Trade Commission for allegedly fixing the prices and terms under which its doctors would contract with payers to provide services for preferred provider organization (PPO) enrollees, has agreed to settle charges that its business practices violated federal antitrust laws. The terms of the proposed consent agreement with California Pacific Medical Group, Inc., doing business as Brown & Toland Medical Group, prohibits the organization from negotiating with payers on behalf of physicians, refusing to deal with payers, and setting terms for physicians to deal with payers—unless the physicians are clinically or financially integrated. The settlement also provides for the termination of contracts that were allegedly obtained illegally. Brown & Toland's network of physicians that contract with health maintenance organizations (HMOs) is financially integrated and was not targeted by the FTC's litigation.

SOURCE: Press release, Federal Trade Commission 2004a.

plans or other third-party payers. Brown & Toland was also accused of directing its physicians to terminate any preexisting contracts with payers, of requiring its physician members to charge specified prices in all PPO contracts, and of approaching other physician organizations to invite them to enter into similar price-fixing agreements (Federal Trade Commission 2004c).

The FTC and the U.S. Department of Justice have challenged hospital mergers as anticompetitive. In the late 1990s and early 2000s, they challenged seven hospital merger cases—and lost all seven. As a result, the FTC formed a new merger litigation taskforce in 2002 to reconsider its hospital merger strategy. It also announced that it would review past mergers to determine if the actions resulted in higher prices.

The FTC and the Department of Justice held joint hearings on impediments to competition in the healthcare field during the summer of 2003 and issued a report in July 2004 calling for continued scrutiny of hospital and physician market behavior and further investigation of the role of quality in the analysis market activities. Their report, titled *Improving Health Care: A Dose of Competition*, can be found at www.ftc.gov/reports/healthcare/040723healthcarerpt.pdf.

In 2004, the FTC challenged the 2000 merger of Evanston Northwest Hospital Corporation (consisting of Evanston and Glenbrook Hospitals) with Highland Park Hospital, all in the affluent suburbs north of Chicago. The complaint alleged that the merger allowed the hospitals to raise their prices "far above price increases of other comparable hospitals" (Federal Trade Commission 2004a). In October 2005, an administrative law judge ordered that Highland Park Hospital be sold within 180 days (Federal Trade Commission 2005). In August 2007, the FTC upheld the anti-competitive findings of the judge but did not require that the hospital be sold.

Dranove, Simon, and White (2002) attempted to empirically test whether the growth of managed care resulted in the consolidation of hospital and physician markets. Consolidation need not result in anticompetitive results, of course. While one reason for merging two hospitals may be to obtain market power to raise prices, another is to achieve economies of scale in operations. Other things equal, an efficiency-based merger results in lower costs and lower prices. Indeed, the growth of managed care may have forced providers to become more cost conscious. Presumably, court rulings against the government antitrust regulators in the late 1990s were partially a result of the courts' conclusions that legitimate efficiency arguments justified the mergers. Thus, the Dranove, Simon, and White study offers insight into whether managed care was responsible for any consolidation, but did not indicate whether the result was anticompetitive, efficiency enhancing, or both.

The hospital component of the study used American Hospital Association (AHA) survey data on hospitals for 1981 and 1994. In each of the 68 largest metropolitan areas, the team constructed a Herfindahl-Hirschman

Index (HHI) value of hospital concentration. The HHI is simply the sum of the squared market shares of each hospital or hospital system operating in the area. The principal advantage of this measure is that it reflects both the number of providers and the dominance of one or more providers. A higher value indicates greater concentration. Methodologically, the biggest challenge to a study of this type is that managed care penetration and hospital or physician consolidation may both be influenced by the same unobserved (to the researcher) change in local conditions. The authors deal with this by using a two-stage statistical technique that can sort out this endogeneity.[1] Dranove, Simon, and White found that the increase in managed care over the period had resulted in greater hospital concentration. The average HHI increased 0.058 points. This is the equivalent of a consolidation from 10.4 to 6.5 equal-sized hospitals in a market. Dranove and colleagues concluded only that managed care had led to consolidation in the hospital market, but they drew no inference about the market power versus efficiency rationale. The Bamezai et al. (1999) study that we examined in Chapter 9 suggested that two-thirds of the cost saving associated with managed care could be achieved with only four hospitals. It is also worth noting that the Dranove study focused on the largest metropolitan markets, where such mergers would be least likely to affect managed care plans' ability to selectively contract.

In their analysis of physician markets, Dranove, Simon, and White (2002) used AMA socioeconomic monitoring survey data over the same years to examine the change in the proportion of physicians in groups of various sizes. They found a large reduction (14 percent) in the proportion of physicians in solo practice associated with greater managed care growth, but no effect on other group sizes or on HMO employment of physicians. Thus, they speculated that the physician consolidation probably reflected efficiency changes, since it was unlikely that the proportionate growth of all groups at the expense of solo practice represented much of an anticompetitive threat. However, it should be noted that they did not investigate the use of physician marketing networks that so concerned the FTC.

More recently, Town and colleagues (2005) reexamined the link between the growth of managed care and hospital consolidation. They examined the more-relevant 1990 to 2000 period. There were 100 or more hospital mergers in 8 of these 11 years and a merger in 40 percent of the market areas in their study. Using sophisticated statistical techniques, they found that growth in HMO penetration had *no effect* on hospital consolidation, and if anything, greater penetration led to somewhat less concentration. Instead,

---

1. Endogeneity exists when an explanatory variable in a regression model is itself at least partially a function of the same forces that determine the left-hand side variable. Two-stage least squares is an econometric technique that uses additional information to purge the explanatory variable of its correlation with the underlying forces.

Town and colleagues speculated that the consolidation was probably driven by excess capacity in local markets that led to many mergers, rather than closures, of failing hospitals.

Summary and Conclusion

Both the managed care backlash and the provider consolidation arguments suggest that health insurance premiums increased as a result of less-successful selective contracting. In the first case, consumer preferences for more choice meant that managed care plans could not direct volume to as narrow a set of providers and, as a consequence, could not negotiate as low a set of prices. In the second case, consolidation of providers either by merger or by the use of marketing networks reduced the number of potential bidders and suggested that managed care plans would not be able to negotiate as favorable a set of prices.

The very limited empirical research on these issues provides only limited insight into the extent to which either or both of these explanations are correct. Research on the managed care backlash predated much of the shift from HMOs to PPOs and did not look at the extent to which even narrow-panel managed care plans allowed subscribers to use services outside the network. The research on hospital and physician consolidation is useful but addressed a somewhat different question. It asked if the growth of managed care led to industry consolidation as providers sought to restrict the number of competitors or to enhance efficiency. Such studies provided some insight into relevant provider markets, but whether or not managed care prompted the consolidation is not the key issue for us. We want to know whether and by how much such consolidation in the healthcare industry resulted in higher prices to managed care plans. This question is still unanswered.[2]

Do Managed Care Plans Have Monopsony Power?

Physicians and hospitals have long argued that they have banded together to fight the market power of large insurers (Muris 2002). The argument is one of alleged "monopsony" power on the part of insurers. Monopsony is the less-well-known cousin of monopoly. With monopoly, a single seller reduces the quantity of the product available on the market (setting marginal revenue equal to marginal cost) and selling the smaller quantity at a higher price. See Figure 11-2a. Here, a profit-maximizing hospital with monopoly power reduces the number of patient days it provides and charges a higher price.

---

2. Many studies have examined the effects of mergers on hospital prices, but all empirically focus on periods prior to the run-up in insurance premiums in the late 1990s and early 2000s. See Morrisey (2001) for a review.

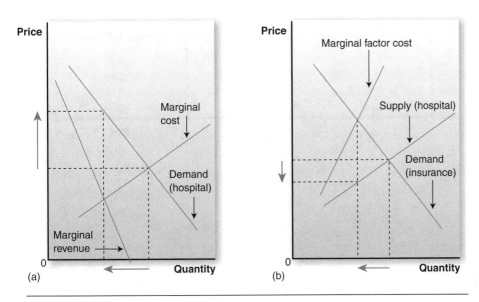

FIGURE 11-2

Comparison of Hospital Monopoly and Insurer Monopsony Power

(a) Price to the hospital rises when the hospital has *monopoly* power.

(b) Price to the hospital declines when the insurer has *monopsony* power.

Thus, when the hospital exercises market power in the hospital market, it extracts a higher price for its services.

In contrast, monopsony exists when there is a single large buyer. Ordinary buyers would pay their suppliers along the marginal cost schedule. If they expand output, they buy more inputs and have to pay each supplier the higher market-determined price for the inputs. Thus, they have to pay not only the higher price for the extra few units but a higher price for all the other units as well. (To see this, consider a competitive nursing labor market. If a hospital tried to hire 10 extra nurses and had to increase the going wage by $5 per hour to get them, it would soon find that it had to pay all its nurses $5 more per hour to keep them.) Monopsonists realize this and appreciate that if they slightly reduce their use of inputs, they will not only save on input costs but also will pay less for all the units of the inputs they use. Strictly speaking, they set marginal revenue equal to "marginal factor cost" (MFC). This is depicted in Figure 11-2*b*. Here, a monopsonist insurer buys hospital services. By reducing the number of hospital days it buys, it can lower the price of all the days. Hospitals have few (literally, no) alternative buyers in this case, and unlike the nurses in the previous example, cannot demand higher payment by threatening to sell their services elsewhere.

There are two views of managed care. One is that through selective contracting, managed care plans have been able to overcome hospital market power and achieve lower prices for hospital services. The other view is that

FIGURE 11-3
Monopoly and
Monopsony
(a)
Monopoly—
Reducing hos-
pital market
power.
(b)
Monopsony—
Imposing
insurer market
power.

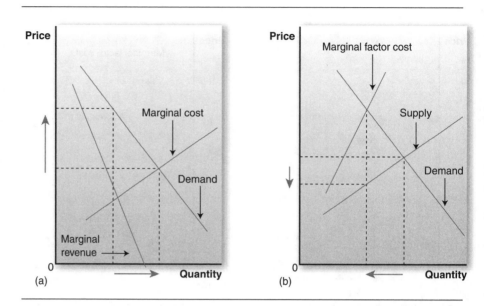

managed care plans have monopsony power and have used it to lower the
prices that they pay hospitals. Mark Pauly (1998) proposed a way to test
whether managed care was thwarting hospital market power or exercising its
own monopsony power. The test is summarized in Figure 11-3. If selective
contracting is effectively eroding hospital market power, then the lower
prices it achieves should result in greater hospital output for managed care
plans. In Figure 11-3*a,* the lower prices would spur greater hospital output
as the hospital market moved closer to a competitive equilibrium. In contrast,
if managed care plans are exercising monopsony power in their local markets,
they should reduce the quantity of hospital services to achieve the lower
prices (see Figure 11-3*b*). Thus, the test is to see if hospital days sold to managed care plans increase (implying less hospital market power) or decrease
(implying insurer monopsony power).

Feldman and Wholey (2001) tested this theory with HMO data from
1985 through 1997. Hospital days were the measure of HMO hospital use,
and the average price paid by each HMO was its hospital expenditures
divided by total days. As with some of the earlier studies discussed, there is a
concern here about endogeneity. The HMO's buying power and its utilization and prices paid may all be subject to the same unobserved (to the
researcher) changes in the local market. The researchers dealt with this by
using a two-stage statistical technique.

Feldman and Wholey's results were straightforward. First, they found
that greater HMO buying power was negatively and significantly associated
with hospital prices. This was no surprise; under both theories, greater HMO
market power should result in lower prices (as seen in Figure 11-3). However, greater HMO buying power also was associated with a *positive* and

significant effect on hospital days. This means that hospital use increased with HMO buying power, results consistent with Figure 11-3*a*. This is a clear refutation of the monopsony model and suggests that, rather than anticompetitive behavior, managed care plans appear to enhance competition in the hospital market. Feldman and Wholey also examined the effects of HMO buying power on hospital ambulatory service prices and utilization but found no statistically significant evidence in either direction. This may have been the result of methodological difficulties in analyzing the ambulatory sector.

Most Favored Nation Clauses

One of the more interesting contract features in some insurer-provider contracts is the "most favored nation" (MFN) clause. The term stems from international trade agreements in which countries are assured that they will not pay any higher import or export taxes than those paid by the "most favored nation." In healthcare, the contract term says that the buyer of hospital (or physician) services gets the benefit of the lowest price that has been given to any other buyer. The provision is controversial because it is said to be anticompetitive. Perhaps surprisingly, some claim that most favored nation clauses benefit the healthcare provider, and others claim that the clauses benefit the insurer.

The first view argues that all hospitals in a market would gain if they would agree to charge a common monopoly maximizing set of prices for their services. This sort of "cartel" arrangement is inherently unstable. Each hospital in the cartel has an incentive to cheat. If it can secretly cut the price to some buyers, it can attract considerably more volume at the expense of its sister institutions. The other hospitals would observe lower utilization, but it would be difficult to determine if this was anything other than random fluctuation. The MFN clause provides an additional set of eyes at every hospital in the form of buyers with this contract provision. If a hospital is secretly giving a discount, the MFN buyer will see the lower price when it exercises its right to examine the hospital books and determine that it is indeed getting the lowest price. In this view, the MFN clause is a mechanism to enforce the provider cartel.

Alternatively, and more commonly, the MFN clause is viewed as a means whereby a large local insurer is able to keep other insurers from negotiating lower hospital prices. In this view, a large insurer insists that it be given the lowest price the hospital gives to any other buyer. If , say, a new managed care plan seeks to selectively contract with a hospital, promising volume in exchange for price, the hospital must give the large insurer the same lower price that it gives the new managed care plan. Alternatively, the hospital must give up its contract (and patients) with the large insurer and cast its lot more

FIGURE 11-4

The Arithmetic
of Discounting
with a Most
Favored Nation
(MFN) Clause

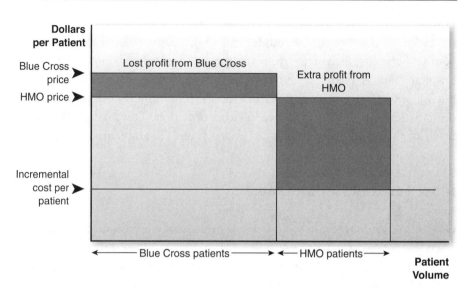

SOURCE: Lynk (2000), "Basics about Most Favored Nation Contracts in Health Care Markets," *Antitrust Bulletin* 45(2): 491–530, Figure 1. Reprinted with permission.

or less with the new managed care plan. This obviously undercuts the ability of the managed care plan to compete on a premium basis with the large local insurer and may keep the managed care plan from entering the market at all.

Finally, there is a view that the MFN clause is not anticompetitive at all but, rather, is simply a mechanism to help an insurer get the best possible price in a world of complex and very diverse hospital prices and costs.

Bill Lynk (2000) provided perhaps the only empirical investigation of the effects of the MFN clause on hospital and insurer markets. The economics of the contract are straightforward (see Figure 11-4). In this model, a hypothetical Blue Cross plan is the large local insurer; it is initially charged the "Blue Cross price" shown in the figure. A new HMO that would provide new patient volume to the hospital asks for the "HMO price" in the figure. The marginal or incremental costs are assumed to be equal per patient to keep the analysis focused on the pricing issues. The shaded area labeled "Extra profit from HMO" indicates profits that the hospital would gain by entering into the new HMO contract. However, with an MFN clause, there is a cost to this new contract. The hospital must give Blue Cross the same lower price. The shaded area labeled "Lost profit from Blue Cross" indicates the magnitude of this cost. It is easy to see from the figure that, depending on the prices negotiated by Blue Cross and the HMO and their respective patient volumes, the hospital may gain or lose as a result of executing the new HMO contract, even in the presence of the MFN clause.

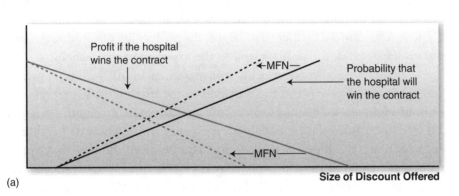

(a)

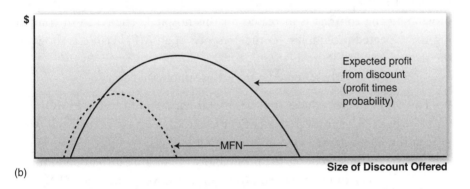

(b)

FIGURE 11-5

The Effect of a Most Favored Nation (MFN) Clause on the Expected Profitability of Discounting

SOURCE: Lynk (2000), "Some Basics about Most Favored Nation Contracts in Health Care Markets," *Antitrust Bulletin* 45(2): 491–530, Figure 3. Reprinted with permission.

This intuition can be easily formalized. See Figure 11-5*a*. The graph has the size of any discount, relative to the Blue Cross price, along the horizontal axis. As you move from left to right, the discount gets larger. The vertical axis has two scales: profit (from an executed contract) on the left and the probability (of winning a contract) on the right. The dark lines represent the market in the absence of an MFN clause. Consider the downward-sloping line. If the hospital gave the HMO no discount (the point at the far left), the hospital would obtain the largest profit. As it gives increasingly large discounts, the profit from the contract declines and ultimately reaches zero if the discounted price was equal to the costs of providing the service. The upward-sloping dark line represents the probability of winning the HMO contract at any size discount. Notice that, as drawn, the hospital has no chance of winning the contract at very small discounts. However, as the size of the discount increases, the probability of winning the contract increases substantially.

Figure 11-5*b* multiplies the profit from the contract by the probability of winning the contract at each potential price discount. The dark line shows the expected profit from various discount levels for the no-MFN-clause scenario. The expected profit is maximized somewhere in the midlevel of potential discounts, at the point where the "hump" is the highest. As you move further to the right, the probability of winning the contract is greater, but the profit is less, so the expected profit declines.

Figure 11-5 also presents the scenario when an MFN clause is present and applies to all or most of the providers in the market. This is represented in both Figures 11-5*a* and 11-5*b* by the dashed lines. In Figure 11-5*a*, an MFN clause causes the profitability line to shift in (downward) because, at each discount, the Blue Cross plan must also be given the new lower price, reducing overall profits. The probability line shifts out (upward) because the MFN clause applies marketwide. Profitability of an HMO contract declines for all of the hospital's competitors, so at any given discount, the probability of winning the contract is increased for this hospital. The result of computing the expected profitability in the presence of an MFN clause is shown by the dashed line in Figure 11-5*b*.

Several hypotheses emerge from this simple theory:

- The MFN clause reduces the size of optimal discount to the HMO. (The peak of the expected profit curve is to the left of where it was without the MFN clause.)
- The MFN clause reduces the profitability of entering into discounting at all. (The peak of the expected profit curve is lower under the MFN clause.)
- Although the profitability of discounting is lower, it is still positive, and therefore, discounting should be seen.

Thus, in some sense, MFN clauses establish a social tradeoff between deep discounts for some and shallow discounts for many.

Lynk (2000) provided two case study evaluations of the effects of MFN clauses. In the first, Blue Cross/Blue Shield of Rhode Island (BCBS) had a large insurance market share. It discovered that it was paying more for physician services than a new insurer, Ocean State HMO. In 1986, it initiated an MFN in its physician contracts. Ocean State sued, but BCBS prevailed in court, and the clause continued intact. In the second, Independence Blue Cross (of Philadelphia) added an MFN clause to its hospital contracts in mid-1992, requiring each hospital to give it as low a price as it gave any non-governmental purchaser. The Department of Justice investigated but withdrew, and the clause remained intact.

Lynk argued that if an MFN clause is harmful to the large insurer's competitors, then (1) the MFN clause should result in lower HMO enrollment, (2) the average net price for hospital services should increase, (3) the average discount should decrease, and (4) average hospital profits should increase due to less-intense discounting.

Lynk compared the trends in non-BCBS HMO enrollment before and after the enactment of the MFN provision in both Rhode Island and Philadelphia. In both instances, he found that enrollment continued upward at essentially the same rates as they had prior to the introduction of the MFN clause, suggesting that the provisions did not lower HMO enrollment. Next, only for the Philadelphia case where the data were available, Lynk reported that hospital net prices were virtually unchanged after the introduction of an MFN. Discount levels increased after the MFN clause was introduced, and average hospital profits were virtually unchanged in the two years following the introduction of the MFN and rose only slightly in the third year. In each instance, the evidence presented suggested that the MFN clause did not do what the anticompetitive theory predicted.

So, if MFN clauses do not keep out HMO competitors, why do large insurers impose the provision? Lynk (2000) argued that they do so to enable them to obtain a more-competitive price from each provider in a market characterized by great uncertainty about price, cost, and quality. He showed that average full billed charges per admission in the Philadelphia market varied by hospital from less than $10,000 to nearly $30,000. Net prices (adjusted for contractual discounts) varied by about half that amount. Billed charges as a percentage of net prices and billed charges as a percentage of operating costs also varied substantially across hospitals.

Under these circumstances, simple price rules can have undesirable effects. If the insurer decided to pay one fixed price to all hospitals, it would find that it was overpaying some hospitals that had lower prices (and costs) and that other, potentially excellent, high-quality hospitals would reject the contract because the offer was below the price that would cover their costs. Alternatively, the insurer could pay a fixed discount on the hospital's charges. Again, this would have the effect of overpaying for services at some hospitals and of having the contract rejected at others. A third approach would require the insurer to obtain detailed cost and quality data from each hospital with which it potentially wished to contract. Aside from the expense of this approach, it is not clear that many hospitals would allow a buyer to rummage through their cost data.

We can liken the problem to buying a new car. Everyone knows that no one pays the sticker price, and no one expects the dealer to actually sell the car below cost. You can go to "Blue Books" and Internet guides, and you can ask to see the invoice. However, the surest way to get a good price is to get information on the lowest price the dealer has accepted from others. That, Lynk says, is a most favored nation clause!

MFN clauses continue to be controversial. As we have seen, there are compelling theories arguing for the anticompetitive and the efficient price explanations, but a theory is only as good as its ability to predict behavior correctly. Lynk's tests refuting the anticompetitive theory are not as strong as they might appear. The two case studies provide pre-post comparisons. While these are informative, they are not the gold standard. We would like to know what happened to enrollment, prices, and profits in otherwise similar markets over the same time period. Further, Lynk has provided no test supporting the efficient pricing theory. Nonetheless, based on his analysis, it is not obvious that MFN clauses necessarily make new insurance entrants worse off.

Chapter Summary

- There are two principal explanations for why health insurance premiums increased in the last decade: a backlash against managed care and a reduction in competition among providers.
- The backlash argument holds that physicians were opposed to restrictions on their practice styles imposed by utilization management techniques and objected to the lower prices negotiated by the plans. Patients were concerned about utilization restrictions, as well as the limited choice of providers in managed care networks. This increased insurance premiums because wider provider choice implies that plans cannot assure sufficient volume to get the lowest prices. Evidence from the late 1990s failed to find much evidence of switching to less-restrictive plans. More recent data suggest much more shifting.
- The reduction in competition argument holds that a wave of hospital mergers and consolidations reduced the number of competitors and allowed hospitals to raise prices to managed care plans. Physicians have been accused of entering into marketing networks that collusively raise the price of their services to insurers. Evidence is mixed on the effects of managed care growth on consolidation among providers. However, there is little research on the effects of the wave of mergers on prices paid by providers. The FTC and the Department of Justice continue to have an active interest in anticompetitive behaviors in the healthcare industry.
- Physicians and hospitals have argued that they have banded together to fight the market power of large insurers. Recent research, however, fails to find evidence of such "monopsony" power. Rather, the pattern of evidence suggests that selective contracting by managed care plans has reduced provider market power.
- "Most favored nation" clauses allegedly harm competition by either enforcing a cartel arrangement among providers that keeps prices high or by restricting the ability of new managed care plans to negotiate lower prices with providers, which benefits large, entrenched local insurers. Alternatively, the clauses are mechanisms to allow insurers to obtain

acceptable prices in markets with considerable uncertainty. The available case study research found no evidence that managed care growth was slowed as a result of the clauses.

Discussion Questions

1. Some have argued that adverse selection is the underlying cause of the decline and revival of health insurance premiums. What would be the effect on average premiums if unhealthy people increasingly joined managed care plans from traditional plans? What is the effect of selective contracting on the cost of coverage for high-risk people in a managed care plan relative to a traditional plan?
2. What role does technological advance play in the escalation of health insurance premiums? Would you expect the growth of managed care to change the trajectory of technology on costs?
3. The Federal Trade Commission has obtained consent decrees from groups who have organized physicians into what we have called marketing networks. What is the harm to competition that is said to arise from these networks?
4. The Department of Justice (DOJ) typically reviews proposed hospital mergers prior to consummation. What is the DOJ looking for? What sort of evidence would likely lead the DOJ to approve a merger? What evidence would give the DOJ concern?

EMPLOYER-SPONSORED HEALTH INSURANCE

12

PREMIUM SENSITIVITY FOR HEALTH INSURANCE

This chapter introduces employer-sponsored health insurance.[1] In Chapter 2, we observed that nearly 62 percent of the under age 65 population in the United States obtains health insurance through the workplace. Many of these do so as employees, others as spouses, dependents, or retirees. Because employer-sponsored coverage is such a dominant and complex feature of private health insurance, we devote several chapters to it. This chapter examines employee premium sensitivity.

There is remarkably little direct empirical evidence regarding the premium responsiveness of employers. The research available on this topic will be discussed in the contexts of the tax treatment of health insurance (Chapter 14), the role of employers as agents for their workers (Chapter 15), and particularly the small group market (Chapter 17).

In contrast, the literature on employees' willingness to change plans when faced with changes in out-of-pocket premiums is extensive. Two findings emerge from this research. First, employees are remarkably price sensitive. It is not much of an exaggeration to say that they would change health plans for a song! This goes a long way in explaining the efforts of managed care plans to negotiate low prices with providers. They risk losing a substantial number of subscribers if other managed care plans are able to negotiate lower prices. Second, even though employees are very price sensitive when considering changing health plans, they are not very responsive in terms of whether or not they have coverage. However, even though this insurance "take-up" elasticity is low, when coupled with the large increases in premiums over the late 1990s, this premium sensitivity may explain much of the drop in coverage.

Early Studies of Premium Sensitivity

Several prices may be relevant when we examine the effect of insurance premiums on the choice of health insurance plan. One approach is to look at the

---

1. Portions of this chapter are drawn from Michael A. Morrisey, *Price Sensitivity in Health Care: Implications for Policy*, 2nd edition. Washington, D.C.: NFIB Research Foundation, 2005. Used with permission.

amount over and above the expected loss from medical expenditures. This follows directly from Chapter 3, where we saw that the risk premium was the maximum that we are willing to pay to avoid the consequences of the uncertain loss. In the insurance vernacular, the actual amount we pay over the expected loss is called the "loading fee." It includes the insurer's administrative costs, reserves, and profit. Employees, however, seldom, if ever, know the loading fee. Feldstein (1974) tried to use such a measure to estimate the effects of premiums on the proportion of the population with private health insurance in a state. Phelps (1973) and Goldstein and Pauly (1976) used the number of employees as a proxy for the loading fee, arguing that larger employer groups faced lower prices. Ultimately, these estimates were too crude to be very useful.

A second approach to examining the effect of insurance premiums on the choice of health insurance plan is to use the total premium the employer pays on behalf of the employee. This is the relevant premium from the insurer's point of view. Moreover, as will be discussed in Chapter 13, employees ultimately pay for employer-sponsored health insurance in the form of lower wages or reductions in other benefits. Thus, it should also be the relevant price to the employee. However, analysts typically argue that because employers tend to split the premium into the "employer's share," paid for with largely unseen wage and benefit reductions, and the "employee's share," paid for by explicit out-of-pocket premiums, it is the out-of-pocket price that affects the employee's decision during the open enrollment period. Inasmuch as employees' nominal wages do not immediately change as a result of their insurance decision, this is not an unreasonable approach.

Welch (1986) was among the first to estimate the effect of the out-of-pocket premium on the choice of health plan. He used Bureau of Labor Statistics data to investigate the extent to which the choice of fee-for-service (FFS) versus health maintenance organization (HMO) enrollment was a function of price differences between the plans offered. Using aggregate firm data, he sought to explain the proportion of workers enrolling in an HMO. He found that a 10 percent increase in the monthly out-of-pocket premium had a short-run effect of reducing the HMO share of the firm's subscribers by 2 percent. The long-run effect was a reduction of 6 percent. Increases in the FFS plan price worked to the HMO's advantage; that is, the alternative plans were substitutes. A 10 percent increase in the FFS out-of-pocket premium, holding the HMO premium constant, increased HMO enrollment by 2 percent in the short run and by 5 percent in the long run. From an insurer's perspective, these estimates suggest that health insurance is quite price responsive. Since the "employer" paid approximately 90 percent of the premiums in these data, the implied elasticities in the short and long runs were −2 and −6, respectively. Thus, a 10 percent premium increase would lead to a 20 percent reduction in the insurers' market share almost immediately and a 60 percent reduction after workers had time to explore options and fully adjust to the new set of premiums.

Long and colleagues (1988) found a relatively large response to changes in out-of-pocket premiums. They used data from approximately 1,500 subscribers to three Minneapolis–St. Paul HMOs in 1984 to examine the effect of relative premium changes on voluntary plan disenrollment. They found that a $5 increase (nearly $10 in 2006 dollars) in an HMO's out-of-pocket premium relative to other premiums resulted in a 66.7 percent increase in disenrollment; a $5 reduction decreased disenrollment by 41.1 percent. Long and colleagues' key contribution, however, was to demonstrate that the extent of price-related disenrollment depended on the availability of substitute plans. Figure 12-1 shows this. A $5 relative premium increase results in approximately 70 disenrollments per 1,000 subscribers in those firms with five HMO choices (the mean for the sample). When only

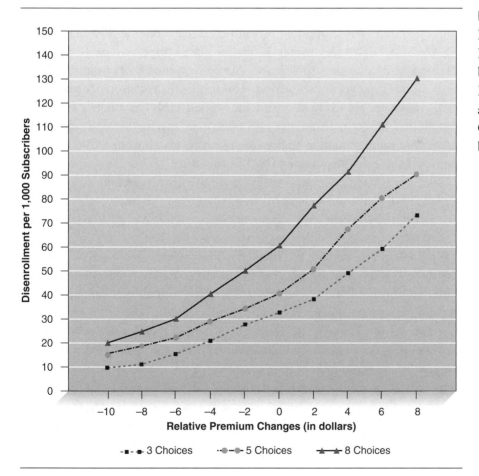

FIGURE 12-1
HMO Disenrollment by Relative Premium and Choices Offered by the Firm

SOURCE: Long et al. (1988), "Employee Premiums, Availability of Alternative Plans and HMO Disenrollment," *Medical Care* 26(10): Figure 1. Reprinted with permission.

three choices were available, the relative premium increase resulted in only 58 disenrollments per 1,000 subscribers. Eight options led to 100 disenrollments per 1,000 subscribers.

Employee Premium Sensitivity

The availability of substitutes complicates the understanding of the effects of out-of-pocket premiums on health plan choice. An employer may offer one or two or several health plan options. However, many employees will also have coverage options available to them through a spouse or a parent. For some employees, Medicaid and State Children's Health Insurance Plans (SCHIP) may also be substitute sources of coverage for their children and, therefore, affect their choice of single versus family coverage. If we ignore these other substitute sources of coverage, we tend to understate the effect of out-of-pocket premiums on the choice of health plan.

The problem can get even more complicated if all plans are not equally good substitutes for each other. A firm may initially offer an FFS plan and an HMO. As discussed in Chapter 3, in addition to price, adverse or favorable selection and consumer preferences may affect choice of insurance plans. Thus, if the employer adds a second HMO to the firm's insurance plan offerings, employees are likely to regard the second HMO as a better substitute for the first HMO than for the FFS plan. This means that it would take a greater premium reduction to get employees to switch from the FFS plan to the new HMO than from one HMO to the other.

Feldman and colleagues (1989) were the first to carefully deal with the availability of substitute sources of coverage outside the employee's own firm. They used 1984 data from 17 firms in Minneapolis–St. Paul to examine the plan choices made by 906 single workers who had no dependents and 2,146 single-parent families and married workers whose spouse was not covered elsewhere. This was made possible by an employee-level survey of coverage options and other household characteristics. The analysis was limited to these two distinct groups of workers because each group was believed to face its own common set of plan options. The authors demonstrated statistically that the inclusion of other workers who had different insurance options led to bias—in this case, to lower estimates of price sensitivity. They also demonstrated that traditional and prepaid group practice plans differed along one fundamental dimension: the freedom to choose a provider. As a result, they categorized independent practice association (IPA) type HMOs as freedom-of-choice plans along with more traditional fee-for-service type insurance plans.

The key result of this study was that employees were less likely to choose health plans with higher monthly out-of-pocket premiums. The size of the effects depended on: (1) the initial enrollment share of the plan raising its price and (2) the share this plan had of overall enrollment in similar plans (i.e., HMO or free-choice plans). Thus, a matrix of answers was obtained, depending on the choices available to the worker.

Table 12-1 presents the results of a $5 increase in out-of-pocket premium for single workers. In 2006 dollars, this would be the equivalent of a $9.60 increase in the monthly premium. Suppose a restricted-choice health plan (e.g., a group model HMO) enrolled 40 percent of the single workers in the firm. And suppose further that this HMO has 80 percent of the total HMO enrollment of single workers in this Minneapolis–St. Paul firm. Then the $5 increase in out-of-pocket premium was estimated to result in a 45 percent reduction in the plan's enrollment share of single workers. This is substantial. The results for those employees with family coverage, but no other source of employer-sponsored coverage, were similar.

As you move down a column in Table 12-1, this HMO is increasingly the dominant provider of managed care at this firm. When it is a small managed care player (at the top of a column), its price increase results in substantial loss of enrollment to other HMOs. When it is the dominant HMO (at the bottom of the column), it only loses enrollment to conventional plans. When you move across a given row, the HMO has constant competition from other

TABLE 12-1
Percentage of Single-Coverage Plan Enrollment Lost as a Result of a $5-per-Month Premium Increase

This HMO's Initial Share of Single-Coverage Workers

This HMO's Share of All HMO Coverage	10	20	30	40	50	60	70	80	90	100
10	100									
20	100	100								
30	100	100	98							
40	96	90	88	84						
50	86	82	78	74	70					
60	79	73	68	64	60	56				
70	67	63	59	55	50	46	42			
80	57	53	49	45	40	36	32	28		
90	48	44	39	35	31	27	22	15	14	
100	38	34	30	25	21	17	13	8	4	0

SOURCES: Morrisey (2005), table 5.1; computed from Feldman et al. (1989).

managed care plans, but declining competition from conventional-type plans. Thus, as you move across the row, the declines in enrollment share are smaller. The sole HMO enrolling all of the single workers faces no loss of enrollment share (lower right), but an HMO with a small enrollment share of single workers facing competition from other HMOs may lose all of its enrollment (upper left). In terms of formal measures of elasticity, these results imply a range of out-of-pocket premium elasticities ranging from –.75 for those with good substitutes to 0 for those with none (Royalty and Solomon 1999).

In follow-up work, Dowd and Feldman (1994/95) examined 1988 to 1993 data on five Minneapolis–St. Paul firms that offered two or more of seven different conventional and managed care plans. Rather than carefully worrying about the choice sets available to workers, Dowd and Feldman simply estimated the enrollment share responses to changes in the relative employee premium contributions of the plans offered. Here, a $5 higher premium contribution ($9.60 in 2006 dollars) was associated with a reduction in single coverage enrollment share of .112 percentage points. This translates into an employee out-of-pocket elasticity of approximately –1.0 (and an elasticity of –7.9 from the insurer's perspective). Given the bias introduced by not accounting for coverage options available through a spouse or parent, this elasticity figure is an underestimate. Royalty and Solomon (1999) criticized both the 1989 and the 1994 to 1995 studies for their inability to adequately control for differences in coverage across plan and firm offerings.

Cutler and Reber (1996) estimated out-of-pocket premium sensitivity among Harvard University faculty and staff. Here, the benefits were reasonably standard across the plans offered, and the researchers found out-of-pocket elasticities in the range of –.30 to –.60.

Buchmueller and Feldstein (1996) examined the extent of plan switching as a result of the introduction of a level-dollar premium contribution plan. In 1994, the University of California system changed its health insurance program from one that set the university's contribution to the average of the four most popular plans to one pegged at the least costly plan. In the new program, if employees wanted the least costly plan, they paid nothing out-of-pocket. However, if they wanted a more-expensive plan, they had to pay an employee premium contribution equal to the entire difference in premiums between the chosen plan and the least costly plan. Buchmueller and Feldstein compared enrollment before and after the change, and their findings are summarized in Figure 12-2. For no change in monthly premium, approximately 5 percent of faculty and staff changed plans. This was presumably due to dissatisfaction with the plan arising from issues other than price, such as undesirable waiting times or perhaps moving to a new home that made the previous plan's network inconvenient. However, over 26 percent of employees changed plans when faced with a $10 increase in premiums, and

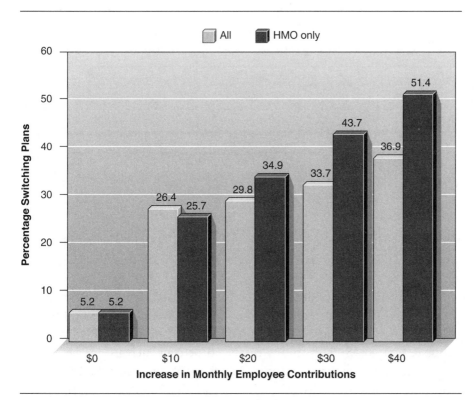

FIGURE 12-2

Effect of Price on Health Plan Switching: Simulation Results

SOURCE: Buchmueller and Feldstein (1996), "Consumer's Sensitivity to Health Plan Premiums: Evidence from a Natural Experiment in California," *Health Affairs* 15(1): Exhibit 3. Reprinted with permission.

nearly 30 percent did so when out-of-pocket premiums increased by $20. Typically, those in HMO plans were more likely to change plans for the same premium increase.

Royalty and Solomon (1999) undertook one of the most thorough studies conducted to date. They examined the extent of premium sensitivity for Stanford faculty and staff from 1994 to 1995. Like Cutler and Reber (1996), they had very consistent benefit packages across plans; like Buchmueller and Feldstein (1996), they examined a firm with level-dollar premium contributions; and like Feldman et al. (1989), they conducted a survey of employees to obtain household information to allow insight into other coverage available, household wealth, and the presence of chronic disease. Employees were offered four health plans: a point-of-service plan (POS), a closed-panel HMO, and two HMO network plans.[2] The plan offerings were designed so that the university's contribution to the plan was a percentage of the lowest-cost plan. Thus, the out-of-pocket premium reflected the cost of more-generous benefits. Since the services covered were essentially the same,

2. A fifth, catastrophic plan was also offered but was chosen by no more than 1.1 percent of the employees in either year of the study. It was not included in the analysis.

TABLE 12-2

Price Elasticities
for Stanford
Health Plans

	POS	Closed-Panel HMO	HMO Network 1	HMO Network 2
Employee perspective	−0.45	−0.43	−0.56	−0.76
Insurer perspective	−2.15	−2.87	−2.83	−3.54

SOURCE: Data from Royalty and Solomon (1999).

NOTES: HMO = Health maintenance organization; POS = Point-of-service.

this meant that the extra out-of-pocket premium bought a wider choice of providers. The POS had the broadest choice, the closed-panel HMO had the least, and the two network plans were somewhere in between.

Table 12-2 shows the out-of-pocket and insurer perspective premium elasticities for each Stanford plan. All of the plans were subject to substantial price sensitivity. The out-of-pocket premium elasticity for the POS plan, for example, was –0.45. This means that a 10 percent increase in the out-of-pocket premium for this plan, other things equal, resulted in a 4.5 percent reduction in the probability of employees choosing the POS plan. It is interesting to note that the two HMO-network plans had the largest elasticities, suggesting that faculty and staff viewed these plans as having better substitutes. The bottom row of Table 12-2 presents the premium elasticities from the "insurer perspective." The top row was derived by dividing the change in premium by the change in the out-of-pocket premium for each plan. The bottom row was calculated by dividing by the change in the total premium. As a result, a given premium change had a much larger impact for the insurer perspective. The POS premium elasticity, for example, was –2.1. A 10 percent increase in premium from this perspective led to a 21 percent reduction in the probability of the plan being chosen. In this case, the out-of-pocket premium changes were really the tail that wagged the dog.[3]

Royalty and Solomon (1999) also provided some useful insights into the effects of other variables on plan choice. Households in which at least one member had a chronic health condition were 4 percentage points more likely to choose the POS with its wider choice of providers and 4 percent less likely to choose the closed-panel HMO. There was no meaningful effect on the network plans. Older workers were also more likely to choose the POS plan. An

---

3. It is worth noting that these results are robust to the inclusion of an earlier year, which allows the model to be estimated with fixed effects. Using the administrative insurance data without the additional information provided by the employee survey yielded smaller estimates of the premium elasticities.

increase of 10 years in age increased the probability of choosing the POS plan by 5 percentage points. Greater family income and higher educational attainment also increased the probability that an employee would choose the POS plan and decreased the probability of choosing the closed-panel HMO. The effects on the network plans were mixed and much smaller in magnitude.

Finally, Royalty and Solomon (1999) examined whether different cohorts of workers had different price sensitivities. For example, those workers with chronic conditions may already have established relationships with one or more specialist physician providers, and it may take a larger change in price to entice them to change health plans. Such was indeed the case. Those with no chronic condition in the household were nearly three times as price sensitive as those with a chronic condition, although the difference was not statistically significant at the conventional levels. There were also substantially higher price elasticities for 30-year-old employees than for 50-year-olds.

The common feature in all of these studies is that there is substantial price sensitivity on the part of employees in choosing health plans. As a consequence, if an insurer's costs are out of line with the competition, it stands to lose significant market share and, presumably, significant profits.

Insurance Take-Up Rates

Since the late 1990s, there has been erosion in insurance coverage through employers. This erosion, however, is not primarily the result of fewer firms offering coverage or declines in eligibility for coverage. Instead, the erosion results from workers who are eligible for insurance coverage but who are declining it. This is shown in Figure 12-3, which reports the various employer-sponsored health insurance rates over the 1988 to 2005 period. The "offer rate" is the proportion of employers offering insurance to their workers. This rate has been relatively stable throughout the period. The "eligibility rate" is the proportion of workers eligible for insurance coverage. (Some workers may not be eligible for coverage because they work part-time or are seasonal employees.) This rate declined in the early 1990s but increased until recently. The "take-up rate" measures the proportion of eligible workers who accept coverage through their employer. This value has declined consistently over the period.

Employees' decision regarding whether or not to accept coverage from their employer is very different from the decision regarding which of the employer's plan offerings to take. Employees may have fewer good insurance substitutes beyond their own employer-sponsored coverage, and as a result, we should expect much less price sensitivity.

Chernew, Frick, and McLaughlin (1997) were among the first to examine the effects of premium contributions on take-up rates among

FIGURE 12-3

Offer,
Eligibility, and
Take-Up of
Employer-
Sponsored
Health
Insurance

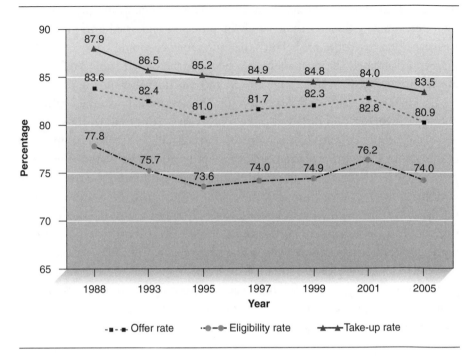

SOURCE: Data from Fronstin (2007).

workers. They examined data from nearly 2,000 small businesses in six cities collected in late 1992 and early 1993. They found that even large subsidies were insufficient to encourage total participation in health plans, even among those with no other source of employer-sponsored coverage. Subsidies as high as 75 percent were estimated to have increased participation only from 89.0 to 92.6 percent and implied an out-of-pocket premium elasticity of –0.07. Blumberg, Nichols, and Banthin (2001) found results similar to that of the Chernew, Frick, and McLaughlin study, using a nationally representative sample. Their take-up elasticity estimate was –0.04. These estimates are both much smaller (in absolute value) than the out-of-pocket elasticities we saw in the choice of plan research.

Using 1999 employer health insurance data, Cutler (2002) sought to explain the drop in take-up rates over the 1990s. He examined business-specific take-up rates as a function of the out-of-pocket premium for the least costly plan offered, as well as wage rates, total insurance premiums, and controls for industry and region. He found a take-up elasticity of –0.12, somewhat larger than that found by Chernew, Frick, and McLaughlin (1997) and Blumberg, Nichols, and Banthin (2001). According to Cutler, for each 10 percent increase in employee premium contributions, the take-up rate declined by 1.2 percent. While this is a small price response, because premium contributions had increased so dramatically over the period, the effect was large enough to explain the entire decline in employer-sponsored coverage. That is, the small price responsiveness, together with large increases in out-of-pocket premiums, led to declines in take-up rates that were large enough to explain the entire drop in employer-sponsored coverage over the period. Cutler argued that a price responsiveness of –.06 was enough to explain the decline in take-up rates.

Gruber and Washington (2005) also investigated the extent of price sensitivity among those offered employer coverage. They argued that the earlier work may have resulted in biased estimates of price responsiveness. The direction of bias in the Chernew and Blumberg estimates depends on whether employers provide low employee premium contributions because workers have preferences for insurance, or on whether they provide low premium contributions to encourage workers with low preferences for insurance to take it nonetheless. Cutler's estimates may be biased because the size of the premium contribution is likely to depend on the tax rate that workers have to pay.

Gruber and Washington investigated a natural experiment that appeared when U.S. postal employees were allowed to pay the employee share of their health insurance premiums with pretax dollars after 1994. This change should be unrelated to worker preferences for insurance and to tax rates of workers. Using 1991 through 2002 data from the U.S. Postal Service and the Federal Employees Health Benefit Plan, Gruber and Washington also found small take-up elasticities. In the family coverage regression, they found a take-up elasticity of –.022 and an overall take-up elasticity of –0.007. These estimates of price responsiveness are even smaller than those found by earlier studies. If these elasticities are closer to the true value, then we must look elsewhere for an explanation for the drop in the take-up rate.

Chapter Summary

- Employees are very price sensitive when it comes to choosing an employer-sponsored health insurance plan. Most studies found the elasticity of plan choice to be in the –.5 to –.75 range. These elasticities imply that a 10 percent increase in the out-of-pocket premium would lead to a 5 to 7.5 percentage point decrease in the probability of an employee taking a given plan. From the insurer perspective, these estimates imply premium elasticities in the range of –2.1 to –3.5.
- Employees' willingness to change plans depends on the number of plans the employer offers and the other plans that may be available to the household through a spouse, parent, or public program.
- Employees do not all have the same degree of premium sensitivity. Those with chronic health conditions, older workers, and those with

higher incomes are less likely to change plans for a given increase in the out-of-pocket premium. This may have to do with established relationships with providers or stronger preferences for particular types of plans.

- The proportion of people covered by employer-sponsored coverage has declined over the last decade. This is largely due to a decline in employees' willingness to accept coverage when offered.

- In contrast to choosing from among several employer-sponsored health plans, the decision to accept or refuse all the plans an employer offers is much less price sensitive. Estimates put the "take-up rate" elasticity in the range of –.04 to –.07, although one study found the rate to be much smaller still. A value of –.07 implies that a 10 percent increase in the out-of-pocket premium would decrease the probability that someone eligible for coverage would accept by 0.7 percentage points. One study concluded that these small elasticities, multiplied by the large increase in out-of-pocket premiums, were sufficient to explain most or all of the decline in employer-sponsored coverage.

Discussion Questions

1. As an insurer, will you be concerned at all about the relative size of the out-of-pocket premium that an employer sets? What sort of actions might you take in the negotiations with the employer over the insurance contract?

2. Suppose your state enacted legislation that provided a subsidy to encourage uninsured workers to accept the health insurance coverage their employers offered. What does this chapter say about the effectiveness of such a program? Do you see any difficulties in the implementation of such a plan?

3. In "level-dollar" premium contribution programs, employers make a fixed contribution to each of the health plans they offer. What is the economic justification for such a program? Who gains and who loses in such a system, relative to one in which employers pay a fixed percentage of the premium? Are there economic reasons why employers may choose to use a fixed percentage approach?

4. Why would employers pay any portion of the health insurance premium of their employees? Do they pay any portion of employees' homeowners or auto insurance policies?

COMPENSATING DIFFERENTIALS

13

This chapter addresses two key questions regarding employer-sponsored health insurance: (1) who pays for the coverage and (2) why employees commonly get health insurance through their employers when employers do not offer coverages like homeowners and auto insurance. The answers provide insight into important public policy and management issues. For example, what are the effects of a state requiring that all firms provide health insurance to their workers? What effect does an increase in the federal income tax rate have on employer-sponsored health insurance? What is the consequence of employers forcing their workers into a managed care plan? What are the consequences of requiring health insurance plans to cover dependents until age 26?

The Nature of the Labor Market

The general view of microeconomics is that workers are paid what they are worth. In the jargon of the discipline, workers are paid their "marginal revenue product." This simply means that, when the labor market is in equilibrium, the wage rate is equal to the value of the extra output produced as a result of the worker's effort.

Employee compensation can take many forms, however. It can be money income, vacation time, sick leave, pension benefits, free parking, pleasant working conditions, health insurance, and so on. The key point to appreciate is that, if workers are paid what they are worth, when something is added to the compensation bundle—say, free parking—then something else must be taken out—for example, some money income. If this did not happen, the employer would be paying more than the worker was worth. Economic theory and common sense say that we do not expect many employers to knowingly do this.

The adjustment to the compensation bundle when something is added is called a compensating differential. If a generous health insurance plan is added to the compensation bundle, other things equal, something must be taken out or the employer is not maximizing profits. The compensating differential works both ways. If, for example, the working conditions are particularly hazardous, such as in the mining or lumberjacking industries, then other things equal, the employer would have to add something, such as money income, to the compensation bundle to compensate for the more-dangerous working conditions.

Thus, the answer to the question of who pays for employer-sponsored health insurance is straightforward: The employee pays in the form of lower wages, fewer other benefits, or both. Employers often make statements to the effect that they do not offer health insurance "because they can't afford it." Such statements, when translated in the light of compensating differentials, would read something like: "I don't believe my employees are willing to give up enough money income to pay for health insurance."

Notice the phrase "other things equal" in the previous examples. This phrase is important to understanding. It means, for example, that the worker is just as productive before and after the inclusion of, say, vacation time in the compensation bundle. We expect wages to be reduced as a result of the inclusion of the benefit. However, if worker productivity increases as well, this increased value of the worker's effort could be reflected in the vacation time and no decrease in wages. The higher productivity that might have resulted in higher wages is instead spent on more vacation time. To put this in another context, from one year to the next, employees may find that their increased productivity goes to pay for more-expensive health insurance, rather than higher wages.

Consider a second example of "other things equal." Suppose we see two workers with differing productivity. The less-productive one receives only money wages. The more-productive one receives both higher wages and health insurance. This is not an example of failed compensating differentials; it is an example of not comparing apples to apples— that is, of not comparing workers of equal productivity.

Why Do Employers Provide Health Insurance?

Once the concept of compensating differentials is understood, we can immediately see the conditions necessary for employers to offer health insurance to their workers. First, employees must value the health insurance. If employees do not value the coverage, they will not consider it a form of compensation and will only see that their wages are lower. Theoretically, these workers would quit and take a similar job offered by employers that provided higher wages and no health insurance.

The second condition necessary for employers to offer health insurance to their workers is that it must be less expensive for an employee to buy health insurance through an employer than to buy it independently. Health insurance may be less expensive through an employer for three reasons. The first is favorable selection. A worker's ability to hold a job is a very low-cost signal to the insurer that the worker is likely to have low claims experience. As we saw in Chapter 3, experience rating results in lower premiums for low-risk individuals. Members of an employed group are likely to have lower claims experience than would a random draw of the population, and certainly lower than a random draw of unemployed people. Moreover, an employer's health insurance plan may have a healthier draw of the population over time as well, if sick employees tend to drop out of the workforce and new healthy employees join.

The tax treatment of employer-sponsored health insurance is the second reason for lower insurance costs through an employer. Compensation provided in the form of health insurance is not subject to federal income tax, Social Security or Medicare payroll taxes, and state income tax. Suppose you are in the 27 percent federal income tax bracket, your state imposes a 5 percent state income tax, and Social Security and Medicare have a combined tax rate of 7.65 percent.[1] For every $100 of compensation paid to you by your employer, you take home $60.35. If instead you received that $100 of compensation in the form of health insurance, you would have the full $100 of coverage. In this example, the U.S. tax system effectively reduces the price of health insurance purchased through your employer by almost 40 percent! If you bought the coverage on your own, under most circumstances you would pay with after-tax dollars, so you would not receive this tax subsidy. We explore the implications of the tax treatment of health insurance more completely in Chapter 14.

The third reason why health insurance is likely to be cheaper if purchased through an employer has to do with administrative cost savings. This category includes a wide range of potential savings. Some are simply savings that occur because the employer's human resources office performs tasks the insurer would otherwise have to do, such as keeping track of which employees are covered and what plan they have and dealing with open enrollment and employees changing health plans. Lower insurer marketing costs are another administrative cost savings. It is almost certainly cheaper to enroll people in groups of 25 or 50 or 1,000, rather than trying to sell to individuals and signing them up individually. Finally, and perhaps of most cost consequence, employers serving as agents for their employees can rationally search longer for a better health insurance value than would individuals. Individuals should search for a better health insurance value until the cost of the extra time spent in search just equals the expected extra savings from continuing to search. In contrast, an employer with 25 or 50 or 1,000 workers can usually afford to search longer because an improvement in the coverage or a reduction in the price will apply to 25 or 50 or 1,000 people.

---

1. The Social Security tax is 6.2 percent each for the employer and the employee on the first $94,200 of income (in 2006). The Medicare tax is 1.45 percent each for the employer and the employee. However, since the profit-maximizing firm pays the marginal revenue product, the worker effectively pays both shares. For ease of exposition, here we only include the "employee's share."

To summarize: Employees buy health insurance through their employers because (1) they value health insurance, and (2) health insurance is less expensive through an employer than otherwise. If either of these conditions is not met, employers probably will not provide coverage. We saw in Chapter 2 that young adults are the least likely to have health insurance. If they consider themselves invulnerable to injury and disease, their demand for coverage is low. They do not value coverage and are more likely to seek out jobs that offer higher wages and little or no health insurance. Others may find that family coverage is less expensive through a spouse than is individual coverage through their own employer. They, too, are more likely to seek out jobs that provide higher wages and little or no health insurance. If a public program provides coverage for children for which employed households are eligible, demand for dependent coverage is likely to be more limited and people probably will seek jobs that provide higher wages and no dependent coverage. This last effect is known as "crowd-out" of private insurance. We explore this topic in more detail in Chapter 23.

Implications of Compensating Differentials

Compensating differentials have a remarkably broad set of policy and management implications. Consider some management implications. Suppose employers decide to cut "their" health insurance costs by substantially raising the copays associated with the use of all covered ambulatory services. Other things equal, this makes the health insurance plan less generous. As a result, we would expect that money wages or some other form of compensation would be increased "to make the employees whole." Thus, it is not at all unusual to see an employer's health insurance plan combine changes, perhaps raising the copay while at the same time increasing the lifetime maximum benefits. This can be viewed as compensating employees for the increased copays. One of the reasons that employers have been relatively conservative in their adjustments to health benefits is that reductions in benefits have to save enough money to make workers "whole" and add something to profits. A change like switching from experience rating to being self-insured probably requires little, if any, compensating differential, but a change like eliminating the dental plan probably does require compensation.

Employers often complain that their health insurance costs are making their products uncompetitive in the global economy. The theory of compensating differentials undercuts this argument, however, since if employers were not paying health insurance premiums, the theory says they would be paying higher wages or more of other benefits. The real issue is not health insurance; it is labor productivity and total compensation.

Given compensating differentials, we would expect to see employers trying to cater to their employees' preferences for coverage and for coverage-wage tradeoffs. In an era of rising health insurance premiums, for example, we would expect employers to try to reduce lesser-valued health benefits, pare back other nonhealth programs, and reduce wage increases as they attempt to make the wide range of tradeoffs that their employees would. In Chapter 15, we explore the limited empirical evidence on how well employers act as "agents" for their employees.

Compensating differentials have a number of implications for public policy. Many states are currently debating whether to require employers to extend health insurance coverage to dependents up to age 26. Some states and more private insurance contracts currently provide for dependent coverage through age 18 or age 22 if the dependent is a full-time student. Compensating differentials imply that workers will pay for this new coverage in the form of lower wages or reductions in other benefits.

Similarly, requiring firms that do not offer health insurance to provide coverage means that workers who currently do not have employer-sponsored health insurance will now have coverage and lower wages or reductions in other benefits. Thus, an employer mandate has much the same effect on uninsured workers as does an individual mandate. In the former, the employer buys health insurance and effectively passes the cost on to workers through compensating differentials. In the latter, the worker pays directly by being required to own an insurance policy. It is worth noting that the theory of compensating differentials also suggests that employment should be little affected by an employer insurance mandate; wages and benefits will adjust, not jobs. There are two exceptions to this: The first is if wages are not free to adjust. For low-income persons affected by minimum-wage laws, wages cannot adjust downward to accommodate the required health insurance coverage. The theory of compensating differentials predicts that many of these individuals would lose their jobs. The second exception is when workers do not value the coverage—in which case, the lower wages and the near worthless health insurance may lead these individuals to drop out of the labor market.

Compensating differentials also have implications with regard to the effect that tax policy has on the provision of employer-sponsored health insurance. If Social Security and/or Medicare taxes were raised to help pay for the cost of the retiring baby boomers, the implication is that these higher taxes would lead workers and their employers to substitute away from money income into more health insurance to avoid some of the net income consequences of the higher taxes.

Evidence of Compensating Differentials

Compensating differentials are one of the strongest predictions to arise from labor economics. As such, it is no surprise that a 2005 survey of health economists indicated that 91 percent of them agreed with the statement that "Workers pay for employer-sponsored health insurance in the form of lower wages or reduced benefits" (Morrisey and Cawley 2006). However, it may come as a surprise that evidence of compensating differentials in health insurance has been difficult to obtain until very recently.

The empirical difficulty in finding evidence of compensating differentials is holding "other things equal," particularly productivity. If individuals have relatively few skills and little education or experience, they may not be very productive in the labor market. They may have a job with low wages and a modest health insurance plan. In contrast, someone with more skills, education, and experience may have both higher wages and a more-generous health insurance plan. If we ignore productivity, comparing the two groups of individuals would lead to the conclusion that there is no compensating differential between wages and health insurance. The problem is that "other things" are not equal.

Empirically, accounting for differences in productivity is very difficult. As an employer, you would like to hire job candidates who are intelligent and creative, understand the business, work well with coworkers and the public, take and carry out orders, meet deadlines, and provide leadership for the tasks at hand. These are the elements of productive workers. Finding such employees is difficult. Suppose that in conducting this talent search, the only information you had on applicants was their age, years of schooling, and if you were really lucky, the number of years of experience in the industry. That is one of the major problems facing research on compensating differentials. Only very crude measures of productivity are available, and as a result, comparisons are biased toward positive relationships between wages and benefits. The problems are compounded because we would also want to control for other job characteristics and the relevant household marginal tax rate, as well as have good measures of the nature of the health insurance actually provided. Data sets with all of this information just do not exist! See Simon (2001), Levy and Feldman (2001), and Jensen and Morrisey (2001) for sophisticated but ultimately failed (or only partially successful) efforts to estimate the magnitude of compensating wage differentials for employer-sponsored health insurance.

There have been an increasing number of successes, however. The Miller (2004) study was the most straightforward. Miller wanted to estimate a wage equation of the general form:

$$\text{Wages} = f\,(\text{Health insurance, Job characteristics,}$$
$$\text{Observed worker characteristics, Unobserved productivity measures})$$

The obvious problem was that he had no measures of unobserved productivity. What he did, however, was look at the change in wages over time for the same workers, some of whom changed jobs and either gained or lost health insurance coverage in the process. If unobserved productivity measures such as creativity, ability to meet deadlines, and so on do not change over time, they drop out of a model that looks at changes in wages. They drop out, but they are implicitly controlled by virtue of looking at the same individuals over time. Thus, Miller actually estimated a model of the form:

$$\Delta \text{ Wages} = f\,(\Delta \text{ Health insurance, } \Delta \text{ Job characteristics,}$$
$$\Delta \text{ Observed worker characteristics})$$

where Δ stands for "change in." Miller used Bureau of Labor Statistics national probability survey data on approximately 3,200 male workers in 1988, 1989, and 1990 and found that workers who lost health insurance over the period had wage increases of 10 to 11 percent. This is good evidence of compensating wage differentials.

Jonathan Gruber (1994b) undertook the most extensive examination of the wage-health insurance tradeoff to date. He investigated the effects of the imposition of state insurance mandates for maternity benefits. In 1979, the federal government required that most group health insurance plans cover maternity care like any other covered medical condition. Before that time, 23 states had done so. Gruber conducted what is called a differences-in-differences-in-differences (DDD) analysis. He compared the change in wages before and after the enactment date of the laws (difference 1), in states that did and did not enact the law (difference 2), for people who would and would not be affected by the law (difference 3). The idea is that the wage changes in unaffected states and for similar but unaffected individuals would control for other factors at work in the states and local labor markets.

The states of New York, New Jersey, and Illinois enacted the maternity care mandate between July 1, 1976 and January 1, 1977. The states of Connecticut, Massachusetts, Ohio, Indiana, and North Carolina were used as controls because they did not enact such laws. Wage data were obtained from the U.S. Census Bureau's Current Population Survey for the two years prior to enactment (1974 and 1975) and two years after (1977 and 1978). The average wage for relevant workers in these states ranged from $5.59 to $6.61, all in constant 1978 dollars. Affected workers were defined as married women of childbearing ages—that is, between the ages of 20 and 40. The unaffected group was defined as all individuals between the ages of 40 and 60 and all single men. Excluded were single women and married men, ages 20–40. Both of these groups, of course, could have been affected by the laws, but their inclusion would only have complicated the comparison.

Table 13-1 shows the results of this DDD analysis. The affected group (married women, ages 20–40) in states that enacted the law had wage decreases of 3.4 percent. Married women, ages 20–40 in states that did not enact the law had wage increases of 2.8 percent. The difference in these two differences was –6.2 percent (–3.4 % minus 2.8%). For the unaffected group (single men, ages 20–40, and all people, ages 40–60) in the states enacting the law, wages decreased by 1.1 percent, suggesting that there were other wage trends going on in the experimental states besides the enactment of maternity benefits laws. For the unaffected group in states that did not enact the laws, real wages declined by 0.3 percent. Thus, the difference-in-differences for the unaffected groups was a decline of 0.8 percent (–1.1% – [–0.3%]). The estimated effect is then the difference in these two overall differences. Gruber (1994b) estimated that wages for the affected group declined by 5.4 percent as a result of the mandated maternity benefit (–6.2% – [–0.8%]). This is rather dramatic evidence of compensating wage differentials that are borne by the affected group.

A third effort to identify compensating differentials associated with employer-sponsored health insurance was undertaken by Louise Sheiner (1999). It is well known that over the life cycle, wages rise rapidly in the early years of an individual's career and then tend to flatten out as that person gets older. The usual explanation for this wage compression is that, in the later working years, there are few increases in productivity. Sheiner's argument was

TABLE 13-1

Estimates of the Effects of Maternity Mandates on Hourly Wages

	Wages before Law	Wages after Law	Time Difference
A. Affected Group: Married Women, Ages 20–40			
States with law	$4.70	$4.54	–3.4%
States without law	$3.93	$4.04	+2.8%
Difference-in-differences			–6.2%
B. Unaffected Group: All People, Ages 40–60, and Single Men, Ages 20–40			
States with law	$5.81	$5.74	–1.1%
States without law	$5.10	$5.09	–0.3%
Difference-in-differences			–0.8%
Difference-in-differences-in-differences			–5.4%

SOURCE: Adapted from Gruber (1994b).

NOTE: Percentage changes are correct. Wage values result from taking the antilog of the published values and rounding to the nearest cent.

that we could look at the age-wage profile across different geographic labor markets. In some of these markets, health insurance costs are high, and in others, they are relatively low. If compensating wage differentials exist, they imply that age-wage profiles should result in lower wages in markets where insurance costs are high than in markets where insurance costs are low. Moreover, the differences should be more pronounced for older workers both because they are likely to have higher claims experience and because the tradeoff is less likely to be masked by changes in productivity. This theory is depicted in Figure 13-1. Wages increase with age, but ultimately level off. The two curves represent the age-wage profile for markets with high insurance cost (the lower curve) and markets with low insurance cost (the upper curve). The increasing spread between the curves reflects the differing compensating wage differential across markets.

Sheiner (1999) tested this model with data from the U.S. Census Bureau's 1989 to 1990 Current Population Survey. To carry it out, she needed information on health insurance costs. Simply using average employer-sponsored premiums across major cities would be problematic, however, because these premiums reflect differences in coverage as well as differences in provider prices and utilization patterns. Instead, she obtained actuarial estimates of the premium for a standard benefits package for a standardized employee group for each of the 244 cities in her study. This measure served as an index of healthcare costs across the markets. She estimated a model of the general form:

$$\text{Wage} = f\,(\text{Age} \times \text{Health costs, Hours worked,}$$
$$\text{Worker characteristics, Region} \times \text{Age})$$

Health costs multiplied by the worker's age captured the hypothesized compensating wage differential that changed with age. Region interacted

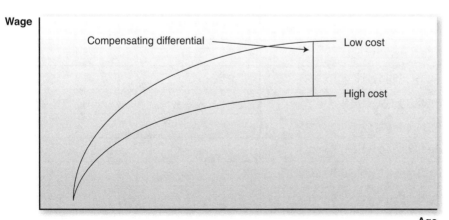

FIGURE 13-1

Age-Wage Profile with Differing Healthcare Costs

with age was intended to capture other features of the local markets than might also be differentially correlated with age. The other factors sought to capture worker productivity.

The results for men are shown in Table 13-2. For each additional year of age, the wage reduction, other things equal, was $113 and was strongly statistically significant. If we reestimate the model, using age groups rather than a continuous age measure, Table 13-2 shows the increasing magnitude of the compensating wage differential as men age. These effects, as Sheiner pointed out, are actually too large to only reflect healthcare costs. She speculated that the model might also be picking up other benefit costs that increase with age and are correlated with healthcare costs. The effects for women were much smaller and less statistically significant. Sheiner attributed this to the much smaller likelihood that women had health insurance through their own employment.

A fourth effort to estimate compensating differentials comes from preliminary work by Bhattacharya and Bundorf (2004). They used the 1989 to 1999 National Longitudinal Survey of Youth to examine the effects of obesity in the labor market. They found that obese individuals with employer-sponsored health insurance received lower wages, while those without employer-sponsored coverage who have individual coverage or no coverage do not. Moreover, they estimated that the size of the wage reduction was roughly in line with the additional medical costs associated with obesity.

Other studies of compensation differentials have focused on, for example, pensions and workers' compensation insurance. Pensions would seem to be an obvious case for compensating differentials. The difficulty is that the wage adjustment is likely to occur over the entire working lifetime. Montgomery, Shaw, and Benedict (1992) and Kotlikoff and Wise (1985) reported evidence of such compensating differentials. As we saw in Chapter 1,

TABLE 13-2

Estimated Effects of Higher Healthcare Costs on the Age-Wage Profile of Men

	Continuous Age	Age Cohorts
Age × Health costs	−$113	
Ages 30–34 × Health costs		−$366
Ages 35–39 × Health costs		−$562
Ages 40–44 × Health costs		−$2,336
Ages 45–49 × Health costs		−$2,088
Ages 50–54 × Health costs		−$4,664
Ages 55–59 × Health costs		−$961

SOURCE: Data from Sheiner (1999).

workers' compensation reflects employment-based insurance against the medical and earnings loss associated with workplace injury and disease. Two studies have used the government-specified levels of earnings compensation to test for compensating wage differentials. Moore and Viscusi (1990) found that each $1 increase in benefits was associated with a 12-cents-per-hour reduction in wages. Gruber and Krueger (1991) found that about 85 percent of workers' compensation costs were borne by workers in the form of lower wages.

A Natural Experiment in Compensating Differentials

Goldman, Sood, and Leibowitz (2005) provided a fascinating window into the nature of the tradeoffs employees make when faced with increasing premiums for employer-sponsored health insurance. If employers are reasonably good agents for their workers, then these are also the sort of compensating differentials we would expect to see them make on behalf of their employees.

Goldman, Sood, and Leibowitz studied a single, large, unnamed firm that employed staff in 47 states and that provided access to data from the years 1989 through 1991. While the data are somewhat old, the time period experienced rapidly increasing health insurance premiums, much as we see today. The researchers restricted their analysis to single employees who signed up for health insurance. This was done to avoid the complications of those who had coverage from another source. Employees in this firm had a particularly flexible compensation program. They received money wages and benefit credits that could be spent on a wide array of benefits, ranging from health insurance options (three fee-for-service [FFS] plans and 47 health maintenance organizations [HMOs] nationwide) to pensions, dental insurance, and long-term disability coverage. The employer made a fixed level-dollar contribution to the health insurance options, pegged at the premium of the least costly plan. Thus, employees faced the full marginal cost of more-generous plans. See Table 13-3 for a summary of the benefits options. Employees could choose to buy more benefit credits with pretax wages or to convert unused benefit credits into taxable wages.

The research question was: How do employees reallocate their compensation bundle when health insurance premiums change? In this case, some HMO premiums had risen by as much as 34 percent year to year, and others had declined by as much as 26 percent. Recall from Chapter 12 that, while workers are very price sensitive to employer-sponsored health insurance options, the elasticity is still in the inelastic region of the demand curve. The elasticity estimates are in the range of –0.5 to –0.75, certainly less than –1.0 (in absolute value). This is important because it says that, when insurance prices increase, employees will try to cut back on the quantity of health insurance

TABLE 13-3

Details of the
Cafeteria
Benefits Plan

Employee Benefit Options Selected:	1990	Compensation:	Average	Minimum	Maximum
Health insurance	100%	Net wages	$26,504	$6,593	$109,303
Life insurance	34%	Health insurance	$673	$0	$1,428
Long-term disability	72%	Other benefits	$286	$0	$5,335
Accident insurance	50%	*Health Insurance Selected:*	*1989*	*1990*	*1991*
Dependent life insurance	1%	FFS catastrophic	6.1%	8.8%	15.0%
Retirement	6%	FFS high deductible	8.5%	10.0%	13.6%
Health expense account	7%	FFS low deductible	42.6%	39.3%	34.0%
Dental insurance	76%	43 HMOs	42.8%	41.9%	37.4%

SOURCE: Data from Goldman, Sood, and Leibowitz (2005).

NOTES: FFS = Fee-for-service; HMO = Health maintenance organization.

they buy, but their total expenditure on health insurance will still increase. They pay for this additional insurance spending by taking less compensation as money income or by reducing the amount of other benefits or both.

Methodologically, perhaps the most difficult aspects of the Goldman, Sood, and Leibowitz study were that there were out-of-pocket premiums for each of the 50 health plans, and all of the HMOs were not available to all employees, due to differing geographic markets. The researchers dealt with this by creating a price index based on the prices of the plans available to workers in each of the relevant states. This limited their analysis in some ways because they could not directly look at shifting across health plans; they could only look at the net effect of a weighted, average, out-of-pocket premium increase on overall insurance expenditures, other benefits expenditures, and on money wages.

Their findings are summarized simply in Table 13-4. A 10 percent increase in weighted, average, out-of-pocket insurance premiums led to a 5.2 percent increase in spending on health insurance. The fact that the increase in expenditures was less than 10 percent indicates that many workers chose to switch to a less costly health plan. The fact that spending increased indicates that the elasticity of demand for health was less than one (in absolute value). Typical employees reallocated their compensation to pay for this extra health insurance spending by taking less in money wages and less in other benefits. More than 71 percent of the extra spending was paid for by reducing

Effect on . . .	Percentage Change
Health insurance expenditures	+5.2%
Other benefits expenditures	−1.5%
Wages	−3.7%

SOURCE: Derived from Goldman, Sood, and Leibowitz (2005).

TABLE 13-4
Effects of a 10 Percent Increase in Weighted, Out-of-Pocket, Aggregate Health Insurance Premiums

money income (the employees bought more benefit credits). The remaining 29 percent was paid for by giving up other benefits.

The upshot of this research is clear. When workers were fully able to choose how to deal with increases in health insurance premiums, they adjusted along all the margins. They switched to relatively less-expensive coverage, and they paid for the still more-expensive insurance by reducing money income and other benefits. This suggests that employers acting as good agents for their employees would do similarly when faced with rising health insurance costs. They would try to eliminate less-valuable coverages, and they would implement compensating differentials, reducing wages (or forgoing raises) and cutting back on some other benefits.

Chapter Summary

- Employees pay for employer-sponsored health insurance in the form of lower wages and/or fewer other benefits.
- Compensating differentials is the term used to describe the adjustment to other forms of compensation when one form is increased or decreased.
- Employees obtain health insurance through their employers because two conditions are met: (1) the employee values health insurance and (2) the insurance is less expensive to obtain through the employer than elsewhere.
- Health insurance tends to be less expensive when obtained through an employer because of favorable selection, the tax treatment of employer-sponsored health insurance, and administrative cost savings.
- The favorable selection arises because the ability to hold a job is likely to be a strong indicator of good health status and lower expected claims experience, leading to lower premiums.
- Health insurance obtained through an employer is not subject to federal or state income taxes or to Social Security or Medicare payroll taxes. As a

consequence, coverage purchased through an employer is likely to be much less expensive than that purchased individually with after-tax dollars.

- Potential administrative cost savings arise from enrollment and related activities carried out by the firm rather than the insurer, from reduced marketing costs associated with group sales, and from economies of scale in searching for the preferred insurance package.
- There is growing empirical support that wages and other forms of compensation adjust when health insurance benefits provided by an employer change.
- Workers tend to pay for mandated health insurance benefits in the form of lower wages and reductions in other benefits, and workers who have higher healthcare expenditures appear to have lower wages, other things equal.

Discussion Questions

1. Recalling what you know about moral hazard and compensating differentials, is it conceivable (or likely) that an employer could increase the copays associated with physician visits and prescription drugs, make workers "whole," and still add something to firm profits as a result?
2. Some policy advocates have called for the end of the exclusion of employer-sponsored health insurance from income and payroll taxes. If this were to occur, do you anticipate that employers would no longer provider health insurance for their workers?
3. Many businesses, particularly small ones, do not provide health insurance for their workers. Why? Given your answer, would you expect there to be any matching of workers and businesses with respect to the offering of health insurance?

TAXES AND EMPLOYER-SPONSORED HEALTH INSURANCE

The tax treatment of employer-sponsored health insurance is a key factor in the structure of U.S. health insurance markets. In this chapter, we explore the cost to taxpayers of the exclusion of employer-provided health insurance from the income and payroll tax base. We demonstrate the effects of the tax exclusion on employers' provision of insurance, and we examine the effects of tax law changes on the extent to which coverage is provided and the generosity of that coverage. In addition, we introduce the role that tax policy plays in determining the size of the employee's premium contribution. This prepares us to discuss the employer as agent in Chapter 15 and consumer-driven health plans in Chapter 16.

The Tax Treatment of Health Insurance

Approximately 62 percent of the under-age-65 population in the United States had health insurance provided to them through the workplace in 2005 (Fronstin 2006). Income provided to employees in the form of health insurance is not subject to federal or state income tax or to Social Security and Medicare payroll taxes. As a consequence, this tax treatment provides a substantial subsidy for the purchase of health insurance through an employer.

Tax Rates on Money Wages

To understand the interplay of income, taxes, and health insurance, begin with the demand and supply curves in Figure 14-1. These reflect the market for labor. Employers are willing to hire hours of labor as shown in the downward-sloping demand curve. Workers are willing to supply hours of labor along the upward-sloping supply curve. In a competitive labor market with no taxes, equilibrium would be at quantity Q_E of hours provided at price (wage) P_E per hour. Suppose a 10 percent tax is imposed on the wage rate per hour worked. This is called an *ad valorum* tax, and it is depicted in Figure 14-1 as "Supply with tax." Since the original supply curve reflects the minimum wage that people would accept to provide the labor, the tax pivots the supply curve upward, indicating that people have to get a wage that reflects both their minimum acceptable wage and the tax.

FIGURE 14-1

Effects of an
Ad Valorum
Tax on Workers

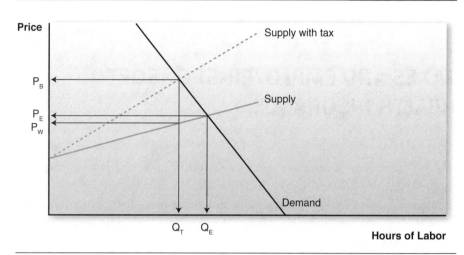

With the tax in place, businesses are still willing to pay along the unchanged demand curve. However, the supply curve inclusive of the tax now crosses the demand curve at a lower quantity (Q_T) and a higher price (P_B). This says that businesses will buy fewer hours of labor when they have to take the tax into consideration. Workers, however, only take home the lower wage (P_W). The difference between P_B and P_W is the amount of tax imposed on each unit of labor.

How much of the tax imposed on labor is due to federal and state income taxes, Social Security taxes, and Medicare taxes? Table 14-1 begins to provide an answer. It presents the marginal tax rates for federal personal income and the "employee shares" of the Social Security payroll tax and the Medicare payroll tax. Social Security and Medicare taxes are based on total income, while the federal income tax is based on "taxable income" and applies only after personal exemptions ($3,300 per person) and the standard deduction ($5,150 for singles and $10,300 for families) have been subtracted from total income. In real life, other factors—most importantly, actual deductions—may also apply. Notice that the Social Security tax rate becomes 0% for total incomes above $94,200 for each worker (in 2006). Social Security does not tax additional income above this level. In contrast, Medicare taxes every additional dollar of income at a fixed rate. The federal income tax imposes a higher tax rate on additional income. Thus, for a single individual, no income tax is owed on the first $8,450 of income, a 10 percent rate applies to income above $8,450 but below $16,001, a 15 percent rate applies to income above $16,000 but below $39,101, and so on. Thus, the marginal income tax rate is higher for increments of additional income. Finally, notice that while the schedule of tax rates appears to be the same in the upper (singles) and lower (families) panels of the table, the income ranges differ. This is because the income tax code specifies income ranges that are twice as wide

TABLE 14-1
Federal
Personal
Income, Social
Security, and
Medicare Tax
Rates, 2006

Total Income	Marginal Income Tax Rate	Marginal Social Security Tax Rate	Marginal Medicare Tax Rate	Combined Marginal Tax Rate
Single Individual Claiming One Exemption and the Standard Deduction				
$0–$8,450	0%	6.2%	1.45%	7.65%
$8,451–$16,000	10%	6.2%	1.45%	17.65%
$16,001–$39,100	15%	6.2%	1.45%	22.65%
$39,101–$82,650	25%	6.2%	1.45%	32.65%
$82,651–$94,200	28%	6.2%	1.45%	35.65%
$94,201–$163,250	28%	0.0%	1.45%	30.45%
$163,251–$345,000	33%	0.0%	1.45%	34.45%
$345,001 or more	35%	0.0%	1.45%	36.45%
Family Filing Joint Return Claiming Three Exemptions and the Standard Deduction				
$0–$20,200	0%	6.2%	1.45%	7.65%
$20,201–$35,300	10%	6.2%	1.45%	17.65%
$35,301–$81,500	15%	6.2%	1.45%	22.65%
$81,501–$143,900	25%	6.2%	1.45%	32.65%
$143,901–$188,400	28%	6.2%	1.45%	35.65%
$188,401–$208,650	28%	0.0%	1.45%	30.45%
$208,651–$356,750	33%	0.0%	1.45%	34.45%
$356,751 or more	35%	0.0%	1.45%	36.45%

SOURCES: IRS and Social Security web sites. The exact sites change regularly. Begin your search with www.irs.gov and www.ssa.gov and look for tax rate and tax base information.

NOTE: Social Security rates apply to the first $94,200 of total income for each worker. Medicare rates apply to total income of each worker. Income tax rates apply only to taxable income, which in this example, equals total income less the relevant exemptions and standard deduction. For a single taxpayer, the exemption equals $3,300, and the standard deduction is $5,150. The family in this example includes two working adults with equal incomes and one child. Their exemptions total $9,900, and their standard deduction is $10,300. Both examples ignore the phase-out of exemptions and deductions at higher income levels.

for families filing jointly compared to singles. This difference shrinks at higher levels and disappears at the highest income range.

Now consider a single woman earning $45,000 in wages. For each additional $100 of income, she must pay $25 in additional federal income taxes, $6.20 in additional Social Security taxes, and $1.45 in additional Medicare taxes. For her, the marginal tax rate is 32.65 percent.

Actually, her marginal tax rate is higher than this—for two reasons. First, all but six states impose a state income tax. If the state tax rate is 5 percent on each additional dollar earned, then the woman in our example faces a marginal tax rate of 37.65 percent.

Second, Table 14-1 only reflects the "employee shares" of the Social Security and Medicare taxes. The "employer shares" are an additional 6.2 percent and 1.45 percent, respectively. Consider Figure 14-2. The basic demand and supply curves are the same as those drawn earlier in Figure 14-1. However, here an *ad valorum* tax is applied to the *employer*, much as the "employer shares" of the Social Security and Medicare taxes are applied to the employer. The end result, however, is completely analogous to that in Figure 14-1: the employees effectively pay the tax. The imposition of the tax drives a wedge between the wages that the business pays and the wages the employees receive. In the case of Social Security and Medicare "employer shares," it is as if the firm pays the employee $107.65, but then takes $7.65 to pay the "employer shares" of the taxes, leaving the employee $100 from which to pay federal and state income taxes and the "employee shares" of the Social Security and Medicare taxes. Thus, in our example, the marginal tax rate inclusive of both shares of the payroll taxes and the 5 percent state income tax is approximately 42 percent.[1]

Taxes and Employer-Sponsored Health Insurance

Suppose that the employer of the woman in our example does not offer health insurance, and the employee goes into the individual market and buys coverage with after-tax income at a cost of $4,248.[2] Alternatively, her employer could have offered this average insurance benefit and lower money wages. So, instead of $45,000 and no health insurance, she could earn $40,752 in money wages plus a $4,248 health insurance plan. Compensation in the form of money wages is taxed (as we have seen); compensation in the form of employer-sponsored health insurance is not. Thus, the woman now pays less income and payroll tax—nearly $1,387 less.[3] Her health insurance plan purchased through her employer effectively cost her $2,489 or 32.65 percent less. The tax system subsidized her employer-sponsored health insurance at a rate equal to her combined marginal tax rate.

This immediately suggests two implications of the tax system. First, people are more likely to buy insurance through their employer because of the tax subsidy. Second, because of the tax subsidy, people are likely to buy

---

1. That is, $(0.25 + 0.124 + 0.029 + 0.05) / (1 + 0.062 + 0.0145) = 0.4208$.
2. Recall from Chapter 2 that the average cost of single coverage provided through an employer in 2006 was $354 per month or $4,248 per year.
3. We conservatively assume that her tax rate is 32.65 percent from Table 14-1 applied to $45,000 and $40,752, respectively.

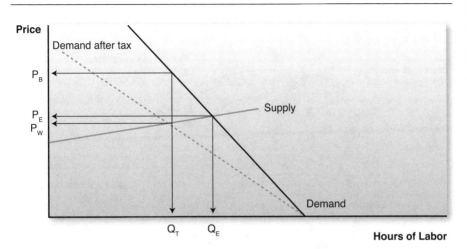

FIGURE 14-2
Effects of an
Ad Valorum
Tax on
Employers

more insurance than they otherwise would have. In the previous example, as long as the woman values health insurance at least at 67 percent of its cost, she is better off buying the coverage. Recall from Chapter 3 that the pure theory of insurance implies that we do not buy coverage for small-magnitude losses or for very small or very large probability events. However, tax subsidies of this magnitude erode those incentives. We are more likely to have coverage with low deductibles and low copays, for example, because of the tax subsidy.

A casual review of the combined marginal tax rates in Table 14-1 demonstrates several important implications of this tax subsidy. First, because of the progressive nature of the federal (and some state) personal income tax systems, the tax subsidy increases with income. Higher-income individuals, with some exceptions, tend to get larger subsidies than do lower-income people. Thus, those with higher incomes are more likely to have health insurance coverage and more likely to have more-generous coverage. Second, an increase in federal, state, Social Security, and/or Medicare tax rates will lead to a greater likelihood that people will have employer-sponsored health insurance coverage and more generous forms of coverage. Finally, if the tax subsidy was eliminated, we would expect fewer people to have coverage and many to have less-generous coverage. Higher-income people would be most affected.

In short, one of the keys to understanding health insurance in the United States is to understand the incentives implicit in the tax, Social Security, and Medicare laws.

Size of the Health Insurance Tax Expenditures

"Tax expenditure" is a term used to describe the tax revenue lost as a result of significant deviations from general principles of taxation. The general tax

FIGURE 14-3

Federal Tax Expenditures for Employer-Sponsored Health Benefits, 2006

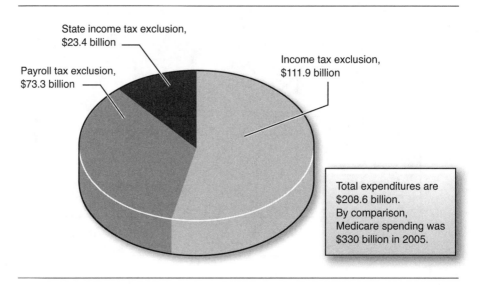

State income tax exclusion, $23.4 billion

Payroll tax exclusion, $73.3 billion

Income tax exclusion, $111.9 billion

Total expenditures are $208.6 billion. By comparison, Medicare spending was $330 billion in 2005.

SOURCE: Data from Seldon and Gray (2006).

principle of importance here is that all compensation should be taxed as the same rate to avoid incentives for people to shift the form in which they receive their compensation. The exclusion of income in the form of employer-sponsored health insurance constitutes a major tax expenditure. Another way to think of this is that the government's "tax expenditure" is the taxpayer's tax subsidy.

Figure 14-3 provides estimates of federal tax expenditures for employer-sponsored health benefits for 2006 (Seldon and Gray 2006). Federal income tax revenues were some $111.9 billion lower because of income taxes forgone as a result of employer-sponsored health insurance. Social Security and Medicare revenues were $73.3 billion lower. Together with state tax expenditures, these totaled $208.6 billion. To put this in some context, in 2005, federal spending on the Medicare program totaled $330 billion. So, annual "tax expenditures" on employer-sponsored coverage were equal to more than 63 percent of Medicare spending.

The tax subsidy has been growing due to the increases in premiums and in the number of people with employer-sponsored coverage (even as the proportion of those with such coverage declines). Bob Helms (2005) reported that the federal and state tax expenditures for employer-sponsored coverage plus the tax subsidy for out-of-pocket medical expenditures totaled more than $200 billion in 2004 and had grown substantially even since 1990 (see Figure 14-4).

FIGURE 14-4

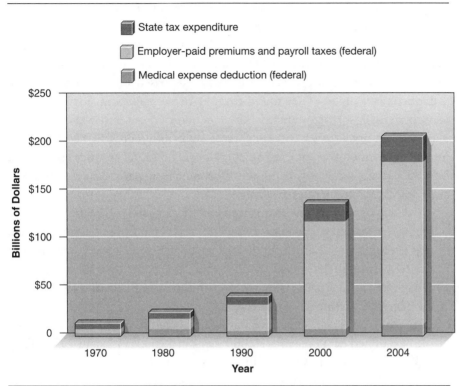

Federal and
State Tax
Expenditures
for Health
Insurance and
Medical
Expenses

SOURCE: Helms (2005), "Tax Reform and Health Insurance," *Health Policy Outlook*. Washington, D.C.: AEI (Jan./Feb.): Figure 2. Reprinted with permission.

Estimates of the Effects of Tax Rates on Health Insurance

Estimating the effects of tax rates on the health insurance decisions within the firm is a daunting challenge. We would need variation in tax rates across individuals, time, and/or political boundaries. If we had data on individuals, there would be concern about the nature of spousal and other nonearned income in the household, which would affect tax rates. If we had data over time, we would need to take into consideration other factors that might have changed along with the tax rates. If we had data across political tax boundaries—states, for example—we would have to worry about why these tax differences exist and what else of relevance differed across the states.

A number of studies, however, have attempted to estimate the effect of tax rates on an employer's decision to offer health insurance coverage and on the proportion of workers with coverage in a firm. Exploiting differences in state income tax rates has been the most popular approach. The results vary substantially, however. Leibowitz and Chernew (1992) used cross-state differences in taxes to compute average after-tax premiums for employees in small firms. They found an elasticity of 2.9 for the tax subsidy. A 1 percent increase in the subsidy increased the probability of offering coverage by 2.9 percent. Gentry and Peress (1994) estimated the average share of workers offered health insurance coverage across cities based on differences in the state income tax rates. They found that a 1 percentage point increase in the (tax) price of insurance reduced the percentage of covered workers by 1.8 percent. Royalty (1999) also used cross-state differences in tax rates, but looked at all employers, not just smaller ones. She found an offer elasticity of only –0.63. Obviously, estimates vary substantially, in part because of the very crude measures of tax rates available.

A set of earlier studies focused on the amount of health insurance offered as a function of tax rates. Long and Scott (1982) used aggregate data on fringe benefits—health insurance in particular—and total compensation from 1974 through 1979 and found that a 10 percent increase in the marginal tax rate led to a 2.2 percent increase in the proportion of total compensation received as fringe benefits, but a 4.1 percent increase in the percentage of total compensation received as health benefits. Sloan and Adamache (1986) examined data on some 10,000 firms in 1968, 1972, and 1977. They found that a 10 percent increase in the tax rate was associated with a 6 percent increase in the proportion of compensation being paid in the form of life and health insurance benefits. Woodbury (1983) used 1977 data on local school districts to estimate the effects of tax rates on the mix of employee compensation. He found that a 10 percent increase in the tax rate was associated with a 16 to 17 percent increase in the proportion of compensation received as life and health benefits. Finally, Hammermesh and Woodbury (1990) examined data on university faculty members for the periods 1984 to 1985 and 1988 to 1989. While they reported results only for aggregate fringe benefits, their research showed considerable price sensitivity: a 10 percent increase in the marginal tax rate resulted in a 17 percent increase in the ratio of benefits to total compensation. Thus, the literature suggests a wide range of estimates with respect to an employer's decision to offer health insurance coverage as a result of differences in individual tax rates, but relatively large (and varied) effects of tax law changes on fringe benefits generally and health insurance in particular.

Gruber and Lettau (2004) conducted the most extensive effort to estimate the effects of tax rates on the probability of a firm offering health insurance coverage and the expenditures on insurance offered. They used wage and nonwage compensation data from the 1983 through 1995 Bureau of Labor Statistics Employment Cost Index (ECI), augmented with data on individual workers from the U.S. Bureau of the Census Current Population Survey (CPS) and data on family taxes from the U.S. Department of the Treasury Statistics of Income (SOI). The ECI provided information on some

203,000 jobs in over 48,000 establishments. The compensation data were the average for all workers holding the sampled type of job. This average worker, of course, could be single or married, and file an itemized or non-itemized return. For each of these possibilities, Gruber and Lettau imputed the average spousal and unearned income based on the state in which the establishment was located, its industry, the occupation classification of the job, and the wage rate, using data from people with similar characteristics in the CPS and SOI. Given these characteristics and family incomes, they computed the relevant marginal tax rate for the household. Then, using the proportions married and itemizing deductions, married and not itemizing, and single itemizing and nonitemizing, they determined the marginal tax rate and the marginal "tax price" of health insurance for the average or median worker in each establishment (see Box 14-1). (We begin to appreciate the difficulties of empirical analysis on this topic!)

Gruber and Lettau found that a 10 percentage point increase in the tax price (meaning a cut in taxes) reduced the probability of a firm offering coverage by 3.6 percent. The annual spending on health insurance was estimated to be reduced by approximately 11 percent in a similar circumstance. The effect on offering coverage is in the lower range of the earlier estimates, and the effect on the amount of spending is in the middle to upper range of the estimates found in the literature.

The effect of tax laws was found to be much greater for smaller firms. The tax subsidy is more important to workers in smaller firms, presumably because many of them do not have a strong demand for health insurance coverage. (In Chapter 17, we discuss the small-group insurance market and make the case that those who value health insurance less intensely disproportionately end up working for firms that have higher relative costs of offering

---

Computing the "Tax Price"

The marginal tax price of health insurance is simply (1 – the marginal tax rate). Thus, back in Table 14-1, if the combined marginal tax rate for a single individual who did not itemize deductions was 32.65 percent, the tax price of employer-sponsored health insurance would be (1 – 0.3265) or 0.6635. Unlike our Table 14-1, however, Gruber and Lettau incorporated the state income tax rate and the "employer shares" of the Social Security and Medicare taxes and were much more sophisticated in their treatment of real-world tax deductions. The average tax price across all taxpayers in their study was 0.644. This also indicates that the average marginal tax rate was 35.6 percent.

coverage.) Thus, the tax subsidy may be an important factor in reducing the effective price of health insurance so that workers and their employers opt to obtain coverage and obtain more-generous coverage. (This tax subsidy, of course, is achieved by raising taxes on money wages.) Gruber and Lettau (2004) estimated that firms with fewer than 100 employees would increase their probability of offering coverage by 0.69 percent when the tax price was decreased by 1 percentage point. The elasticity with respect to the generosity of coverage was even greater: a 1 percent decrease in the tax price increased the annual spending on health insurance by 1.3 percent. The spending increase came about, for example, if employers and their employees chose to add dental coverage, lower copays on the drug plan, or implement a smaller deductible on the use of covered health services. There is little research on which coverages adjust. The theory presented in Chapter 3 suggests that coverage for smaller claims and for very low or very high probability events would be reduced. Gentry and Peress (1994) did find that dental and vision coverages were more responsive to tax rate differences.

Effects of Eliminating the Tax Subsidy for Employer-Sponsored Health Insurance

Health economists and some policy advocates regularly call for the elimination of the tax subsidy provided by the exclusion of health insurance compensation from the definition of taxable income. The argument is twofold. First, since the personal income tax is progressive, imposing larger tax rates on those with higher incomes, the tax subsidy is regressive. So, more-affluent groups benefit more than the less well off. Second, the subsidy distorts decision making, encouraging people with the subsidy to buy deeper and more-extensive insurance policies than they would if they faced the full price. This increased demand has the further implication that it raises the premium for health insurance coverage, thereby making it more difficult for lower-income persons to buy coverage.

Gruber and Lettau (2004) estimated the effect on coverage and health insurance spending through employers if the tax exclusion were eliminated. It is important to note at the outset that this simulation goes way beyond the range of Gruber and Lettau's data. It extrapolates the results for a relatively narrow range of tax rates to the extreme point where insurance would be taxed at the same rate as money income. Nonetheless, the estimates are interesting.

The foregoing estimates suggested that the total elimination of the tax subsidy in the federal and state income tax laws and in Social Security and Medicare would reduce the probability that a firm offered any coverage by 15.5 percent. The change in the annual cost of providing coverage, conditional on providing any, was 28.6 percent. Taking into account both the reduction in plan offerings and the reduction in spending, Gruber and Lettau estimated that spending on employer-sponsored health insurance would be reduced by 45 percent. (Some of this, of course, would be counterbalanced by increased purchase of individual coverage by some employees who dropped coverage.) This is obviously a huge amount, but it highlights the importance of tax policy in the U.S. private health insurance system.

Taxes and Employee Premium Contributions

Our discussion of taxes and health insurance may have raised at least two issues with thoughtful readers. Both are related to the tax treatment of employee premium contributions for health insurance obtained through an employer. The first is that many employers offer flexible spending accounts (FSAs). These plans cover the employee premium contribution, effectively making the employee's contribution pretax. What effect does this have on employer-sponsored health insurance? The second is that, in the absence of an FSA, the tax laws seem to imply that employee premium contributions should not exist; the entire premium should be paid "by the employer" with the employee's pretax earnings. Yet, employers do not seem to do this routinely.

We will discuss these issues in more detail in Chapter 15 on employers as agents for their employees, and in Chapter 16, when we discuss consumer-driven health plans. However, tax policy issues of relevance to both questions are briefly highlighted here.

Firms can set up FSAs for their employees under Section 125 of the tax code. Under these programs, an employer can determine the maximum amount an employee may contribute. These amounts, typically set between $5,000 and $10,000 of pretax income, go into a special account held by the employer. The employee can use these dollars for out-of-pocket medical care expenses, such as the price of an uninsured dental office visit, the copay on a physician visit, or new prescription contact lens. It is less well known that these plans also pay the employee premium contribution of an employer's health insurance plan. The employee does nothing to achieve this outcome. In essence, the employer passes the employee's premium contribution through the FSA, making it pretax, before paying for the insurance premium. (Note that what we are calling the pass-through does not reduce the amount the employee may have contributed to the account.)

The FSA extends the tax subsidy to this portion of the premium. Thus, if the employee is in the 32.65 percent marginal tax bracket, the spending account reduces the premium contribution by 32.65 percent. Paying the employee premium contribution through an FSA has the effect of reducing toward zero the price sensitivity of employees to premiums. Dowd and colleagues (2001) are the only ones who have examined this issue. Using a 1994 survey of large U.S. city and county governments, they found that elasticity of plan choice was reduced by about 56 percent. We saw in Chapter 11 that higher employee premium contributions led to switching of health plans and a movement toward the lower-priced plans. The Dowd et al. (2001) estimates suggest that these efforts are substantially undermined when an FSA is present.

The second issue is that, in the absence of FSAs, the tax treatment of employer-sponsored health insurance would seem to imply that there should be no employee premium contributions. The entire premium should be paid with pretax dollars, reducing employee wages and taking full advantage of the tax laws. This intuition is correct. Employers can lower their labor costs while leaving employees no worse off, or alternatively, workers can be made better off with no additional cost to the employer if the entire premium is paid on behalf of the employee with pretax dollars. Yet, most firms do impose premium contributions.

As we will see in Chapter 15, two factors drive the size of the employee premium contribution. One is the size of the tax subsidy for employer-sponsored health insurance. The other is the desire to sort workers into health plans that best reflect their tastes and preferences. As an example of the latter, a two-earner household may prefer to obtain family coverage from one employer, with the commensurate lower wages, and take higher wages and no insurance from the other employer. A higher employee premium contribution helps achieve this. Gruber and McKnight (2003) found that the size of the tax subsidy was an important determinant of whether the "employer paid" the entire health insurance premium. A 10 percent increase in the tax price (that is, a reduction in the tax rate) was associated with a 1.7 percent reduction in the probability that a firm would pay the entire premium. Thus, tax policy affects not only the probability of employers offering health insurance coverage, and the generosity of that coverage, but it also affects the split between the "employee contribution" and the "employer contribution" to the premium.

Chapter Summary

- Federal and state personal incomes taxes, together with Social Security and Medicare payroll taxes, are major factors underlying the employer provision of health insurance in the United States.
- Employer-sponsored health insurance is not subject to these taxes, and this exclusion provides an incentive for employers and their employees to shift compensation from taxed money wages to untaxed health insurance.
- Higher tax rates lower the "tax price" of health insurance and increase both the probability that a firm will offer coverage and the generosity of the coverage provided.

- A recent study found that a 10 percentage point decrease in the tax price (an increase in tax rates) would lead to a 3.6 percent increase in the probability that a firm would offer coverage and an 11 percent increase in insurance spending among firms offering coverage. Smaller firms were found to be the most responsive to tax law changes.
- Tax policy also affects the size of the employee premium contribution. When tax rates are higher, the size of the out-of-pocket premium will be smaller.
- Flexible spending accounts (FSAs), among other advantages, extend the pretax treatment of employer-sponsored health insurance to the employee premium contribution. The effect is to reduce employees' price sensitivity to different plans offered by employers.

Discussion Questions

1. The Social Security and Medicare programs are predicted to face financial crisis before 2020. One way of dealing with this problem would be to raise payroll taxes. What effects would this have on the market for employer-sponsored health insurance?
2. You are a consultant specializing in employee benefit programs. Suppose there is a relatively large and permanent reduction in the federal personal income tax rate. What sort of changes to their health insurance offerings would you encourage your clients to consider as a result of this congressional action?
3. Some policy advocates have called for the taxation of employer-sponsored health insurance as just another form of employee compensation. At least one study has suggested that expenditures on employer-sponsored health insurance would decrease by as much as 45 percent. Would you anticipate that spending on medical care would be reduced by 45 percent as well? Would you anticipate any change in medical care spending?

15

EMPLOYERS AS AGENTS

An agent is someone who acts on behalf of another. In health economics, we typically think of physicians as agents for their patients. As agents, physicians use their knowledge and expertise to diagnose, select, and apply treatment in a fashion that reflects the preferences and willingness to pay of their patients. Perfect agents do this without regard to their own preferences or financial incentives. As a matter of economics, however, as in real life, we expect agents to be imperfect.

Many employees buy health insurance through their employers. To what extent do employers serve as agents for their employees? That is, to what extent do employers use their knowledge and expertise to obtain insurance coverage that reflects their employees' preferences? In this chapter, we explore this issue. The chapter begins with some descriptive evidence on the extent to which employees approve of the quality of the plans their employers offer and employees' preferences for different mixes of wages and benefits.

We then introduce what is known as a labor market "sorting model," which suggests that the reason why employers offer very different health insurance plans is that workers have preferences for different forms and extents of coverage. We also look at the empirical evidence concerning the labor market's success in matching workers' preferences with employers' offerings.

The labor market today includes a majority of married couples in which both partners are employed outside the home. These two-earner households are likely to have many more wage-health insurance tradeoffs available to them. A new line of empirical research has examined the effects of two-earner households on insurance coverage obtained through an employer. The results suggest that, when making health insurance decisions, employees do consider the range of options available to them.

This presents a challenge to employer-agents. They must provide insurance coverage that meets a wide range of preferences, taking into consideration the incentives implicit in the tax laws, and still provide a compensation bundle that does not overpay or underpay employees. Employee premium contributions for health insurance play an important role in sorting employees into benefit plans that reflect their own preferences for coverage and the availability of substitute sources of coverage through spouses, parents, and government programs. Indeed, one explanation for the growth of employee premium contributions is that it is an accommodation to the prevalence of two-earner households and the wider range of insurance options available to them.

Finally, employees expect employer-agents to take health plan quality into consideration and to make information about health plan quality available when employees are choosing among offered plans. We explore the limited empirical evidence on the effects of health plan quality information on plan choice by employers and employees.

Employee Perceptions of Employer Plans

As discussed in Chapter 13, a necessary condition for employers to offer health insurance is that the workers value the coverage. This suggests that worker preferences should be an important factor in whether or not an employer offers coverage and in the nature of that coverage. Health benefits consultants often report results of employee surveys that show health insurance to be the most valued fringe benefit. Such surveys, however, seldom directly address the issue of whether the health plans offered are the ones that the workers themselves would have chosen. Two relatively recent surveys, however, offer some insight into the nature of health insurance coverage based on questions of plan quality and tradeoffs workers themselves would make.

A survey commissioned by the Commonwealth Fund (2001) found that nearly three-quarters of employees with employer-sponsored health insurance thought their employers did a "good job" of selecting quality health plans, while 10 percent said employers did a "mixed job," and 13 percent said employers did a "bad job."

The Employee Benefits Research Institute (Fronstin 1999) conducted a national survey of 1,004 employees with employer-sponsored coverage and asked them how satisfied they were with the wage-health benefits tradeoff their employers offered. The results are summarized in Figure 15-1. Slightly more than two-thirds of employees were satisfied with their existing tradeoff. However, one in five would have preferred more health insurance and lower wages, while 8 percent would have preferred lower benefits and higher wages. The labor market appears to do a remarkably good job of matching preferences, but the outcome is far from perfect.

Labor Market Sorting

Goldstein and Pauly (1976) developed the basic model of worker sorting in the employer-sponsored health insurance market. The idea is pretty simple. Suppose workers are perfectly interchangeable but have different preferences for health insurance. Then, in a frictionless labor market, we would expect employers to offer only one health insurance plan, if any. Workers would

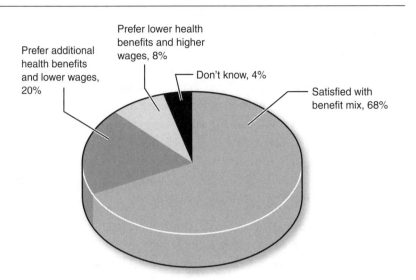

Prefer lower health benefits and higher wages, 8%

Prefer additional health benefits and lower wages, 20%

Don't know, 4%

Satisfied with benefit mix, 68%

FIGURE 15-1

Satisfaction with Current Wage-Benefit Composition, 1999

SOURCE: Fronstin (1999), "Employment-Based Health Insurance: A Look at Tax Issues and Public Opinion," *EBRI* Brief no. 211: Chart 3. Reprinted with permission.

choose to work for the firm with the wage-insurance package tradeoff that best fits their preferences. The sorting is complete.

This simple model yields some useful implications. It suggests, for example, that if employers have different costs of providing health insurance, then those employers with the highest costs will be the ones not offering a health insurance plan. They will also be the employers that attract workers who do not value coverage. The model also suggests that employers offering a wage-insurance tradeoff that is inferior to that offered by others will not attract any workers.

The labor market is much more complex, of course. Workers do not have homogeneous skills, and the production processes of firms may require workers with many different skills and preferences for insurance. This suggests that the diversity of preferences among workers will lead employers to offer multiple plans. The number of plans offered will depend on the diversity of worker preferences and the costs of offering additional plans. These costs include the objective risk associated with offering plans to small numbers of workers if these workers cannot be effectively pooled with others. (Recall the discussion of objective risk in Chapter 5)

There are frictions in the labor market. Workers and employers face significant search costs in findings jobs and employees that match skills and wage-insurance tradeoffs. Given the costs of search, we should expect that some, perhaps many, workers are not in jobs that ideally match their preferences for the wage-insurance tradeoff. In the end, given the costs of search, we expect workers to choose the employer with the wage-insurance tradeoff that yields the greatest utility.

Monheit and Vistnes (1999) directly tested the idea that the labor market sorts workers and employers based on worker preferences for insurance coverage. They used the 1987 National Medical Care Expenditure Survey, a nationally representative survey of some 36,000 individuals. They limited their analysis to single individuals to avoid the complications of coverage available through a spouse and joint decision making by couples about jobs and coverages. A unique feature of this survey was a set of questions asking about preferences for health insurance. Specifically, the survey asked the extent to which the respondent agreed that:

1. "I'm healthy enough that I really don't need health insurance."
2. "Health insurance is not worth the money it costs."
3. "I'm more likely to take risks than the average person."

Table 15-1 reports the proportion of employed people with insurance coverage offered by their employers who agreed and disagreed with the previous three statements. Overall 77.2 percent of single workers had employer-sponsored coverage offered to them. Those who agreed that they did not really need health insurance were 6.3 percentage points less likely to have been offered coverage than were those who disagreed. Those who agreed that health insurance was not worth the cost were 9.7 percentage points less likely to be offered coverage than were those who disagreed. By comparison, there was no statistically significant difference in coverage offering among those who agreed or disagreed that they were more likely to take risks than the average person. These results suggest that worker preferences may indeed play a part in job and coverage decisions.

Monheit and Vistnes then estimated a regression model in which having a job with insurance *offered* was a function of the wage difference between jobs with and without coverage, expected out-of-pocket medical expenses, the costs of search, and the insurance preference measures. They concluded that those who had strong preferences for coverage were 14 percentage points more likely to have a job offering coverage than were those with weak preferences for insurance, other things equal. (Those with strong preferences for insurance agreed with both statements 1 and 2 presented earlier; those with weak preferences disagreed with both of the statements.) By comparison, the usual employment and demographic characteristics yielded a 17 percentage point increase in the probability of having a job offering coverage. This suggests that worker preferences are as important as other characteristics in explaining why some workers do not have jobs offering health insurance coverage.

There has been an effort to explore the effect of worker heterogeneity on the number of health plans and the number of health plan types that

	Percentage of Single Workers with Jobs Offering Health Insurance
All single workers	77.2%
Worker Preferences:	
Don't Really Need Health Insurance	
Agree	71.8%
Disagree	78.1%*
Health Insurance Is Not Worth the Cost	
Agree	69.3%
Disagree	79.0% †
More Likely to Take Risks	
Agree	76.4%
Disagree	77.5%

TABLE 15-1
Worker Preferences and Employer-Sponsored Health Insurance

SOURCE: Data from Monheit and Vistnes (1999).

*, † Difference between agree and disagree significant at the 95 and 99 percent confidence levels, respectively.

employers offer. Moran, Chernew and Hirth (2001) used 1993 to 1994 survey data on employers to estimate the extent to which the *variance* in worker characteristics in a firm explained the breadth of plan offerings. Thus, they were interested in whether a wider range of ages and incomes in a firm affected the number and types of plans offered. They found that the more diverse the workforce with respect to age, income, and gender, the more likely the employer was to offer more plans and more plan types. The effects were relatively small, however. An increase of two standard deviations in age diversity (a very large increase) was associated with an 8.6 percent increase in the probability of offering more than one plan and a 12 percent increase in the probability of offering more than one plan type.

Two-Earner Households

Only 24 percent of married women participated in the labor market in 1950. By 2000, approximately 65 percent of married couples under age 65 had both partners in the labor force (Abraham and Royalty 2005). Two-earner households present new opportunities for health insurance coverage and new challenges for employers sponsoring coverage. In a two-earner household, the family may be able to choose coverage from one or both employers. Spouses could each have individual coverage. They could obtain family coverage from one or both places of employment. They could take coverage through one spouse and higher income and no coverage through the other. Or, of course, they could go without health insurance altogether. From the employer's perspective, some employees in two-earner households may not want coverage at all, preferring higher wages, while others in such households may want generous family coverage and lower wages. The range of preferences is likely to be considerable broader than it was when households typically had only one income earner.

Abraham and Royalty (2005) provided the most comprehensive overview of the effects of two-earner households on employer-sponsored health insurance coverage. Using the 1997 Medical Expenditure Panel Survey (MEPS), they found that, controlling for other factors, having two earners in a household increased the probabilities that a worker would have coverage and that the entire family would have coverage by between 10 and 20 percentage points, depending on whether they controlled for household income.[1] In addition, workers in these families, on average, had nearly 1.3 more plans from which to choose and were 22 percentage points more likely to have a plan with freedom in the choice of provider.

Abraham and Royalty (2005) also examined the effect of two-earner households on the probability that part-time and self-employed workers and workers in small firms had employer-sponsored-insurance coverage. Of course, these coverages may come from the worker's own employer or through the spouse's employer. The results are summarized in Table 15-2. Part-time employees are much less likely to be offered employer-sponsored coverage. Abraham and Royalty estimated that, other things equal in the MEPS data, part-time workers were nearly 47 percentage points less likely to have employer-sponsored coverage than were full time workers. However, 77 percent of this difference was offset if there were two earners in the household. Thirty-six percent of the lower probability of being without employer-sponsored coverage as a self-employed individual was offset by being in a two-earner household, and over half of the lower probability of not having employer-sponsored coverage for those employed in small establishments was offset by being part of a two-earner household.

---

1. A two-earner household may have higher income relative to a single-earner household, and this greater income may directly result in a higher probability of having coverage. Thus, Abraham and Royalty (2005) present alternative estimates that do and do not control for household income.

	Without Controlling for Income		Controlling with Income	
	Marginal Effect	Percentage Offset	Marginal Effect	Percentage Offset
Part-time—One-earner household	–.466*		–.392*	
Part-time—Two-earner household	+.361*	77%	+.310*	79%
Self-employed—One-earner household	–.460*		–520*	
Self-employed—Two-earner household	+.168*	36%	+.188*	36%
Small establishment—One-earner household	–.286*		–.254*	
Small establishment—Two-earner household	+.165*	58%	+.124*	49%

TABLE 15-2
One- and Two-Earner Household Effects on the Probability of Vulnerable Workers Having Employer-Sponsored Health Insurance Coverage

SOURCE: Data from Abraham and Royalty (2005)

*Coefficient is statistically significant at the 99 percent confidence level.

> *Overall, we find that the average effect of having two earners leads to a dramatic improvement both with respect to access and choice set generosity. . . . [H]ouseholds with vulnerable workers, including part-time, self-employed, and workers in small firms, tend to fare worse on all dimensions, but that having a second earner serves to mitigate a significant proportion of the negative effects.*
>
> *—Abraham and Royalty (2005, p.182)*

Abraham and Royalty did not examine how these results came about. It is fairly obvious that part-time workers obtained coverage through the employer-sponsored family coverage of their spouse. What is less clear is whether they have coverage because of their spouse's plan or whether they were able to take the part-time job (or be self-employed, or work for a small firm that did not offer coverage) because the spouse already had a job offering coverage. In a world of compensating wage differentials, either scenario would imply that one spouse took lower wages and health insurance, while the other took higher wages and no coverage.

Employee Premium Contributions

Recall from earlier in the chapter the simple Goldstein and Pauly (1976) model of employer-sponsored health insurance. In that model, workers sorted themselves across firms based on their preferences for health insurance and the wage-insurance tradeoff that employers offered. There was no employee premium contribution; the employer simply paid for whatever health insurance was offered and reduced wages to reflect the premium. Arguably, the reason for this is that, once workers have sorted themselves out across firms, each firm's workforce had homogeneous preferences for the exact coverage the firm offered. The compensating wage adjustment was trivial; it was simply the amount of the health insurance premium and applied to everyone.

As we have seen, in the real world, preferences differ, and firms employ workers with differing alternative sources of insurance coverage. One way to deal with this would be to have precise compensating wage differentials tailored to the preferences of each worker. Those workers who want an expensive, traditional, fee-for-service plan with a wide choice of providers, low deductibles, and low copays would receive lower wages that reflected that choice. Others who prefer a narrow-panel health maintenance organization (HMO) would have fewer dollars deducted from their wages to reflect their less-expensive choice. Those who have excellent coverage through their spouse would forgo coverage from their own employer and would have no premium deducted from their pay. A straightforward way to deal with this would be for employers to post the full premiums for each plan offered. Employees could then choose which plan they wanted, and employers would deduct the premium before giving employees their pay.

This is actually the world we might see if it were not for the current federal and state income tax laws that tax money compensation but not compensation in the form of health insurance. As we saw in Chapter 14, these laws provide incentives to pay for the insurance with pretax dollars. The incentives that arise from preference diversity on the part of employees are in conflict with the incentives inherent in the tax laws. We would expect that when employees have common preferences for coverage, there would be no employee premium contribution. This would allow the firm and its employees to take full advantage of the special tax treatment of health insurance. On the other hand, when workers have very different preferences for health insurance, we would expect to see employee premium contributions that take some advantage of the tax laws while still allowing for the differing preferences of the workforce. The firm might use compensating wage differentials to pay the value of the lower-cost plans and employee premium contributions for the extra cost of the higher-cost plans.

Employee premium contributions are a way of sorting employees into the plans that they prefer, given their circumstances, and still accomplishing the compensating wage differential. For example, suppose a firm employs a number of workers, many of whom are married and some of whom are in two-earner households. Some employees, both single and married, want family coverage. Some, both single and married, want single coverage. Some want no coverage at all from this employer. The firm may require a relatively small premium contribution for single coverage and a much larger contribution for family coverage. The "employer's share" of the cost of single coverage may be paid through a reduction in wages for all employees (the compensating wage differential). Those employees wanting family coverage pay a larger premium contribution. Those who have access to less-expensive family coverage through a spouse's health insurance plan decline all of these offers and take home somewhat higher wages, reflecting the premium contributions they did not make.[2]

We have characterized the use of employee premium contributions as an effort to pay higher wages to employees who have other, better, health insurance options and who therefore do not value coverage from their employer. Dranove, Spier, and Baker (2000) characterize it instead as essentially a bribe by employers to encourage their employees to obtain coverage through their spouse if they can. Both approaches argue that the employee premium contribution will increase with more options available to two-earner families. As yet, no empirical work can differentiate between the two characterizations.

Empirically, Dranove, Spier, and Baker used data from the 1993 to 1994 Robert Wood Johnson Employer Health Insurance Survey. They found that firms with more female employees and with more part-time workers had higher employee premium contributions. They viewed these as measures of workers more likely to have other sources of insurance coverage.

Vistnes, Morrisey, and Jensen (2006) used over 84,000 establishments from the 1997 to 2001 Medical Expenditure Panel Survey to directly test the effects of two-earner households on the size of the marginal employee premium contribution (EPC) for family coverage. That is, the EPC is the difference between the family and single premium contributions. Vistnes,

---

2. Typically, the employee premium contribution is set at much less than the cost of single coverage. Part of this reflects the tax exclusion of employer-sponsored health insurance, but part of it also may reflect the value of having insurance options available in the next open enrollment period. However, to the extent that the firm is unable to find a way to adequately compensate employees who do not want coverage, we would expect to see more instances among two-earner households in which one spouse works in a firm that does not offer health insurance at all. This is consistent with our earlier discussion of the Monheit and Vistnes (1999) study.

Morrisey, and Jensen argued that, when there is a larger proportion of two-earner households in the employer's labor pool, the marginal EPC will be larger. In addition, if women or younger workers are disproportionately second-earners in the family, they may not value family health insurance as highly as the primary earner. If so, they would presumably prefer wages to insurance coverage. A higher EPC accomplishes this. Vistnes, Morrisey, and Jensen estimated a series of fixed-effects regression equations in which the EPC was a function of worker heterogeneity, local labor market conditions, the cost of health insurance, the generosity of public insurance programs, and tax laws.

The key result is summarized in Figure 15-2. The marginal employee premium contribution (EPC) for family coverage increased with the proportion of women employed by the firm, but only in communities in which there was a substantial concentration of two-earner households. In these data, the average firm was in a market in which approximately 30 percent of workers were in two-earner households. This is the middle line in Figure 15-2. The marginal EPC also rose substantially with the share of female workers when 50 percent of the employers' labor pool was in two-earner households. This is the upper line in Figure 15-2. However, when only 10 percent of the employment pool was in a two-earner household, the marginal EPC did not rise with the percentage of women; in fact, it declined slightly. This is the bottom line in Figure 15-2. This suggests that it is not the proportion of women per se that leads to higher out-of-pocket premiums, but the larger share of women who are likely to be in two-earner households. Analogously, Vistnes, Morrisey, and Jensen found that when there was a high proportion of two-earner households in the market, the marginal EPC increased with the proportion of younger workers.

Gruber and McKnight (2003) provided a more-general empirical analysis of employee premium contributions. Using 1982 to 1996 Current Population Survey data, they found that employee premium contributions rose with insurance premiums, reflecting the increased value of worker sorting when insurance is more expensive. They also found that the EPC was higher when the local Medicaid program was more generous in its eligibility. Over the 1980s, the Medicaid program was expanded to allow children in households with higher incomes to participate. We would expect that, as Medicaid became more generous, rational parents would enroll their eligible children in the program and take home higher money wages by dropping family coverage. The Gruber and McKnight (2003) study found this to be the case. Finally, as we saw in Chapter 14, Gruber and McKnight also found that the size of the employee premium contribution increased when tax rates fell.

Buchmueller et al. (2005) examined the effects of the more-recent State Children's Health Insurance Program (SCHIP) on the size of the employee premium contributions set by employers. The SCHIP program

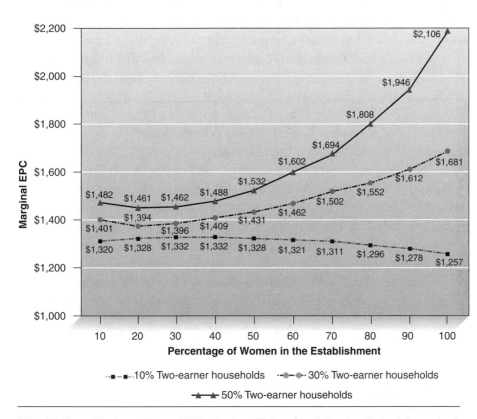

FIGURE 15-2

Predicted Annual Marginal Employee Premium Contribution (EPC) by Percentage of Women in the Establishment for Selected Percentages of Two-Earner Households in the Market

SOURCE: Vistnes, Morrisey, and Jensen (2006), "Employer Choices of Family Premium Sharing," *International Journal of Health Care Finance & Economics* 61(2): 25–47, Figure 4. Reprinted with kind permission from Springer Science and Business Media.

extends eligibility for public health insurance to children in "working poor" families. Prior to its introduction in 1997, the family income level making a 15-year-old child eligible for public insurance ranged from 10 percent to 225 percent of the federal poverty line. By 2000, the range was from 100 to 400 percent of the poverty level. These typically large expansions in eligibility across states might be expected to affect employer-sponsored coverage. Under the worker sorting theory, we would expect that at least some newly eligible families would want to shift the children to the SCHIP program, reduce their spending on employer-sponsored family health insurance coverage, and take home more of their compensation in the form of money income. This would be accomplished by raising the marginal employee premium contribution for family coverage. The alternative characterization (Dranove, Spier, and Baker 2000) is that employers raise the employee premium contribution to encourage eligible families to enroll their children in SCHIP rather than in one of the employer's plans.

Like the Vistnes, Morrisey, and Jensen (2006) study, the Buchmueller et al. (2005) study also used the 1997 to 2001 MEPS data. It found that the effects on the size of the employee premium contribution depended on the extent to which the potential labor pool was eligible for SCHIP coverage. Specifically, they found that a hypothetical firm with 20 percent of its potential workforce eligible for SCHIP coverage would raise the marginal out-of-pocket cost of family coverage by $119 (2001 dollars) over the period, controlling for other factors. When 50 percent of the potential workforce was eligible for SCHIP, there was an associated increase in the marginal family employee premium contribution of $351 per year. There was no effect on the premium contribution for single coverage.

Buchmueller and colleagues also found that when 20 percent of the potential workforce was eligible for SCHIP, the proportion of workers with family coverage declined by 1.4 percentage points. When 50 percent was eligible for SCHIP, family enrollment declined by 4.6 percentage points. This sort of response to expansions in public coverage has come to be called "crowd-out." We examine the evidence in more detail when we discuss Medicaid and the SCHIP programs in Chapter 23. Here, it is enough to see that employers, as agents, adjust the out-of-pocket premium contributions to reflect the public (as well as private) insurance options likely to be available to their employees.

Information on Plan Quality

As agents, employers are expected to identify plans with quality levels demanded by their employees and to either use this information in selecting plans offered or provide the quality information to their employees to assist them in selecting among the plans offered.

Since the early 1990s, the Health Plan Employer Data and Information Set (HEDIS) has been available to provide information to employers on the quality of managed care plans and to assist plans with quality improvement (National Committee for Quality Assurance 1993). The data collection effort was undertaken by a group of large employers and HMOs, and the measures of quality include patient satisfaction as well as measures of surgical care (such as the number of cesarean sections and cardiac catheterizations per 1,000 members), preventive care (such as the immunization and mammography screening rates), and physician quality measures (such as the proportion of physicians who are board certified). The elements and their measures go through periodic updates. However, it is not clear how many employers use the measures when selecting plans.

Some employers provide HEDIS data or other summaries of plan quality to their employees during the open-enrollment periods, and a handful of studies have tried to gauge how effective the efforts have been in influencing plan choice. Chernew and Scanlon (1998) examined the effect of providing HEDIS data on the choice of plans to workers in one large Fortune-100 firm during the open-enrollment period in the autumn of 1994. They limited their analysis to managed care plans because HEDIS scores are not available for fee-for-service plans. They also limited the analysis to active worker, nonunion, single employees to avoid retiree, labor-contract issues and complexities arising from plan choice available through spouses. Nonetheless, they analyzed the choices of over 12,500 employees. In each of five dimensions of HEDIS scores, they ranked plans as being in the top 25 percent of the plans in the region. They then regressed plan characteristics, including whether or not there was a "superior" ranking in each of the five quality dimensions on the enrollment share of each plan in each of the firm's locations.

Their results were instructive. First, there was little correlation between superior rankings across dimensions. Being superior in one dimension did not imply that the plan was superior in others. In fact, the measure of physician quality was slightly negatively correlated with patient satisfaction. Second, only one of the superior ratings had a positive, statistically significant effect on enrollment. Plans rated superior in the prevention dimension had larger enrollment shares. Finally, one quality measure that was statistically significant was of the wrong sign. "Superior" patient satisfaction was associated with smaller enrollment shares. Chernew and Scanlon (1998) suggested that this may have been an artifact of how satisfaction was measured in HEDIS. It included measures of waiting time for various types of appointments. Short waiting times were indicative of superior quality. However, Chernew and Scanlon quipped that it may be that patients view short waiting times the same way they view an empty restaurant—as not a good sign! The issues with providing quality measures involve constructing measures that users understand and find relevant. More recently, Beaulieu (2002) and Scanlon et al. (2002) found modest effects of providing health plan quality information on plan switching.

The most encouraging findings to date are those of Wedig and Tai-Seale (2002). They investigated the effects of the federal government's efforts to provide health plan quality information to their own employees in the Federal Employees Health Benefit Program (FEHBP). In 1994 and 1995, federal employees were surveyed about their experiences with their health plan. They were asked about overall satisfaction, access to medical care, overall quality of care, doctors available through the plan, coverage and information provided by the plan, customer service, and simplicity of paperwork. The results were tabulated and shared with current and new employees during the open-enrollment periods in 1995 and 1996. Unfortunately (for the government), the 1995 survey results only reached 25 percent of the employees. All received them in 1996. Wedig and Tai-Seale used the difference in the estimates across the two years as their measure of the effects of the dissemination of plan quality information.

Several findings are worthy of note. First, unlike Chernew and Scanlon (1998), Wedig and Tai-Seale found that the FEHBP measures of quality were highly correlated—so much so that they were able to use only two measures: (1) overall plan quality and (2) coverage and information provided. If confirmed in other studies, this would suggest that a small set of measures, rather than a large, complicated set, could be useful for consumers. Second, Wedig and Tai-Seale found that the dissemination of plan information did influence choice. A one standard deviation increase in the report-card measure of overall quality of care increased the likelihood of plan selection by more than 50 percent. It is always hard to interpret effects described in this way, but at the mean, a one standard deviation improvement in reported overall quality was an increase of 5.7 percent on a mean value of 87.45. This suggests that the estimated impact was indeed rather large. Moreover, as we might expect, the results were larger for new hires, who probably knew less about the plans offered than did existing employees. Third, the measure of plan coverage also affected plan choice, but only for existing workers, not for new hires. The authors suggested that this may have resulted from the existing workers being, on average, 10 years older and likely to have somewhat poorer health status, making coverage issues more relevant. Finally, Wedig and Tai-Seale found that the dissemination of quality information increased the price sensitivity of plan choice. This is what we would expect. In the absence of information on quality, price may serve as a proxy measure of quality. A higher price leads workers to buy less because of the true price effect, but if quality is also higher for more-expensive services, the incentive to switch plans is likely to be mitigated. When quality is better known (and controlled for in the analysis), we should get an estimate closer to the true price effect.

Chapter Summary

- Employers serve as economic agents for their employees, purchasing health insurance that employees themselves would purchase if they had the same knowledge and purchasing power. In general, a large majority of people with employer-sponsored health insurance report being satisfied with their coverage.
- Labor markets attempt to sort workers into firms such that workers obtain the wage-insurance tradeoff they prefer. The sorting is less than complete because worker preferences differ, search is costly, and there are economies in pooling similar risks.
- Many employers offer more than one health insurance option to appeal to the preferences of their employees. Unless compensating differentials

function at the individual level, employee premium contributions serve as a mechanism to sort employees into plans they prefer.

- Employee premium contributions will be larger when preferences differ substantially. One key reason for differences in employee preferences is the availability of alternative sources of coverage through a spouse or through a government program. Evidence indicates that premium contributions are larger when there are more two-earner households in the labor force and when the labor force had greater access to expanded public insurance programs.

- As economic agents, some employers have collected and disseminated information on health plan quality. While early evidence was not very encouraging, more-recent work suggests that information on plan quality can affect employee decision making and make employees more price sensitive as well.

Discussion Questions

1. What would be the consequences of a firm offering a health insurance plan that its employees did not desire?
2. Suppose Congress expanded veterans' benefits to provide medical care for all people who had served in the military to the level currently provided to those with service-connected disabilities. What effect would this have on the size of the employee premium contributions set by employers?
3. In Chapter 14 (and also in Chapter 16), we discuss flexible spending accounts (FSAs), which allow employee premium contributions to be paid with pretax dollars. What effect would a newly introduced flexible spending account have on the size of employee premium contributions in a firm?
4. Why would access to easily understood and credible information on the quality of health plans increase the price sensitivity of health insurance for employees?

SPECIAL TOPICS IN HEALTH INSURANCE

HEALTH SAVINGS ACCOUNTS AND CONSUMER-DRIVEN HEALTH PLANS

This chapter describes new initiatives in health insurance. These are predominately health savings accounts (HSAs) and consumer-driven health plans (CDHPs), which typically wrap around an HSA. These models combine a high-deductible health insurance plan with a tax-sheltered savings account. The rationale behind these plans is that consumers are responsible for much of the price of initial medical care expenditures. As a result, they have incentives to shop more carefully for health services, both in terms of finding providers who offer the preferred set of services and in terms of negotiating with providers for lower prices. At the same time, the high-deductible insurance provides protection against catastrophic medical events. The key premise underlying CDHPs and HSAs is that individual consumers will become prudent shoppers for healthcare, weighing the value of an interaction with the healthcare system with the price of that interaction.

There is little hard research on these new insurance vehicles, but there has been work done on their forerunners: medical savings accounts (MSAs). In this chapter, we describe the features of the new insurance plans and then review the existing research. We also review the evidence on the extent to which consumers actually shop for health services.

Health Savings Accounts

Congress created health savings accounts (HSAs) as part of the Medicare reform package that established the Medicare prescription drug program in December 2003. An HSA is essentially a tax-sheltered financial account into which individuals or their employers may contribute funds and from which individuals may withdraw money to pay for qualified health services. As such, HSAs have features common with flexible spending accounts (FSAs) and medical savings accounts (MSAs), each of which we describe shortly.

To be eligible to own an HSA, an individual or family must have a "qualified" high-deductible health insurance plan. The deductible must be at least $1,050 for an individual and $2,100 for a family in 2006. The insurance plan may have copays or coinsurance features in addition to the deductible, but under the legislation, the maximum out-of-pocket expenditure for

BOX 16-1

HSA Limits Eased after 2006

In December 2006, Congress amended the HSA laws to allow annual contributions up to the size of the health plan deductible and permitted one-time-only rollovers of unused FSA balances and one-time transfers from individual retirement accounts (IRAs), up to the maximum annual contribution.

covered services by an individual in any one year is $5,250 and $10,500 for a family. The minimum deductibles and the maximum out-of-pocket limits are adjusted for inflation each year by the U.S. Department of the Treasury. While the deductible must apply to all covered health services, there is an exception for preventive services; the health plan may cover these on a first-dollar basis.

The contributions that individuals make to an HSA are limited to 100 percent of the deductible in the health plan they have to a maximum of $2,700 for an individual and $5,450 for a family (in 2006). Thus, if you had an eligible high-deductible plan with a $2,000 deductible, you could put up to $2,000 in an HSA that year (see Box 16-1). HSA contributions can be made by individuals, employers, or both.

The contributions are not subject to federal income tax or to the Social Security and Medicare payroll taxes, even if you do not itemize deductions. Moreover, the distributions from the HSA are not taxable if they are used for qualified medical expenses. Qualified medical expenses are broadly defined but ordinarily do not include the premiums for health insurance plans (including dental and vision plans). HSA distributions can be used, however, to pay insurance premiums for COBRA coverage (see Chapter 18) or for coverage while receiving unemployment compensation. The rationale for excluding insurance premiums is straightforward. The objective of HSAs is to give consumers incentives to be prudent purchasers. If people could pay their health insurance premiums with HSA distributions, they might be inclined to buy first-dollar coverage and undermine the incentives to shop wisely for services. There is an exception for preventive services.

A key feature of HSAs is that any unused portion of the account can be carried forward without penalty to be used for qualified expenses in later years. Thus, there is no "use it or lose it" provision that gives people incentives to buy health services and supplies late in the year to avoid losing any remaining dollars in their spending account.

Moreover, individuals own their HSA and can transfer it from one employer to another when they change jobs. Subscribers can invest HSA

BOX 16-2

For More Information on HSAs

For a readable summary of HSA provisions, see *All about HSAs,* published by the U.S. Department of the Treasury in December 2005 and available at: http://www.treasury.gov/offices/public-affairs/hsa/pdf/hsa-basics.pdf.

funds in a wide variety of ways: money market funds, mutual funds, certificates of deposit, etc. The earnings accrue tax free. If they have an HSA through an employer, the employer may limit the investment opportunities. Even so, any balance in the account moves with employees at the end of employment. However, if subscribers withdraw money from an HSA to use on nonqualified expenditures, the withdrawal is subject to the appropriate marginal tax rate plus a 10 percent penalty. At age 65, however, individuals can make nonqualifying withdrawals and only pay the appropriate tax rate with no additional penalty (see Box 16-2).

Medical Savings Accounts

Medical savings accounts (MSAs) were introduced into the tax code as a demonstration program in 1996. Their features are similar to HSAs, but the various cutoffs and limits occur at different values. The key distinction, however, is that MSAs are only available to individuals and to employees of firms with fewer than 50 workers. Moreover, enrollment was limited to 750,000 nationwide, and the original legislation had provisions that would have terminated the program in 2000.

MSAs have had limited appeal. Indeed, a survey of small businesses conducted in 2003 found that only 5 percent of small employers offered an MSA to their employees (Morrisey 2003). Advocates would say this is because of both the limitations on eligibility and the sunset provision that was to end the program in 2000. MSAs are likely to disappear with the introduction of the more-generous features of the HSAs.

Flexible Spending Accounts

Flexible spending accounts (FSAs) are only tangentially related to the HSAs and MSAs. There is no requirement that a high-deductible health plan be offered; indeed, an employer need not offer any health insurance plan to still offer an FSA. However, FSAs are only available through an employer. An FSA is a tax-sheltered account held by an employer. Employees may contribute any amount up to the maximum established by the employer to such an account, and the money may be used for any qualified health service. However, unlike HSAs or MSAs, if the money in the account is not expended in 12 (or 15) months, the money is no longer available to the employee. "Use it or lose it" applies.

As we discussed in Chapter 15, employers may pass the employee premium contribution for employer-sponsored coverage through an FSA, effectively making those contributions tax sheltered. Employers also can establish what is sometimes called a "premium-only plan." This sort of FSA only covers the employee premium contribution, and employees are not allowed to make contributions that would be used for uncovered medical expenses.

Consumer-Driven Health Plans

A consumer-driven health plan (CDHP) is the current term used to describe a health plan that has a high deductible and an HSA. The plan may have a preventive services component, information on appropriate use of health services, and a network of preferred providers.

Figure 16-1 provides a simplified numeric example. The CDHP shown in the figure includes a health insurance plan with a high individual

FIGURE 16-1
Consumer-Driven Health Plan

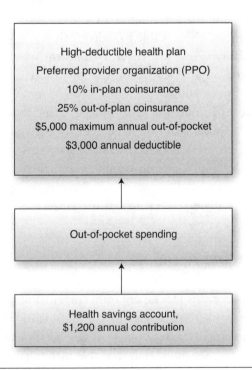

deductible of $3,000. Once that annual deductible is reached, the health plan's preferred provider organization (PPO) will begin paying for any covered health services. If subscribers use a provider who is a member of the PPO's panel of providers, there is 10 percent coinsurance; that is, subscribers pay 10 percent of any bill. If subscribers receive care from a nonpanel provider, they must pay 25 percent of the bill. The health plan also includes a $5,000 maximum out-of-pocket limit. This means that once subscribers have incurred annual out-of-pocket expenses of $5,000, through a combination of the deductible and coinsurance payments, they no longer have to pay anything out-of-pocket for covered services. Most individuals will not reach the annual $3,000 deductible, and as a result, will pay for all of their health services out-of-pocket. However, some will have substantial medical expenditures. They will satisfy the deductible and will have coverage for their catastrophic health problem.

The CDHP also has an HSA. In this case, individuals and their employers each contribute $600, or $50 per month, to the HSA. (Under the HSA rules, the employer, the employee, or both can contribute to an HSA. Recall, too, that in reasonably well functioning labor markets, it does not matter who contributes; the contributions will come ultimately from the worker's productivity.) HSA contributions are not taxed at the federal level.

Now consider Year 1 healthcare expenditures. Suppose a subscriber visits an internist (at a price of $75), has a PSA test ($50), visits a specialist ($150), and has $100 in prescription drugs, thereby incurring health spending of $375. These bills are paid out of the HSA, leaving a balance of $825.

Now consider Year 2 healthcare expenditures. Another $1,200 is contributed to the HSA, and $825 is carried forward from Year 1. In addition, the fund also has any earnings that accrued on the HSA balances. To keep the math simple, we assume that the balances earned $25 after operational fees were deducted. Thus, in Year 2, the subscriber has $2,050 available in the HSA. Suppose this year he falls from the roof of his house, has an ambulance fee of $350, is hospitalized with a bill of $3,150, has physician bills of $1,200, and uses prescription drugs (painkillers among others) costing $500. Total expenses are $5,200.

In this situation, the subscriber pays $3,000, satisfying the deductible. Of this $3,000, $2,050 comes from his HSA, and the remaining $950 is out-of-pocket. The subscriber's health insurance plan pays 90 percent of the remaining $2,200 in medical bills ($5,200 − $3,000) because all of the medical services were in-plan use. So, the subscriber pays an additional $220 out-of-pocket. Thus, of the $5,200 total expenses, the subscriber's PPO pays $1,980, $2,050 is paid out of the subscriber's HSA, and the subscriber pays $1,170 out-of-pocket. In Year 3, $1,200 is again deposited into the subscriber's HSA.

The Year 2 just described was an unusual year. An alternative Year 2 could have resulted in no medical expenses at all. In that case, the subscriber's HSA balance would have continued to accrue earnings, and the entire amount would roll over to the next year. In this scenario, Year 3 would have a new contribution of $1,200 plus the $2,050 in the HSA from the prior year, plus the new earnings of, say, $100, for a total available of $3,350. Once the balance in the HSA reaches $5,000, the subscriber does not have any out-of-pocket expenses. And the HSA can continue to grow, subject only to the annual contributions, earnings on the balance, and of course, any medical-related withdrawals.

Finally, proponents of CDHPs argue that the plans will provide information to help consumers made informed decisions about routine care. They assert that fully implemented plans will have contracts with centers of excellence for tertiary care and incentives for high-quality efficient care for chronic care and more-expensive acute-care services.

There are several issues to consider with respect to CDHPs. Among them are the following:

- The HSA can be considered a tax-sheltered investment tool. It has the advantage that both dollars contributed *and* those withdrawn for allowed purposes are free of federal taxation. Indeed, on reaching age 65, the funds can be withdrawn for nonhealth uses and be subject only to ordinary income tax rates. (Savvy investors might stack a CDHP on top of an FSA, using the FSA for routine health services expenses and using the HSA for investment and true catastrophic medical events.)
- The CDHP is supposed to encourage consumers to shop among providers for greater value and to forgo those health services that do not appear to be worth the full cost. To what extent do CDHPs reduce healthcare spending? Are consumers able to shop among providers for value? To what extent do consumers forgo truly beneficial health services to preserve their HSA investment?
- The insurance firm potentially has much greater ability to negotiate prices than does an individual consumer. To what extent do the prices subscribers pay reflect the prices the managed care plan/insurer has negotiated with providers versus the list prices of those providers?

There are no complete answers to these questions, but research conducted on MSAs does provide some insight into the effects of HSAs. In addition, research studies that are now somewhat dated have examined consumer searches for such health services as dental and eye exams and eyeglasses. These latter studies are of particular interest because they report the effects of the (then) newly allowed consumer advertising. If CDHPs are to be serious competitors in the health insurance market, we would expect to see increased advertising of price on the part of providers.

The Economics of HSAs

Larry Ozanne (1996) provided a straightforward explication of the economics of an HSA, although he did this in the context of the MSAs that were authorized in the mid-1990s. Consider three alternative health insurance plans:

1. **Comprehensive.** This conventional health insurance plan has a $200 deductible, a 20 percent coinsurance requirement, and a $1,000 stoploss. While such plans are now uncommon, this was a typical fee-for-service type plan as late as 1990.
2. **Catastrophic.** This health plan pays for all covered health services once a $2,000 annual deductible is satisfied.
3. **HSA/MSA.** This plan includes the catastrophic plan and a tax-sheltered saving account with a $2,000 contribution. In addition, the subscriber has a 20 percent marginal tax rate.

The three plans are diagramed in Figure 16-2. The horizontal axis has annual medical spending that the subscriber might incur. The vertical axis has

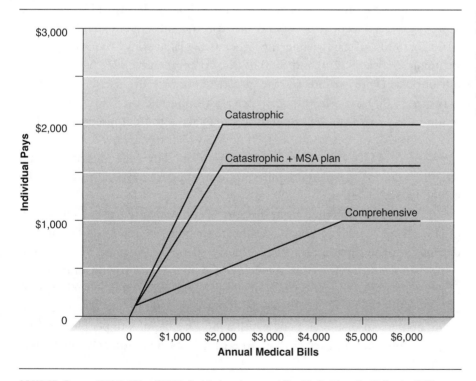

FIGURE 16-2

The Economics of Health Savings Accounts (HSAs)

SOURCE: Ozanne (1996), "How Will Medical Savings Accounts Affect Medical Spending?" *Inquiry* 33(3): Figure 3. Reprinted with permission.

NOTE: The "Catastrophic + MSA plan" label in the figure corresponds with the "HSA/MSA" plan in the text discussion. MSA = Medical savings account.

the out-of-pocket expenditures that the individual pays. The first $200 of the comprehensive plan is a deductible, and the subscriber has to pay this out-of-pocket with after-tax dollars, so the diagonal line rises at 45 degrees. Once the deductible is paid, the subscriber pays 20 cents on the dollar, so the line rises much less rapidly until the subscriber has expended $4,200 and paid $1,000 out-of-pocket. Any further medical services will cost the subscriber nothing out-of-pocket.

The catastrophic plan requires the subscriber to pay the first $2,000 out-of-pocket, so the line rises at 45 degrees until $2,000 has been expended. After that, the subscriber pays nothing out-of-pocket.

Finally, the HSA/MSA plan also has the $2,000 deductible, but these health services expenditures are paid from the tax-sheltered HSA/MSA. So, instead of paying $1 for each $1 of medical spending, subscribers only effectively pay 80 cents on the dollar because they are in a 20 percent marginal tax rate. Thus, the first $2,000 of spending under the HSA/MSA is effectively subsidized at the marginal tax rate, and the graph of the HSA/MSA lies below that of the catastrophic only plan.

Now consider the incentives to spend on health services under each plan. The spending incentives depend on where the subscriber is on the medical spending continuum. Between $0 and $200, the HSA/MSA plan has a slightly greater incentive to spend because the subscriber would only pay $160 for $200 of care, while the other two plans would require $200 of spending. Between $200 and $2,000, the comprehensive plan has the lower out-of-pocket prices and so the greater incentive to spend. However, between $2,000 and $4,200, both the catastrophic and the HSA/MSA plans require less out-of-pocket expenditure than does the comprehensive plan, and because of the tax break, the HSA/MSA plan has greater incentives for spending than does the pure catastrophic plan. For expenditures beyond $4,200, none of the plans require any out-of-pocket expenditures, so the incentives are identical.

If everyone switched from this sort of comprehensive plan to this form of HSA/MSA, would aggregate healthcare spending be reduced? The answer depends on the distribution of healthcare spending. Ozanne (1996) used some data from the American Academy of Actuaries to provide an estimate. Figure 16-3 shows the proportion of adults by the magnitude of their healthcare spending in 1995. Most people spend very little in any given year. In 1995, 50 percent of adults spent less than $500; a handful of people had very large expenditures, but fewer than 4 percent had expenditures of more than $15,000.[1]

---

1. To put this in a more current context, simply adjusting for general inflation means that $15,000 in 1995 is the equivalent of $19,832 in 2006 dollars.

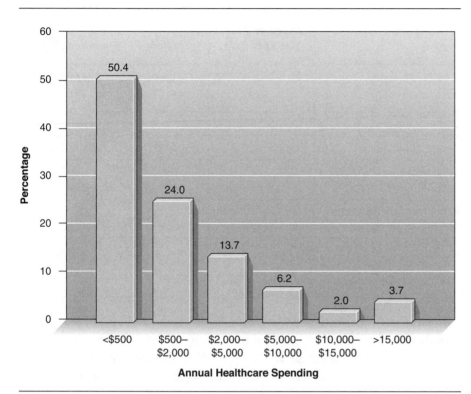

FIGURE 16-3
Distribution of
Healthcare
Claims, 1995

SOURCE: Data from Ozanne (1996).

Ozanne then computed how much a subscriber would spend out-of-pocket under each health plan for each spending category and multiplied it by the proportion of adults in the category. This told him the expected marginal price of care with each plan. These results are shown in Table 16-1. On average, the typical subscriber to the comprehensive plan would pay 48 cents on the dollar of expected spending. A pure catastrophic plan implies an expected out-of-pocket price of 74 cents. The HSA/MSA plan depends on the subscriber's marginal tax rate. For the 20 percent rate used in the example, the expected out-of-pocket price is 60 cents on each dollar of actual expenditure.

The final step in the simulation was to estimate how responsive subscribers were to out-of-pocket prices. Ozanne (1996) used the RAND Health Insurance Experiment (RAND-HIE) to obtain these estimates (see Chapter 7). The RAND-HIE found an overall elasticity of –0.2. Ozanne also used a smaller elasticity of –0.1. With the RAND-HIE estimate, if everyone switched from comprehensive coverage to catastrophic only, the aggregate reduction in healthcare spending would be 8.4 percent. Obviously, if health services utilization is less responsive to price, the results are smaller. Note,

TABLE 16-1

Effects of
Catastrophic
and HSA/MSA
Plans on
Spending

	Expected Price per $1 of Care	Change in Spending (%)	
		Elasticity = −0.1	Elasticity = −0.2
Comprehensive	$.48		
Catastrophic alone	$.74	−4.3	−8.4
Catastrophic + HSA/MSA, 20% marginal tax rate	$.60	−2.2	−4.4
Catastrophic + HSA/MSA, 50% marginal tax rate	$.37	+2.5	5.0

SOURCE: Ozanne (1996), "How Will Medical Savings Accounts Affect Medical Spending?" *Inquiry* 33(3): Table 4. Reprinted with permission.
NOTE: HSA = Health savings account; MSA = Medical savings account.

too, that the 8.4 percent is the maximum savings. If instead everyone moved from comprehensive coverage to an HSA/MSA, the savings would be in the neighborhood of 4.4 percent. This is because the (20 percent) tax subsidy implicit in the HSA erodes the impact of facing the full out-of-pocket prices.[2]

Importantly, Ozanne estimated that, if subscribers were in a 50 percent marginal tax bracket, the expected price of each additional dollar of expenditure would be 37 cents. This is less than that of the comprehensive plan; therefore, spending should increase! Ozanne's estimate was that spending would increase by 3 percent in aggregate.

Thus, three things emerge from this model:

1. Catastrophic coverage health plans reduce spending on health services relative to a comprehensive conventional health plan.
2. The addition of a tax-sheltered HSA/MSA to a catastrophic plan reduces the incentives to decrease spending.
3. The incentive to reduce spending relative to the comprehensive plan depends on the marginal tax rate. This also implies that HSAs/MSAs are more attractive to people facing higher marginal tax rates.

There are some obvious limitations to this study, two of which are particularly important. First, the comparison is made relative to conventional

---

2. Keeler et al. (1996) also estimated the effects of MSAs. They concluded that aggregate expenses would decline by 0 to 13 percent, depending on plan design, if everyone under age 65 was enrolled. Given that not everyone would join, their selection model predicted that aggregate spending would range from an increase of 1 percent to a decline of 2 percent.

coverage, which is rare nowadays. Relative to a closed-panel HMO that has negotiated substantially lower provider prices, it is not clear that the HSA model would yield savings. Second, the results depend on the elasticity estimates of the RAND-HIE. That study was not designed with the view that individual consumers would negotiate with providers over price or look for alternative internists, specialists, or drugstores if they did not receive sufficient value for the dollar. If advocates are right that CDHPs will eventually revolutionize how consumers shop for medical care, then the elasticity estimates embodied in Ozanne's estimates are understated, and the savings could be greater.

Enrollment in HSAs and CDHPs

Greg Scandlen has been one of the stronger advocates of HSAs. As the legislation was being passed in late 2003, he analyzed the potential growth. First, he predicted that banks and third-party administrators as well as insurers would rapidly develop products because there was no sunset provision and the HSAs were available to all (Scandlen 2003). Second, he expected those individuals with nongroup coverage to rapidly shift to HSAs. While these individuals cannot deduct the insurance premium, they can buy policies with high deductibles and contribute to a large HSA, thereby minimizing premium expenses and maximizing the size of the tax-sheltered HSA. Third, Scandlen expected only limited response from the small-group market. While they may eventually be prime candidates, he argued that the small-group market is seldom an early adopter of new forms of insurance. (This is correct; see Chapter 17.) Fourth, he expected the midgroup market (those firms with 100 to 1,000 employees) to adopt HSAs relatively quickly, raising deductibles relative to more-conventional (PPO type) coverages and making contributions to employee HSAs. This shift would leave employer spending on insurance largely unchanged. Employees could contribute additional amounts to their HSAs. Finally, Scandlen did not expect self-insured larger employers to aggressively offer HSAs. He argued that many of them already offered health reimbursement accounts (HRAs).[3]

In contrast (or at least in the longer run), Goldman, Buchanan, and Keeler (2000) expected to see substantial shifts to HSA-like accounts in the small-group market. They used 1993 Current Population Survey data and service elasticity estimates from the RAND-HIE to simulate the effects of the

---

3. An HRA is similar to an FSA but instead of the employee contributing to the account, the employer makes the contribution.

introduction of an MSA into employee groups of 50 or fewer workers. In their model, small firms had the option of offering a conventional 80/20 coinsurance plan with a $250 deductible, an MSA with $1,500 individual and $3,000 family deductible, an HMO with no copays, or no coverage at all. In the simulation, household medical spending was used to determine which sort of plan, if any, would be most beneficial to the household. Random groups of households were combined into small firms, and the "voting" of each household was used to determine which plan, if any, the firm offered to its employees. The voting simply was a reflection of which plan type would be most beneficial to the household. Goldman, Buchanan, and Keeler concluded that the MSA would attract 56 percent of all workers offered a plan. Most of this enrollment would come at the expense of conventional plans, and there would be only a very modest increase (2 percent) in coverage among those who did not have coverage.

Actual Estimates of Early Enrollment

The Employee Benefit Research Institute (Fronstin and Collins 2005) conducted an online survey of insured people between late September and mid-October of 2005. They found that 1 percent of insured adults had a CDHP, and an additional 9 percent had a high-deductible plan that was eligible for an HSA. Claxton et al. (2006a) reported that 4 percent of insured workers were in a CDHP-type plan in 2006.

Table 16-2 and Figure 16-4 show the size of the deductibles typically included and the enrollment by household income category. While HSA-eligible plans typically had individual deductibles of less than $2,000 and family deductibles of $2,000 to $3,000, CDHPs subscribers had larger deductibles, typically above $2,000 for individual and $3,000 for family. There is little difference in the income distribution of comprehensive, CDHP and HSA-eligible plan subscribers. While CDHP subscribers were statistically more likely to have incomes above $150,000, the difference with other plans was small. Although not statistically significant, CDHP subscribers were also more likely to have incomes below $49,000 than were those with comprehensive coverage. The CDHP subscribers were also more likely to report being in excellent or very good health and less likely to be obese, to smoke, or to not exercise regularly. The estimates of enrollment distribution by income, age, and health status reported by eHealthInsurance.com (2005) (for calendar year 2004 and focusing only on HSA-eligible plans) and by Blue Cross and Blue Shield (2005) (for August 2005) mirrored these data but did not show statistically significant differences across categories.

	CDHP	High-Deductible Health Plans
Individual		
$1,000–$1,999	39%	64%
$2,000–3,499	49%	23%
$3,500+	10%	8%
Family		
$2,000–$2,999	31%	50%
$3,000–$4,999	43%	22%
$5,000+	24%	20%

TABLE 16-2

Distribution of Deductibles in CDHPs and HSA-Eligible Plans, 2005

SOURCE: Data from Fronstin and Collins (2005).

NOTE: High-deductible health plans do not have an HSA. CDHP = Consumer-driven health plan; HSA = Health savings account.

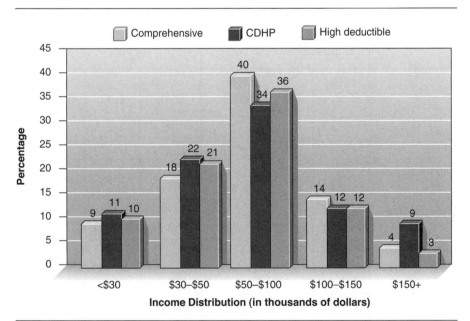

FIGURE 16-4

Income Distribution of Subscribers to CDHPs and High-Deductible Plans, 2005

SOURCE: Data from Fronstin and Collins (2005).

NOTE: High-deductible plans do not have an HSA. CDHP = Consumer-driven health plan.

More-Rigorous Research on CDHPs

Given the recent introduction of CDHPs, it is not surprising that there has been almost no rigorous effort to examine health plan choice or the effects of CDHPs on utilization and expenditures. The exception is a series of papers by Parente, Feldman, and Christianson (2004a, 2004b).

Parente, Feldman, and Christianson (2004a) examined the first-year effects of offering a CDHP to University of Minnesota faculty and staff in 2002. Employees had a choice of two versions of a CDHP, a PPO, an HMO, and a tiered health system that directly contracted with providers. Table 16-3 reports the premiums and enrollment across these plans. Parente, Feldman, and Christianson then used a conditional logit regression model to estimate the effects of various employee characteristics and preferences on plan choice, controlling for the size of the employee premium contributions. Since only about 4 percent of employees were enrolled in the CDHP options, it is a mistake to put too much emphasis on these findings. Nonetheless, Parente, Feldman, and Christianson found that:

- Chronic illness of the employee or a family member had no effect on CDHP choice but was associated with a greater probability of enrolling in the PPO.

TABLE 16-3
Biweekly Premiums and Enrollment in University of Minnesota CDHP, 2002

	Employee-Only Coverage			Family Coverage		
	Total Cost	EPC	Total Enrollment	Cost	EPC	Enrollment
HealthPartners (HMO)	$137.84	$0.00	5,027	$344.59	$20.67	3,967
Patient choice (tiered care)	$147.63	$9.79	2,091	$365.80	$41.88	2,808
PreferredOne (PPO)	$189.61	$51.77	731	$467.83	$143.91	997
Definity (CDHP)	$150.50	$12.66	349	$323.51	$51.59	346
Enrollment			8,198			8,118
Total enrollment						16,316

SOURCE: Data from Parente, Feldman, and Christianson (2004a).

NOTE: CDHP = Consumer-driven health plan; EPC = Employee premium contribution; HMO = Health maintenance organization; PPO = Preferred provider organization.

- Those with higher incomes and those preferring a national provider network were more likely to choose a CDHP option.
- Employees were more likely to choose plans with smaller employee premium contributions, and those with a chronic condition in their household were more price sensitive than others.

In their second paper, Parente, Feldman, and Christianson (2004b) examined the claims experience of a large, unnamed employer who offered a CDHP (along with a PPO and an HMO) beginning in 2001. Three groups of employees were studied: (1) those who were in the PPO from 2000 through 2002, (2) those who were enrolled in the HMO over the same period, and (3) those who switched from either the PPO or the HMO into the CDHP in 2001. What they found was a somewhat mixed bag with respect to claims and utilization. By 2002, the CDHP cohort had lower expenses than the PPO group, but higher expenses than the HMO cohort. Physician visits and prescription drug use and expenditures were lower in the CDHP cohort than in either the PPO or HMO groups. In contrast, physician expenditures and hospital admission rates and costs were higher in the CHDP cohort than in either the PPO or HMO cohorts.

Consumer Search for Health Services[4]

The presence of generous health insurance coverage will influence the price that consumers pay for services. When consumers pay the full price of services they purchase, they are able to keep all of the gains that arise from efforts to seek out lower prices. When faced with little cost sharing, consumers have reduced incentives to search for lower prices because they only receive a fraction of the gains. See Phelps (2000) for a detailed discussion of the underlying economics of search as it applies to healthcare.

Consumer-driven health plans encourage consumers to search for greater-valued, or at least, lower-priced health services. They do this by requiring relatively large deductibles. Consumers pay all of the first-dollar costs of care, albeit with a tax subsidy.

Unfortunately, there has been little empirical research on search in healthcare. Newhouse and Phelps (1976) analyzed 1963 survey data on the use of medical services. For physician fees, they found that a 10 percent increase in out-of-pocket payment resulted in a 1.5 to 2.0 percent reduction

---

4. This section of the chapter draws heavily on Chapter 3 of Michael A. Morrisey, *Price Sensitivity in Health Care: Implications for Policy*, 2nd edition. Washington, D.C.: NFIB Research Foundation, 2005. Used with permission.

in the price of physician services used. A linear extrapolation suggests that paying the full price for physician services would decrease fees by 18 percent.

Sloan (1982) used 1977 and 1978 Physician's Practice Cost Survey data. Like Newhouse and Phelps, he examined the effects of insurance coverage on various physician fees with a two-stage model. He concluded that a 10 percent decrease in the proportion of insured patients reduced follow-up office visit fees by 1.8 percent; fees for follow-up hospital visits declined 0.3 percent. In contrast, Grembowski and Conrad (1986) examined 1980 data on persons with dental coverage. They found that differences in the extent of coverage had virtually no effect on the prices paid for dental services.

The RAND-HIE also examined the effect of coinsurance on provider choice. It examined the use of specialists and the fees charged (Marquis 1985). The results indicated essentially no statistically significant effects of differences in coinsurance on the decisions to use a private physician, a specialist rather than a generalist, or an internist rather than another specialist. The study did find statistically meaningful differences in physician prices, but these effects were so small as to be effectively meaningless. The study also investigated physician choice and fees by the subset of enrollees who reported that they had changed their usual source of care. These results were similar to those of the entire sample.

These findings suggest, first, that the relatively large effects that Newhouse and Phelps (1976) and Sloan (1982) found were driven primarily by adverse selection. Those with greater likelihood of using healthcare chose health insurance or health insurance plans with less cost sharing.

While the literature is mixed and tends not to strongly support the search theory, it is important to note the limitations of the literature. First, while less cost sharing provides reduced incentives for price search, it subsidizes the search for higher-quality care. Thus, the minimal differences of the RAND-HIE study may reflect some offsetting effects. Second, limitations on advertising in the medical care sector are well known. If price information were made more readily available, the results might be different. The classic studies of advertising for optometric services by Benham (1972) and Feldman and Begun (1978) support this view. Benham (1972) found that the price of eyeglasses was 25 to 100 percent higher in states that prohibited advertising. Feldman and Begun (1978) used 1976 data to examine the effects of advertising bans on the price of optometric examinations. Prices were 16 percent higher in states that banned optometric and optician price advertising. Marquis (1985) tried to address this issue indirectly. However, she found that those with higher education and, presumably, better ability to use information had similar specialty and physician fee responses to different coinsurance levels as did the others. Finally, the short duration of the RAND-HIE experiment may have not given enrollees sufficient incentive to seek out alternative providers.

Chapter Summary

- Health savings accounts (HSAs) allow individuals or their employers or both to contribute money to a tax-sheltered account that can be used to pay for qualified health services. Unspent balances can be rolled over from year to year. Such accounts can only be established if combined with a high-deductible health insurance plan.
- A consumer-driven health plan (CDHP) is a high-deductible health plan with an HSA.
- The attractiveness of HSAs and other tax-sheltered accounts, such as medical savings accounts (MSAs) and flexible spending accounts (FSAs), increases with the marginal tax rate of the subscriber. As of 2005, approximately 1 percent of insured adults had a CDHP, and another 9 percent were estimated to have high-deductible plans that were eligible for an H.S.A. Early research on HSAs provides modest evidence consistent with higher-income people enrolling in high-deductible plans. However, lower-income people also appear somewhat more likely to enroll.
- A key issue with CDHPs is the extent to which people will actually search for greater value or at least lower-priced health services. The limited evidence on this issue suggests only modest effects and is quite dated, but it does imply, however, that provider advertising may be key.

Discussion Questions

1. What does the theory of the demand for insurance presented in Chapter 3 suggest about the demand for CDHPs and HSAs?
2. Most of the existing research has been on MSAs and has compared them to conventional health insurance plans. How effective in controlling spending do you think CDHPs and HSAs will be, relative to PPOs? Relative to narrow-panel HMOs? What factors do you believe are the most important in your analysis?
3. Suppose a CDHP uses an HMO or PPO as the high-deductible insurer. Suppose, too, that the prices that the managed care plan has negotiated with providers are available to subscribers as they seek to satisfy the deductible. Do you think this will aid or hinder the CDHP's ability to control costs as its advocates envision?

THE SMALL-GROUP MARKET

The small-group market has various definitions but typically is defined as firms with 50 or fewer employees. The fact that employees in small firms are less likely to have employer-sponsored health insurance has led to a number of policy initiatives to regulate or subsidize the market. In this chapter, we describe the small-group market and the nature of coverage offered, explore reasons for the less-common coverage, and review the effects of many of the reform initiatives.

The Extent of Coverage

Figure 17-1 presents trends in small-group coverage from 1996 through 2005. Approximately 60 percent of firms with fewer than 200 employees offered health insurance in 2005. However, not all firms were equally likely to offer coverage. Those with 25–199 employees were almost as likely as

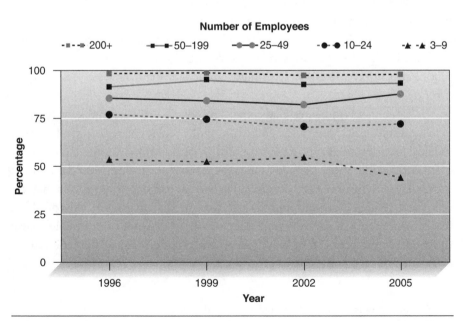

FIGURE 17-1
Percentage of Small Firms Offering Coverage, by Firm Size

SOURCE: Data from Claxton et al. (2006b).

TABLE 17-1

Percentage of Small Firms Offering Medical Savings Accounts (MSAs) and Flexible Spending Accounts (FSAs), and Reimbursing Workers for Purchased Coverage, 2003

Firm Size

	1–9 Employees	10–19 Employees	20–249 Employees	All
Offer an FSA	6.5%	14.9%	24.1%	9.1%
Offer an MSA	4.2%	5.6%	10.2%	5.0%
Reimburse employees for some or all of the premium for insurance purchased on their own	11.4%	16.6%	17.5%	12.5%

SOURCE: Data from Morrisey (2003).

large employers to offer coverage. The smallest of small businesses—those with fewer than ten workers—were much less likely to offer insurance coverage, however. This group has seen the greatest decline in the probability of offering coverage since the beginning of the twenty-first century. Over the longer term, this is also the group that has shown the greatest volatility in its provision of coverage (Morrisey, Jensen, and Morlock 1994). Moreover, the vast majority of small businesses have fewer than ten employees, so it is this subgroup that deserves the greatest attention.

Based on a 2001 survey of small employers, the Kaiser Family Foundation (2002) reported that small firms that paid average wages or salaries of less than $26,400 were less likely to offer coverage. Similarly, firms that employed larger proportions of workers with only an elementary or high school education and those with high employee turnover were less likely to offer health insurance.

Table 17-1 indicates that small employers are very unlikely to offer tax-sheltered health insurance elements. Only 5 percent reported offering a medical savings account (MSA) in 2003, and similarly, only 16 percent offered a flexible spending account (FSA). Most surprising, over 12 percent of small businesses say they do not offer health insurance per se, but they do reimburse employees who purchase coverage on their own. All of these responses suggest that small employers are often unaware of or unable to use the available tax breaks that would allow them to reduce their compensation costs and/or to pay their workers more.[1]

---

1. In some circumstances, workers believe that they are better off making larger Social Security tax payments with higher implicit retirement income in the future than in avoiding higher taxes today.

Small Employers and Managed Care

Unlike larger firms, small employers that offer health insurance coverage tend to only offer a single plan. In 2003, 83 percent of small businesses providing coverage indicated that they offered only one plan (Morrisey 2003). This does not vary much by firm size; even among those firms with 20 to 249 employees, 80 percent still only offered one plan. The Kaiser Family Foundation (2002) found that 43 percent of small employers indicated that substantial administrative cost was the major reason why they only offered a single plan. Much more common was that the "firm gets a better deal if all employees are in one plan" (63 percent) and "health plan rules require all or nearly all employees be in the same plan" (52 percent). These incentives/requirements presumably reflect efforts by insurers to minimize adverse selection that could arise if only "sicker" workers enrolled. Some insurers only require that workers have coverage somewhere, not that all have coverage through a given plan.

While small firms may only offer a single plan, there is considerable diversity in the types of health insurance plans they offer. As Table 17-2 indicates, small firms are most likely to offer a preferred provider organization (PPO). Importantly, however, while national estimates suggest that only about 3 percent of insured workers have conventional coverage, this figure is close to 25 percent among employees of small firms. In some sense, the small-group market represents the last vestige of conventional coverage.

Three rationales are sometimes offered for why small firms disproportionately offer conventional coverage. The first is that small firms are not very

TABLE 17-2 Types of Coverage Offered by Small Firms Providing a Single Plan, 2003

Firm Size	1–9 Employees	10–19 Employees	20–249 Employees	All
Conventional	25.6%	23.6%	16.9%	23.9%
PPO	45.7%	45.1%	47.8%	45.9%
HMO	22.1%	20.6%	26.0%	22.5%
POS	0.0%	4.9%	5.1%	1.6%
Other	4.5%	2.0%	1.7%	3.7%
Don't know	2.0%	3.9%	2.5%	2.4%

SOURCE: Data from Morrisey (2003).

NOTE: HMO = Health maintenance organization; POS = Point-of-service; PPO = Preferred provider organization.

responsive to the prices they face for insurance coverage. Thus, lower managed care premiums would not lead many of them to change plan types. The second is that small businesses have very lean administrative staffs and are unable to devote many resources to identifying better or lower-priced health plans. Thus, they are slow to respond to newer forms of coverage. The third is that small firms tend to be manual rated by conventional insurers (see Chapter 5). Many managed care plans, particularly health maintenance organizations (HMOs), do not use manual rating, and for some time, federally qualified plans were only allowed to community rate. Thus, some have claimed that the absence of state limitations on allowable forms of underwriting have kept managed care firms out of the small-group market for fear of adverse selection.

Morrisey and Jensen (1997) provided some insight into these issues. They examined the extent to which small firms with fewer than 50 employees offered HMOs or PPOs between 1993 and 1995. They found a relatively modest price response; a 10 percent decrease in managed care premiums relative to conventional premiums increased managed care enrollment by 2.4 percent. There was no statistically significant effect of state underwriting restrictions on the probability of a small firm offering a managed care product. However, Morrisey and Jensen did find that knowledge seemed to matter. This was not because insurance agents suddenly began approaching small businesses. Rather, it appeared that the earlier shift to managed care among larger employers provided information to smaller employers and accommodated their shift to HMOs and PPOs. Morrisey and Jensen found that each 1 percentage point increase in prior year HMO or PPO marketwide penetration resulted in a 1.4 percent increase in the probability that a small firm would offer a managed care product. That is to say, small businesses are not innovators with respect to health insurance offerings but do follow the lead of larger employers. Thus, as discussed in Chapter 16, if consumer-driven health plans become popular, we do not expect the small-group market to take the lead, but we do expect that they would follow.

Reasons Why Small Employers Do and Do Not Offer Health Insurance Coverage

Morrisey (2003) found that small employers offered a number of reasons for why they do not offer health insurance coverage. These are summarized in Figure 17-2. The reasons fell into four broad categories. First, many employers reported that they cannot afford to provide coverage either now or in the future. This, of course, is inconsistent with the view that workers pay for coverage in the form of lower wages. One interpretation is that many small employers simply "got it wrong." This may be too harsh. If the firms are

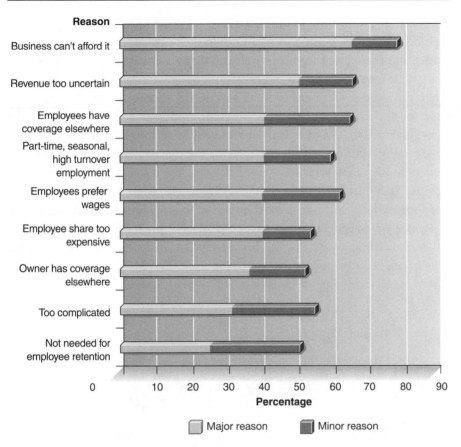

FIGURE 17-2

Reasons
Why Small
Employers
Do Not Offer
Health
Insurance
Coverage, 2003

SOURCE: Data from Morrisey (2003).

employing workers at or near the legal minimum wage, wages cannot adjust to pay for the insurance. Moreover, there is some risk in providing coverage if premiums rise after wage-insurance decisions have been made. If many small employers have very limited cash flow, unanticipated premium increases may make it risky for them to provide coverage. It may also be the case that the cost issue is simply a short-hand response for other reasons.

Second, a number of small-employer responses suggested that employees do not value the coverage sufficiently. These included responses such as "employees have coverage elsewhere," "employees prefer wages," "employee share too high," and "not needed for employee retention." All of these are consistent with the discussion of compensating differentials in Chapter 13. They are also consistent with the work of Monheit and Vistnes (1999) discussed in Chapter 15, which found that small firms that did not offer coverage often employed a disproportionate share of workers who did not strongly value coverage.

A third set of reasons for small firms not providing health insurance coverage related to the administrative costs of providing that coverage. These included both the "hassle factor" of dealing with coverage as a small business owner and the administrative complexity that arises with high turnover.

The fourth reason for not providing coverage related to insurance coverage for owners themselves. Small business owners may seek health insurance for themselves and their family. One option is coverage through the individual market. Another is to provide coverage to their workers largely as a means of getting less costly coverage for themselves. Approximately 38 percent of small employers said they did not offer coverage in their business because they already had personal coverage elsewhere. Little research has been focused on relating any of the specific reasons for not providing health insurance coverage to particular types or sizes of small firms.

Small employers that *do* provide health insurance coverage offered four general reasons for doing so (see Figure 17-3) (Morrisey 2003). Two of

FIGURE 17-3

Reasons Why Small Employers Do Offer Health Insurance Coverage, 2003

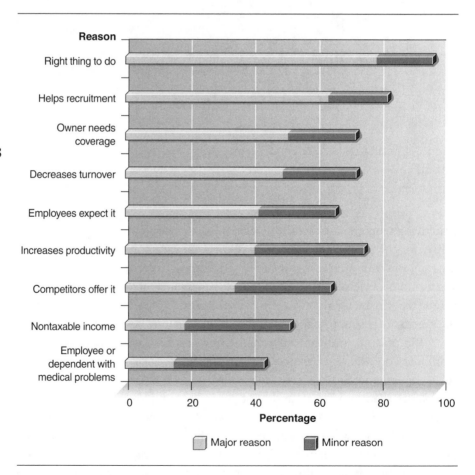

SOURCE: Data from Morrisey (2003).

these are mirror images of the reasons discussed for *not* providing coverage. First, a number of small-employer responses indicated that workers value the coverage or that the firm would lose employees to competitors if it did not offer what the employees want. Second, group coverage provides a source of personal insurance coverage for the owner who has no other coverage. Small employers also indicated that offering coverage enhances productivity. There is little research establishing a productivity effect, and while it may be true, employers may simply be observing the effects of favorable selection of healthier, risk-averse workers into their organizations. Finally, the most common reason given for offering coverage was that "it's the right thing to do." Unfortunately, this can mean anything from a statement of high principle to a summary of the labor market that small employers face.

Price Sensitivity in the Small-Group Market

Since the early 1990s, a number of studies have examined the effects of premium changes on the probability that a small firm will offer coverage. Some studies have examined the effects of state government or private foundation demonstration projects designed to expand coverage. Others have relied on responses to hypothetical questions about the price of coverage. The best of the studies have used state or national data to estimate price elasticities. Unfortunately, the studies have yielded a wide range of estimates.

Estimates Based on Experimental Demonstrations
Uniformly, the findings from several demonstration projects in which uninsured firms were offered a premium subsidy were that the programs were not effective. In one project, conducted by the state of New York in 1989, small firms newly providing coverage were offered a 50 percent premium discount. Thorpe et al. (1992) found that the percentage of small firms offering coverage increased by only 3.5 percent as a result of the subsidy. Several demonstration projects funded by the Robert Wood Johnson Foundation beginning in the mid-1980s also offered premium subsidies to small businesses. Barrand and Helms (1991) and Helms, Gauthier, and Campion (1992) reported that employer responses to the programs were modest at best. The implied price elasticities from these demonstration projects ranged from –0.1 to –0.7.

These demonstration efforts may not have offered reliable estimates for several reasons. First, as Morrisey and Jensen (1996) noted, only 9 percent of small employers in the demonstration states were aware of the subsidy. Second, the subsidies were for only a limited time. As we saw in the survey responses in Figure 17-2, fear of not being able to offer coverage in the future was a common reason for not offering coverage currently. Third, the demonstration programs often prohibited the business owner from participating in the coverage. The earlier survey responses indicated that the owner's ability to obtain personal coverage was reported as a significant factor in offering coverage through the business. Thus, if owners were unaware of the program, knew that the premium subsidy would be of relatively short duration, and were not able to participate in the coverage themselves, it is not surprising that they were not very responsive to the incentives.

Estimates Based on Responses to Hypothetical Questions

Morrisey, Jensen, and Morlock (1994) used survey questions about hypothetical situations to gauge the premium sensitivity of small employers' demand for insurance. Specifically, they asked small, uninsured firms in 1993 about their interest in purchasing coverage at various prices. Over the range of price offers, the implied premium elasticity was –0.9; that is, a 1 percent reduction in the premium increased the probability of offering coverage by 0.9 percent. Thorpe et al. (1992) also questioned small employers in the New York demonstration project. They found an implied offer elasticity of –1.6. There are good reasons to discount this approach. Hypothetical questions elicit hypothetical answers, and responses may be biased by whatever market or policy influence respondents think they may have.

Estimates Based on Offer Decisions in Real Markets

Jensen and Gabel (1992) found that, among firms with 50 or fewer workers, price had a substantial impact on the decision to offer coverage. Using 1985 and 1988 data from two surveys of small employers and differences in state premium tax rates to proxy for the price of insurance, they found that a 1 percent increase in premiums reduced the probability of offering coverage by 2.6 percent.

Leibowitz and Chernew (1992) used the premium for a standard insurance package offered by a nationwide small-group insurer as their estimate of the price of coverage in different markets. Based on a 1989 survey of small employers, they concluded that a 1 percent increase in price reduced the probability of offering coverage by 2.9 percent.

A key problem with both of these studies was the measure of the price of insurance. For those with coverage, the price is obvious; it is what they pay. For those without coverage, the answer is much less obvious; it is the relevant price they explicitly or implicitly turned down. Feldman and colleagues (1997) set the standard for small-group studies by using characteristics of firms offering coverage to estimate the determinants of the premium. The characteristics included the size and age of the small firm, its industry, and the characteristics of its workforce. They then fit characteristics of firms not offering coverage to these estimates to impute an average premium that the uninsured firms would have been offered. In essence, Feldman and colleagues used a regression approach to mimic the underwriting that an insurer might undertake in the small-group market.

Feldman and colleagues used 1993 Robert Wood Johnson Foundation (RWJF) Employer Survey data from Minnesota on firms with fewer than 50 employees to estimate price response. They concluded that small firms were quite price sensitive. At the mean, a 1 percent decrease in the single-coverage premium was associated with a 3.9 percent increase in the probability of offering coverage. Family coverage was more responsive: a 1 percent decrease increased the probability of offering coverage by 5.8 percent.

Marquis and Long (2001/2002) also used the 1993 RWJF Employer Survey but had data from ten states and did not include Minnesota. Their analysis focused on those small firms with fewer than 100 employees, in contrast to the fewer than 50 employees threshold that Feldman et al. (1997) used. While Marquis and Long's estimation strategy was analogous to that of Feldman et al., it employed a richer set of explanatory variables in the premium estimation equation. Marquis and Long concluded that the small-group market was characterized by low price sensitivity, in the neighborhood of –0.14. This implies that a 1 percent decrease in the premium would increase the probability of offering coverage by about 0.14 percent. This is consistent with earlier demonstration studies that found very low price response. Marquis and Long tested for differences in price responsiveness among those firms with fewer than ten employees and found no statistically significant difference.

Finally, Hadley and Reschovsky (2002) examined a later RWJF Employer Survey with data from 1997. They, too, followed the Feldman et al. (1997) methodology in estimating the demand for coverage, but unlike the Feldman et al. study, they used the predicted premium for all of their observations. In addition, they examined whether premium elasticities are difference across small firms of different sizes and with differing percentages of workers near the minimum wage. Their results are summarized in Table 17-3. They found a range of offer elasticities that declined as the size of the firm increased. Firms with 50 to 99 workers were very unresponsive to changes in premiums: a 1 percent decrease in premiums increased the offer rate by 0.03 percent. In contrast, smaller firms were much more responsive: for those with fewer than ten employees, a similar decrease in price increased the offer probability by 0.63 percent.

Thus, the range of estimates, even among only rigorous empirical studies is quite wide, ranging from –0.2 to –3.9. However, the Hadley and Reschovsky study appears to be the most useful. It employed the strong Feldman et al. (1997) model, used more-recent data, and was the most careful about the endogeneity of the estimated premium. Moreover, it provided some insight into why the earlier studies differed in their findings. Aside from the states considered and some issues of methodology, the Feldman et al. (1997) study only examined firms with fewer than 50 workers, while the Marquis and Long (2001/2002) study focused on firms with 100 or fewer workers and found results less elastic than did Feldman et al., consistent with

TABLE 17-3
Predicted
Premiums,
Offer Rates,
and Elasticities
for Small
Employers

	Premium	Offer Rate	Elasticity
Establishment Size			
<10 employees	$176	0.40	−0.63
10–24 employees	$162	0.69	−0.30
25–49 employees	$151	0.83	−0.24
50–99 employees	$150	0.92	−0.03
Percentage of Low-Wage ($7/hour) Workers			
>75%	$178	0.22	−1.18
50%–75%	$175	0.37	−0.58
<50%	$169	0.57	−0.30

SOURCE: Data from Hadley and Reschovsky (2002).

the range of findings in the Hadley and Reschovsky work. Moreover, since larger small firms almost always offer coverage, like truly large employers, their decision to offer coverage is little affected by the range of premiums considered. However, recall from our discussion of tax rate changes in Chapter 14 that while the offer decision is somewhat influenced by the effective price, the nature of the coverage is likely to change more dramatically with changes in the premium.

Reforms in the Small-Group Insurance Market

Because employees in small firms are less likely to be offered health insurance through their employer, states have implemented a number of policy initiatives to affect this market. These can be considered in three broad categories: (1) bare-bones coverage laws, (2) premium limitations, and (3) underwriting provisions.

So-called bare-bones laws were introduced to try to minimize the deleterious impacts of some insurance regulation enacted by state legislatures. As we will discuss in more detail in Chapter 18, all of the states have enacted laws that require health insurers to cover particular services (such as alcohol abuse treatment), particular providers (such as chiropractors), and particular categories of people (such as adopted children), if they sell insurance in the state. Large firms can avoid these state insurance regulations by being self-insured under the terms of the federal ERISA (Employee Retirement Income Security Act) legislation. However, small firms find it much more difficult to self-insure. Arguably, the insurance coverage mandates require small firms to provide coverage they otherwise would not, thereby raising the costs of coverage and encouraging workers and their employers to forgo coverage altogether. However, as Morrisey and Jensen (1996) noted, the bare-bones legislation in many states also included provisions that made insurance less attractive, such as covering fewer than 30 days of inpatient care.

Bare-bones laws were enacted by several states to exempt small firms of a certain size, often those with fewer than 25 employees, from having to provide the mandated coverages. In 1989, only one state had enacted a bare-bones exemption; by 1995, 43 states had done so (Jensen and Morrisey 1999b). The argument was that this provision would make health insurance more affordable for small businesses and encourage them to begin or continue to offer coverage.

The second category of small-group reforms—premium regulations—either established rating bands or limited the use of certain underwriting provisions. Using manual rating, an insurer sets different premiums for different firms based on its underwriting standards. Rating bands establish legally allowed ranges by which high-risk premiums can exceed standard rates. High-risk rates, for example, may be allowed to be no more than 100 or 150 percent higher than standard rates. The argument is that these limits will result in lower premiums for higher-risk small groups. However, insurers may drop out of the higher-risk market. States may also restrict the variables that an insurer uses to classify risks in the small-group market. They may require that only community rating or rating based on age and sex be allowed. While these provisions may make coverage less expensive for higher-risk groups, they will likely increase premiums for lower-risk groups, who now find their risk pool expanded to include the higher-risk employer groups. Jensen and Morrisey (1999b) reported that only one state had enacted either of these rating restrictions in 1989, but 45 states had done so, in one form or another, by 1995.

Finally, small-group reform may have included provisions for guaranteed issue, guaranteed renewal, portability, and/or limits on the use of preexisting condition clauses. Guaranteed issue laws mean that if a small firm wishes to buy coverage at an insurer's established rates, the insurer cannot refuse to sell the coverage. Guaranteed renewal means that a small group cannot be denied the renewal of an insurance policy if it is willing to pay the established premium. Neither of these provisions limits the size of the premium the insurer may charge, however. By 1995, 38 and 43 states, respectively, had enacted guaranteed issue and guaranteed renewal provisions (Jensen and Morrisey 1999). The rationale for these laws is that they allow firms to purchase or continue to maintain coverage if an insurer chooses to redline them. That is, these laws prevent an insurer from saying it will not provide coverage in a particular neighborhood or that it will not cover people in a particular profession, occupation, or industry. They also prevent the insurer from dropping a small group that has experienced high claims.

Portability allows an individual to move from one employer to another without having to again satisfy waiting periods or preexisting condition waiting periods with the new employer if equivalent waiting periods were satisfied with the old employer. A waiting period is an initial time period, perhaps 6 or 9 months, before a new employee may submit a claim. Such contract provisions are implemented to limit adverse selection in which individuals take a job with coverage so that they or a family member may receive covered care for an already existing condition. Waiting periods for preexisting conditions serve the same purpose. Three states had portability laws in 1989, and 11 had limitations on waiting periods; by 1995, 43 and 45 states, respectively, had such laws. For the most part, the portability and waiting period provisions were superseded by the federal Health Insurance Portability and Accountability Act of 1996 (HIPAA).

A series of studies investigated the effects of these reforms on the provision of health insurance by small employers. Zuckerman and Rajan (1999) used the U.S. Census Bureau's Current Population Survey from 1989 through 1995 to examine the effects of state insurance reforms on coverage. After controlling for demographic and market characteristics, they found: (1) that no package of small-group reforms had a statistically significant effect on the proportion of people without coverage and (2) that states that enacted guaranteed renewal and rating restrictions, but not guaranteed issue and portability reforms, saw declines in the proportion of people with private coverage (although this finding was not statistically significant at the conventional levels).

Jensen and Morrisey (1999b) used 1989 to 1995 small-employer survey data to examine the effect of small-group insurance reforms on the probability that a firm with fewer than 50 workers offered coverage. The reforms included guaranteed issue and renewal, portability, waiting periods, preexisting condition limitations, and bare-bones exclusions. Rating restrictions were highly correlated with other laws and could not be studied separately. Jensen and Morrisey found generally no statistically significant effects of the laws, either as a group or separately, on the probability that a small firm would offer health insurance coverage, but the presence of preexisting condition limitations did increase the likelihood that a small firm would offer coverage.

Hing and Jensen (1999) used the national 1994 Employer Health Insurance Survey data on nearly 18,000 small employers to examine the effects of small-group reform. They found that full reform, in effect for at least three years, resulted in small employers being "slightly" more likely to offer coverage. However, employee participation in small-group plans was no higher. Their employer survey asked: "Can the insurer refuse to cover employees or their dependents under this plan who have particular health problems or conditions?" There was no difference in responses among employers in states with reform packages and those without. "Full reform" was defined as requiring guaranteed issue and renewal, portability, limitations on preexisting conditions clauses, and the use of rating restrictions. Partial reforms—that is, those excluding rating restrictions—appeared to reduce the probability of coverage for the smallest of small businesses. While the reforms had virtually no effect overall, small firms in redlined industries were much more likely to offer coverage in states with full reforms.

Marquis and Long (2001/2002) examined "second-generation" small-group reforms, focusing on the effects on health insurance offer and enrollment rates in small-employer plans, on premiums, and on the variability and increase in premiums. They concluded:

> Overall, we find no effect of small-group reform on any of the outcomes; the sign of the effect is not consistent across reform states, the estimates rarely attain statistical significance, and they show no consistent pattern across the outcomes within each state. (p. 365)

Thus, the clear consensus is that the small-group reforms, separately or as a group, had almost no effect on overall coverage decisions. There are at least three reasons why this has been the case. First, with many of the reforms, there were mixed incentives. Limiting the use of health factors in underwriting, for example, may make insurance premiums lower for those with health problems, but it will raise premiums for healthier people. Thus, some of the effects were offsetting. Second, it may be that many of the laws did not address pervasive problems. Morrisey and Jensen (1996), for example, reported that very few firms had limitations on preexisting conditions that would have been affected by state laws. Finally, it may be that insurers in the small-group market have found ways to avoid the binding conditions of many reforms. Hall (1999) described how the careful choice of the premium for standard coverage, for example, can allow an insurer to effectively broaden the range of rates charged, even in a state with rating restrictions.

Small-Group Coalitions and Association Health Plans

A final issue in the small-group market is the ability of local coalitions and association health plans to make health insurance less expensive in the small-group market. Coalitions are groups of small employers who come together and pool their employees into a larger group in the hope of obtaining the sorts of lower premiums that large employers enjoy. They were relatively popular in the 1980s and have declined since. However, small employers often raise the possibility of banding together locally to provide lower-cost health insurance. Association health plans (AHPs) are nationwide insurance plans that sell coverage to small employers, but like self-insured large employers, are exempt from state insurance regulation and, arguably, able to sell coverage more cheaply. AHPs require action by Congress and have been on the small-business policy agenda for the last several years.

Employer Coalitions

The motivation for coalition health plans is the observation that objective risk is reduced when group size increases. Recall Chapter 5. Thus, the argument is that, by banding together, a number of small groups can effectively be a large group and get the lower premiums that arise from the reduction in risk. This insight is correct as far as it goes.

However, two factors make coalitions unlikely to be successful based purely on pooling. The first is that objective risk depends on the size of the expected loss and the variance in that loss, as well as the number of covered lives. If the coalition were to combine a number of small groups, each of which had the same expected loss and each drawn from the same distribution of claims experience, the larger-group argument would apply. On the other hand, if the small groups have very different claims experience, the pooled group would be larger, but the expected loss may or may not change. Moreover, the variance almost certainly will increase, thereby increasing objective risk. Thus, a coalition is likely to be successful only if it is able to combine small groups with similar claims experience. Successful coalitions are very careful about which small groups they allow into their pool or set up multiple pools to reflect the differing claims experience. In essence, this means that successful coalitions engage in an underwriting exercise designed to put small groups into their appropriate risk class.

This immediately raises the second obstacle to a successful coalition. A number of existing insurers already specialize in the small-group market. They pool small groups based on their expected claims experience. To be successful, a coalition of small employers has to undertake the same insurance functions, including underwriting, as these established carriers do and do so more cheaply. Unless the coalition has a comparative advantage in some aspect of the small-group insurance business or is able to undercut the prices charged by an entrenched insurer with market power, it is unlikely to be able to do better than the market.

McLaughlin, Zellers, and Brown (1989) sought to describe and evaluate the effectiveness of the healthcare coalition movement in the mid-1980s. There were two types of coalitions: (1) those that were community-wide and included providers as well as employers, and (2) employer-only coalitions. Both were intended to reduce healthcare costs. While no formal evaluations were conducted, the McLaughlin, Zellers, and Brown conclusion was that "there is little evidence that they are succeeding" (p. 81). Their decline as organizations suggests that participants did not find them effective.

Association Health Plans

Under current law, a professional association in a state—say, the state florists' or realtors' association—may offer health insurance as long as it follows the state's insurance laws. This typically means that the association must be licensed by the state to sell insurance, must have sufficient reserves, and must abide by other statutes that may regulate the nature of the coverage it offers, the premiums it charges, and how it conducts its marketing. A national florists' or realtors' association could also sell insurance to its members, as long as it met the insurance regulations in each of the states. Congress has been considering legislation since at least the early 2000s that would allow AHPs to avoid most of the state insurance regulations, much as firms that are self-insured under the terms of ERISA are exempt from state regulation (see Chapter 18).

The rationale is twofold: First, AHPs would be exempt from state insurance mandates that require coverage for specific services, providers, and categories of subscribers. This would arguably reduce the cost of health insurance to small-employer groups. Second, AHPs may be able to better pool similar risk groups and take advantage of the cost savings of larger groups. This saving might arise, for example, because an AHP is made up of only its members, and the national scope may allow it to recruit similar-risk individuals or small groups into its insurance pool more easily than existing market participants. Thus, if most florist shops or real estate agencies employ similar distributions of employees, their claims experience may be similar, and a common insurance pool may result in lower risk, and therefore, lower premiums. Finally, an AHP may have lower administrative costs, perhaps because of its ongoing relationship and communication with its members.

There has been little research on this topic. Work by Baumgardner and Hagen (2001/2002) is the exception. They developed a simulation model to estimate the likely impact of AHPs on the probability of someone having insurance coverage and whether the individual was previously uninsured. As with all simulations, Baumgardner and Hagen had to draw on the literature to make assumptions about the size of the key parameters. In this case, the major issues were: (1) the price responsiveness of small employers and (2) the extent to which exemption from state insurance mandates reduce health insurance premiums. Baumgardner and Hagen used elasticities from the lower end of the range—from –0.3 to –2.0—and they assumed that then-current mandates increased the costs of small-group coverage by 1 to 15 percent. Using their midrange assumptions, they concluded that AHPs would have a relatively large effect on the small-group market, enrolling approximately 4.6 million people in 1999. However, most of this would come at the expense of existing insurers; fewer than 500,000 people would be newly insured.

The Small-Group Market: Diverse and Complex

As we have seen, small firms are less likely to offer health insurance than larger firms, and this is largely a phenomenon of the smallest of the small businesses. We have also seen that these smallest of small businesses have a larger insurance price sensitivity than somewhat larger firms and that efforts to subsidize coverage and to change the underwriting and other features of the small-group market have not had much impact on the decision to offer coverage.

Recently published work by Kronick and Olsen (2006), reporting on the results of detailed survey work in San Diego, California, offered some important insight as to why the small-group market is so unresponsive. The short answer is that many workers in small businesses that do not offer coverage nonetheless have coverage. Kronick and Olsen successfully interviewed some 2,830 businesses with between 2 and 50 full-time employees and achieved an unheard-of 79.5 percent response rate. Of these, 26.5 percent did not offer coverage. Like the national surveys, substantially more of the businesses with two to nine workers did not offer coverage (66.4 percent). However, Figure 17-4 shows that, among the businesses not offering coverage, many workers nonetheless had coverage. Thirty-six percent of firms not offering coverage had no uninsured workers; another 14 percent had only one. There are several reasons for this. One of particular note is that the small-business owner is often included among the workers. If within a two-person business the owner had nongroup coverage, for example, the results in Figure 17-4 would be one uninsured worker.

Employees in small businesses not offering coverage held several types of coverage. Over 19 percent, for example, had nongroup coverage. Just over 18 percent had coverage through a spouse or other relative; 3 percent had Medicaid or Medicare coverage. Smaller businesses had larger proportions of workers with nongroup or spousal coverage. These results are consistent with the diverse reasons given by small employers for offering or not offering coverage. They are also consistent with the work by Abraham and Royalty (2005) on the nature of insurance coverage in two-earner households examined in Chapter 15.

The small-group market is made up of a diverse set of firms with a wide range of workers, many of whom have alternative sources of health insurance coverage. It is perhaps not surprising that this market has been so little affected by broad-brush efforts at reform.

FIGURE 17-4

Distribution of
the Number of
Uninsured
Workers in San
Diego Small
Businesses That
Do Not Offer
Coverage, 2001

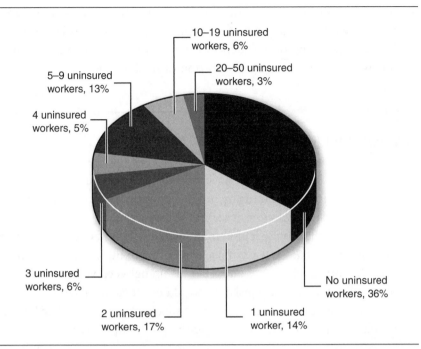

10–19 uninsured
workers, 6%

20–50 uninsured
workers, 3%

5–9 uninsured
workers, 13%

4 uninsured
workers, 5%

3 uninsured
workers, 6%

2 uninsured
workers, 17%

1 uninsured
worker, 14%

No uninsured
workers, 36%

SOURCE: Kronick and Olsen (2006), "A Needle in a Haystack? Uninsured Workers in Small Businesses That Do Not Offer Coverage," *Health Services Research* 41(1): 40–57, Figure 4. Reprinted with permission courtesy of Wiley–Blackwell Publishing Ltd.

Chapter Summary

- Small businesses are less likely to sponsor health insurance for their employees than are larger firms. This is largely a phenomenon of the smallest of the small businesses; only 48 percent of those with fewer than ten employees offered coverage in 2005.
- Small-employer decisions to offer coverage relate to employee willingness to give up other forms of pay and to employer concerns about the cost of coverage.
- Small firms are much more likely than large firms to offer a single health plan. While small firms most commonly offer PPOs, they also are the most likely firms to offer a conventional health insurance plan. The limited evidence to date suggests that the cost of obtaining information leads smaller firms to follow the health insurance actions of larger firms, rather than be leaders themselves.
- The price elasticity of demand for health insurance by small firms decreases with the size of the firm. Estimates in the neighborhood of –0.63 for firms with fewer than ten employees suggest that even relatively large decreases in premiums would only have a modest effect on the decision to offer coverage.

- State efforts to reform the small-group market have focused on bare-bones coverage laws, premium limitations, and underwriting provisions. There is little empirical evidence that any of these initiatives have had much of an impact on the proportion of small employers offering coverage.

Discussion Questions

1. Suppose the local metropolitan small-business association decides to offer health insurance to its members. Under what circumstances would this effort result in premium savings to its members?
2. Why do you think state legislation limiting waiting periods for preexisting conditions had so little impact on coverage in the small-group market? Do you think there is any relationship between your answer and the probability that a state legislature would enact such a law?
3. Suppose a state wanted to encourage small employers to offer health insurance and did so by subsidizing the premium for two years. What effect do you think this would have on the proportion of small firms offering coverage? Why?

HEALTH INSURANCE REGULATION

This chapter describes the extent and nature of regulation of the health insurance industry in the United States and summarizes the research on the regulation's effects on the provision and cost of health insurance.

At the federal level, the key legislation includes:

- The 1945 McCarran-Ferguson Act, which explicitly leaves insurance regulation to the states and grants limited federal antitrust immunity to the "business of insurance"
- The 1954 amendments to the Internal Revenue Code, which exclude employer-sponsored health insurance from the definition of income for purposes of federal taxation
- The 1974 Employee Retirement Income Security Act (ERISA), which exempts self-insured employers from state health insurance laws
- The 1986 Consolidated Omnibus Budget Reconciliation Act (COBRA), which provides continuation of coverage for most persons separated from an employer

Several other relevant federal statues deal with benefits mandates. The most notable of these is the 1996 Health Insurance Portability and Accountability Act (HIPAA), which limits waiting periods when individuals move from one job to another.

There is considerably more insurance regulation at the state level. The Council for Affordable Health Insurance (2006) reported that, at the close of 2005, there were some 1,843 state insurance laws mandating the coverage of specific types of services or providers or categories of individuals. In addition, there are laws restricting underwriting provisions and the composition of provider networks, among others. The states also impose taxes on premiums collected. The key question with respect to these laws is whether they have an impact on the extent of coverage and the cost of care.

Federal Regulation of Health Insurance

The states have always enjoyed primary responsibility for the regulation of insurance. Recall the Chapter 1 discussion of the creation of state enabling legislation for Blue Cross plans that initially ran afoul of state insurance laws.

This view was challenged in 1944 when the Supreme Court ruled in *U.S. vs. the South-Eastern Underwriters Association* that insurance was interstate commerce and therefore subject to federal regulation. The McCarran-Ferguson Act of 1945 was enacted to reestablish state primacy. It clarified the states' authority to tax, license, and regulate insurance companies, regardless of the insurance company's state of incorporation, and also gave the states authority to allow insurance companies to engage in cooperative rate making. In addition, it explicitly exempted "the business of insurance" from federal antitrust laws as long as the states regulated those activities.

The rationale for this last exemption was that insurers needed reasonably large amounts of data to determine the distribution of claims and to set premiums that would be less subject to wide fluctuations due to the experience of a small number of covered lives. Over the years, there has been ongoing interest in the repeal of or an amendment to the McCarran-Ferguson Act to allow greater antitrust oversight. Most of this attention has focused on the liability and life insurance markets. Patricia Danzon (1983) argued that, even in these fields, there is relatively easy entry and exit from the market and, therefore, little reason for antitrust concern. In the health insurance market, the ability of self-insured employers to enter the market without restrictions from state regulators suggests even greater ease of entry and even greater restraints on health insurance carriers' ability to raise premiums above competitive levels.[1]

The 1954 amendments to the Internal Revenue Code comprise a second major set of federal laws dealing with health insurance. As discussed in Chapter 14, these statutes effectively codified and clarified the special rulings that the Internal Revenue Service (IRS) had made over the years to the effect that health insurance provided through an employer was exempt from federal personal income and Social Security (and later, Medicare) taxation. This legislation provides greater incentives for people to purchase health insurance through their employers and to buy broader and deeper coverage than they otherwise would have because of the implicit tax subsidy that is created.

The third important federal law with respect to health insurance is the 1974 Employee Retirement Income Security Act (ERISA). This law was largely focused on providing incentives for employers to prefund defined benefit pension plans and on creating the Pension Benefit Guarantee Corporation to federally insure defined benefit pension plans. With respect to health insurance, ERISA broadly preempts state law to establish exclusive federal regulation of self-insured health insurance plans:

---

1. For a recent discussion of the issues attendant to the reform of the McCarran-Ferguson Act, see the June 2006 hearings before the Senate Judiciary Committee (http://judiciary.senate.gov/hearing.cfm?id=1952).

ERISA expressly permits states to continue to enforce all state laws that regulate the business of insurance, but it prohibits states from declaring an employee benefit plan that is covered by ERISA to be an insurance company or engaged in the business of insurance. (Federal Trade Commission/Department of Justice 2004, chap. 5, p. 4)

Thus, self-insured plans are exempt from state insurance mandates, premium taxes, and other regulations.

The intent of ERISA appears to have been to allow large employers operating in several states to be free of conflicting and overlapping regulations. As we saw in Chapter 5, self-insured plans are conceptually no different than retrospectively experience-rated plans but are not subject to state insurance regulation. Moreover, they are now very prevalent. The available estimates suggest that at least half of insured workers are in a self-insured plan (Gabel, Jensen, and Hawkins 2003). Later in the chapter, we discuss the broader effects of ERISA in the context of its effects on state insurance regulations.

An insurance mandate is a law that requires an insurer to provide a specific coverage if it is to sell any insurance within the jurisdiction of the law. The 1979 Pregnancy Discrimination Act was one of the first federal insurance mandates. It specified that a woman unable to work for pregnancy-related reasons is entitled to disability benefits or sick leave on the same basis as employees unable to work for other medical reasons. In addition, any health insurance provided at work must cover expenses for pregnancy-related conditions, just as it covers expenses for other medical conditions. Firms with fewer than 15 workers are exempt from the law on the argument that mandates increase the cost of insurance and lead small firms in particular to forgo coverage for their employees.

The most significant federal insurance mandate was enacted as part of the 1986 Consolidated Omnibus Budget Reconciliation Act (COBRA). COBRA allows qualified individuals to continue to receive health insurance coverage through a former employer for up to 18 to 36 months. Qualified beneficiaries must pay 102 percent of the full premium for each month of coverage. Employees are generally covered for up to 18 months if they were voluntarily or involuntarily terminated for any reason other than gross misconduct. Spouses or dependents of terminated employees are eligible for 18 months of coverage if the employee was terminated as noted earlier, but are eligible for 36 months of coverage if the employee's Medicare coverage, divorce, legal separation, or death causes the spouse or dependent to otherwise lose employer-sponsored coverage. In addition, dependent children can be covered if they are no longer eligible under the dependent-child provisions of the employer's policy. Typically, a qualifying individual has 60 days after notification from the employer to elect coverage. Firms with fewer than 20 employees are exempt (see U.S. Department of Labor 2005 for more details).

COBRA eligibility often occurs when the individual has reduced financial resources; the premiums are set by law at 102 percent of the full premium and, by definition, are paid with after-tax dollars. Thus, as you might anticipate, COBRA coverage is subject to substantial adverse selection. Figure 18-1 shows that, from 1994 through 2004, COBRA claims experience was never less than 145 percent of that of active workers. *Medical Benefits* (2005a) reported that, in 2004, 20.4 percent of those eligible for COBRA coverage elected to exercise their option. On average, those eligible for 18 months of coverage purchased coverage for 9.6 months, and those eligible for 36 months purchased coverage for 17.6 months.

In 1996, Congress enacted several federal benefits mandates. The Health Insurance Portability and Accountability Act (HIPAA) is the most well known. It requires that waiting periods for preexisting conditions be limited to no more than 12 months. Moreover, it requires that a new employee be given credit for continuous coverage held through a former employer. Thus, if you had employer-sponsored coverage through a former employer for, say, 8 months and then immediately moved to a new employer who had a 12-month waiting period, the 8 months spent under the earlier employer's plan would count toward satisfying the 12-month requirement. It is also of note that pregnancy is not a preexisting condition under HIPAA, and newborns are not subject to preexisting condition clauses if covered within 30 days. The rationale for the legislation is that it prevents "job-lock"; that is, it keeps people from being locked into undesirable jobs for fear that they or their dependents will lose needed health insurance coverage.

FIGURE 18-1

Average COBRA Claims as a Percentage of Average Active Worker Claims

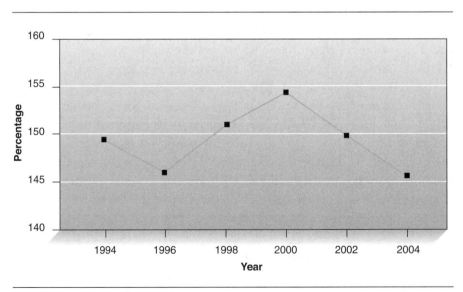

SOURCE: Data from *Medical Benefits* (2005a).

It is unlikely that HIPAA had much impact on access to coverage. By the time HIPAA was passed in 1996, some 45 states had already enacted their own legislation to limit the extent to which insurers could use preexisting conditions. These laws typically apply to firms that are too small to self-insure under ERISA. However, even among small firms, very few had waiting periods that were constrained by a 12-month limit. In 1993, only 3 percent of conventional plans and 4 percent of preferred provider organizations (PPOs) offered by small employers had preexisting condition waiting periods that were 12 months or longer (Jensen and Morrisey 1999b).

The Mental Health Parity Act of 1996 requires that the annual or lifetime dollar limits on mental healthcare coverage be no lower than they are for covered medical care. However, insurance plans are allowed to set differing limits on the number of visits, for example. Small employers with fewer than 50 workers are exempt, and larger employers are exempt if they can show that their health insurance premiums increased by at least 1 percent. At this writing, the law is scheduled to expire on December 31, 2007.

The 1996 Newborns' and Mothers' Health Protection Act requires that insurance plans allow maternity stays of at least 48 hours and at least 96 hours in the event of a cesarian section delivery. While research on the federal law is lacking, a recent study by Webb and colleagues (2001) examined the effects of a similar Pennsylvania law enacted in July 1996. The Webb et al. study found that the median length of stay for vaginal deliveries in the 12-month postlegislation period increased from 35 to 47 hours, compared to a 12-month prelegislation period. Median charges for maternity care for these patients increased by $1,063.

Finally, the Women's Health and Cancer Rights Act was enacted in 1988. It requires that if a health plan covers mastectomies, it also must cover reconstructive breast surgery.

With the exception of the COBRA legislation, which went well beyond the provisions of state statutes at the time, most federal mandates tend to mimic existing state laws. The open question with respect to the spate of federal mandates is whether or not they reflect a move to federalize health insurance regulation in piecemeal fashion or whether these laws are simply the outcomes of the special political considerations of their day.

State Regulation of Health Insurance

The states have imposed considerable regulation on health insurance plans. First, of course, are the typical conditions required of life and casualty insurers in the state. They must meet solvency and reserve requirements. These are imposed to assure that an insurance carrier will have the necessary resources to pay claims, often incurred years after the premiums are collected

TABLE 18-1

Domestic Premium Tax Rates in Selected States, 2006

State	Tax Rate	State	Tax Rate
Alabama	1.60%	Massachusetts	2.00%
California	2.35%	Minnesota	2.00%
Colorado	1.00%	Mississippi	3.00%
Connecticut	1.75%	New York	1.50%
Florida	1.75%	Ohio	1.00%
Georgia	2.25%	Texas	1.75%
Maryland	2.00%	Virginia	2.25%

SOURCE: Internet search.

NOTE: Virtually every state has enacted what are called "retaliatory taxes" on foreign insurers as well. "Foreign" insurers, by definition, have their headquarters in another state. If state X imposes a higher tax rate on foreign insurers than on domestic ones, then other states retaliate by assessing a tax rate equal to the higher rate on insurers from state X doing business in their state.

in the case of life and liability insurers. Many states require that proposed insurance rates be filed with the state insurance commissioner before they are introduced; a few states require these rates to be approved prior to implementation. In addition, many states impose premium taxes of 1 to 3 percent on the premiums collected in their state (see Table 18-1).

The states have been considerably more active in regulating health insurance. They have enacted provisions for mandated benefits and mandated benefit options. They have imposed line-of-business mandates, as well as additional taxes to cover state high-risk pools. Mandated benefits laws require that, if a firm sells health insurance coverage in a state, it must include coverage for specific categories of services, providers, or individuals. Mandated benefit option laws require that the insurer must give its clients the option to purchase a specific coverage. Line-of-business mandates apply to specific types of insurance. They may require managed care plans, for example, to include specific categories of providers in their networks, or they may specify the underwriting rules that must be used in the small-group or individual insurance markets. Finally, the state may provide coverage for high-risk individuals and assess a tax on the state's insurers to pay for some of the plan's costs.

The number of state mandates has grown dramatically since the mid-1970s. Jensen and Morrisey (1999a) reported that, by 1996, there were some 860 such laws that applied to Blue Cross/Blue Shield plans. Figure 18-2 shows the trend in state mandates over the 1949 to 2002 period. However, while the figure reports laws applying to all carriers, it includes only those mandates that cover services and providers; it excludes those that extend cov-

FIGURE 18-2

Number of
New State
Insurance
Mandates, by
Decade

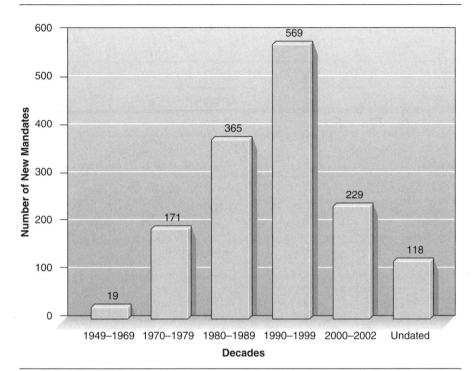

SOURCE: Data from Laugesen et al. (2006).

NOTE: This compilation excludes mandates applying to specific groups of individuals.

erage to groups of individuals. The most comprehensive list of state mandates is probably that of the Council for Affordable Health Insurance (2006). It reported that, by the end of 2005, the states had enacted some 1,843 insurance mandates.

Table 18-2 shows the most common mandates. Among these are service mandates, such as maternity stay, mammography screening, and diabetic supplies; and provider mandates, such as coverage for chiropractors, optometrists, and psychologists. Finally, there are mandates that extend coverage to specific cohorts of individuals, such as newborns and handicapped dependents. Among the newest mandates are those that extend coverage to age 25 (in New Mexico) and to age 30 (in New Jersey) for unmarried resident dependents or those who are full-time students. Many readers of this text may be amused that these laws are sometimes called "slacker mandates" (Council for Affordable Health Insurance 2006)!

There is considerable variation across the states with respect to the enactment of these laws. Minnesota is the most prolific, with some 62 mandates in 2005. Iowa, the District of Columbia, Alabama, Utah, and Vermont have the fewest, with between 13 and 23.

TABLE 18-2

Twenty Most Common Conventional Mandates, 2005

Mandates Regarding . . .	Number of States	Mandates Regarding . . .	Number of States
Newborns	51	Emergency services	43
Maternity stay	50	Optometrists	43
Mammogram	50	Adoptive children	42
Breast reconstruction	48	Conversion to nongroup	42
Diabetic supplies	47	Mental health parity	42
Chiropractors	46	Mental health general	40
Alcoholism dependents	45	Handicapped	39
Psychologists	44	Off-label drug-use	37
Continuation/ dependents	44	Dentists	36
Continuation/ employees	44	Podiatrists	35

SOURCE: Data from Council for Affordable Health Insurance (2006).

Why Have State Mandates Become So Popular?

States may choose to enact mandates for three economic reasons. The first is a lack of knowledge on the part of consumers and their employer-agents. The argument is that a particular service provides considerable benefits, well worth the cost, but that potential consumers lack this knowledge, and there are substantial costs associated with making this knowledge known to them. Therefore, the mandate gives consumers the coverage they themselves would have purchased, had they only known. Little evidence supports this view.

The second rationale is one of severe adverse selection with substantial cost differences. The argument is that many people value the benefit provided by the mandate, even though they may not ever have to use it. However, those who do use it, use it extensively. If only one firm offered the benefit, it would be flooded with those individuals who will actually use the service, and the premium would be pushed so high that few, if any, of the unlikely users would be willing to buy. However, if the cost was spread across all the willing buyers—those likely and those unlikely to use the benefit—then even the unlikely users would be willing to pay the extra premium. The argument is that a mandate achieves this purpose. This argument is the classic one for the market failure of health insurance and was formalized by Rothschild and Stiglitz (1976). However, here, too, there is little empirical evidence to show that this event is common enough to explain the flood of state insurance mandates.

The third explanation has to do with the political economy of state laws. Typically, as consumers, we have some interest in all the laws that the state legislature might consider. However, the costs of advising and influencing the legislature are relatively high. So, for most proposed pieces of legislation, we rationally do nothing. In contrast, if a law would substantially enhance or harm our livelihood, we find that it pays to take a more-active role. This is the public-choice view of legislation developed by Stigler (1971), among others. It argues that the relevant proponents and opponents of legislation will tend to be suppliers whose potential gains or losses are large enough for them to organize to support or oppose legislation. See Jensen and Morrisey (1999a) for a review of the empirical literature on the enactment of state insurance laws.

The argument is that various healthcare suppliers tend to support mandates that will increase the demand for their services. They are opposed by insurers who face declines in the demand for coverage when the costs rise (and risk seeing more of their business convert to self-insurance) and by employers who act as agents for their employees in opposing most mandates. The probable explanation for the increase in state insurance mandates after the mid-1970s is ERISA. This law preempted self-insured employers from state insurance laws. Thus, prior to 1974, when a mandate was proposed, proponents and opponents presented their case before the legislature, which balanced the views of both groups. After ERISA, larger, self-insured employers were no longer affected and, as a consequence, did not waste political capital on insurance mandates. The result was the growth in mandates evident in Figure 18-1.

Many states have become concerned about the growth of state mandates and have reacted by creating pre- or postreview processes for state benefit mandate laws. Bellows, Halpin and McMenamin (2006) reported that, as of September 2004, 26 states had established a formal review process. However, there is no evidence to date (one way or the other) that the processes have affected the enactment of state insurance mandates.

The Economics of Mandates

The intent of mandates is to increase the number of persons who are covered by particular provisions. Thus, the first question is whether mandates actually expand coverage. The issue is not clear-cut because the labor/health insurance markets can adjust in several ways. At one extreme are large employers that are unaffected because they are self-insured under ERISA. Some additional firms may switch from purchasing insurance to being self-insured to avoid the consequences of particularly expensive mandates. At the other extreme are small employers who may be exempted from specific mandates or that may be exempted by virtue of "bare-bones" laws that exclude them from all or most of the mandates in their state (see Chapter 17). In the middle are employer groups that are affected. They may purchase coverage with the mandates and by means of compensating differentials pass the costs on to their employees. Employees may choose to decline coverage individually, or the employer may drop coverage entirely due to the now-higher premium. In addition, there is some question as to whether mandate laws are actually enforced. To further complicate the story, the mandated coverage may simply reflect coverage that most people in the state already have. If so, the enactment of the mandate may merely reflect the existing coverage preferences of those in the state, rather than actually driving people in the state to adopt some new coverage.

Mandates and the Extent of Coverage

There appears to be no rigorous research that directly addresses the issue of how many more people may (or may not) be covered by a particular insurance mandate. However, the existing literature allows us to begin to bracket the potential for increase.

First, state mandates do not apply to federal insurance programs. Thus, the roughly 12 percent of the U.S. resident population that is over age 65 and covered by Medicare are not affected. Those covered by Medicaid and by other federal programs, such as the U.S. Department of Veterans Affairs (VA), also are not affected. Overall in 2005, Medicaid and other federal programs constituted approximately 19 percent of the under-age-65 U.S. population (see Table 18-3).

Second, an additional 17.9 percent of those under age 65 are uninsured and would be unaffected, at least initially, by a state coverage mandate.

Third, those employees and their dependents who are covered by a self-insured employer-sponsored plan also are not subject to a state insurance mandate. Data from the 2001 Kaiser/HRET Employer Health Benefits Survey (Gabel, Jensen, and Hawkins 2003) suggest that 50 percent of insured workers are in self-insured plans. Since 62 percent of those under age 65 are covered by an employer-sponsored plan, the implication is that roughly 31 percent are unaffected.

Finally, there is some concern about whether state insurance mandates are actually enforced. Jensen, Roychoudhury, and Cherkin (1998) examined the effects of chiropractic coverage mandates and found that 17 percent of enrollees in purchased plans that were subject to a state chiropractic coverage mandate nonetheless appeared to lack this coverage entirely.

Type of Coverage	Percentage of Population
Medicaid	13.5%
Other public programs	5.5%
Uninsured	17.9%
Enrolled in self-insured plan	31.0%
Total	67.9%

SOURCE: Data from Fronstin (2006).

TABLE 18-3
Proportion of the Under-Age-65 U.S. Population Unaffected by State Insurance Mandates

The extent of government coverage and the number of the uninsured, and the self-insured will vary from state to state, but these data suggest that approximately two-thirds of those under age 65 will not be affected by a mandate. Among the remaining one-third, many may (or may not) already have the coverage.

Probability of an Employer-Sponsored Plan Becoming Self-Insured Due to State Mandates

A handful of studies have examined the conditions under which a firm—or more appropriately, an employer-sponsored plan—is self-insured. The evidence of the effects is mixed and dependent on the period under study. Jensen, Cotter, and Morrisey (1995) used early and mid-1980s data to examine the probability that a firm would be self-insured. The early data showed that the initial movement toward self-insurance was motivated to some extent by an attempt to avoid state regulation. Taken as a group, state mandates together with state premium taxes were sufficient to explain 68.5 percent of the shifts from purchased to self-insured coverage during the 1981 to 1984 period. Mandates for mental health coverage and state continuation of coverage laws were associated with greater probabilities of being self-insured. The laws had no effect in the 1984 to 1987 period, however. Garfinkel (1995) used 1989 data and found offsetting results. Alcohol abuse treatment mandates increased the probability of self-insurance, but mental health coverage mandates reduced the probability. Park (1999) examined 1994 data and found no effect of state regulatory factors. Finally, using 1993 to 1999 data, Jensen, Morrisey, and Gabel (2003) found no statistically significant effects of mandates on the probability that a firm's conventional, PPO, health maintenance organization (HMO), or point-of-service (POS) plan was self-insured. Instead, the decision to self-insure appeared to be linked to an effort to avoid conflicting state laws.

The Effects of State Mandates on Insurance Premiums

The effect of mandates on insurance premiums is not easily determined either. The appropriate questions are: (1) How much higher (or lower) are the premiums when the mandate is imposed on those who otherwise would not have purchased the coverage? and (2) How much higher (or lower) are the premiums for those who otherwise did purchase the coverage? Simply comparing the premiums for those with and without the coverage has the problem of adverse selection.

In early work, Jensen and Morrisey (1990) showed that some services often subject to mandates were expensive elements in an employer-sponsored conventional insurance package. Chemical dependence coverage was associated with 9 percent higher premiums, and mental health coverage with 13 percent higher premiums. This analysis, however, was unable to disentangle the effects of adverse selection in plan offerings. Aces, Winterbottom, and Zedlewski (1992) looked directly at the costs of mandates and found that, among firms that offered insurance, premiums were 4 to 13 percent higher as a result of mandated benefit laws after controlling for characteristics of the firm and basic aspects of plan coverage.

The Effects of State Mandates on Wages and Coverage Decisions

To the extent that an insurance mandate does raise premiums, the theory of compensating differentials that we examined in Chapter 13 says that employees will pay for the coverage in the form of lower wages and/or reductions in other forms of compensation. The strongest evidence that workers pay for health insurance came from a study in which Gruber (1994b) compared the differences in wages before and after the law, of affected and unaffected workers, in states that did and did not enact a maternity benefits mandate. He concluded that wages were lower in the states that enacted the law and were sufficiently lower to cover the actuarial cost of the coverage. This is strong evidence that employees pay for mandated benefits.

It is also possible that if mandates increase premiums, then some individuals and firms will choose to forgo insurance coverage altogether. Sloan and Conover (1998) examined this issue using Current Population Survey data from the U.S. Census Bureau. They found that the larger the number of state service mandates, the larger the probability that an individual would be uninsured. The probability that an adult would be without coverage increased by 0.004 percentage points with each mandate present. Sloan and Conover extrapolated and applied this to the national uninsured rate and concluded that the elimination of all state insurance mandates would reduce the proportion of uninsured people by one-fifth to one-quarter. While the usual care must be exercised with such extrapolations, the results are broadly consistent with earlier work by Goodman and Musgrave (1987) that concluded that the elimination of state insurance mandates would reduce the proportion of uninsured by 14 percent.

Mandates and Employer Service Offerings

Another way to gauge the effects of mandates is to examine the extent to which coverage differs between employer-sponsored plans that are and are not subject to a mandate. Thus, several authors have compared self-insured plans with purchased plans in states with and without mandates.

Morrisey and Jensen (1993) examined alcohol abuse, drug abuse, and mental health coverage in the late 1980s. They concluded that self-insured firms were about as likely to offer these benefits in states with these mandates as were firms with purchased plans. Similarly, self-insured firms were about as likely as those with purchased plans to offer these benefits in states that did not have the mandates. The overall probability of offering the benefit, however, was lower in states without the mandate.

Data from the mid-1990s similarly revealed that, in states with chiropractic or mental health coverage mandates, self-insured firms were just as likely (or indeed more likely) to include such benefits in their plans as were firms with purchased plans (Jensen, Roychoudhury, and Cherkin 1998; Jensen et al. 1998). In a 1993 study of self-insured plans, Aces et al. (1996) found that the coverage offered by self-insured plans was nearly identical to that contained in purchased plans. There are two interpretations of these findings. One is that the laws encouraged self-insured plans to provide the coverage, even though they were not required to do so. Alternatively, it may be that the legislatures were encouraged to enact the benefits mandates *because* the coverage was already common within the state. To date there is no study to disentangle the direction of impact. However, we saw in the discussion of the federal benefits mandates that Congress tended to enact laws that were already common within the states. It is perhaps a small leap to also conclude that state legislatures enact mandates because the coverage is already common within the state.

Line-of-Business Laws

Small-Group Underwriting

In addition to benefits mandates, most states have enacted laws designed to address specific lines of insurance. Perhaps the most prominent are the laws dealing with permissible underwriting practices in the small-group market. We investigated these in Chapter 17. The upshot was that there is virtually no evidence that the laws affected the availability of coverage in the small-group market.

Any Willing Provider and Freedom of Choice Laws

As managed care plans began to proliferate in the late 1980s, a number of states began to adopt so-called "any willing provider" (AWP) and "freedom of choice" (FOC) laws. AWP laws say that a managed care plan covered under the statute must allow into the provider network any covered provider willing to abide by the terms and conditions of the provider contract. FOC laws require that a managed care firm allow subscribers to step outside of its panel of providers and use a provider of their choice without having to pay the full price for care. By 1995, at least 30 states had some form of AWP law, and 19 had an FOC law. The laws were most likely to apply to pharmacies and HMO networks. See Table 18-4.

The laws are typically characterized as a means of enhancing competition by allowing more providers to be in a managed care plan's network. However, the economics of the laws suggest that the effect is to reduce competition and increase the cost of healthcare services. Indeed, the Federal Trade Commission (FTC) has advised at least one state of the potentially anticompetitive effects of such laws (Federal Trade Commission 2004b). Recall from Chapter 9 that the key to managed care is selective contracting. The plan trades the promise of higher patient volume for lower prices from hospitals, physicians, and pharmacies. The plan meets this promise by directing subscribers to in-plan providers.

Under an AWP law, the managed care plan can no longer assure patient volume. Once a pharmacy and the plan agree on a price, for example, other

TABLE 18-4
Number of
States with
AWP/FOC
Laws, 1995

	Physicians	Hospitals	Pharmacy
Any Willing Provider (AWP)			
HMO	11	9	25
PPO	11	7	22
Freedom of Choice (FOC)			
HMO	5	5	16
PPO	6	5	18

SOURCE: Data from Morrisey and Ohsfeldt (2003/2004).

NOTE: HMO = Health maintenance organization; PPO = Preferred provider organization.

pharmacies can demand to be part of the contract by agreeing to the same terms and conditions. But once there are additional providers, the plan cannot assure the volume. As a result, no pharmacy has an incentive to offer such a low price; it cannot be assured of an increase in volume. Thus, AWP laws, at least in concept, strike at the comparative advantage that managed care plans have enjoyed.

Under an FOC law, a similar but less-dramatic shift occurs. With an FOC law, out-of-plan providers can provide care and be at least partially reimbursed by the managed care plan. As a consequence, no provider has as strong an incentive to offer a lower price because the potential volume gain is eroded by the new entrants to the network.

Work by Marsteller et al. (1997) and Ohsfeldt et al. (1998) suggested that the laws were typically enacted as "preventive strikes" in states that did not yet have significant managed care penetration. Vita (2001) used state health-spending data over the 1980 to 1988 period in a fixed-effects regression methodology. He concluded that states with high AWP/FOC regulatory intensity had per capita healthcare costs that were $35 to $50 higher per year. High regulatory intensity states were those that covered more managed care plan types and more types of providers. Morrisey and Ohsfeldt (2003/2004) used a similar methodology and found that states with higher regulatory intensity had HMO penetration rates that were 6 percentage points lower. Both of these effects appear to be too big to be true, given the relatively modest opposition to the laws raised by the managed care industry. Most likely, the methodologies were unable to fully account for the tendency of the laws to be enacted in states with low managed care penetration.

Chapter Summary

- The federal Employee Retirement Income Security Act (ERISA) has had a major impact on health insurance markets by preempting state insurance regulation of self-insured employer-sponsored health plans.
- State insurance mandates require that health plans offered in the state must include coverage for specific types of services, providers, and individuals. The number of these mandates has increased dramatically since the mid-1970s.
- In the median state, less than 40 percent of the under-age-65 residents are likely to be affected by a group insurance mandate because they are in self-insured plans, covered by a federal program, or uninsured.
- To the extent that a state mandate raises premiums, theory and evidence suggest that employees with coverage will pay in the form of lower wages or other forms of compensation.

- Evidence suggests that as much as one-fifth to one-fourth of the uninsured can be attributed to the presence of state insurance mandates that raise the cost of insurance.
- Many states have enacted any willing provider (AWP) and freedom of choice (FOC) laws, which serve to inhibit a managed care plan's ability to successfully selectively contract with providers for lower prices.

Discussion Questions

1. A former administrator for the Centers for Medicare and Medicaid Services (CMS) noted that the states have only a minor role to play in healthcare reform due to the presence of ERISA. Why is this likely to be true?
2. Why is the average claims experience of COBRA-covered individuals so much higher than the average experience of active workers?
3. What is "job-lock"? How is it supposed to be minimized by HIPAA? To what extent would COBRA limit "job-lock"?
4. Proponents of any willing provider (AWP) laws often argue that these laws enhance competition. Opponents argue that these laws keep prices high. Discuss.

THE INDIVIDUAL INSURANCE MARKET

Individual insurance plays a small role in the current U.S. health insurance market. Only 6 to 7 percent of those under age 65 report having such coverage. Yet, it bulks large in the view of many health reform advocates. Some see it as the market of choice once the link between employment and health insurance is dissolved. Others see it as a mechanism to reduce the ranks of the uninsured by means of tax credits. People currently in the market, however, often see it as transitory coverage from and to employer-sponsored insurance, while other purchasers see it as a longer term source of coverage.

In this chapter, we review the existing literature on the characteristics of those with individual or nongroup coverage, the nature of that coverage, and its providers. We also explore the role of the Internet in the individual market. Finally, we examine the tax credit proposal and the estimates of its impact on coverage.

Who Has Individual Coverage?

The best work on the extent of coverage in the individual insurance market comes from Ziller and colleagues (2004). They examined the 1996 to 2000 panel of the Survey of Income and Program Participation (SIPP) from the U.S. Census Bureau. This survey included a nationally representative sample of nearly 40,200 households that were interviewed every four months for four years! Thus, the researchers were able to identify characteristics of those with coverage but also report on the duration of coverage and the nature of transitions into and out of individual coverage.

In the first month of the survey in 1996, 5.9 percent of the population ages 18–65 were estimated to have "privately purchased" health insurance. Figure 19-1 demonstrates a key feature of these individual insurance purchasers: They tended to be employed. Nearly three-quarters of those with individual coverage were employed. Those employed part-time (fewer than 40 hours per week) were twice as likely as those working full-time to have individual coverage. However, because there are more full-time workers, full-time workers represent nearly two-thirds (62.2 percent) of those with individual coverage. Those who were self-employed were over seven-times more likely to buy individual coverage than were those who worked for someone else (22.3 percent vs 3.2 percent). Seventy-two percent of those employed

FIGURE 19-1
Employment
Status of
Those with
Individually
Purchased
Health
Insurance,
1996

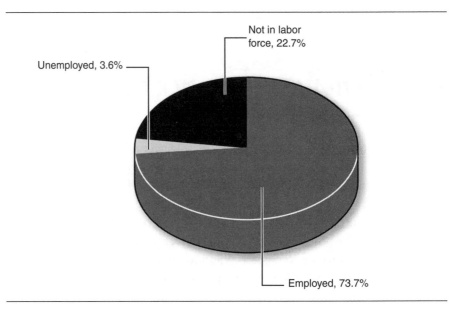

SOURCE: Data from Ziller et al. (2004).

people with individual coverage worked for firms with fewer than 25 employees. Thus, for the most part, the individual market is dominated by people who work full-time for themselves or for others, but typically in a smaller firm. Of course, just over one-fourth are not employed.

While people across the age spectrum purchased individual coverage, the SIPP data indicated that individual coverage was disproportionately held by those who were middle-aged. This is demonstrated in Figure 19-2. The left panel of the figure reports the proportion of individuals buying nongroup private coverage by age group. The right panel reports the distribution by age of those with nongroup private coverage. Over 46 percent of those who had purchased coverage were between 45 and 64 years old. In addition, nearly 60 percent of those with individual coverage had at least some college education, while 9 percent had only an elementary education. Just over 15 percent of those with individual coverage had incomes below the federal poverty line in 1996. Converted to 2006 dollars, the poverty level for a single individual was the equivalent of $9,908. However, 45.4 percent of purchasers had incomes of 300 percent of the poverty level or higher. Sixty-four percent of those purchasing coverage indicated that their health status was "excellent" or "very good," while 11.8 percent indicated that it was "fair" or "poor." Ziller and her colleagues suggested that the health status data may indicate that underwriting to avoid adverse selection may be successful in this market. Others have suggested that higher-risk persons migrate to public programs. See the discussion of work by Hadley and Reschovsky (2003) a little later in the chapter.

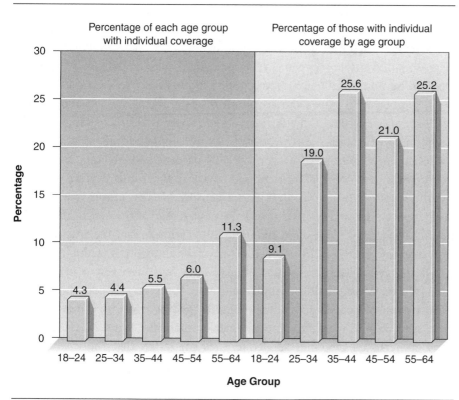

FIGURE 19-2

Age Distribution of Individually Purchased Coverage, 1996

SOURCE: Data from Ziller et al. (2004)

The individual insurance market appears to hold a rather stable share of the population. The Current Population Survey (CPS) from the U.S. Census Bureau and the Medical Expenditure Panel Survey (MEPS) from the U.S. Department of Health and Human Services both suggested that about 5 percent of the ages 18–65 population had individual coverage over the late 1990s (Pauly and Percy 2000). More recent CPS data, from 2005, suggested that the individual market may have grown. These data indicated that about 7 percent of the under-age-65 population had individual coverage (Fronstin 2006). Moreover, those in the ages 18–24 cohort were even more prominent purchasers than those in their 50s and early 60s (Fronstin 2005).

Reasons for the differences between the SIPP and CPS surveys may have to do with the precise nature of the questions asked and the duration of individual coverage, as well as actual secular changes in coverage. However, only the SIPP data are able to look at episodes and duration of coverage. Over the 1996 to 2000 period, 13 percent of the SIPP survey participants purchased individual coverage at least once (Ziller et al. 2004). Typically, obtaining and dropping individual coverage was related to obtaining employer-sponsored coverage. Sixty-eight percent of those obtaining individual coverage said they did so because they had lost employer-sponsored coverage. Another 14 percent had lost public coverage. Nearly 70 percent ended their individual coverage when they were covered by an employer-sponsored plan; 15 percent obtained public coverage. Younger and healthier persons were more likely to be uninsured when they dropped individual coverage.

Figure 19-3 shows the distribution of the median time people in the SIPP survey panel had individual coverage. There is clearly variability in the duration of coverage. Nearly one-half (48 percent) had individual coverage for less than 6 months. However, over 18 percent had coverage for one to two years, and another 17 percent had coverage for over two years. It is also worth noting that these data are "right censored." This means that some of the people in the survey continued to have coverage at the end of the survey period; in fact, over one-third did. The implication is that the true distribution is shifted to the right because many of the individuals in this one-third had coverage for longer than was observed during the survey window.

Thus, while small, the individual market appears to play three roles. First, it provides coverage to many middle-aged people who are either self-employed or who work for others, typically in smaller firms. The regression work undertaken by Ziller and colleagues suggested that those who were

FIGURE 19-3

Duration of
Time with
Individual
Coverage,
1996–2000

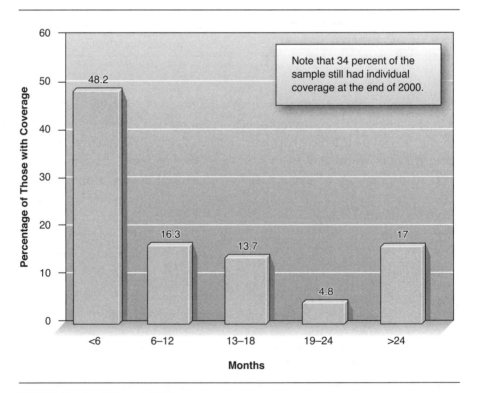

Note that 34 percent of the sample still had individual coverage at the end of 2000.

SOURCE: Data from Ziller et al. (2004).

self-employed tend to have 20 percent longer periods with individual coverage. In this sense, it appears to provide stable, ongoing coverage for those who are in the latter part of their careers, perhaps working in their own small businesses as they plan for their retirement. Second, individual coverage provides transitional coverage for a short period of time, often for less than one year, for those moving from one employer-sponsored plan to another. Third, it provides spells of coverage for the otherwise uninsured. Some people acquire individual coverage and then drop it to return to uninsured status. This group tends to be unemployed and younger, and to have lower income. While it is unclear from the SIPP data, this group may include young adults who are transitioning from parental coverage to first jobs that do not include employer-sponsored coverage. It is conceivable that some of these individuals purchase coverage because of impending health problems.

Insurance Providers in the Individual Market

The general view of the individual market is that the coverage is more expensive per unit of coverage than in the group market and that there is substantially more manual rating. Health status is thought to be used as a factor at least at initial enrollment to overcome potentially severe adverse selection. Very little hard data exist to substantiate these views, however.

Pauly and Percy (2000) summarized some of the only available data on the relative prices of nongroup coverage compared to group coverage. They reported the loading ratios for group and nongroup coverage for various types of health insurance companies from the mid-1990s. The loading ratio is the amount of aggregate premiums divided by the sum of claims paid. These comparisons obviously do not compare the full premiums for identical coverage. However, the loading ratio can be thought of as the amount over and above the expected claim that the insurers in the respective markets have charged. Table 19-1 shows that, in the group market, this ratio was in the neighborhood of 1.17; premiums exceeded claims paid by roughly 17 percent. In contrast, the average ratio in the nongroup market was nearly 1.75 but has declined steadily over the years.

Chollet, Kirk, and Chow (2000) described the structure of the individual insurance market in the late 1990s. They reported a market dominated by a few sellers. In 1997, the largest three insurers had at least 50 percent of the market in every state and at least 75 percent of the market in 28 states and the District of Columbia. Seven states reported having four or fewer insurers in the individual market. However, many states had many insurers with very small market shares. In 32 states, the smallest 50 percent of insurers had 10 percent of the market or less. Blue Cross/Blue Shield tended to be the dominant insurer in most states and had a national market share in the

TABLE 19-1

Loading Ratios
for Health
Insurance

Commercial Insurance for Hospital and Medical/Surgical Insurance

Year	Group	Nongroup
1970	1.02	2.10
1975	1.13	1.97
1980	1.22	1.65
1985	1.34	1.68
1990	1.18	1.53
1995	1.15	1.50

Accident and Health Insurance Lines of Life/Health Insurers

Year	Group	Nongroup
1988	1.16	1.78
1990	1.27	1.75
1995	1.21	1.66

SOURCE: Data from Pauly and Percy (2000), tables 7 and 8.

individual market of nearly 50 percent. The remainder was split about evenly between health maintenance organizations (HMOs) and commercial insurers. As noted later in the chapter, there is some suggestion of a significant increase in non-HMO managed care plan offerings more recently.

Commentators have noted the heterogeneity that is present both in the policies that are offered and the people who select coverage. Chollet and Kirk (1998) conducted field studies in ten states and observed that benefits, cost sharing, and prices varied widely. Some insurers offered a single benefit design with a number of deductible and cost-sharing options; others offered major differences across plan choices. It was not unusual to see products excluding maternity and mental health coverage. When these were present, they almost always required separate and higher deductibles, copays, and separate annual and lifetime limits on coverage. It was not uncommon for insurers to deny coverage. Buntin, Marquis, and Yegian (2004), for example, suggested that denials ranged from 8 to 18 percent of applications.

Pooling in the Nongroup Market

The heterogeneity of the individual policies offered obviously reflects concern over adverse selection. Several researchers have investigated the extent of "pooling" in the individual market. By this they mean the extent to which the individual market combines people with different risks. From this perspective, refusing to insure high-risk individuals and using medical underwriting would result in less "pooling." The group of insured individuals would then be more homogeneous.

The evidence with respect to the extent of pooling in the individual market is conflicting. Saver and Doescher (2000) used 1987 data from the National Medical Care Expenditure Survey to estimate the effects of demographic, geographic, and health status measures on the purchase of nongroup coverage. They found that health status measures had only a weak ability to predict nongroup purchase. This suggests substantial pooling of risks. Herring and Pauly (2001) used 1997 data from the Community Tracking Study Household Survey sponsored by the Robert Wood Johnson Foundation. They regressed the nongroup premium on predicted medical expenses and a set of control variables and found that premiums increased with expenditures but by less than a proportionate amount. This, too, suggests relatively weak medical underwriting and substantial pooling.

There are institutional reasons to think that the extent of pooling is relatively great. First, Pauly and Nichols (2002) argued that the contribution of agents and brokers in the individual insurance market is to provide information to potential purchasers, helping them find lower-priced policies. To the extent that insurer underwriting practices differ, the effect of agents is to increase pooling. Second, underwriting is undertaken at initial enrollment and is seldom repeated once individuals are enrolled. Moreover, since the passage of the 1996 Health Insurance Portability and Accountability Act (HIPAA), sellers of individual coverage are required to guarantee renewal. Buntin, Marquis, and Yegian (2004) indicated that re-underwriting typically does not to occur unless individuals change insurance products or the carrier closes the line of business. Thus, even if there is substantial sorting of risks at initial enrollment, pooling would increase over time as some insured individuals develop chronic health problems.

Marquis and Buntin (2006) confirmed this conjecture with data from three large California nongroup health insurers. They found that "our results by and large support the conclusion that there is considerable risk pooling in the individual market" (p. 1979). They did find some separation of risks.

TABLE 19-2

Health Status
of Insurance
Purchasers,
1998–2001

	Nongroup Insurance	Employer-Sponsored Health Insurance	No Insurance	Public Insurance
All	4.8%	71.2%	18.3%	5.7%

Policyholder's Health (% distribution)

	Nongroup Insurance	Employer-Sponsored Health Insurance	No Insurance	Public Insurance
"Excellent" with no chronic conditions	23.6%	17.7%	15.3%	8.9%
"Excellent" with 1+ chronic conditions	8.8%	6.6%	5.7%	5.8%
"Very good" or "Good" with no chronic conditions	28.6%	30.2%	28.5%	20.0%
"Very good" or "Good" with 1+ chronic conditions	16.4%	18.0%	13.6%	12.9%
"Very good" or "Good" with 2+ chronic conditions	15.7%	18.5%	15.5%	21.4%
"Fair" or "Poor"	6.9%	9.0%	21.4%	31.0%

SOURCE: Data from Hadley and Reschovsky (2003).

Higher-risk individuals were less likely to purchase individual coverage, more likely buy plans with generous coverage, and more likely to pay higher premiums than were those in better health. However, those who had been enrolled for more than two years, on average, had worse health status than those at initial enrollment. Much of this appeared to result from underwriting occurring only at initial enrollment and not subsequently.

Hadley and Reschovsky (2003), however, argued that selection bias on the part of potential purchasers may also explain the existing research. That is, those who have high health risks may not buy individual coverage and may instead migrate to public or employer-sponsored coverage. As evidence of this likely selection bias, Hadley and Reschovsky reported data from the 1998 to 1999 and 2000 to 2001 Community Tracking Study Household Survey for those ages 18–64. These data are summarized in Table 19-2.

The data clearly suggest that those in poorer health are much more likely to be in a public insurance program such as Medicaid and somewhat more likely to have employer-sponsored health insurance than are those who purchase nongroup coverage. This suggests that, if we look at the determinants of choice, excluding those with public and employer-sponsored health insurance coverage, we are likely to get results that show substantial risk pooling, but it is actually pooling over a relatively narrow range of expected losses.

Hadley and Reschovsky estimated nongroup insurance premiums, accounting for the type of coverage taken using a selection-adjusted model. That is, their analysis incorporated information on the disproportionate probability that someone in fair or poor health would likely be in a public or employer-sponsored health insurance program. In so doing, they found that health status has a relatively large effect on nongroup insurance premiums. A single person with a "minor" health problem was estimated to pay a premium 15 percent higher than a person in "excellent" health with no chronic conditions. (A "minor" health problem was defined as being in "excellent," "very good," or "good" health and having no more than one chronic condition.) Those with a "major" health problem paid premiums that were 43 to 50 percent higher than individuals in "excellent" health. (A "major" health problem was defined as being in "very good" or "good" health and having two or more chronic conditions, or being in "fair" or "poor" health.) In addition, smokers paid 16 percent higher premiums, other things equal.

The statistical relationship between self-reported health status and premiums suggests that insurers in the nongroup market were able to identify those with health problems through their underwriting mechanisms and charge them higher premiums. It also suggests that if those with poorer health status are able to sort themselves into public and employer-sponsored plans, the remaining health status differences are not particularly noteworthy in premium determination for the nongroup market.

This is important for ongoing policy debates. If we assume that high-risk people will remain in or migrate to public and employer-sponsored plans, then we can use estimates of the demand for individual coverage that focus on those currently uninsured or already in the individual market. That research suggested that the individual market would do a reasonably good job of providing coverage for these individuals. Alternatively, if we assume that public or employer-sponsored options would not be options for higher-risk individuals, then we would focus more on Hadley and Reschovsky's findings. Their work suggested that high-risk people would be unable to find individual coverage except at high (i.e., risk-adjusted) premiums.

The Individual Market and the Internet

One of the biggest shortcomings of the existing literature on the individual health insurance market is that the research was conducted before the Internet was a serious option for obtaining information and premium quotes.

In the individual market, the Internet has become a routine source to which people can turn for a sense of the coverages available and the premiums charged. You can, of course, purchase coverage over the Internet. Table 19-3 presents information on the monthly premium for health insurance in a

TABLE 19-3

Examples of Monthly Premiums for Individual Health Insurance Coverage, 2006

Health Insurance Quotes from eHealthInsurance.com for Female Nonsmoker Born in October 1982 and Living in:

City	Zip Code	Premium	Plan
Baltimore, Md.	21210	$93.26	UnitedHealthcare Plan 100
Birmingham, Ala.	35206	$104.38	UnitedHealthcare Plan 100
College Station, Tex.	77845	$120.56	UnitedHealthcare Plan 100
Evanston, Ill.	60208	$123.58	UnitedHealthcare Plan 100
Iowa City, Iowa	52240	$95.99	UnitedHealthcare Plan 100
San Diego, Calif.	92109	$88.00	HealthNet Simple Choice 25
Seattle, Wash.	98105	$74.00	Regence Blue Shield Preferred Plan 2500

Health Insurance Quotes from eHealthInsurance.com for Male Nonsmoker Born in October 1946 and Living in:

City	Zip Code	Premium	Plan
Baltimore, Md.	21210	$435.12	UnitedHealthcare Plan 100
Birmingham, Ala.	35206	$490.21	UnitedHealthcare Plan 100
College Station, Tex.	77845	$568.56	UnitedHealthcare Plan 100
Evanston, Ill.	60208	$580.36	UnitedHealthcare Plan 100
Iowa City, Iowa	52240	$450.77	UnitedHealthcare Plan 100
San Diego, Calif.	92109	$434.00	HealthNet Simple Choice 25
Seattle, Wash.	98105	$274.00	Regence Blue Shield Preferred Plan 2500

SOURCE: Data from http://www.ehealthinsurance.com.

NOTE: The UnitedHealthcare Plan 100 has $2,500 deductible with no copays or coinsurance for most services provided by network providers. Maternity care is not covered. There is a 12-month waiting period for preexisting conditions and $3 million lifetime maximum. Other exclusions and limitations apply. The other plans are similar, except the Seattle plans which also require a 20% coinsurance rate after satisfying the deductible.

number of cities across the country and was drawn from eHealthInsurance.com in September 2006. The web site lists a variety of health insurance plans from a number of different companies, depending on the market area. The premium "offers" in Table 19-3 are for two individuals, both of whom are nonsmokers: (1) a woman born in October 1982 and (2) a man born in October 1946. The former is in the age range of a typical student in a graduate health insurance course; the latter is in the age range at which an individual might consider becoming self-employed or starting a second career prior to Medicare eligibility. They represent the two age ranges most likely to buy individual coverage.

Given the insurance theory in Chapter 2, the selected plans in Table 19-3 cover high-magnitude loses. All of the plans have a relatively high individual deductible of $2,500. The fine print indicates that they exclude maternity care and have a 12-month waiting period on preexisting conditions. The UnitedHealthcare Plan 100 was used as a benchmark only because it was available in most of the markets selected. Cheaper plans, typically with higher deductibles, were available, as were more-expensive offerings. A casual review of the plans offered on the web site showed most to be preferred provider organizations (PPOs) or networks of providers. It is worth noting that plans were not offered through this web site in several states, particularly in the Northeast. This is likely a result of state insurance law restrictions on Internet sales, underwriting provisions, or premium restrictions. (It is, of course, conceivable that plans affiliated with this web site simply did not do business in these states for other reasons.)

The female graduate student in our example could typically get this coverage for about $100 per month. The older man would have to pay something in the neighborhood of $500 per month.

Pauly, Herring, and Song (2002a) undertook some of the first work using Internet nongroup premium offerings as a basis of research. They were interested in whether the dispersion (or range) of premiums differed for high- and low-risk individuals and whether the dispersion of premium offers was different than the dispersion of premiums actually purchased. More importantly, they were also interested in whether people could save money on individual coverage by using the Internet.

They investigated these questions by using the Community Tracking Study Household Survey from 1996 and 1997 to provide data on the actual premiums paid by those with individual premiums. They then rolled these premiums forward to 2001, using a premium-predicting regression equation, and compared the web-based offers with the rolled-forward actual premiums. The Internet premiums were obtained from eHealthInsurance.com, the same source used for compiling Table 19-3. Given that source, their only measure of risk was age. They defined "low risk" as people ages 18–44 and "high-risk" as people ages 45–64.

Pauly, Herring, and Song's first finding was that the dispersion of Internet "offer" prices did not vary between low-risk and high-risk people. However, the dispersion of actual prices was smaller for high-risk persons. This is what we would expect from search theory. High-risk people will have higher claims experience, and therefore, their insurance will cost more. This gives them greater incentives to search for lower prices. The fact that the dispersion of actual prices is smaller for high-risk persons suggests that they searched more before settling on a particular product.

Pauly, Herring, and Song's second finding was that the premium sensitivity was lower for actual premiums than for offered premiums. This, too, is consistent with search theory and implies that greater search effort (particularly on the part of high-risk people) offset some of the expected higher medical claims expense they would incur.

Finally, Pauly and colleagues examined whether people could save money with Internet searches for health insurance. Their answer was that it depends. If you compare the actual price paid with the *median* price offered on the Internet, on average all types of individuals would have paid higher prices by using the Internet. However, people do not typically search for the median price; they search for a low price. When the study compared the tenth percentile offer price (i.e., not the lowest price, but near the bottom of the distribution of prices), young people (i.e., the low-risk individuals) would have paid less using the Internet than the premium they actually paid. However, higher-risk people would still have paid more through the Internet than they actually paid by traditional searching. Thus, the evidence suggests that younger people had been less aggressive searchers and would have gained more from Internet searching.

> In short, it is possible to save money by using the Internet, but there are no guarantees.
>
> —Pauly, Herring, and Song (2002a, p. 18)

Tax Credits in the Individual Market

One approach to dealing with the problem of the uninsured is to provide an income tax credit. Currently, those who have employer-sponsored coverage can treat their health insurance as untaxed income. Those with individual coverage can deduct a portion of their premiums under some circumstances. A number of policy advocates have proposed providing a refundable income tax credit for the purchase of health insurance. Whereas a tax exemption such as with employer-sponsored coverage increases in value as you reach higher marginal tax rates, a tax credit is defined in terms of a constant tax subsidy. Some proponents have suggested a $1,000 tax credit. This means that you could spend as much as you liked on individual health insurance, but your federal income tax liability would be reduced by $1 for each dollar purchased, to a maximum of $1,000. A refundable credit is one that would be paid even if your tax liability was less than $1,000. Under this plan, any policy purchased with a premium of $1,000 or less has a tax-adjusted, or net premium, of zero.

Pauly, Herring, and Song (2002b) provided estimates of the likely take-up of insurance under this sort of plan. They again used the 1996 to 1997 Community Tracking Study Household Survey to generate the characteristics of likely purchasers. The Community Tracking Study has nearly 6,100 people without health insurance and provides information on the age, gender, zip code, and smoking status of each participant. Pauly, Herring, and Song used the eHealthInsurance.com web site to get premium "offers" for people with those characteristics in 2001. The issue is how many of the uninsured would purchase basic coverage if they had a $1,000 refundable tax credit. The study defined a basic policy as one with a $1,000 deductible or less. The web site allowed them to obtain a range of premium "quotes" for each individual.

Pauly and colleagues argued that if individuals could get coverage for a net price of zero (premium minus the tax credit), they should be counted as getting coverage under the proposal. Obviously, the researchers could have obtained a high estimate of the number of covered individuals by matching each observation to the least costly basic plan found on the web site. This is rather unrealistic, however, inasmuch as the lowest cost plan may have provisions that make it undesirable. Instead, the study team identified the entire range of premium offerings that had a $1,000 deductible or less for each individual and used the premium at the 25th percentile premium as the relevant price. For some individuals, the 25th percentile premium was relatively low; for others, it was higher. Various points on the distribution of the 25th percentile premium are presented in Table 19-4. For example, the least expensive 10 percent of the individuals had a (25th percentile) premium of $683 or less. Their net price would be zero, and they were counted as buying coverage. From the table, it is clear that at least 25 percent of the uninsured would face a zero net premium and would have coverage under the proposal. In fact, some percentage between 25 and 50 percent would actually face a zero net price.

Of course, with a tax credit, even those who have to pay something to purchase insurance have a subsidy. We would expect at least some of them to buy subsidized coverage. How many depends on the elasticity of demand for individual coverage. Using Pauly, Herring, and Song's more-conservative

Distribution	Web-Based Premium	Net Price	
			TABLE 19-4
			Distribution of
10th percentile	$683	$0	25th Percentile
			Premiums for
25th percentile	$873	$0	Uninsured
50th percentile	$1,252	$252	Individuals
			under a $1,000
75th percentile	$1,995	$995	Tax Credit in
90 percentile	$2,952	$1,952	2001

TABLE 19-5

Simulated Take-up Rates, Given a $1,000 Refundable Tax Credit in 2001

Premium Assumption	Take-up Rate
Internet premiums, 25th percentile—$1,000 deductible plans	56%
Internet premiums, 10th percentile—$1,000 deductible plans	62%
Internet premiums, 25th percentile— $250 deductible plans	21%

SOURCE: Data from Pauly, Herring, and Song (2002b).

estimate, Table 19-5 presents estimates of take-up rates under various assumptions about coverage. The top row reflects the assumptions underlying Table 19-4: $1,000 deductible policy and take-up defined at the 25th percentile of "offer" premium. It implies that 56 percent of the uninsured would have basic coverage under this proposal. A larger share of the uninsured could be covered if we assume that people would buy a lower-priced policy—one at the 10th percentile of the offers they find on the web site. Under this scenario, 62 percent could be covered. Finally, if we assume that only more-generous coverage is appropriate, the last row of Table 19-5 indicates that, with no more than a $250 deductible, 21 percent of the uninsured population would likely have health insurance under a $1,000 tax credit in 2001.

There are additional issues to consider with such a tax credit proposal, of course. The first is the extent of "crowd-out" from employer-sponsored coverage. If the tax credit is added to the existing tax rules, some people with employer-sponsored coverage will drop that coverage and take individual coverage through the tax credit. Employer-sponsored coverage would be crowded-out. We could *replace* the employer-sponsored tax exclusion with a tax credit, as some have proposed. Alternatively, we could limit eligibility for the tax credit to lower-income individuals and families in an effort to limit such crowd-out.

Moreover, Hadley and Reschovsky (2003) raised the concern that such a tax credit would only be sufficient to attract younger, healthier members of the uninsured. Their estimates, examined earlier in the chapter, found that individuals with major and minor health conditions faced premiums that were approximately 45 and 15 percent higher, respectively, than those with excellent health. The concern is that these people would find the tax subsidy too small to buy effective coverage and would decline to purchase any. This has led some to suggest that any tax credit should be risk adjusted.

What We Do Not Know about the Nongroup Market?

Little is actually known about the individual insurance market and the potentially large role it could play in the future. Pauly and Nichols (2002) summarized a series of unresolved issues about this market. The first issue is how well the nongroup market works. Some look at the evidence and see a wide range of choices and coverages tailored to individual preferences and risk profiles. Others see a market in which higher-risk people are unable to buy coverage or are only able to buy it at prices that are too high, relative to other premiums or to their incomes.

The second issue is what would happen if there were an infusion of a large number of people into the market as a result of a tax credit or a substantial change in the tax policy affecting employer-sponsored coverage. Presumably, this increased demand would lead to lower loading fees and more mass-marketed products. Pauly and Nichols noted that the mass marketing of auto insurance resulted in loading fees that dropped by up to one-third, and this may be possible in the individual health insurance market as well.

The third issue is how the provision of a tax credit would affect the employer-sponsored market. Insurance theory suggests that employer-sponsored coverage would become less generous if the open-ended existing tax credit were replaced with a tax credit. As we noted in Chapter 14, some simulation work suggests that this effect could be large. The related question is: what happens to the purchase of group coverage? That would seem to depend on whether there were limitations on the eligibility of the tax credit. If there were narrow limits, the crowd-out effects would likely be small, regardless of other features. However, if group insurance provides other advantages, as suggested in Chapter 13, any disruption of the group market would likely be small. Most people would continue to get their (now less-generous) coverage through their employer.

Chapter Summary

- The individual or nongroup health insurance market in the United States currently consists of 6 to 7 percent of the under-age-65 population. Very little research has been undertaken on this segment of the private insurance market.
- The individual health insurance market is heterogeneous. Most people with individual coverage tend to be in the labor force; many of them are older and self-employed. These people often maintain the coverage for longer periods of time. Others purchase the coverage to transition from or to employer-sponsored coverage. Still others purchase spells of coverage in between periods without insurance.
- The individual health insurance market in most states is dominated by a few insurers, usually including Blue Cross/Blue Shield. The smallest 50 percent of insurers typically share less than 10 percent of the individual market.

- Individual insurance plans have loading ratios that are often three times that of group policies. However, there appears to be substantial variation in the nature of coverage and the degree to which various underwriting factors and preexisting condition clauses are used. The market also appears to be less extensively regulated than the small-group market.
- The Internet has become a much more important source of premium and coverage information in the nongroup market. Early evidence suggests that some individuals—particularly, younger, healthier people—can benefit from Internet searches for coverage.
- Policy advocates see a major role for the individual health insurance market either as a replacement for employer-sponsored coverage or through targeted tax credits designed to encourage people to buy coverage.

Discussion Questions

1. Visit a web site such as eHealthInsurance.com, and obtain premium quotes for yourself in your current zip code. What premium are you quoted for a $2,500 deductible policy with no other cost sharing? If you did not have employer-sponsored coverage, would you find this premium and coverage attractive? Would a policy with a $4,000 deductible be more or less attractive? How about one with a $250 deductible and 20 percent coinsurance? Why?

2. Our discussion of health savings accounts (HSAs) in Chapter 16 suggested that they may be particularly attractive in the individual market. Why would this be so? Which segment of the individual market is likely to find HSAs most attractive?

3. Suppose the tax subsidy for employer-sponsored health insurance ended, and there was a large influx of subscribers into the individual market. What sort of changes, if any, would you expect to see in this market?

HIGH-RISK POOLS

Some people are unable to purchase private health insurance due their health status. This can occur for the obvious reason that their expected claims experience simply exceeds their resources. In this circumstance, not only can they not buy health insurance, they cannot pay for their likely use of health services. A more nuanced view, however, helps identify more of the issues. According to the standard insurance theory discussed in Chapter 3, the uninsurables can be thought of as having risk premiums that are not large enough to compensate an insurer for providing coverage. This may be because the individuals have very little risk aversion and, therefore, are unwilling to pay much more than the expected loss to avoid the consequences of that loss. Alternatively, the probability of individual loss may be very high. Insurance theory says that, under such circumstances, people will have small risk premiums and will not be very willing to purchase coverage.

Moreover, in the case of expected high claims experience, any significant variance and relatively few covered lives in a risk pool mean that an insurer faces substantial objective risk (recall Chapter 5). These circumstances suggest that the insurer would either quote a high loading fee on top of the expected loss to reflect this risk or simply avoid the risk entirely by not offering coverage.

Many states have tried to assist with the problem of insurance coverage for the uninsurable. In this chapter, we investigate these programs. In essence, the states have created publicly run health insurance plans for those who cannot obtain insurance elsewhere. In the process, the states have to deal with issues of eligibility, coverage, and premiums. Because these programs have claims expenditures that exceed the premium revenues collected, the states must find ways to cover the losses. In the chapter, we summarize the approaches that states take in forming their high-risk pools, and we also explore the potential size of the pool of uninsurables, the extent of premium sensitivity among purchasers, and the length of time people stay in high-risk pools. As with the individual insurance market, the research on high-risk pools is very limited.

How Many Uninsurables Are There?

The short answer to the question "How many uninsurables are there?" is that we do not know. Certainly everyone who is uninsured is not uninsurable.

Some simply are not willing to pay a risk premium that others would gladly pay. Few would define these people as uninsurable. Moreover, providing a subsidy to those who are unwilling to pay even modest risk premiums would provide incentives for everyone to understate their willingness to pay.

Frakt, Pizer, and Wrobel (2004, p. 74) provided a working definition of the uninsurable as those under age 65 who are "uninsured and who could not work, were limited in the type of work they could do, or received any disability or worker's compensation." This approach, together with Current Population Survey data from the U.S. Census Bureau for 1995 through 2001, led them to suggest that about 1 percent of the total population and 6 percent of the uninsured population fit the definition. These estimates are consistent with a recent report by the California Managed Risk Medical Insurance Board (2006), which cited their actuaries as estimating that between 2.5 and 6 percent of the population was both uninsured and uninsurable.

State High-Risk Pools

As of 2006, there were 34 states that had implemented a high-risk pool (Communicating for Agriculture 2006). The first pools were created in Minnesota and Connecticut in 1976. Table 20-1 provides the most recently available compendium of the number of people covered by state. It is immediately obvious that most high-risk pools are very small. Only three had more than 10,000 enrolled, and fifteen had fewer than 2,000. However, Minnesota, Nebraska, Oregon, and Wisconsin cover at least 20 percent of the estimated number of uninsurables in their states.

Eligibility

Depending on the state, high-risk pools are open to up to three categories of eligible populations: (1) the medically uninsurable, (2) those eligible under the Health Insurance Portability and Accountability Act (HIPAA), and (3) Medicare beneficiaries seeking supplemental coverage.

The principal purpose of state high-risk pools is to provide coverage for those who are either unable to obtain coverage in the private market or who face high premiums—that is, the medically uninsurable. Achman and Chollet (2001) provided an excellent overview of eligibility and coverage circa 2000. Operationally, the states have defined eligibility based on experience in the private market. Depending on the state, the individual must have been turned down for coverage by one or two insurance plans or must have been quoted premiums that are substantially above standard rates. In some states, these rates must be 150 to 300 percent of the private-sector rates for those in good health. Many states allow participation if the person has been

State	Total	High-Risk Pool Enrollees	
		Relative to Number Uninsured	Relative to Number Uninsurable
Total	115,688	0.45%	8%
Alabama	2,431	0.37%	5%
Alaska	395	0.33%	4%
Arkansas	2,270	0.55%	7%
California	17,343	0.25%	6%
Colorado	1,536	0.25%	5%
Connecticut	1,719	0.51%	8%
Florida	709	0.03%	1%
Illinois	10,120	0.58%	10%
Indiana	6,475	0.89%	11%
Iowa	271	0.11%	2%
Kansas	1,283	0.43%	6%
Louisiana	1,088	0.13%	2%
Minnesota	25,892	6.14%	54%
Mississippi	2,231	0.49%	7%
Missouri	889	0.16%	3%
Montana	1,687	0.99%	12%
Nebraska	5,023	3.03%	36%
New Mexico	1,063	0.25%	5%
North Dakota	1,307	1.68%	18%
Oklahoma	1,922	0.32%	3%
Oregon	5,833	1.22%	21%
South Carolina	1,451	0.25%	3%
Texas	8,600	0.18%	4%
Utah	1,106	0.37%	5%
Washington	2,333	0.29%	4%
Wisconsin	10,042	1.90%	21%
Wyoming	669	0.87%	11%

TABLE 20-1
High-Risk Pool Enrollees by State, 2000

SOURCE: Frakt, Pizer, and Wrobel (2004),"High-risk Pools for Uninsurable Individuals: Recent Growth, Future Prospects," *Health Care Financing Review* 26(2): 73–87, Table 2.

BOX 20-1

HIPAA and High Risk Pools

Interest in state high-risk pools increased after the passage of the Health Insurance Portability and Accountability Act (HIPAA) in 1996. As discussed in Chapter 18, the federal HIPAA legislation limited waiting periods for pre-existing conditions. As part of this, it also required states to guarantee health insurance portability. States can meet this obligation in a variety of ways, and failure to do so brings on federal oversight. One way that states can provide portability is to allow HIPAA eligibles to participate in the state's high-risk pool.

offered coverage only with a restrictive rider, and several states deem individuals to be eligible if they have certain medical conditions, such as Hodgkin's disease or AIDS.

HIPAA requires that those losing group coverage are to have access to individual coverage. Some 23 states (in 2000) used their high-risk pool as "last-resort" coverage to satisfy this requirement (Frakt, Pizer, and Wrobel 2004). See also Box 20-1. This component of the state's program can be relatively minor, as in Minnesota where only 1 percent of participants are HIPAA eligible, to Montana where more than half are (Achman and Chollet 2001). The Alabama high-risk pool was established exclusively for HIPAA eligibles, but the person must have exhausted COBRA (Consolidated Omnibus Budget Reconciliation Act—see Chapter 18) continuation coverage to be eligible for the Alabama program.

Achman and Chollet (2001) reported that 11 states allow Medicare beneficiaries to participate in their pools. Typically, the purpose is to allow these individuals to purchase Medicare supplementary coverage (see Chapter 21). Some of these states only allow those who are Medicare disabled to participate, and one state—Mississippi—only allows those who were in the high-risk pool prior to Medicare eligibility to continue in the program. The importance of this component also varies by state. Over one-third of the enrollees in the Washington, Wisconsin, and Wyoming programs are Medicare beneficiaries. It is much less of a factor in other states.

It is important to note that, while the state programs establish rules of eligibility, from time to time, they close their programs to new enrollees, and in such cases, waiting lists are common. Florida closed its program to new enrollees in 1991, and it remains closed at this writing. While it once had some 7,500 enrollees, it now enrolls approximately 500 (AcademyHealth 2006). Frakt, Pizer, and Wrobel (2004) indicated that the California program could sell only as many high-risk policies as it could finance with its allocation from the state's tobacco settlement moneys. In 2000, there were approximately 4,000 people on the waiting list, and these people expected to wait about a year for coverage. The waiting list had been eliminated by 2005, due to a pilot program that increased insurance industry participation in the financing of the program. The board that provides oversight to the program expects the waiting lists to return, however (California Managed Risk Medical Insurance Board 2006). Communicating for Agriculture (2006) indicated that the Louisiana and Illinois programs place limits on the number of new enrollees who are medically uninsurable, but not on those who are eligible due to HIPAA.

Duration of Coverage

There is little generalized evidence on the duration of enrollment in high-risk pools. Stearns and Mroz (1995/96) provided some of the only data. They examined eight states (Connecticut, Florida, Iowa, Minnesota, North Dakota, Nebraska, Washington, and Wisconsin) over the early 1990s. They found that disenrollment rates ranged from 15 to 40 percent, depending on state. Typically, about 70 percent of enrollees were estimated to be in the program after one year, about 50 percent after two years, and roughly one-third after four years.

Stearns and Mroz (1995/96) found that nonpayment of premium was the most frequent reason for disenrollment. Among those who voluntarily disenrolled, disenrollment rates decline with age, after age 20. However, disenrollment increased with the number of people in the family, perhaps suggesting attaining access to employer-sponsored coverage through a spouse or parent. As discussed in more detail later in the chapter, price is an important factor in participation in a high-risk program.

Coverage

Most states offer a variety of coverage options in their high-risk programs. Achman and Chollet (2001) reported that of the 29 programs they tracked, almost all offered a variety of coverage options. Some included indemnity and preferred provider organization (PPO) plans; a few offered health maintenance organizations (HMOs). Most plans had a number of deductible options, often ranging from $500 to $5,000 or even $10,000. Most of these plans had coinsurance arrangements once the deductibles were covered. Coinsurance rates ranged from 10 to 20 to 30 percent of covered expenses.

Importantly in a high-risk population, virtually all of the programs in the Achman and Chollet study had lifetime limits. For most programs, this was $1,000,000, but Indiana and Tennessee (in their TennCare program at the time) had no limits. In contrast, Wyoming had limits of $350,000 to $600,000, depending on the plan selected. Some states also imposed a limit on the length of time a person can be covered. California, for example, allowed coverage under its high-risk pool for a maximum of 36 months.

Achman and Chollet also found that, with the exception of HIPAA eligibles, all of the states had waiting periods for coverage. As of 2000, most were for six months, but eight states required a twelve-month waiting period before coverage for preexisting conditions was effective. Typically, the states also used a six-month "look-back period" in which they could identify preexisting conditions. These conditions served to limit adverse selection, at least to some extent. People who have exhausted their eligibility in one state would have to wait for six to twelve months before being eligible for coverage in a new state (depending on how a state interprets its lifetime maximum).

According to Achman and Chollet, the programs also typically limited the coverage for mental health and maternity care. The former limit undoubtedly stems from the large price elasticity associated with mental health coverage, as discussed in Chapter 7, and the latter limit results from fear of adverse selection. Riders are sometimes available in the states for these coverages.

Premiums

While the eligibility is limited and the coverage is not generous, the premiums in state high-risk programs are limited. State legislation typically requires the premiums to be no more than 125 to 150 percent of the average premium for similar coverage of standard risks in the individual insurance market (Communicating for Agriculture 2006). Table 20-2 provides premium information for four states in 2006. These states were selected to provide some geographic representation, to reflect states with large programs (Minnesota and Texas) as well as smaller ones, and to feature newer programs (Texas and New Hampshire) relative to others.

Several observations are immediately apparent when we compare the rates across states. First, the states use differing underwriting factors. Colorado and Texas impose different rates for men and women, and both use area within the state as a factor. Minnesota, New Hampshire, and Texas have different rates for smokers and nonsmokers. Coverage also differs significantly. Each state has a different lifetime maximum. One state covers maternity care; two explicitly do not.

These features explain only some of the variation in premiums for high-risk pool plans. A $1,000 deductible plan for a 30-year-old woman ranges from $2,313 in Minnesota to $6,552 in Colorado. The Colorado plan covers maternity care, for example, but has a much lower lifetime maximum. The Colorado plan also has explicit premium reductions for those with sufficiently low income. One of the key additional factors is the premium cap that was established in state law. In Minnesota, the premium may be no more than 125 percent of comparable coverage; in Colorado, the premium is capped at 150 percent. The low Minnesota premiums may explain why Minnesota had 50 percent more enrollees in 2000 than did the next largest state's enrollment (Frakt, Pizer, and Wrobel 2004).

	$1,000 Annual Deductible	$5,000 Annual Deductible
Age 30		
Colorado[*]		
Male	$3,181	$1,676
Female	$5,404	$2,847
Minnesota[†]	$2,313	$1,387
New Hampshire[‡]	$2,472	$1,596
Texas[§]		
Male	$4,848	$2,544
Female	$6,552	$3,456
Age 50		
Colorado[*]		
Male	$12,728	$6,706
Female	$12,560	$6,618
Minnesota[†]	$4,528	$2,675
New Hampshire[‡]	$6,096	$3,924
Texas[§]		
Male	$8,736	$4,620
Female	$9,240	$4,860

TABLE 20-2
Selected Annual
Premiums for
High-Risk Pool
Coverage, 2006

SOURCE: Data from: http://www.healthinsurance.org/riskpoolinfo.html.

NOTES: Other terms and conditions apply to all policies.

[*]Colorado: Denver area; maternity is covered with a 20 percent coinsurance; $1 million lifetime maximum; 40 and 50 percent premium reductions are available for lower-income individuals.

[†]Minnesota: Nonsmoker rates; summary plan description is silent on maternity coverage; $2.8 million lifetime maximum.

[‡]New Hampshire: Nonsmoker rates; managed care plan; maternity is not covered; $2 million lifetime maximum.

[§]Texas: Dallas area; nonsmoker rates; managed care; maternity is not covered; $1.5 million lifetime maximum.

Losses in High-Risk Pools

While the coverage is limited and the premiums are high (at least relative to standard-risk individual contracts), all of the state high-risk pools lose money. Figure 20-1 reports data compiled by Achman and Chollet (2001) on the loss ratios of the 29 states in their study. The loss ratio is defined as the claims paid divided by the premium revenues collected. Even the state with the best financial performance in 1999—Oklahoma—paid out $1.14 in claims for every dollar it collected. The large Minnesota program paid out $1.96 in claims for every dollar of premium. Losses are even larger when operating costs are included. Communicating for Agriculture (2006) suggested that, in 2003, premiums tended to cover about 55 to 59 percent of total costs.

FIGURE 20-1

Medical Loss Ratios for State High-Risk Pools, 1999

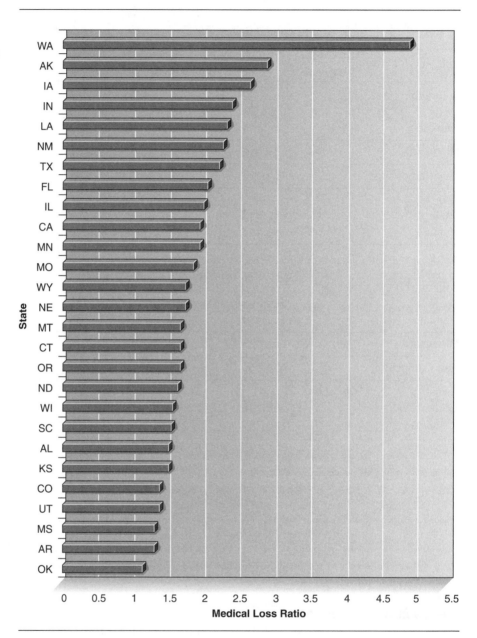

SOURCE: Data from Achman and Chollet (2001).

The states pay for these losses in a variety of ways. Most states impose a tax on health insurers doing business in the state. Of the 29 states in the Achman and Chollet (2001) study, 22 assessed high-risk pool losses to state insurers. These losses are usually apportioned according to each insurer's share of health insurance revenue reported to the state. Thus, if a firm had 20 percent of the aggregate private insurance premium revenue in the state, it would be assessed 20 percent of the losses in the state high-risk pool. Recall from Chapter 18 that employer-sponsored plans that are self-insured under the Employee Retirement Income Security Act (ERISA) are exempt from state insurance regulation and are, therefore, exempt from assessments to fund a state high-risk pool.

Over half of the states that assess losses on insurers allow insurers to use these assessments as offsets against state taxes. This essentially transfers the liability from the insurers to the state treasury.

Effects of Premiums on Risk Pool Enrollment

Remarkably little rigorous research has examined the effects of individual premiums on participation and duration of enrollment in state high-risk pools. Stearns and Mroz (1995/96) estimated disenrollment equations for each of the eight state programs they studied. For a 50-year-old male with the lowest deductible policy offered by each state in 1988, they found disenrollment elasticities that varied from 0.6 to 15.9. A disenrollment elasticity of 4.98 in the Minnesota program, for example, meant that a 1 percent increase in the premium resulted in a 4.98 percent increase in disenrollment relative to what it would have been with no premium change. The authors caution against cross-state comparisons because of differences in coverage by state. We can only conclude that the size of the premium clearly matters but that the magnitude of the premium responses depends on the "details" of coverage.

More recently, Frakt, Pizer, and Wrobel (2004) estimated risk pool enrollment equations. They sought to explain reported enrollment in each state's high-risk pool over the 1981 to 2000 period as a function of the premium, the size of the lowest deductible, the presence of multiple deductible options, the size of the uninsured pool of potential buyers in the state, and the per capita income of the uninsured in the state. The data on the latter two variables were drawn from the Current Population Survey by the U.S. Census Bureau. The model also included year fixed effects (i.e., it included variables to control for the average effect of each year). The premium data were not routinely available, so they were proxied by the state's allowed percentage markup multiplied by the Medicare per capita expenditure in the state. The "allowed percentage" is simply the share of the average individual insurance premium that the state is allowed to use in establishing the risk pool's rates. As noted earlier, these tend to be in the range of 125 to 150 percent of the average individual premium for comparable coverage, although some are higher.

Frakt, Pizer, and Wrobel (2004) estimated an elasticity of –1.9, implying that a 10 percent increase in the high-risk pool premium would reduce enrollment by 19 percent. The researchers then used simulation methods to assess the effect of all states with risk pools setting their markup at 125 percent rather than something higher. They concluded that this would increase total enrollment in the state plans by about 17,500 people in 2000 and increase the percentage of the uninsurable with high-risk coverage from 8 to 11 percent.

Chapter Summary

- Approximately 6 percent of the under-age-65 population are thought to be uninsurable in the sense that they are uninsured and have health problems that keep them from working.
- Thirty-four states had high-risk pools in 2006. Eligibility is open to some combination of medically uninsurables, HIPAA eligibles, and Medicare beneficiaries.
- The high-risk pools can be described as having restrictive eligibility, typically low enrollment, limited coverage with significant deductibles and sometimes limiting lifetime maximums, and waiting periods for preexisting conditions.
- Premiums typically are set by statute to be no more than 125 to 150 percent of the average premium for equivalent coverage in the private individual insurance market.
- All of the state high-risk pools collect less in premiums than they spend in medical claims. The shortfalls are usually covered by assessments on state health insurers, who are often able to use these payments to offset other state tax liabilities.

Discussion Questions

1. Some states use gender and region of the state to set rates for their high-risk pool; others do not. What differences across states do you anticipate in the nature of premiums and enrollment based on underwriting rules?
2. Suppose a state were to enact a new high-risk pool for its uninsurables. What effects, if any, would you expect to see in the employer-sponsored group market and the individual insurance market in that state as a result of the new program?
3. All state high-risk pools lose money. Discuss the advantages and disadvantages of three alternative funding mechanisms.

MEDICARE, MEDICAID, AND PRIVATE COVERAGE

AN OVERVIEW OF MEDICARE

The Medicare program provided benefits to some 35.8 million elderly beneficiaries and another 6.7 million disabled beneficiaries in 2005 (Boards of Trustees, Federal Hospital and Insurance and Federal Supplementary Medical Insurance Trust Funds 2006). In some sense, it is the largest health insurer in the United States. However, unlike private health insurance, only 15.5 percent of Medicare revenues come from premiums. Most of its revenues come from taxes. In this chapter, we provide an overview of the coverage and financing of the two Medicare trust funds and put these in the context of the Social Security funds. The Medicare Hospital Insurance (HI) trust fund largely covers hospital services, while the Medicare Supplementary Medical Insurance (SMI) trust fund covers ambulatory care and prescription drugs.

This chapter has a twofold purpose. The first is to simply describe Medicare—a large and important program. The second is to set the stage for Chapter 22, in which we discuss retiree coverage. Approximately 93 percent of Medicare's elderly beneficiaries have some form of health insurance coverage in addition to traditional Medicare. This additional coverage takes the form of privately purchased supplemental coverage, employee-sponsored retiree coverage, Medicaid, and Medicare Advantage. Medicare Advantage, occasionally called Medicare Part C, is the current name for Medicare managed care options. It is paid for from Part A and Part B programs and typically provides greater benefits, but fewer provider options, than traditional Medicare.

Social Security: Medicare in Context

Social Security was enacted in 1935 as part of President Franklin Roosevelt's New Deal program. Persons age 65 and older who had paid Social Security taxes for a sufficient period of time were eligible for monthly cash benefits. (People born after 1929 are required to work for ten years to be eligible for benefits.) In 1939, the program was expanded to include cash benefits for the spouse and minor children of retired workers and for dependents of prematurely deceased workers. Revenues collected through the Social Security payroll taxes are paid into a government-run trust fund. The moneys are used to pay benefits, and reserves are invested in special U.S. government securities.

The cash benefits were increased substantially in the 1950s and were indexed for inflation, beginning in 1975. The program was expanded in 1954 and again in 1956 to provide cash benefits for workers with disabilities. When this change was enacted, a second trust fund was established. So today there is the Old Age and Survivors Insurance (OASI) trust fund and the Disability Insurance (DI) trust fund. At the close of 2005, some 40.1 million people received OASI benefits, and 8.3 million received DI benefits. These trust funds had assets of approximately $1.66 trillion and $196 billion, respectively (Boards of Trustees 2006).

Medicare was enacted in 1965 during President Lyndon Johnson's administration. As noted in Chapter 1, Medicare's structure looks much like private health insurance in the 1960s. That is, there are essentially two types of coverage: one for hospital services and one for physician services, much as a person then might have obtained hospital coverage through Blue Cross and physician services through Blue Shield. Medicare Part A provides coverage for hospital services; revenue and expenses flow through the Hospital Insurance (HI) trust fund. Physician and other ambulatory services are covered under Medicare Part B. The revenues and expenses of this program flow through the Supplementary Medical Insurance (SMI) trust fund. As we discuss later in the chapter, the HI trust fund is financed analogously to the OASI and DI funds; the SMI fund is not. At the close of 2005, approximately 42 million people were covered by Medicare. The HI fund had assets of $286 billion, and the SMI fund had $24 billion (Boards of Trustees 2006).

Medicare beneficiaries may choose to obtain coverage through a Medicare managed care plan. This option is now called Medicare Advantage and is more formally known as Medicare Part C. As discussed at some length in Chapter 6, Medicare Advantage plans are paid a capitated amount based on the average Part A and Part B (combined) expenditures per beneficiary, adjusted for location and demographic and health conditions of beneficiaries.

In December 2003, during President George W. Bush's administration, Congress expanded the Medicare program to include coverage for prescription drugs. The program allowed Medicare beneficiaries who chose to participate to purchase subsidized private drug coverage. This expansion, called Part D, is financed in the same fashion as Part B and is part of the SMI fund. Figure 21-1 provides a road map of the four trust funds and the coverage they provide.

Medicare Hospital Insurance Coverage

Typically, people become eligible for Medicare Part A in the same way as they become eligible for Social Security: they work for ten years in jobs covered by the program. They also typically become eligible to receive benefits when

FIGURE 21-1
Social Security and Medicare Overview

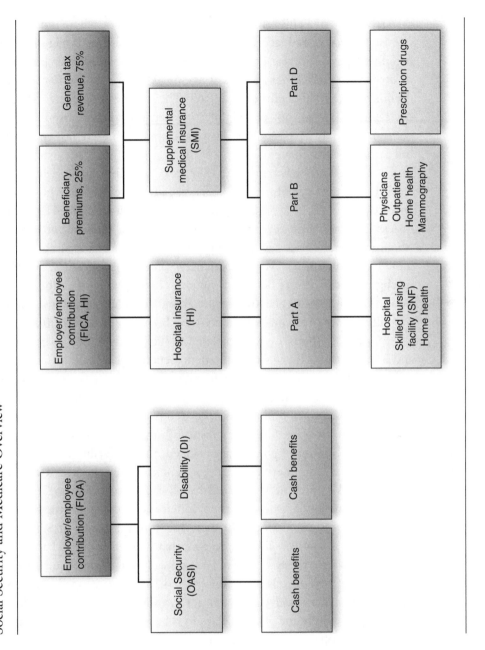

they reach age 65. This is in contrast to Social Security, where individuals may choose to receive reduced benefits as early as age 62, and eligibility for full benefits depends on year of birth. Under Social Security, those born in 1937 or earlier can receive full benefits at age 65. However, those born after 1959 do not receive full benefits until age 67. Thus, some people have Social Security benefits but are not yet eligible to receive Medicare hospital insurance, while others may have Medicare hospital insurance but are not yet eligible for full Social Security benefits.

Those who have reached the age of eligibility but who have not worked the sufficient number of years may purchase Medicare hospital insurance coverage. In 2007, the premium for this coverage was $410 per month or less, depending on the number of years worked. Only about 1 percent of Medicare beneficiaries pay a premium for Part A coverage; almost all are eligible by virtue of their work experience. Some under-age-65 individuals can be eligible for Medicare hospital insurance coverage due to disability or inclusion in the end-stage renal dialysis program. At the close of 2005, there were 42 million Part A Medicare beneficiaries (Boards of Trustees 2006).

Medicare Part A covers hospital, skilled nursing home, home health, and a handful of other largely inpatient benefits. The key to understanding this coverage, however, is the "spell of illness." Individuals are covered for 90 days of hospital care and 100 days of skilled nursing facility (SNF) care per spell of illness. A spell of illness is unrelated to any particular malady. Instead, a spell of illness begins when the person is hospitalized, and it ends when the person has been out of a hospital or skilled nursing facility for 60 days.

Box 21-1 summarizes the major benefits covered under Medicare Part A. A hospital deductible is associated with each spell of illness. In 2007, the deductible was $992. Once this is paid, there is no copay for the first 60 days of hospital care, but days 61 through 90 require a copay of $248 per day. There is also a one-time lifetime reserve that will cover days 91 through 150 of a hospital stay; these days may be used only once and require a copay of $496 per day. SNF care is covered for up to 100 days per spell of illness. This care is viewed as a lower-cost substitute for hospital care. A beneficiary must have spent a minimum of three days in a hospital for a related illness to be eligible. No copays are required for the first 20 SNF days; days 21 through 100 require a copay of $124 per day.

Note that the hospital deductible and copays have nothing to do with the size of the payment that a hospital may be paid for services under the prospective payment system. If a person were admitted for a stroke under a new spell of illness, the Centers for Medicare and Medicaid Services (CMS) would pay the hospital the rate for DRG-14 (a stroke), less the $992 deductible that the hospital would collect from the beneficiary (see Box 21-2).

The various copays are all tied by law to the size of the hospital deductible. The hospital copay is 25 percent of the deductible, the lifetime

BOX 21-1

Coverage under Medicare Part A

- Per spell of illness:
  - Up to 90 days on inpatient hospital care
    $992 deductible per spell of illness (in 2007)
    $0 copay for days 1–60
    $248 copay for days 61–90[*]
  - Up to 100 days of skilled nursing facility care following a three-day or

    longer hospitalization
    $0 copay for days 1–20
    $124 copay for days 21–100[†]
    60-day inpatient lifetime reserve
- Lifetime reserve of 60 additional inpatient hospital days
  $496 copay for each day[‡]
- Up to 100 home health visits following a three-day or longer
  hospitalization
- Lifetime limit of 100 days of inpatient psychiatric care
- Hospice care
- Blood

reserve copay is 50 percent of the deductible, and the SNF copay is 12.5 percent of that same deductible. Thus, when the CMS determines the deductible each year, the copays are automatically adjusted as well. The deductible itself is based on the deductible from the preceding year, adjusted for the percentage increase used in updating the payment rates for hospitals. For 2007, this adjustment factor was 3.4 percent (*Federal Register* 2006).

Medicare Part A also covers up to 100 home health visits. These visits must require part-time or intermittent skilled nursing care or physical or speech therapy to homebound persons. There is no deductible or copay associated with these services, but they must follow a minimum three-day hospital stay.

Medicare Supplementary Medical Insurance

Everyone who is eligible for Medicare Part A also is eligible to participate in the Medicare supplementary medical insurance (Part B) program. It is little known, but those who did not work long enough to be covered by Part A but are otherwise eligible may purchase Part B coverage even if they do not

BOX 21-2

Implications of a Spell of Illness

The hospital deductible under Medicare Part A is *not* per year or per hospitalization. It is per spell of illness. This has important implications for how much beneficiaries pay for hospital care and how much hospital coverage they actually have. Suppose your grandmother were hospitalized in late January for a hip replacement and was hospitalized for four days. She would be responsible for the $992 deductible. If she were hospitalized in early March for a pulmonary problem, this would be regarded as the same spell of illness; she would not pay the deductible. If instead she had been hospitalized in May, after being out of the hospital (and an SNF) for 60 days, the pulmonary admission would have required payment of the deductible.

If your grandmother were admitted continuously for 90 days, she would pay the deductible associated with the first day of hospitalization and $248 each for days 61 through 90. If she continued to stay beyond the ninetieth day, she would tap into her lifetime reserve days, paying $496 for each day.

The more-typical example, however, is an individual who is in and out of a hospital but is not out for at least 60 days. This person exhausts the 90 days of coverage without ever triggering a new spell of illness. Thus, if your grandmother had the hip replacement, the pulmonary admission, a heart attack, and other medically unrelated admissions, without being out of a hospital (or an SNF) for 60 days, she could end up using her lifetime reserve days and ultimately exhaust her Medicare coverage for this spell of illness.

purchase Part A. Part B is purely voluntary. However, virtually everyone purchases coverage. Indeed, over 94 percent of Medicare beneficiaries take Part B coverage (Boards of Trustees 2006). This should be no surprise; the coverage is heavily subsidized. The monthly standard premium paid by beneficiaries was $93.50 in 2007. By law, this amount is designed to cover 25 percent of the costs of the Part B program; the remaining 75 percent is paid from federal general tax revenues. In addition, those with incomes below 135 percent of the federal poverty line and with limited assets are eligible for further subsidies that cover some or all of the premium.

As a result of the Medicare Modernization Act, beginning in 2007, higher-income beneficiaries were charged higher premiums. At the end of a three-year transition period, those with higher incomes will pay 35, 50, 65, or 80 percent of the full cost of Part B, depending on their income. In 2007,

BOX 21-3

Coverage under Medicare Part B

- $131 annual deductible (in 2007)
- 20% coinsurance rate applicable to Medicare reasonable fees
  - Physician services, including office visits and a one-time physical for new beneficiaries
  - Durable medical equipment
  - Outpatient hospital services
  - Outpatient mental health services
  - Clinical laboratory and diagnostic tests
  - Outpatient occupational, physical, and speech therapy
  - Home healthcare not preceded by a three-day hospital stay
  - Some preventive screening services[*]
  - Blood

[*]Limitations and the deductible and coinsurance may apply.

those beneficiaries filing individual tax returns with taxable income between $80,000 and $100,000 (and those with joint returns with incomes between $160,000 and $200,000) paid premiums of $105.80 per month. The CMS anticipates that approximately 4 percent of Medicare beneficiaries will have to pay the higher premiums (Centers for Medicare and Medicaid Services 2006a).

The major components of Part B coverage are physician services, durable medical equipment, outpatient hospital services, laboratory services, and some preventive services, among others (see Box 21-3). Most Part B services require payment of an *annual* deductible. This deductible was originally set at $50 in 1966 and was raised periodically until set at $100 in 1991. This was raised to $110 in 2005 and has been indexed to inflation since then. In 2007, the deductible was $131. In addition, beneficiaries pay a 20 percent coinsurance rate on most covered Part B services (see Box 21-4).

Medicare Advantage Coverage

Medicare Part C provides coverage through Medicare-approved managed care plans. Over the years, this program as been referred to as Medicare HMOs and Medicare+Choice and currently is known as Medicare Advantage. In 1999, approximately 17.3 percent of Medicare beneficiaries were enrolled in one of the Medicare Part C plans, the high-water mark for the program. Enrollment declined to a low of 12.6 percent in 2003 and has

BOX 21-4

Balance Billing under Medicare

Since the beginning of the Medicare program, Medicare has paid 80 percent of the reasonable cost of covered physician services. The Part B coinsurance feature requires the beneficiary to pay the other 20 percent. The reasonable cost is determined by the Medicare fee schedule.

However, what happens when physicians charge more than what Medicare considers a reasonable amount? In this case, physicians have two choices: They can "accept assignment," meaning that Medicare pays them directly for its share of the reasonable amount. Physicians then bill the patient for the other 20 percent and forgo any additional payment. Alternatively, physicians can "reject assignment." In this case, Medicare pays the patient for the amount it owes. Physicians then "balance-bill" the patient for the entire amount—the amount Medicare would pay, the coinsurance share, and any additional charges. As such, physicians face a tradeoff: the assurance of getting paid 80 percent of the allowed amount paid directly by Medicare or some probability of getting paid more, less, or nothing by the patient.

In the past, physicians could choose at every occasion of service whether they would or would not accept assignment. Economics suggests that they would be much more likely to accept assignment for patients who were unable or unlikely to pay their bills and reject assignment for those patients who could or would pay their bills. In 1986, only approximately 60 percent of Medicare payments to physicians were made under assignment (Colby et al. 1995). Beginning in 1984, however, Congress began making balance-billing less attractive to providers. Physicians were eventually required to accept or reject assignment on all or none of their Medicare patients, and the amount they could change over and above the Medicare fee schedule was limited to 9.25 percent. In 1999, 97.5 percent of physician claims were on an assignment basis (Iglehart 2002). Today, it is extremely rare for a Medicare beneficiary to be balance-billed.

rebounded since. According to Gold (2006), in December 2005, 14 percent of beneficiaries were in Medicare Advantage plans. Gold attributed much of the increase in enrollment to expanded payment levels under the Medicare Modernization Act of 2003 (MMA).

The current Medicare Advantage program allows Medicare beneficiaries to enroll in participating health maintenance organizations (HMOs), preferred provider organizations (PPOs), and private fee-for-service (PFFS) plans. The latter are non-network capitated plans. Medicare pays the PFFS a fee per enrolled Medicare beneficiary per month; the beneficiary can receive care from any provider willing to accept the PFFS fee schedule. The Medicare Payment Advisory Commission (2006) reported that all Medicare beneficiaries had a Medicare Advantage plan available to them in 2006.

Under the MMA, Medicare Advantage plans submit bids to Medicare on the price they will accept for Medicare Part A and Part B services, for supplemental benefits (if any), and for Medicare Part D drug benefits. These bids are compared to benchmark prices that the CMS has established in each county. If the bid is above the benchmark, Medicare beneficiaries enrolling in the plan pay a monthly premium. If the bid is below the benchmark, Medicare keeps 25 percent of the difference, and the remaining 75 percent is rebated to the plan. The plan, in turn, must disperse these savings to the enrolled beneficiaries in the form of reduced Part A and Part B cost sharing, reduced Part B or Part D premium sharing, or enhanced benefits. Medicare Payment Advisory Commission (2006) reported that 95 percent of plan bids were below the benchmark and, as Figure 21-2 shows, the plans were most likely to use most of their rebates to reduce Part A and Part B cost sharing and to expand benefits. Plans are also free to enhance benefits beyond the amount of the rebate. Thus, even if a plan's bid is below the benchmark, it may still enhance benefits such that beneficiaries pay an additional monthly premium.

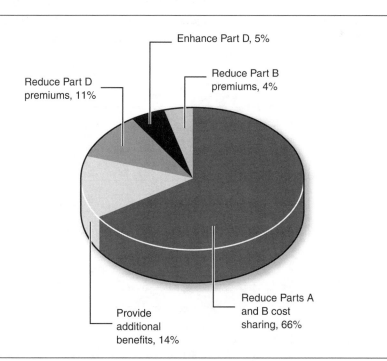

FIGURE 21-2
Medicare Advantage Plans' Use of the Largest Share of Bid Rebates

SOURCE: Medicare Payment Advisory Commission (2006), "Report to Congress: Increasing the Value of Medicare," Figure 9-2.

Medicare Prescription Drug Coverage

Medicare Part D coverage was enacted in December 2003 as part of the MMA and became operational January 1, 2006. The program is voluntary and privately run. Anyone eligible for Part B coverage is also eligible for Medicare prescription drug coverage. Enrollees can purchase stand-alone drug coverage to complement traditional Medicare, or they can enroll in a Medicare Advantage plan that offers drug coverage. The stand-alone plans are sold by many private insurers. (The CMS web site [www.cms.hhs.gov] lists the approved plans in each area.) The total cost of Part D coverage and the beneficiary's premium depends on the plan chosen. In 2006, the national average premium was expected to be about $32.20 per month (Boards of Trustees 2006). However, the CMS reported that the actual average premium in 2006 was less than $24 per month (U.S. Department of Health and Human Services 2006a).

Figure 21-3 summarizes the nature of the "standard benefits" available under Part D. Beneficiaries who chose to participate in 2006 faced a $250 annual deductible. Once the deductible was satisfied, Medicare paid 75 percent, and the beneficiary paid 25 percent of the next $2,000 in covered prescription drug expenses. There was no Medicare coverage for expenditures between $2,250 and $5,100. This is the so-called "donut hole" in which the beneficiary has no Medicare coverage. Beyond $5,100, Medicare paid 95 percent of any covered prescription drug expenditures during the

FIGURE 21-3
Standard
Medicare
Part D
Coverage, 2006

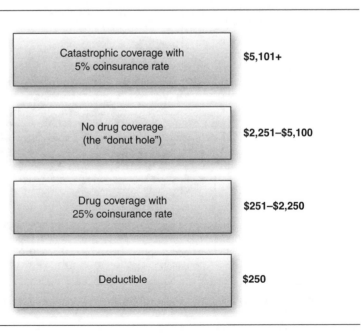

year. This odd arrangement of benefits reflects the compromise in Congress through which the program provided catastrophic coverage in accord with insurance principles and first-dollar coverage in accord with political principles, while not exceeding estimated spending levels that were acceptable to Congress and the president. The level of the deductible and the thresholds for the various phases of the coverage are adjusted each year to reflect inflation.

However, beneficiaries do not have to select the standard benefits. They may purchase plans that provide a smaller deductible and that provide coverage for all or part of the "donut hole." The plans may also differ with respect to the specific drugs that are covered in the formulary and the specific local drugstores that participate in each plan. In the summer of 2006, the CMS reported that approximately 87 percent of those beneficiaries who purchased coverage selected a plan with more-generous coverage than the standard plan (U.S. Department of Health and Human Services 2006a).

Currently, many Medicare beneficiaries obtain retiree health insurance coverage through their former employer. Congress was concerned that many of these plans would drop prescription drug coverage with the advent of Part D. Therefore, they provided a subsidy of 28 percent for drug spending in the range of $250 to $5,000 if the employer retiree plan offered prescription drug coverage that matched or exceeded the Part D benefit.

In addition, Part D legislation provides that Medicare beneficiaries with incomes below 135 percent and between 135 and 150 percent of the federal poverty line are eligible for a waiver or reduction of the deductible, elimination of the "donut hole," and reduced coinsurance rates. In 2006, the poverty line for an individual was $9,800 and $13,200 for a family of two (U.S. Department of Health and Human Services 2006b). The Congressional Budget Office estimated that about one-third of beneficiaries would qualify under the low-income provisions (Antos and Calfee 2004).

As of mid-June 2006, approximately 78 percent of Medicare beneficiaries had prescription drug coverage from Medicare or a former private or federal government employer. About one-third of these had coverage through the stand-alone program, with others obtaining drug coverage through Medicare Advantage, the employer drug coverage subsidy, automatic Medicare-Medicaid enrollment, or federal employee/military retiree coverage. Approximately 75 percent of those eligible for the low-income subsidy also had obtained drug coverage (U.S. Department of Health and Human Services 2006a).

Figure 21-4 summarizes the distribution of benefit payments across Medicare covered services. In 2006, hospital inpatient services constituted 34 percent of spending, physicians and other suppliers received almost 25 percent of expenditures, and the new Part D prescription drug program accounted for 5 percent. The Congressional Budget Office (CBO 2007) estimated that by 2016 prescription drug benefits will comprise 17 percent of

FIGURE 21-4

Medicare Benefit Payments by Type of Service

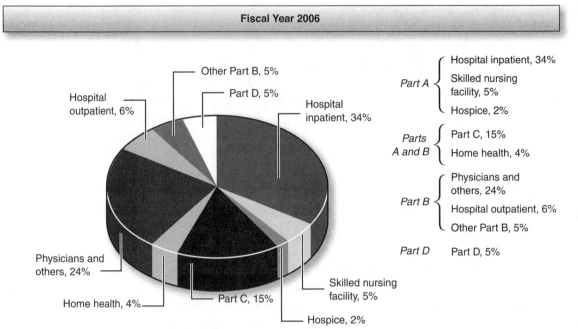

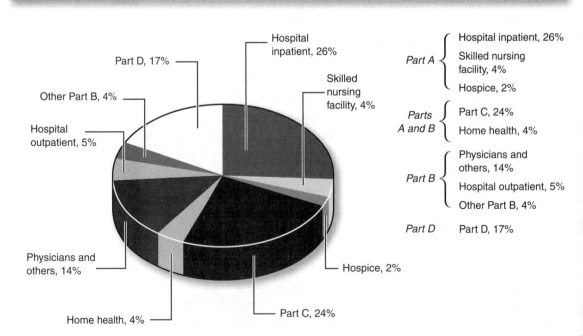

SOURCE: Data from Congressional Budget Office (2007).

spending, with disproportionate reductions in shares seen in hospital and physician services. The CBO also projected that Medicare Advantage programs will increase from 15 to 24 percent of spending.

Financing Social Security and Medicare

The OASI, DI, and HI trust funds are all funded from payroll taxes assessed on current workers. Often called "FICA contributions" (for Federal Insurance Contribution Act), these taxes are nominally imposed equally on employers and employees. The tax base and the tax rate have increased over time with expansions of benefits and increases in costs. Table 21-1 presents trends in the maximum earnings subject to FICA taxes and the rates imposed. The tax rates listed are paid by both employers and employees. Self-employed individuals pay double these rates and, of course, it is worth noting (as demonstrated in Chapter 14) that employees effectively pay both the employee and the employer shares because they must produce enough to allow the employer to pay wages, benefits, and taxes associated with their employment.

Two observations regarding these trends are notable. First, the maximum earnings subject to the FICA tax have increased over the lifespan of the programs. Part of this is due to inflation. The $3,000 maximum in 1937 is roughly the equivalent of $42,000 in 2006 dollars. However, the remaining increases and the increases in the tax rates are the result of expansions in the generosity of the programs, the growth of the elderly population, the decline in the working-age population and, for the HI trust fund, increases in the costs of medical care. Second, note that in 1991 the tax base for the Medicare HI trust fund was de-coupled from the tax base for the Social Security trust funds and became unlimited in 1994.

In contrast, the Medicare SMI trust fund is financed with both beneficiary-paid premiums and general tax revenues. Both Part B and Part D ordinarily require the beneficiary to pay 25 percent of the cost of the coverage. The other 75 percent comes from federal personal and corporate income taxes.

The FICA taxes are insufficient to cover the projected costs of the OASI, DI, and HI trust funds over time. Each year, the Social Security and Medicare trustees project the short-range outlook for the trust funds. For each future year, they estimate the revenues and expenses for each of the funds and compute the "trust fund ratio" for each. The ratio is simply the assets at the beginning of each year divided by the expected expenditures for the year times 100. The ratios for the trustees' "intermediate assumptions" about revenues and expenses are presented in Figure 21-5. At the close of

TABLE 21-1

Trends in Maximum Taxable Earnings and Applicable Tax Rates for OASI, DI, and HI Trust Funds

Year	Maximum Earnings Subject to OASI and DI	Maximum Earnings Subject to HI	Applied to Both Employer and Employee:		
			OASI Tax Rate	DI Tax Rate	HI Tax Rate
1937	$3,000	—	1.000	—	—
1947	$3,000	—	1.000	—	—
1957	$4,200	—	2.000	0.250	—
1967	$6,600	$6,600	3.550	0.350	0.500
1977	$16,500	$16,500	4.375	0.575	0.900
1987	$43,800	$43,800	5.200	0.500	1.450
1991	$53,400	$125,000	5.600	0.600	1.450
1994	$60,600	Unlimited	5.260	0.940	1.450
1997	$65,400	Unlimited	5.350	0.850	1.450
2000	$76,200	Unlimited	5.300	0.900	1.450
2001	$80,400	Unlimited	5.300	0.900	1.450
2002	$84,900	Unlimited	5.300	0.900	1.450
2003	$87,000	Unlimited	5.300	0.900	1.450
2004	$87,900	Unlimited	5.300	0.900	1.450
2005	$90,000	Unlimited	5.300	0.900	1.450
2006	$94,200	Unlimited	5.300	0.900	1.450

SOURCE: Social Security Administration web sites: www.ssa.gov/OACT/ProgData/oasdiRates.html and www.ssa.gov/OACT/COLA/cbb.html

NOTES: DI = Disability insurance; HI = Hospital insurance; OASI = Old age and survivors insurance.

2005, the HI trust fund had a ratio of 144. This means that there were assets equal to 144 percent of the expected expenditures. The DI and OASI funds were in better shape.

In fact, as Figure 21-5 shows, the HI trust fund is expected to have expenditures that exceed assets in 2012, and the assets will be exhausted in 2018. The DI and OASI funds are projected to be exhausted in 2025 and 2042, respectively. Thus, it is the Medicare HI trust fund—not Social Security—that is in the greatest financial peril.

Given the impending retirement of the baby boomers beginning in 2010, it may seem surprising that it is the Medicare HI trust fund that is in greatest jeopardy. There are three reasons for the decline in the assets of the

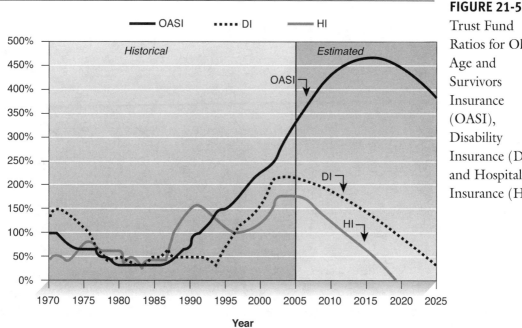

FIGURE 21-5

Trust Fund Ratios for Old Age and Survivors Insurance (OASI), Disability Insurance (DI), and Hospital Insurance (HI)

SOURCE: Palmer and Saving (2006), http://www.ssa.gov/OACT/TRSUM/tr06summary.pdf. "A Message to the Public," Chart A.

Medicare HI trust fund. First, the impending retirement of the baby boomers will increase the number of people eligible for Medicare (and Social Security) benefits, increasing expenditures. Second, these retirements will leave fewer active workers to pay into the trust funds. In 2005, there were approximately 3.9 workers per beneficiary; by 2018, there will be approximately 3.0. As a result, revenues into the funds will decline. Third, the Medicare HI fund will also face substantially higher healthcare spending per beneficiary, due to rising trends in utilization, longevity, and medical care prices.

The SMI trust fund does not face the same financial stress, but this is only because it is financed from general tax revenues and beneficiary premiums. Retirement of the baby boomers and increasing medical expenses simply mean that premiums and, in particular, the allocation from general tax revenues increase! Indeed, because of the addition of Medicare Part D, SMI expenditures will grow more rapidly than any other portion of Medicare.

Figure 21-6 presents the Medicare Trustees' projections in 2006 of the trends in tax revenue, transfers, and deficits as a percentage of gross domestic product (GDP) that result from their intermediate case assumptions for the overall Medicare program. Note that these are all premised on existing laws. They do not assume any changes in benefits or taxes that have not already been enacted (Palmer and Saving 2006). Moreover, because the

FIGURE 21-6

Medicare Expenditures and Noninterest Income by Source as a Percentage of Gross Domestic Product (GDP)

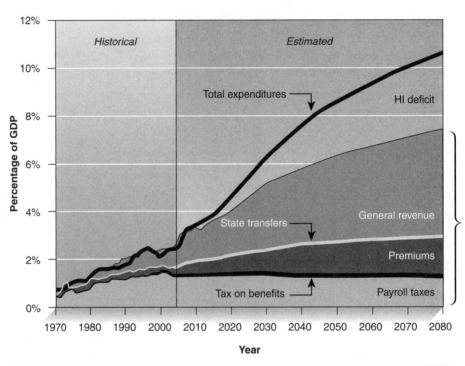

SOURCE: Palmer and Saving (2006), http://www.ssa.gov/OACT/TRSUM/tr06summary.pdf. "A Message to the Public," Chart D.

figure is defined in terms of GDP, it reflects current estimates in the growth of the U.S. economy over the same period.

Begin at the bottom of Figure 21-6. "Payroll taxes" fund Part A. These revenues increased as a percentage of GDP between 1966 and about 2000, reflecting higher tax rates, the expanding tax base, and the growing taxable incomes of active workers. However, after 2000, they level off and decline as a percent of GDP, due to the retirement of the baby boomers. "Taxes on benefits" are a minor share of revenue but increase due to the relative affluence of some future retirees. "Premiums" are the share of Part B and Part D premiums paid by Medicare beneficiaries. These increase, reflecting baby boomer retirees' greater use of ambulatory and prescription drug benefits, which translates into higher premiums. "State transfers" are minor but reflect the payments that states make for certain Medicaid recipients. "General revenue" transfers reflect the single largest source of funds in the years to come. These are the 75 percent share of Part B and Part D spending covered by general revenues. Indeed, as the Medicare Trustees put it "Soon after the Part D program becomes fully implemented in 2006, general revenue transfers are expected to constitute the largest single source of income to the Medicare program as a whole—and would add significantly to the Federal Budget pressures" (Boards of Trustees 2006, page 13). Finally, the "HI deficit" reflects the shortfall in the Part A trust fund. For a number of years, this deficit would be satisfied by redeeming the government securities held by the HI trust fund, putting even further pressure on the rest of the federal budget.

Consider the period 20 to 30 years from today. At that point, most of you reading this text will be in your midforties to midfifties—your most productive earning years. At that point, under current law and the Medicare Trustees' actuarial assumptions, the Medicare program will constitute 6 to 8 percent of GDP—that is, 2 to 2.5 times its share today. Thus, you will pay virtually all of the amounts identified in Figure 21.6, except those marked "premiums" and "tax on benefits." You will almost certainly pay for any solution to the Medicare deficit that involves higher taxes.

Chapter Summary

- Medicare coverage is provided through two trust funds. The Hospital Insurance (HI) trust fund provides coverage for Part A services, largely inpatient hospital care and skilled nursing facility and home healthcare covered after a stay in the hospital. The Supplementary Medical Insurance (SMI) trust fund provides coverage for Part B ambulatory services and Part D prescription drugs. Revenues from both the HI and SMI funds pay for Part C, Medicare managed care plans.
- Eligibility for Medicare largely comes from working for ten years, paying FICA payroll taxes, and reaching age 65. Individuals may also purchase coverage on reaching age 65.
- Medicare HI is funded with payroll taxes paid by current employees and their employers. Each nominally pays 1.45 of worker earnings. Medicare SMI is funded by voluntary beneficiary premium contributions for Part B and for Part D coverage, essentially matched three to one by general tax revenues.
- The Medicare HI fund is currently projected to exhaust its assets in 2018. The SMI fund's revenues are always approximately equal to its expenditures because premiums and allocations of general tax revenues are adjusted to make this so.
- Under current law and the actuarial assumptions of the Medicare Trustees, the Medicare program is expected to grow from about 3 percent to 6 to 8 percent of the U.S. gross domestic product within 20 to 30 years.

Discussion Question

Robert Reischauer (1997), now with the Urban Institute, has summarized several alternative big-idea approaches to solving the Medicare problem:

- Replace the existing Medicare program with a program in which beneficiaries get a large-deductible Medicare policy; once the annual deductible is satisfied, the beneficiary has full coverage.
- Replace the existing Medicare program with a voucher program in which Medicare gives each beneficiary a subsidy to buy private health insurance.
- Replace the existing Medicare program with a redefined set of core covered services and allow private insurers to bid with Medicare to provide these services. Allow beneficiaries to purchase supplemental coverage if they choose.
- Keep the existing Medicare program but cut prices to providers and raise copays, deductibles, and premiums to beneficiaries.
- Replace the existing Medicare program with a government-run program similar to the current Veterans Affairs system.

Any of these, of course, could be undertaken in the context of higher taxes as well. Discuss some of the advantages and disadvantages of each approach from the point of view of beneficiaries and taxpayers.

RETIREE COVERAGE

Virtually all Americans age 65 and older have coverage through the Medicare program. However, in 2003, all but about 7 percent also had some coverage in addition to traditional Medicare (American Association of Retired Persons [AARP] 2004). This coverage includes employer-sponsored retiree coverage, Medigap plans purchased individually, Medicare Advantage plans, and Medicaid.

In this chapter, we examine retirees' non-Medicaid coverage. After briefly discussing the distribution of coverage, we look at the nature of employer-sponsored and Medigap coverages, the relative costs of these benefits, and the effects of the federal regulation that standardized the benefit packages. Employer-sponsored retiree coverage is provided by larger employers and is typically more generous than Medicare, but it has become less prevalent over time. We discuss the reasons for this, as well as the alternative mechanisms for coordinating retiree benefits with Medicare. We also examine the extent to which these private coverages affect Medicare expenditures. We then look at Medicare Advantage coverage and its changes over time. The chapter concludes with a discussion of price sensitivity for retiree coverage and competition between Medigap and Medicare Advantage plans.

Distribution of Supplemental Coverage

Figure 22-1 reports the percentages of Medicare beneficiaries with various types of supplementary coverage in 2003. Nearly 40 percent of Medicare beneficiaries had employer-sponsored coverage. This coverage can be of two types. The first is coverage provided by an employer to an active worker who happens to be over age 65. This coverage reflects the options that employees have at their place of employment. The one complicating factor is that, for active workers, Medicare is a "secondary payer." This means that, when a claim is filed, the employer coverage will pay according to it benefits structure, and Medicare will then pay some or all of the remainder. We discuss the coordination of benefits between Medicare and private plans later in the chapter.

The second form of employer-sponsored supplementary coverage is retiree coverage, which larger employers often provide. Employees usually become eligible much as they do for private defined benefit pensions—that

FIGURE 22-1

Distribution of
Medicare
Beneficiaries,*
by Type of
Supplemental
Coverage, 2003

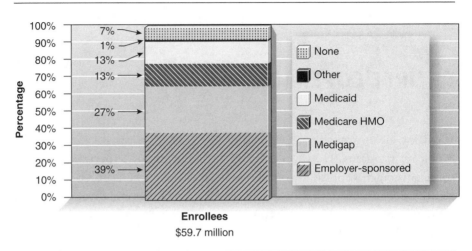

SOURCE: American Association of Retired Persons (2004), "Out-of-Pocket Spending on Health Care by Medicare Beneficiaries Age 65 and Older in 2003," *Data Digest*. Washington, D.C.: AARP, September, Figure 5.
*Noninstitutionalized Medicare beneficiaries, age 65 and older.

is, after they have worked for a sufficient number of years for the firm. This coverage may begin before age 65 and may end when the individual becomes eligible for Medicare. However, more typically, it continues along with Medicare coverage. Again, the coverage typically reflects the options that are available to employees during their active working years. In the case of retiree coverage, Medicare is the primary payer immediately.

According to Figure 22-1, approximately one-quarter (27 percent) of Medicare beneficiaries had Medigap coverage in 2003. This insurance is typically purchased by an individual, who chooses from one of ten allowable coverage plans. Most of these plans, and certainly the most popular ones, only cover the out-of-pocket expenses of covered Medicare services. That is, they cover expenses like the Medicare Part A deductible and the coinsurance associated with Part B physician services, but they do not, for example, cover more inpatient hospital days than does Medicare.

Figure 22-1 indicates that, in 2003, 13 percent of beneficiaries had a private Medicare plan, which means coverage through a Medicare managed care plan (now called Medicare Advantage plans). As we saw in Chapter 21, Medicare pays Medicare Advantage plans a capitated amount per month to cover all of the beneficiary's Part A and Part B services. These managed care plans, however, typically provide more covered services than does traditional Medicare. Thus, enrollees may have coverage for annual physicals and prescription drugs, as well as lower cost-sharing levels than those in traditional Medicare. These plans may charge an additional premium for the supplementary services.

In 2003, 13 percent of Medicare beneficiaries were also covered by the Medicaid program. Medicaid provides coverage to these individuals because they have sufficiently low income that they are: (1) eligible for Supplemental Security Income, in which case Medicaid provides a full range of Medicaid benefits and pays the Medicare Part B premium and cost-sharing requirements; (2) "qualified Medicare beneficiaries," in which case there are no Medicaid benefits, but Medicaid does pay the Part B premium and cost-sharing requirements; (3) "specified low-income beneficiaries," in which case Medicaid pays their Part B premium; or (4) covered under an optional state Medicaid program.

As Figure 22-1 shows, 7 percent of beneficiaries had no supplemental coverage in 2003. Using older data, Khandker and McCormack (1999) reported that those without a Medicare supplement of some kind tended to be disproportionately male and African American, with lower income and a health status that was better than those on Medicaid but generally worse than those with private supplements. Those with Medigap coverage were more likely female and had somewhat higher incomes, education, and health status, while those with employer-sponsored retiree coverage were more likely to be male and white, with higher education, income, and health status.

Employer-Sponsored Retiree Coverage

As noted earlier, nearly 40 percent of current Medicare beneficiaries have employer-sponsored retiree benefits. This percentage, however, both overstates and understates the picture of employer-sponsored retiree coverage. It overstates the coverage because it reflects past decisions by employers to provide coverage to current retirees. Increasingly, retiree coverage is not offered to current employees. It understates the coverage because many people retire before they are eligible for Medicare but obtain postretirement, pre-Medicare coverage through a former employer. Thus, even though they are not covered by Medicare, they have employer-sponsored retiree coverage.

As demonstrated in Table 22-1, employer-sponsored retiree coverage is primarily a large-firm phenomenon. Only about 5 percent of firms with fewer than 200 workers provided the coverage in 2004, while 60 percent of those with 5,000 or more employees did so. The proportion of larger employers (those with 200 or more employees) that offer retiree coverage has been fairly stable over the 1990s and 2000s, with estimates ranging from 40 to 35 percent (Kaiser Family Foundation 2005).

The proportion of larger employers offering retiree coverage is considerably reduced from prior years, when as many as two-thirds of such firms offered the benefit. The reasons for this decline are not well analyzed. Some

TABLE 22-1

Percentage of Firms Offering Retiree Health Benefits by Firm Size, 2004

Firm Size	Percentage Offering Retiree Health Benefits
3–199 employees	5%
200–999 employees	31%
1,000–4,999 employees	43%
5,000 or more employees	60%

SOURCE: Data from Kaiser Family Foundation (2005).

have suggested that the decline is the result of a change in accounting rules that requires corporations to report on their balance sheets the liability associated with the promise of retiree coverage. As a matter of economics, this seems an unlikely explanation. Savvy investors would have understood the nature of the liabilities even without the accounting rule change, even if most investors did not, and it is these savvy investors who tend to drive the equity market. Moreover, the accounting explanation does not incorporate compensating wage differentials. If workers are promised retiree health benefits, this implies that life-cycle wages will be lower as a result. Simply eliminating retiree benefits should impose alternative labor compensation costs on employers.

The more likely explanation has to do with the changing nature of the labor force. If workers are more mobile today, it suggests that many of them do not work sufficient years with one employer to qualify for retiree health benefits. If so, the promised (but not vested) benefits are of little value to them. Thus, they would prefer the cash. In some sense, this is analogous to the shift from defined benefits to defined contribution pension funds that the U.S. economy has witnessed over the last two decades. Rather than being promised a pension based on years of service and earnings at retirement (a defined benefit pension), mobile workers today are more likely to get a defined contribution pension, in which the amounts put into a retirement account stay with employees, regardless of their job. If this speculation is correct, then firms with high turnover are the ones more likely to have shifted from defined benefit to defined contribution pensions and also to have dropped retiree health insurance coverage.

Larger employers are changing the nature of the wage/retiree coverage tradeoff. The Kaiser Family Foundation (2005) reported that larger employers are increasing retiree premium contributions and copayments, among other things. One interpretation of these actions in the context of compensating differentials is that the current costs of retiree health insurance

FIGURE 22-2
Percentage of
Large Firms
That Offer
Retiree Health
Benefits to
Early Retirees
and Medicare-
Eligible
Retirees,
1997–2001

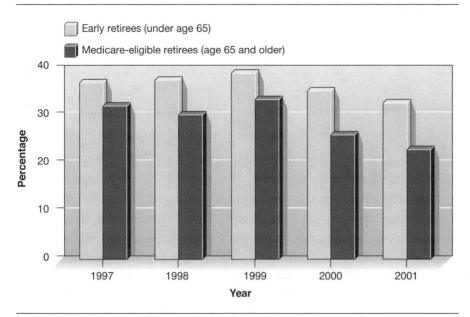

SOURCE: McCormack et al. (2002), "Trends in Retiree Health Benefits," *Health Affairs* 21(6): Exhibit 2. Reprinted with permission.

NOTE: Includes large firms (200 employees or more) that offer coverage to either early retirees or Medicare-eligible retirees, as well as to active employees.

exceeded the future value of the anticipated costs when the wage adjustments occurred.

Early Retirees

Employer-sponsored coverage may include early retirees (those not yet eligible for Medicare) and Medicare-eligible people. The latter may or may not have yet retired, of course. Figure 22-2 reports the trends over the late 1990s and early 2000s in early-retiree and over-age-65 coverage provided through employers. It is clear that the decline in coverage for those over age 65 has been steeper.

The Kaiser Family Foundation (2006b) reported that the average total monthly premium for early retirees averaged $552 in 2006 and that the retiree typically paid 41 percent of the premium out-of-pocket. In contrast, the premium for Medicare-eligibles was only $270 per month, on average, of which the retiree paid approximately 41 percent out-of-pocket. Undoubtedly, the reason for the lower premiums is that Medicare-eligibles include many true retirees for whom Medicare is the primary payer. As such, the claims experience of the employer-sponsored plan is substantially lower.

Coordinating Benefits

When individuals have coverage from two health insurers, the insurers typically have agreements about which plan pays and how much. The reason for these arrangements has to do with "true" moral hazard. The insurers do not want beneficiaries to be made better off as a result of an illness or injury. Thus, the coordination rules serve to limit payment to no more than the total amount of the medical care expenses.

There are three alternative methods of coordination between Medicare and employer-sponsored retiree coverage are: (1) the coordination-of-benefits method, (2) the carve-out method, and (3) the exclusion method. The carve-out is by far the most common. Under all of the methods, the primary insurer pays whatever its policy requires. The coordination methods relate to how much of the remaining claim is paid by the secondary insurer. With retiree coverage, Medicare is the primary insurer, and the employer-sponsored plan is secondary.

Under the coordination-of-benefits method, the employer plan considers the Medicare payments to first apply to the deductibles and copays that the retiree would have had to pay under the employer plan and then to what the employer plan would have had to pay. Thus, under this model, the retiree often has no out-of-pocket liability. The most recent data available (1988) suggest that approximately 34 percent of employers providing retiree coverage used this coordination method (Morrisey 1993).

Under the carve-out method, the employer plan considers Medicare payments to first apply to what it would have paid and any remaining Medicare payments reduce the retiree's out-of-pocket liability. The employer's claim liability, of course, is reduced substantially. Indeed, this method tends to minimize the liability of the employer plan. In 1988, 46 percent of employers, but 80 percent of retirees, were in employer-sponsored plans that used the carve-out method.

Under the exclusion method, the employer plan considers any remaining balance after Medicare's payment to be the relevant claim. It applies its deductibles and copays to this balance. Under this arrangement, the retiree is almost always responsible for the out-of-pocket charges associated with the employer plan, regardless of what Medicare pays. Approximately 19 percent of employers used the exclusion method in 1988.

Thus, retirees typically will pay the most out-of-pocket when the carve-out method is used and least when the coordination-of-benefits method is applied. We might also expect that the total premium for retiree coverage would be lowest for the carve-out method as well. If retirees pay for this coverage through compensating differentials, we would expect smaller adjustments, other things equal, when the carve-out method is used. Box 22-1 provides an example.

BOX 22-1

Impact of Alternative Coordination Methods

Suppose your grandfather is covered by traditional Medicare and has retiree coverage through his former employer. He has an acute injury that requires a stay in a hospital that costs $6,000 and physician charges that total $2,000, for a total bill of $8,000. To keep the example simple, further suppose that this injury constitutes a new spell of illness under Medicare, that your grandfather has not yet paid any of the Part B annual deductible, and that the physician is a participating provider and, therefore, accepts the Medicare fee schedule as payment in full.

In 2007, the Medicare hospital deductible was $992, and the Part B annual deductible was $131. Thus, Medicare would pay $6,503 on behalf of your grandfather [($6,000 hospital bill − $992 Part A deductible) + .80 ($2,000 physician bill − $131 Part B deductible)]. Under Medicare alone, your grandfather would be responsible for $1,497.

Suppose that his employer retiree coverage is traditional conventional coverage that has a $500 annual deductible on all covered services, and once that is satisfied, the patient is responsible for 20 percent of the bill. Thus, if your grandfather only has the employer-sponsored coverage, the plan would pay $6,000, that is, [.80 ($8,000 − $500)]. Your grandfather's out-of-pocket expense would be the remaining $2,000.

Now here is how the alternative coordination methods would affect your grandfather's liability:

- *Coordination-of-benefits method.* Medicare is always the primary payer for a beneficiary with retiree coverage. Thus, it will pay its $6,503 share of the bill. With the coordination-of-benefits method, the employer-sponsored plan will consider Medicare payments to first apply to your grandfather's share, with any residual applying to the firm's share. This means that the employer plan will pay $1,497, and your grandfather will have no bill to pay.
- *Carve-out method.* In the carve-out method, the employer plan will consider Medicare's payments to first apply to any payments it would have had to pay, with any residual being applied to the retiree's share. In this example, the employer's bill would have been $6,000, but Medicare paid $6,503 (more than the employer plan would have owed), so the employer plan would pay nothing in this example, and your grandfather would owe $1,497, that is, [$2,000 − $503].
- *Exclusion method.* The exclusion method applies the employer plan to the remainder after Medicare has paid its $6,503. Thus, your grandfather would be responsible for $699; that is, 20 percent of the remaining balance after he satisfied the employer's $500 deductible. The employer plan would pay $798.

Prior to the Medicare Modernization Act taking effect in 2006, most employer-sponsored retiree health insurance plans provided prescription drug coverage. Kaiser Family Foundation (2005) data for 2002 suggest that approximately 97 percent of those with an employer-sponsored supplement had prescription drug coverage. This high participation rate explains why the Medicare prescription drug program that we examined in Chapter 21 provided a subsidy to employers if they continued to offer drug coverage that was at least as good as that offered by stand-alone Medicare drug benefits.

Medigap Coverage

Medigap coverage is perhaps the most well known of the supplemental coverages available to Medicare retirees. Individuals can typically purchase one of ten plans (A–J), whose design was mandated by Congress in the Omnibus Budget Reconciliation Act of 1990. The coverages provided in these ten plans are summarized in Table 22-2. What is clear from the table is that the coverage in most Medigap plans is not extensive. The plans cover the Part A and Part B copayments, the Part A spell of illness deductible, and depending on the plan, prescription drugs and a few other items. For the most part, Medigap pays the first-dollar payment obligations of Medicare beneficiaries. The plans seldom provide coverage for services not already provided by Medicare.

Chollet (2003) provided some sense of the popularity of these policies in 2001 (Figure 22-3). Plans F and C were clearly the most popular but covered essentially only out-of-pocket Medicare-related charges.

FIGURE 22-3

Distribution of Medigap Enrollment by Plan, 2001

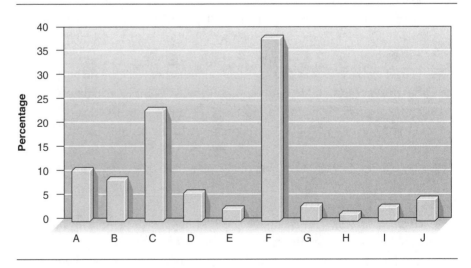

SOURCE: Data from Chollet (2003).

TABLE 22-2

Benefits Offered under Approved Medigap Policies

	Medigap Plans									
Benefits	A	B	C	D	E	F	G	H	I	J
Core benefits*	•	•	•	•	•	•	•	•	•	•
SNF coinsurance†		•	•	•	•		•	•	•	•
Part A deductible		•	•	•	•	•	•	•	•	•
Part B deductible		•				•				•
Part B excess charges						High‡	Low‡		High‡	Low‡
Foreign travel			•	•	•	•	•	•	•	•
At-home recovery				•			•		•	•
Prescription drugs								Low§	Low§	High§
Preventive medical care					•					•

SOURCE: Rice, Graham, and Fox (1997), "The Impact of Policy Standardization on the Medigap Market," *Inquiry* 34(2): 106–116, Table 2. Reprinted with permission.

NOTES: *Core benefits include coverage of all Part A (hospital) coinsurance for stays over sixty days, the 20 percent Part B coinsurance, and the Part A and B blood deductible.

†SNF = Skilled nursing facility.

‡Low excess charge coverage pays 80 percent of the difference between the physician's charge and the Medicare allowable rate; high coverage pays 100 percent of the difference.

§Low prescription drug coverage has a $250 annual deductible, 50 percent coinsurance, and a maximum annual benefit of $1,250; high coverage is similar except that it has a $3,000 maximum annual benefit.

The implementation of the Medicare Part D prescription drug program affects the Medigap market in two ways. First, the legislation does not allow new purchases of Medigap coverage with prescription drug benefits. Thus, plan types H, I, and J are no longer sold to new subscribers. However, two new plans—K and L—that allow seniors to buy catastrophic coverage are now available. Second, seniors with traditional Medicare, a Medigap policy, and a now stand-alone drug plan may find that Medicare Advantage plans, which typically integrate all of these coverages, are more appealing.

Medigap Underwriting

Medicare beneficiaries cannot be denied Medigap coverage if they apply within the first six months after they become eligible for Medicare Part B. However, the policies are manually underwritten and state regulated. Robst (2006) used a Centers for Medicare and Medicaid Services (CMS) survey of state insurance commissioners to explore the nature of Medigap premiums and the nature of the underwriting. He found that, in 2000, Plan F had an average annual premium for 65-year-olds of $1,229 (in 2000 dollars), which rose to an average of $1,724 for 85-year-olds. Regressing premiums on plan characteristics and underwriting features, Robst found no meaningful premium differences across male and female beneficiaries. However, "issue-age" policies were cheaper than "age-attained" policies for younger purchasers. This is as we would expect because an issue-age policy holds a constant premium into the future, while an age-attained policy increases with the individual's age. Community-rated Medigap policies were much more expensive compared to age-attained policies for younger Medicare beneficiaries, but much less expensive for older beneficiaries. This simply reflects the usual effects of combining dissimilar risks that we discussed in Chapter 5. Guaranteed-issue plans are plans in which individuals cannot be refused coverage. In Robst's study, policies with this feature were substantially more expensive across the age spectrum to account for the risk of adverse selection.

Medigap Regulation

When Medigap policies were first available, regulation of the policies was left to the states. A few states implemented minimum coverage standards in the early 1970s. In 1978, the National Association of Insurance Commissioners (NAIC) adopted ten model plans. Congress encouraged the states to adopt these models with the 1980 Baucus Amendments, and by 1984, all of the states had done so. There was concern that beneficiaries misunderstood the nature of the Medicare coverage and that insurers were taking advantage of these uninformed older consumers. As a result, effective in 1992, Congress required that only the model policies recommended by the NAIC could be sold.

Rice, Graham, and Fox (1997) argued that these reforms stabilized the Medigap market to the extent that low-value benefits were eliminated, the prescription drug options had greater annual maximums, and the premium ranges were narrower.

Finkelstein (2004) examined the effects of the minimum coverage standards on the probability that a Medicare senior would have an individual supplemental insurance policy over the 1976 to 1986 period. Using data from the National Health Interview Survey, she concluded that the standards reduced the probability of coverage by 4.9 percentage points in the first two years after enactment and by 8 percentage points (a nearly 25 percent reduction in Medigap coverage) after 3 or more years. Moreover, she found no evidence that there was a substitution into other forms of coverage. Thus, while some people had better coverage as a result of the minimum standards, others gave up their coverage, presumably due to the higher premiums associated with the improved coverage.

In the 1990s, several states enacted underwriting restrictions on the Medigap market. Seven required community rating, and three banned attained-age underwriting. Bundorf and Simon (2006) examined the effects of these changes on enrollment. Using the 1992 to 1999 Medicare Current Beneficiary Survey, they found that the laws had no effect on the probability of coverage but did change the mix of coverage. The changes led to higher rates of coverage among high-risk individuals and lower rates among low-risk individuals. The effects were relatively small. Mandatory community rating increased coverage by 2.8 percentage points for high-risk individuals and lowered coverage by 2.5 percentage points for low-risk individuals. These changes coincided with a shift away from Medicare managed care coverage and an increase in the proportion of Medicare beneficiaries with no supplemental coverage.

Effects of Supplemental Coverage on Traditional Medicare

Supplemental Medicare insurance coverage has obviously important implications for the private insurance market. However, it has big implications for Medicare as well. Medicare expenditures are higher as a result of the various supplements. The reason has to do with moral hazard.

To the extent that Medicare beneficiaries have to pay some portion of the price of a physician visit or a laboratory test out-of-pocket, they will use somewhat fewer visits and tests than they otherwise would have. Medigap plans and employer-sponsored coverage that reduce or eliminate the out-of-pocket payments encourage beneficiaries to slide down the demand curve and consume more Medicare-covered services.

Khandker and McCormack (1999) provided some of the most detailed analysis of the effects of supplemental coverage. They examined the 1991 through 1993 Medicare Current Beneficiary Survey. This survey of nearly 5,300 beneficiaries asked questions about the nature of any non-Medicare coverage. Of particular value, the survey responses were linked to the Medicare claims data. Thus, the study had access to the actual expenditures for covered Medicare services. Khandker and McCormack used a two-part model to examine the probability of healthcare use and the amount of use conditional on using any and were able to use information on self-reported health status to attempt to control for selection bias. They obtained separate estimates for those with different types of supplements. The results are presented in Table 22-3.

TABLE 22-3

Effects of Supplemental Coverage on Total Medicare Spending

	Medigap	ESHI	Medigap + ESHI	Medicaid	Medicare Only
Predicted probability of spending	0.870	0.875	0.893	0.863	0.740
Predicted level of spending, given use	$2,780	$2,947	$3,136	$3,119	$2,710
Total effect relative to Medicare only	1.151	1.226	1.322	1.285	1.000

SOURCE: Data from Khandker and McCormack (1999).

NOTE: ESHI = Employer-sponsored health insurance.

The first row of the table shows that those with Medigap coverage had an 87 percent predicted probability of using any Medicare-covered services and (from the second row) were predicted to spend $2,780, on average, if they had any expenditures. Compared with those with traditional Medicare coverage only (third row), those with Medigap plans had 15.1 percent more Medicare spending. Those with employer-sponsored coverage had nearly 23 percent higher spending, and those few (7 percent of respondents) with both employer-sponsored retiree coverage and a Medigap plan had over 32 percent higher spending. Those who were dual-eligible under Medicaid also had higher Medicare expenditures—over 28 percent higher, controlling for other factors. This is not the only study to find substantial increase in Medicare spending as a result of supplemental coverage. In a review of the literature, Atherly (2001) reported on 13 studies, 11 of which found higher Medicare spending and 2 that showed no effects. Clearly, the presence of retiree coverage increases Medicare costs.

Medicare Advantage

Medicare managed care plans have been available since the 1970s, and as we saw in Chapter 6, were paid on a capitated basis using the Adjusted Average Per Capita Cost (AAPCC) model. Managed care options were expanded in 1997 with the Balanced Budget Act, and the CMS developed a payment system that better reflects beneficiary health status with Hierarchical Condition Categories (HCCs) that has been phased in during the 2000s. The

Medicare Modernization Act further expanded the available options and modified the way Medicare Advantage plans are paid.

Under Medicare Advantage, enrollees can choose from among five different types of health plan arrangements (Centers for Medicare and Medicaid Services 2006b):

1. A health maintenance organization (HMO) that typically has a closed panel of providers but may have a point-of-service option
2. A preferred provider organization (PPO) that typically allows enrollees to use nonplan providers for an extra copay
3. A Private Fee-for-Service (PFFS) plan in which enrollees can typically go to any physician or hospital that agrees to accept the plan's payment terms
4. A Medicare medical savings account (MSA), similar to a health savings account (HSA), in which the beneficiary has a high deductible and an HMO, PPO, or PFFS, together with an account into which Medicare deposits money
5. A Special Needs Plan (SNP) designed for those who may live in a nursing home, are dually eligible for Medicaid, or who have specific chronic or disabling conditions

The plans typically provide Part D drug coverage along with the other services they cover, although they are not required to do so.

Since the Medicare Modernization Act, Medicare Advantage plans now enter into a bidding process with Medicare. The CMS establishes a benchmark payment level per beneficiary in each county or region to provide the full range of Medicare Part A and Part B services. If the Medicare Advantage plan submits a bid below the benchmark, the CMS will keep 25 percent of the difference and rebate the other 75 percent back to the plan. The plan must return this rebate to its Medicare subscribers in the form of additional services, lower copays, and/or lower Medicare Part B or Part D premiums. If the plan's bid is above the benchmark, it can charge the Medicare subscriber for the difference. In addition, once the plan enrolls subscribers, Medicare will adjust the actual payment for each based on the HCC methodology.

The Medicare Payment Advisory Commission (2005) reported that approximately 95 percent of Medicare Advantage plans provided bids that were below the benchmark. The average monthly rebates in 2006 averaged $80 for HMOs, $30 to $50 for PPOs (depending on whether they were regional or local), and $40 for PFFS plans. As mentioned in Chapter 21, in 2006, Medicare Advantage plans used the largest proportion of their rebates to reduce Part A and Part B cost sharing, followed by the provision of additional benefits.

The Kaiser Family Foundation (2005) reported that the vast majority (95 percent) of Medicare Advantage enrollees in 2005 were enrolled in an

HMO. PFFS plans had 1 percent of enrollment, and PPOs had the remainder. Medicare MSAs were not available until 2007.

Enrollment in Medicare managed care plans has varied widely over time and across the country. Enrollment peaked in 1998 with approximately 17 percent of beneficiaries enrolled; it declined to 11 percent in 2004 and had reached 13 percent by 2005 (Kaiser Family Foundation 2005). The Kaiser Family Foundation further reported that enrollment projections varied widely, with the Department of Health and Human Services estimating that 30 percent of beneficiaries would be in a Medicare Advantage plan by 2013, while the Congressional Budget Office estimated that only 16 percent would do so.

Medicare Advantage is also a regionalized phenomenon. As of 2005, fewer than 1 percent of Medicare beneficiaries were enrolled in an HMO or PPO in 17 states, but at least 20 percent were enrolled in six states: Arizona, California, Colorado, Oregon, Pennsylvania, and Rhode Island. One-fourth of Medicare Advantage enrollees lived in California (Kaiser Family Foundation 2005).

Price Sensitivity of Medicare Advantage

Enrollment in Medicare Advantage obviously depends in part on an additional premium that may be assessed. There has been no published work on this topic that incorporates the changes brought about by the Medicare Modernization Act. However, Atherly and colleagues (2004) used 1998 Medicare Current Beneficiary Survey data to examine the effects of extra Medicare Advantage premiums on plan choice. They found that a typical Medicare HMO would lose about .62 percentage points of market share with a $10 increase in its monthly premium. (The consumer perspective elasticity of plan choice was –0.13, and the insurer perspective elasticity was –4.57.) The study team also found that beneficiaries were responsive to plan characteristics, particularly having coverage for prescription drugs. Thus, where the CMS sets the benchmark payment level and the ability of plans to provide prescription drug coverage appear to be key to how dramatically Medicare Advantage plan enrollment grows.

Competition between Medigap and Medicare Advantage

Because access to employer-sponsored retiree coverage is typically determined before people retire, most of the short-run competition in the retiree market is between Medigap plans and Medicare Advantage. McLaughlin, Chernew, and Taylor (2002) used the 1996 to 1997 Community Tracking Survey to examine the interaction of Medigap and Medicare managed care at 56 sites in 30 states. They found substantial variation in premiums across markets, insurers, and coverages. As importantly, there was a strong positive correlation between Medigap premiums and Medicare HMO enrollment. A one standard deviation increase in the average Medigap premium (from $236 per year to $291) was associated with an increase in Medicare HMO participation of 8 percentage points.

The advent of new forms of Medicare managed care options, together with Medicare prescription drug benefits, suggests that these estimates of substitution may no longer be reliable. However, older citizens have increasing experience with managed care plans through their working lives and may be more willing to consider such options on retirement. Morrisey and Jensen (2001) used the Health and Retirement Survey to explore the type of coverage that active workers, ages 57 to 63 in 1996, selected on transitioning to retiree coverage in 1998. They found that 87 percent of those with active-worker HMO coverage (and who had a choice of plan types when they retired) took HMO coverage, 73.8 percent of those with PPO coverage chose PPO coverage on retirement, and 47.5 percent of those with traditional coverage chose to continue with traditional coverage. These transitions suggest that future retirees with even greater experience with managed care plans may be amenable to Medicare Advantage type plans, just as those with employer-sponsored retiree coverage are disproportionately likely to remain in managed care plans.

Chapter Summary

- Fewer than 10 percent of Medicare beneficiaries lack some supplemental form of health insurance coverage.
- The largest employers commonly offer employer-sponsored retiree coverage, which typically provides coverage analogous to that provided to active workers. Coordination of coverage with Medicare makes retiree coverage less expensive than that held by active workers.
- Medigap coverage is typically purchased individually and covers the out-of-pocket expenses associated with covered Medicare services.
- Supplemental coverage increases traditional Medicare's claims experience due to moral hazard. Effectively lower out-of-pocket prices increase Medicare expenses by 15 to 32 percent.
- Medicare Advantage is Medicare managed care coverage offered by private insurers. Insurers bid to provide coverage relative to a CMS-established benchmark. Most bids are below the benchmark, and as a result, most plans offer lower cost sharing and/or enhanced benefits relative to traditional Medicare. Plans received risk-adjusted payments for the beneficiaries they actually enroll.

- The implementation of the Medicare prescription drug program is having significant effects on the supplemental retiree health insurance market.
- Medigap and Medicare Advantage are effectively substitutes for each other.

Discussion Questions

1. Why would an employer offer retiree health benefits?
2. What effects do you think the Medicare prescription drug program will have on the Medigap market? On the employer-sponsored retiree health insurance market? On the Medicare Advantage market?
3. Is Medigap coverage a "good buy" for seniors? Is it consistent with the theory of the demand for insurance we studied in Chapter 3? If not, why would it be so popular?

MEDICAID, "CROWD-OUT," AND LONG-TERM CARE INSURANCE

Medicaid is a joint federal-state program enacted along with Medicare in 1965. Unlike Medicare, however, Medicaid is a needs-based program designed to provide health insurance coverage to low-income families and, in particular, pregnant women, children, the elderly, and those with disabilities. Substantial expansions of Medicaid in the mid to late 1980s and again in 1996 extended coverage to children in households with higher incomes. Because it is a joint federal-state program, Medicaid coverage varies considerably from state to state.

This chapter provides a broad description of the Medicaid program, both with respect to eligibility and covered services. We discuss the evidence on "crowd-out"—the extent to which Medicaid expansions have affected the private insurance market. We also examine the effect that Medicaid has had on the development of the long-term care insurance market. Finally, we review the analysis on the future growth of the Medicaid program. It is important to note, however, that no short chapter can do justice to the range of programs available under Medicaid. Interested readers should consult the web site for the Centers for Medicare and Medicaid Services (CMS) and, in particular, the individual state Medicaid web sites for program details.

Medicaid Overview

The Medicaid program consists of more than a score of somewhat related programs with differing eligibility conditions. However, the programs essentially provide coverage for four groups of low income people: (1) pregnant women and adults in families with children, (2) children, (3) the elderly, and (4) individuals with disabilities. In 2004, approximately 16 percent of the U.S. population received Medicaid services (Kaiser Family Foundation 2006a).

The federal government has established categories of services that must be covered by state Medicaid programs and also has identified optional services that a state may choose to offer. Within these strictures, the states have considerable flexibility with respect to the level of mandatory services they provide, as well as to whether they provide any of the optional services.

In addition, the states have considerable flexibility with respect to the eligibility criteria they apply for covered services.

Federal-State Funding

The share of Medicaid medical spending that federal sources cover is determined by the relative per capita income of the state. The matching formula is:

$$\text{Federal share} = 1.0 - [(\text{State per capita income}^2 / \text{Federal per capita income}^2) \times 0.45]$$

Per capita incomes are the average of the preceding three years, and the federal share is constrained by law to be no less than 50 percent and no more than 83 percent. Thus, the federal share in a poor state such as Mississippi is approximately 75 percent, while an affluent state such as Illinois has a federal match closer to 50 percent. The federal match on most administrative costs is limited to 50 percent. The Kaiser Family Foundation (2006a) reported that, overall, federal sources covered 57 percent of total Medicaid costs in 2004.

Eligibility under the Categorically Needy Programs

In general, eligibility is determined by being a member of a covered group and having sufficiently low income. Children and families were originally eligible under the categorically needy program because they were eligible for Aid to Families with Dependent Children (AFDC) in their state of residence. However, with the welfare reforms enacted during President Bill Clinton's administration, the direct link between welfare and Medicaid eligibility was severed. Now, families with dependent children are eligible for Medicaid if they would have met the requirements for welfare coverage in 1996, when the welfare reforms were enacted. These conditions are defined by the federal poverty line (FPL) and the level of the FPL the state has established for eligibility. Table 23-1 shows the 2006 FPL for families of one to six members. It is worth noting that no state has pegged its eligibility criterion at 100 of the FPL. Most set it around 45 percent of the line, although some set it as low as 15 percent.

The categorically needy program was expanded through a series of laws passed in the mid to late 1980s. These are often called SOBRA expansions for the Sixth Omnibus Budget Reconciliation Act of 1988, which was one of the key statutes. The expansions provided coverage for pregnant women and children up to age 6 who had family incomes up to 133 percent of the FPL. They also phased in coverage for children ages 6–19 with family incomes up to 100 percent of the FPL. That phase-in was complete in 2002. The states have the option of expanding the coverage to children up to 185 percent of the FPL.

Number of Persons in Family or Household	Federal Poverty Line
1	$9,800
2	13,200
3	16,600
4	20,000
5	23,400
6	26,800

TABLE 23-1
Federal Poverty Line, 2006

SOURCE: http://aspe.hhs.gov/poverty/06poverty.shtml.

NOTE: Each additional person adds $3,400. Values are for the 48 contiguous states and the District of Columbia.

The categorically needy program of Medicaid also provides coverage for individuals who are blind, elderly, or disabled if they are covered by federal Supplementary Security Income (SSI). The SSI program has income and asset limitations. In 2006, the benefit rate was approximately 73 percent of the FPL—$7,236 per year for a single individual. Moreover, an individual could earn up to $1,291 per month before the SSI benefit was totally phased out. The asset limitations were $2,000 for an individual and $3,000 for a couple. Several states have more-restrictive eligibility limitations.[1]

The categorically needy Medicaid program also provides coverage to people in nursing homes, hospitals, posthospital extended care, and intermediate-care facilities/mental retardation facilities if they have income below 300 percent of the SSI limit. There are asset limitations as well, but these typically exclude the home if a spouse or dependent is living there or if the intent is to return to the home. If assets are above the allowed threshold, the individual or couple is required to "spend-down" their assets to become eligible for Medicaid.

Eligibility under the Medically Needy Programs

Currently, 34 states and the District of Columbia have implemented an optional Medicaid medically needy program. These programs typically do one or both of the following: First, they often provide coverage for people ages 19–20 who otherwise would not be Medicaid-eligible or who are eligible because the medically needy program has a higher income threshold. Second, and more generally, the medically needy programs allow individuals who have too much income but who also have high medical expenses to spend-down

---

1. See "Understanding Supplemental Security Income," http://www.ssa.gov/notices/supplemental-security-income/text-understanding-ssi.htm.

to eligibility. These people become eligible because, after adjusting their income for their medical spending, they meet the income threshold. Given these eligibility criteria, those covered under the medically needy programs tend to have higher healthcare spending than other Medicaid-covered groups (Crowley 2003).

Eligibility for Certain Medicare-Eligible Groups

In addition to those who may be Medicaid-eligible because they reside in a nursing home or other medical facility, three groups of Medicare beneficiaries are eligible for Medicaid. The first, as mentioned earlier, are those who are eligible because they are also eligible for SSI. They receive full Medicaid benefits, and Medicaid pays their Part B and D premiums and the cost sharing associated with the use of covered Medicare services. Second, "qualified Medicare beneficiaries" have incomes below 100 percent of the FPL and must also satisfy an asset limitation. If they qualify, Medicaid pays their Part B and Part D premiums and Medicare cost sharing. However, no other Medicaid services are provided. Finally, "special low-income beneficiaries" have incomes between 100 and 120 percent of the FPL. Medicaid pays their Part B and Part D premiums only.

Medicaid Recipients and Expenditures

Figure 23-1 provides a sense of the distribution of the nearly 60 million people who received Medicaid services in 2006. Nearly half of those receiving services were children. However, individuals with disabilities and the elderly were much more intensive users of Medicaid, together comprising over 68 percent of expenditures.

This relationship is made clear by examining the average expenditure per recipient in 2003. Expenditures for children and adults averaged $1,410 and $1,799, respectively. However, average expenditures on behalf of the individuals with disabilities and the elderly were $11,659 and $10,147 respectively. Moreover, as is shown in Figure 23-2, much of the expenditure for the elderly and those with disabilities was for long-term care services. Indeed, Medicaid is estimated to have paid 44 percent of all nursing home spending in 2004 (Kaiser Family Foundation 2006a).

Medicaid Covered Services

Medicaid specifies certain mandatory services that state programs must cover. There are also a number of optional benefits, any number of which a state may choose to include in its program. Box 23-1 (on page 354) lists these

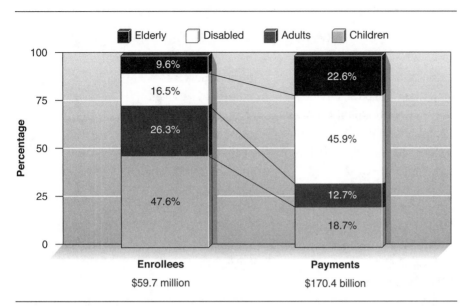

FIGURE 23-1
Distribution of Medicaid Enrollees and Payments, 2006

SOURCE: Data from Congressional Budget Office (2006).

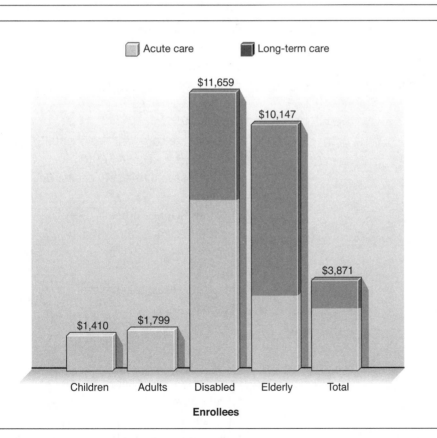

FIGURE 23-2
Medicaid Payments per Enrollee by Acute and Long-Term Care, 2003

SOURCE: "Medicaid at a Glance—Fact Sheet," (#1066-06) The Henry J. Kaiser Family Foundation, March 2007. This information was reprinted with permission from the Henry J. Kaiser Family Foundation. The Kaiser Family Foundation, based in Menlo Park, California, is a nonprofit, private operating foundation focusing on the major health care issues facing the nation and is not associated with Kaiser Permanente or Kaiser Industries.

BOX 23-1

Medicaid Covered Services

Mandatory Services	Optional Services
Inpatient hospital services	Podiatrists services
Outpatient hospital services	Optometrists services
Rural health clinic and federally qualified health center (FQHC) services	Chiropractors services
	Psychologists services
	Medical social worker services
Laboratory and X-ray services	Nurse anesthetists services
Nurse practitioners services	Private duty nursing
Nursing facility (NF) services and home health services for individuals age 21+	Clinic services
	Dental services
	Physical therapy
Early and periodic screening, diagnosis, and treatment (EPSDT) for individuals under 21	Occupational therapy
	Speech, hearing, and language disorders
	Prescribed drugs
	Dentures
Family planning services and supplies	Prosthetic devices
	Eyeglasses
Physicians' services and medical and surgical services of a dentist	Diagnostic services
	Screening services
	Preventive services
Nurse-midwife services	Rehabilitative services
	Intermediate care facilities/mentally-retarded services (ICF/MR)
	Inpatient psychiatric services for under age 21
	Christian Science nurses
	Christian Science sanitoriums
	Nursing facility (NF) services for under age 21
	Emergency hospital services
	Personal care services
	Transportation services
	Case management services
	Hospice care services
	Regulatory care services
	TB-related services
	Inpatient and NF services for 65+ in institutions for mental diseases (IMDs)

SOURCE: Centers for Medicare and Medicaid Services 2000, p. 9.

covered services. The states, however, maintain considerable discretion about the level of benefits to provide within each of the mandated or optional services they offer. Alabama, for example, covers 16 inpatient hospitals days, 3 nonemergency hospital outpatient visits, and 14 physician visits per calendar year as part of its mandatory benefits.

Medicaid Managed Care

Managed care plays a significant role in Medicaid. By 2003, approximately one-half of all Medicaid recipients—some 27 million individuals—were in a managed care program (Hurley and Retchin 2006). The vast majority of these recipients are women and children; managed care is much less common among the disabled and elderly Medicaid populations. One reason for this is that many states require that children and pregnant women be enrolled in a health maintenance organization (HMO) or other form of Medicaid managed care plan.

The Medicaid managed care market has some key differences from the private market. As Draper, Hurley, and Short (2004) reported, some managed care plans have specialized in the Medicaid market. This involves several features. First, the plans tend to have narrower networks, unlike the expanded networks that arose as a result of the managed care backlash in the private sector (see Chapter 11). However, these narrower networks often have to include federally qualified health centers and traditional Medicaid inpatient providers in the community. The plans also maintain relatively broad service offerings.

Second, while commercial plans have moved away from utilization management, Medicaid managed care plans have not. Part of this reflects an inability to use anything other than nominal copays to limit moral hazard (see Box 23-2).

Finally, while Medicaid managed care plans have continued to use capitation more aggressively than have plans that focus on the private market, whether they have been able to selectively contract with providers is unclear. Early work by Leibowitz, Buchanan, and Mann (1992) demonstrated that Medicaid populations voluntarily enrolled in a managed care plan had substantially lower Medicaid expenditures than did those who were assigned to a managed care plan or who were voluntarily in a fee-for-service arrangement. They concluded that apparent Medicaid cost savings from Medicaid managed care was, in fact, the result of favorable selection. If the savings are the result of favorable selection, then requiring all Medicaid eligibles to participate in the managed care program will not save money. As we saw in Chapter 9, the key to cost containment in managed care is selectively contracting on a price basis. It is not clear that Medicaid managed care plans have done this.

BOX 23-2

Copayments under Medicaid

In 2005, Congress gave states the authority to charge copayments up to 10 percent of the cost of services for those individuals with family income between 100 and 150 percent of the FPL. Those with higher incomes may be charged up to 20 percent. However, total cost sharing may not exceed 5 percent of the family's income (Congressional Budget Office 2006). It is not clear, however, how many Medicaid managed care plans have introduced increased cost sharing.

State Children's Health Insurance Plan (SCHIP)

The State Children's Health Insurance Plan (SCHIP) was created as part of the 1997 Balanced Budget Act. In essence, it provides federal matching funds for the provision of health insurance to lower-income children up to 300 percent of the poverty line. The legislation provides a capped amount of funding for each state through 2007. If they choose to participate, the states have three ways to provide coverage: (1) they can expand their existing Medicaid program, (2) they can create a new separate program, or (3) they can develop a combined Medicaid-private program. As of 2001, 19 states had expanded their Medicaid program, 15 had created a separate program, and the remainder had taken a combination approach (LoSasso and Buchmueller 2004). One of the reasons why many states adopted a separate private program was a concern that Medicaid was stigmatizing. It was believed that parents with eligible children would be more likely to enroll their children in private programs.

The National Health Policy Forum (2004) reported that 40 states have expanded eligibility for children up to at least 200 percent of the FPL as a result of SCHIP. If the states expanded their Medicaid program, the benefits offered had to be the same as those in their state program. If they took another, private, option, the benefits could be:

- benchmark coverage—analogous to the Blue Cross/Blue Shield coverage or the state employees benefit package available in the state;
- benchmark equivalent coverage—coverage that was actuarially equal in value to the benchmark option;
- the same as plans offered by Florida, New York, or Pennsylvania that were in place prior to the legislation; or
- a plan of their own creation approved by the CMS (National Health Policy Forum 2004).

The states may impose premium sharing and copays on services, but the payments may not exceed 5 percent of the family's income. The cost of the program is shared by federal and state taxpayers. In general, the federal match on SCHIP is 15 percentage points higher than for Medicaid, within the range of 65 to 83 percent of total costs up to the dollar cap established for each state. If the state's allocation is not spent within three years, the moneys are reallocated to other states.

Medicaid "Crowd-out"

"Crowd-out" exists when a public program such as Medicaid causes people to drop private coverage and shift to the public program. We alluded to crowd-out in Chapter 15 when we discussed higher out-of-pocket premiums for employer-sponsored family coverage in states with generous Medicaid programs. The argument was that some families substitute public coverage for private. Here we examine the phenomenon directly.

Cutler and Gruber (1997) undertook some of the best work on the issue of Medicaid crowd-out. They used the U.S. Census Bureau's Current Population Survey (CPS) to examine the effects of the SOBRA expansions in coverage for children ages 7–19 between 1987 and 1992. They found that the decline in private coverage as a result of the expansions was roughly 50 percent. That is, for every two children who gained Medicaid coverage, one gave up private coverage.

Other ways to measure crowd-out are sometimes employed. However, as Cutler and Gruber showed, these measures understate the extent of crowd-out. For example, using the same CPS data, they estimated that 22 percent of the expansion in Medicaid over the period was offset by reductions in private coverage. The flaw in this approach is that Medicaid enrollment may have increased for other reasons besides the SOBRA expansion. Crowd-out also has been measured as the proportion of those with private coverage who lost it as a result of the expansion. Cutler and Gruber estimated this to be approximately 15 percent. However, private coverage may change for any number of reasons besides the substitution effect.

SCHIP and Crowd-out

More recently, LoSasso and Buchmueller (2004) examined the effects of the SCHIP expansion on coverage and crowd-out. Using much the same methods as Cutler and Gruber, they found that approximately 9 percent of the children meeting the income eligibility criteria gained insurance coverage through SCHIP. They also concluded that, if anything, the straight Medicaid expansions were more effective that the separate programs. Thus, they concluded that the stigma of Medicaid was not an issue, or at least no different under the separate programs. They argued that the growth in coverage was more likely the result of explicit outreach programs that SCHIP used.

However, over 46 percent of those who gained SCHIP coverage gave up private coverage. The extent of crowd-out was about the same as that found in the earlier Medicaid SOBRA expansion. Not surprisingly, those eligibles with higher family incomes were more likely to move from private coverage to SCHIP. They are the ones more likely to have had employer-sponsored coverage. Thus, one obvious way to reduce crowd-out is to target the program to only low-income families.

Another way to reduce crowd-out is to impose waiting periods before coverage takes effect. LoSasso and Buchmueller (2004) found that a five-month waiting period essentially eliminated crowd-out, but it also reduced the take-up rate by 3.7 percent. Work by others suggests that premium sharing can also be an effective means of reducing crowd-out (Davidson, Blewett, and Call 2004). The SCHIP out-of-pocket premium reduces the gains from dropping private coverage.

Long-Term Care Insurance and Medicaid

The trade association for health insurers—America's Health Insurance Plans (2004)—estimated that, in 2002, there were some 6.4 million private long-term care policies in force. Approximately 80 percent of these were sold in the individual market. However, these sales constituted only about 2.2 percent of the U.S. population. While you might assume that the elderly purchase such policies, the average age of those with coverage through the individual market was 60 years, and 45 years for those purchasing coverage through an employer. Finkelstein and McGarry (2003) reported that, based on the Health and Retirement Survey, only 10 percent of those over age 65 had a long-term care policy in 2000.

Figure 23-3 shows the reported average annual long-term care insurance premium in 2002. Premiums increase with the age at which they are purchased. Policies typically are sold with an "elimination period," which is simply the number of days that an individual is in a nursing home before coverage begins. It is analogous to a deductible. The policies typically also cover such long-term care services as assisted living and home health. "Inflation protection" in Figure 23-3 refers to a 5 percent increase in the benefit each year. A "nonforfeiture clause" means that, if the premium is not paid, the policy will remain in force with reduced benefits. Unfortunately, no studies have yet examined the price sensitivity of long-term care insurance.

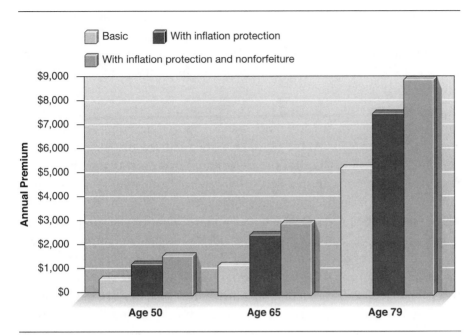

FIGURE 23-3

Average Annual Long-Term Care Insurance Premium, 2002

SOURCE: Data from America's Health Insurance Plans (2004).

NOTE: Basic coverage includes a $150-per-day benefit and four years of coverage after a 90-day elimination period.

A number of arguments have been advanced for why the long-term care insurance market has not developed more significantly. These arguments have focused on both the demand and supply sides of the market.

On the demand side, it is often argued that people misperceive their likelihood of using long-term care services, that they believe that Medicare covers such care, or that their family will take care of them. In fact, if a person lives long enough, the probability of spending time in a nursing home increases dramatically. Liang et al. (1996) estimated that, on average, someone alive at age 65 will spend 14 percent of their remaining life in a nursing home. By age 85, this proportion rises to 50 percent, and by age 90, to just over 70 percent. Medicare does provide some long-term care services: up to 100 days of skilled nursing home care per spell of illness and substantial amounts of home health and hospice care. However, most nursing home care is not delivered in skilled facilities but in facilities that provide much less intense levels of care. Moreover, while spouses or family members commonly provide caregiver services, the earlier Liang et al. estimates belie their ability to fully substitute out of commercial care-giving services.

On the supply side, the arguments are that insurers lack reliable information on the extent of moral hazard and adverse selection. The information on moral hazard in the long-term care services market is indeed weak. As we saw in Chapter 7, very few studies of private nursing home demand have been undertaken, but those that have suggest substantial price sensitivity, with elasticity estimates in excess of −1.0 in absolute value. Thus, we would expect either substantial use of various forms of copayment (such as the elimination periods noted earlier) or high premiums designed to accommodate this increased usage.

Finkelstein and McGarry (2003) examined the extent of adverse selection in the long-term care insurance market. Using data from the 1995 Asset and Health Dynamics (AHEAD) Survey, they showed that there is adverse selection. After controlling for the factors used by insurers in predicting the use of nursing homes, respondents' self-reported probability of being in a nursing home within five years was still predictive of both the use of nursing homes and of the purchase of long-term care insurance. This implies asymmetric information and the presence of adverse selection. However, Finkelstein and McGarry also found that individual preferences for bearing risk also mattered—and in the opposite direction. Those who were more cautious—that is, more risk averse—were more likely to buy the coverage but less likely to use it. The net effect was that both types of people tended to buy long-term care coverage, and the aggregate effect was the appearance of no adverse selection.

However, the primary reason for the lack of a large private market in long-term care insurance is again crowd-out. In this case, people do not buy coverage because they already have it; it's called Medicaid.

As we noted earlier, an older person can become eligible for Medicaid nursing home services in a variety of ways. In each case, there are income and asset limitations on eligibility. The binding constraint is usually thought to be the asset limitation. There are many anecdotes of people impoverishing themselves either by spending their assets on nursing home care until they become eligible for Medicaid or by transferring their assets to family members or friends in the years prior to their eligibility for Medicaid. There was concern that this effort also served to impoverish the community-dwelling spouse of someone entering a nursing home. For this reason, the Medicare Catastrophic Coverage Act of 1988 (MCCA) liberalized the income and asset rules when there was a community-dwelling spouse. Most importantly, it excluded the homestead from the asset considerations when there was such a spouse, and it allowed the spouse to keep all income in his or her name and a portion of the income that was in the spouse's name.

Sloan and Shayne (1993) examined the extent of such impoverishment before and after MCCA, and by extension, the extent to which people had Medicaid coverage for long-term care. They used the National Long-Term Care Survey and information on state Medicaid policies in 1987 and in 1991. They then simulated the extent to which people with disabilities would have to spend-down their assets to be eligible for nursing home care. It is worth noting that their definition of disabilities is relatively modest: those with one or more limitations in activities of daily living. They argued convincingly that individuals with disabilities are the relevant population. Those seniors in better health are likely to be able to legally transfer assets before their health deteriorates sufficiently to be disabled.

Sloan and Shayne's findings, shown in Table 23-2, clearly show that, post-MCCA, nearly 78 percent of those at risk of entering a nursing home were already on Medicaid or were immediately eligible. Another 5 percent were eligible within six months. The detail of the table is also instructive. The MCCA had a relatively small but important impact on eligibility. It increased the percentage of people immediately eligible or eligible within six months by 8.7 percentage points. Virtually all of this increase came from increased eligibility among married people. This is as we would expect because the key feature of the MCCA was to protect the income and assets of a community-dwelling spouse.

The upshot of all of this for the purchase of long-term care insurance is clear. The reason most people do not buy long-term care insurance is that they already have it. Based on the Sloan-Shayne estimates, over 80 percent of those likely to use a nursing home will be eligible for Medicaid immediately or within six months of entry.

More recently, Brown, Coe, and Finkelstein (2006) examined the crowd-out effects of Medicaid on private long-term care insurance. They

	Before Medicare Catastrophic Coverage Act of 1988			After Medicare Catastrophic Coverage Act of 1988			
	Single	Married	All	Single	Married	All	
Already on Medicaid	24.0%	10.1%	18.7%	24.0%	10.1%	18.7%	**TABLE 23-2** Percentage of Disabled Elderly Eligible for Medicaid on Admission to a Nursing Home
Immediately eligible	48.5%	43.3%	46.4%	48.9%	75.1%	59.0%	
Eligible in 1 to 6 months	7.8%	11.3%	9.2%	7.8%	1.3%	5.3%	
Eligible in 6 to 30 months	7.2%	13.4%	9.6%	7.5%	3.1%	5.8%	
Eligible in 30 to 120 months	4.7%	9.1%	6.4%	4.6%	1.6%	3.8%	
Not eligible in 120 months	7.8%	12.8%	9.7%	7.2%	7.7%	7.4%	
	100.0%	100.0%	100.0%	100.0%	100.0%	100.0%	

SOURCE: Sloan and Shayne (1993), "Long-term Care, Medicaid, and Impoverishment of the Elderly," *Milbank Quarterly* 71(4) 575–599, Table 2. Reprinted with permission.

concluded that, in the presence of Medicaid and controlling for other relevant factors, between 66 and 90 percent of people would not buy long-term care coverage. They showed that there is some sensitivity to the asset threshold that Medicaid imposes to determine eligibility. A $10,000 decrease in qualifying assets would increase private long-term care coverage by 1.1 percentage points.

The Future of Medicaid

The Congressional Budget Office (2006) reported that, under current law, federal Medicaid benefits payments are projected to more than double between 2006 and 2016. The period beyond that is even more problematic.

Figure 23-4 shows the CBO estimates of the determinants of Medicaid spending growth over the 27 years from 1975 to 2002. Overall, slightly more than one-third (37 percent) of spending growth can be attributed to increases in the number of covered individuals. This includes both increases in the populations covered by the program and expansions in eligibility. However, nearly two-thirds of spending growth is attributable to the same medical care cost drivers that affect all of healthcare.

The distribution across eligibility groups is instructive as well. The bulk of the growth in adult care came from increases in the number of recipients. The largest group here is the expansion in eligibility for pregnant women. Since the duration of their eligibility is relatively brief, costs were less

FIGURE 23-4
Share of Medicaid Cost Growth from Increases in Recipients and Inflation-Adjusted Cost per Recipient, 1975–2002

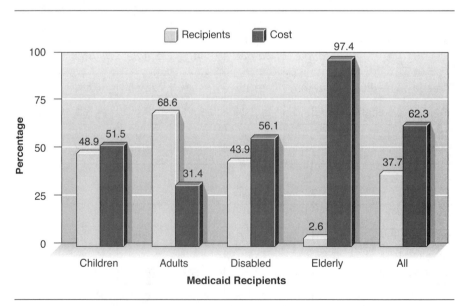

SOURCE: Computed from Congressional Budget Office (2006).

of a factor. In contrast, virtually all of the growth in expenditures for the elderly was the result of increases in inflation-adjusted costs. This reflects the increasing costs of nursing home and other long-term care services. The CBO (2006) estimated that long-term care expenditures grew at an average 7.7 percent, more rapidly than hospital and physician services, but slower than prescription drug costs.

Over the ten-year span from 2006 to 2016, federal spending on Medicaid is projected to increase by 112 percent (CBO 2006). Spending per recipient will increase fairly consistently across the eligibility groups, with the exception of the elderly, for whom it will grow more slowly. This simply reflects the shift in much of the prescription drug costs from Medicaid to Medicare as a result of Medicare Part D. Enrollment growth for children and adults is expected to be quite modest (3.5 and 3.8 percent, respectively) over the entire ten-year period. In contrast, enrollment growth for the high-cost disabled and elderly groups is projected to be 29.3 and 31.6 percent, respectively.

Thus, just as the aging of the baby boom generation begins to affect Social Security and Medicare in the next ten years, it also begins to affect Medicaid. However, over this period, baby boomers will be relatively young and healthy. They probably will not have a considerable influence on Medicaid (or Medicare) until later.

Figure 23-5 presents the CBO's projections of Medicaid, Medicare, and Social Security spending as a share of the gross domestic product (GDP), thereby adjusting for anticipated growth in the U.S. economy overall. The values are for 2050. They show Medicaid spending growing over 2.67 times from its 2006 level, nearly comparable to Medicare's growth and much faster than the growth of Social Security. In 2050, Medicaid may comprise 4 percent of GDP and Medicare 8.6 percent.

The values shown in Figure 23-5 for Medicaid are particularly problematic. The CBO assumed that enrollment in the program would grow at the same rate as the general population. On the one hand, this seems unlikely, given the 30 percent growth figures for enrollment of the elderly and individuals with disabilities that the CBO projected over the 2006 to 2016 period. On the other hand, some have argued that health status will continue to improve over time. Still others disagree. To further complicate the story, the CBO assumed that healthcare costs would rise less rapidly than they have historically and made no assumptions about cutbacks (or expansions) in optional services that states may impose as Medicaid spending increases. In short, the future of Medicaid, like that of Medicare, promises to be an exciting ride.

FIGURE 23-5

Comparison of
Projected
Spending for
Medicaid,
Medicare, and
Social Security
as a Percentage
of Gross
Domestic
Product (GDP)

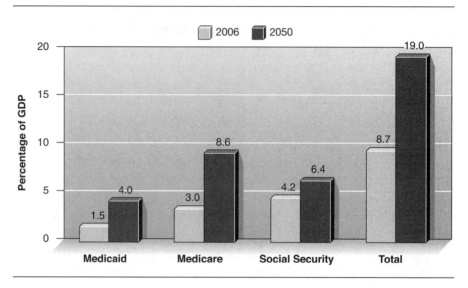

SOURCE: Data from Congressional Budget Office (2006).

Chapter Summary

- Medicaid is a joint federal-state need-based program to provide medical services to low-income populations, and in particular, pregnant women, children, the elderly, and individuals with disabilities.
- The states exercise considerable flexibility with respect to the criteria for Medicaid eligibility, the generosity of services, and the inclusion of optional services.
- While children make up nearly half of the enrolled Medicaid population, the elderly and those with disabilities expend nearly 70 percent of the costs.
- Medicaid expansions have sought to cover people with somewhat higher family incomes. There is evidence of substantial private insurance "crowd-out" as a result of these expansions, typically on the order of one person giving up private coverage for every two gaining public-sector benefits.
- Under current laws, long-term care insurance is unlikely to be a major market. Estimates suggest that nearly 80 percent of likely nursing home residents are already on Medicaid or will be immediately eligible on entering a nursing home.
- Medicaid faces the same burgeoning cost projections as does Medicare and for the same reasons: the aging and retirement of the baby boom generation.

Discussion Questions

1. Under what conditions would a Medicaid managed care program likely be successful in restraining Medicaid costs?
2. Some have proposed that more children would be enrolled in SCHIP (or Medicaid) if their parents could also be enrolled. Leaving aside the issue of the extent to which children would enjoy first-time coverage, what effect would this have on parental coverage? How large a crowd-out effect would you anticipate?
3. In 2006, Congress enacted legislation that prevents persons with a home valued at more than $500,000 from qualifying for Medicaid; states can raise this limit to $750,000. (Homesteads of whatever value are exempt when a community-dwelling spouse or other dependent is living there.) In addition, Medicaid will "look back" for five years instead of three in determining whether assets have been transferred in anticipation of Medicaid eligibility. What effects do you expect this action to have on Medicaid eligibility and the demand for long-term care insurance?
4. Suppose you are a reasonably wealthy individual. Under what circumstances would you buy long-term care insurance rather than investing in other assets?

AN ENDNOTE—A COURSE SUMMARY

This text has provided a broad and reasonably deep discussion of health insurance in the United States. However, for all of the detail, only six key issues need be considered in any discussion of health insurance. If you have mastered the course, then anytime a management or policy question arises with respect to health insurance, you will immediately consider which of the following issues apply. In spite of your best efforts to suppress it, identifying the relevant issue will cause the underlying economics to be recalled, and the implications of the management or policy question will almost always appear. Try it!

- The demand for insurance
- Adverse selection
- Moral hazard
- Selective contracting
- Compensating differentials
- The tax treatment of health insurance

REFERENCES

Abraham, J. M., and A. B. Royalty. 2005. "Does Having Two Earners in the Household Matter for Understanding How Well Employer-Based Health Insurance Works?" *Medical Care Research and Review* 62 (2): 167–86.

AcademyHealth. 2006. "High-Risk Pools." *State Coverage Initiatives.* [Online at http://www. statecoverage. net/matrix/highriskpools.htm.]

Aces, G., S. H. Long, M. S. Marquis, and P. F. Short. 1996. "Self Insured Employer Health Plans: Prevalence, Profile, Provisions, and Premiums." *Health Affairs* 15 (2): 266–78.

Aces, G., C. Winterbottom, and S. Zedlewski. 1992. "Employers' Payroll and Insurance Costs: Implications for Play or Pay Employer Mandates." In *Health Benefits and the Workforce.* Washington, DC: U.S. Department of Labor.

Achman, L., and D. Chollet. 2001. *Insuring the Uninsurable: An Overview of State High-Risk Health Insurance Pools.* Publication 472. New York: The Commonwealth Fund.

Altman, D., D. Cutler, and R. Zeckhauser. 2003. "Enrollee Mix, Treatment Intensity, and Cost in Competing Indemnity and HMO Plans." *Journal of Health Economics* 22 (1): 23–45.

American Association of Retired Persons. 2005. *The Medicare Program: A Brief Overview.* Washington, DC: American Association of Retired Persons, February.

———. 2004. "Out-of-Pocket Spending on Health Care by Medicare Beneficiaries Age 65 and Older in 2003." *Data Digest.* Washington, DC: American Association of Retired Persons, September.

American Hospital Association. 2006. *Hospital Statistics,* Chicago: American Hospital Association.

American Medical Association. 2001. *Physician Socioeconomic Statistics, 2000–2002 Edition.* Chicago: American Medical Association Center for Health Policy Research.

———. 1998. *Socioeconomic Characteristics of Medical Practice 1997/98.* Chicago: American Medical Association Center for Health Policy Research.

America's Health Insurance Plans. 2004. *Long-Term Care Insurance in 2002.* Washington, DC.

Anderson, R. V. 1986. "Presentation to Business Coalition on Health, Harford Connecticut." Presented at the Group Health Association of America annual meeting, Minneapolis, MN, June 2.

Antos, J., and J. E. Calfee. 2004. "Of Sausage Making and Medicare." *Health Policy OutLook.* Washington, DC: American Enterprise Institute, January–February.

Atherly, A. 2001. "Medicare Supplemental Insurance: Medicare's Accidental Stepchild." *Medical Care Research and Review* 58 (2): 131–61.

Atherly, A., B. E. Dowd, and R. Feldman. 2004. "The Effects of Benefits, Premiums, and Health Risk on Health Plan Choice in the Medicare Program." *Health Services Research* 39 (4, Part 1): 847–64.

Autor, D. H., and M. G. Duggan. 2003. "The Rise in the Disability Rolls and the Decline in Unemployment." *Quarterly Journal of Economics* 118 (1): 157–205.

Bamezai, A., J. Zwanziger, G. A. Melnick, and J. M. Mann. 1999. "Price Competition and Hospital Cost Growth in the United States (1989–1994)." *Health Economics* 8 (3): 233–43.

Barrand, N. L., and W. D. Helms. 1991. "Testimony before the Subcommittee on Health, Committee on Ways and Means, United States House of Representatives." 101st Congress, 1st Session.

Batata, A. 2004. "The Effects of HMOs on Fee-for-Service Health Care Expenditures: Evidence from Medicare Revisited." *Journal of Health Economics* 23: 951–63.

Baumgardner, J. R., and S. A. Hagen. 2001/2002. "Predicting Response to Regulatory Change in the Small Group Health Insurance Market: The Case of Association Health Plans and HealthMarts." *Inquiry* 38 (Winter): 351–64.

Beaulieu. N. D. 2002. "Quality Information and Consumer Health Plan Choices." *Journal of Health Economics* 21: 43–63.

Bellows, N. M., H. A. Halpin, and S. B. McMenamin. 2006. "State-Mandated Benefit Review Laws." *Health Services Research* 41 (3, part 2): 1104–23.

Benham, L. 1972. "The Effects of Advertising on the Price of Eyeglasses." *Journal of Law and Economics* 15: 337–352.

Bhattacharya, J., and M. K. Bundorf. 2004. "The Incidence of the Healthcare Costs of Obesity." Stanford University Working Paper presented at the Annual Health Economics Conference, Birmingham, AL, April 2004.

Blendon, R. J., M. Brodie, and D. E. Altman. 1998. "Understanding the Managed Care Backlash." *Health Affairs* 17 (1): 80–95.

Blendon, R. J., M. Brodie, J. M. Benson, D. E. Altman, L. Levitt, T. Hoff, and L. Hugick. 1998. "Understanding the Managed Care Backlash." *Health Affairs* 17 (4): 80–94.

Blue Cross and Blue Shield Association. 2005. *Consumer Directed Health Plans in Practice: Perspectives from the Consumers and the Blues.* http:// bcbshealthissues. com/events/ consumer/sullivan_ presentation. ppt#2274,1,Consumer-Directed Plans In Practice.

Blumberg, L., L. Nichols, and J. Banthin. 2001. "Worker Decisions to Purchase Health Insurance." *International Journal of Health Care Finance and Economics* 1 (3/4): 305–25.

Boards of Trustees, Federal Hospital and Insurance and Federal Supplementary Medical Insurance Trust Funds. 2006. *2006 Annual Report of the Boards of Trustees of the Federal Hospital Insurance and Supplementary Medical Insurance Trust Funds.* Washington, DC.

Brodie, M., L. A. Brady, and D. E. Altman. 1998. "Media Coverage of Managed Care: Is There a Negative Bias?" *Health Affairs* 17 (1): 9–25.

Brown, J. R., N. B. Coe, and A. Finkelstein. 2006. "Medicaid Crowd-out of Long-Term Care Insurance Demand: Evidence from the Health and Retirement Survey." National Bureau of Economic Research Working Paper 12536 (September).

Buchmueller, T. C., P. Cooper, K. Simon, and J. Vistnes. 2005. "The Effect of SCHIP Expansion on Health Insurance Decisions by Employers." *Inquiry* 42: 218–231.

Buchmueller, T. C., and P. J. Feldstein. 1996. "Consumer's Sensitivity to Health Plan Premiums: Evidence from a Natural Experiment in California." *Health Affairs* 15 (1): 143–51.

Buchmueller, T. C., K. Grumbach, R. Kronick, and J. G. Kahn. 2005. "The Effect of Health Insurance on Medical Care Utilization and Implications for Insurance Expansion: A Review of the Literature." *Medical Care Research and Review* 62 (1): 3–30.

Bundorf, M. K. and K. I. Simon. 2006. "The Effects of Rate Regulation on Demand for Supplemental Health Insurance." *American Economic Review, Papers and Proceedings* 96 (2): 67–71.

Buntin, M. B., M. S. Marquis, and J. M. Yegian. 2004. "The Role of the Individual Health Insurance Market and Prospects for Change." *Health Affairs* 23 (6): 79–90.

Bureau of Labor Statistics. 2006. *Occupational Outlook Handbook, 2006–07 Edition.* Bulletin 2600. Washington, DC: U.S. Government Printing Office. [Online at www.bls.gov/oco/print/ocos074.htm.]

California Managed Risk Medical Insurance Board. 2006. "California Major Risk Medical Insurance Program 2006 Fact Book." [Online information.] www. mrmib.ca.gov/MRMIB/MRMIPFBV3_23_06.pdf

Center for Studying Health System Change. 2003. "Behind the Times: Physician Income: 1995–99." *Data Bulletin: Results from HSC Research*, no. 24. Washington, DC: Center for Studying Health System Change.

———. 2002. "Kinder and Gentler: Physicians and Managed Care, 1997–2001." *Tracking Report*, no. 5. Washington, DC: Center for Studying Health System Change.

Centers for Medicare and Medicaid Services. 2006a. "Fact Sheet: Medicare Premiums and Deductibles for 2007." Washington, DC: Centers for Medicare and Medicaid Services. [Online at www.cms.gov/apps/media/press/release.asp?Counter=1958.]

———. 2006b. "Medicare and You 2007." Washington, DC: Centers for Medicare and Medicaid Services. [Online at www.medicare.gov/publications/pubs/pdf/10050.pdf.]

———. 2005. "Medicaid at a Glance." Publication CMS–11024–05. Washington, DC: Centers for Medicare and Medicaid Services. [Online at www.cms.hhs.gov/MedicaidGenInfo/Downloads/MedicaidAtAGlance2005.pdf.]

———. 2004a. "Chapter 7: Payment to Medicare+Choice (M+C) Organizations." *Medicare Managed Care Manual.* [Online information.] www.cms.hhs.gov/manuals/downloads/mc86d07.pdf.

———. 2004b. "Program Information on Medicaid & State Children's Health Insurance Program (SCHIP)." Office of Research, Development and Information. [Online information.] www.cms. hhs.gov/TheChartSeries/04_Medicaid_Facts_Figures.asp#TopOfPage

———. 2000. *A Profile of Medicaid: Chartbook 2000.* Washington, DC: Centers for Medicare and Medicaid Services, September.

Chassin, M. R., J. Kosecoff, R. E. Park, C. M. Winslow, K. L. Kahn, N. J. Merrick, J. Keesey, A. Fink, D. H. Solomon, and R. H. Brook. 1987. "Does Inappropriate Use Explain Geographic Variations in the Use of Health Care Services?" *Journal of the American Medical Association* 258: 2533–37.

Cherkin, D. C., L. Grothaus, and E. H. Wagner. 1989. "The Effect of Office Visit Copayments on Utilization in a Health Maintenance Organization." *Medical Care* 27: 669–79.

Chernew, M., K. Frick, and C. G. McLaughlin. 1997. "The Demand for Health Insurance Coverage by Low-Income Workers: Can Reduced Premiums Achieve Full Coverage?" *Health Services Research* 32 (4): 453–70.

Chernew, M., and D. Scanlon. 1998. "Health Plan Report Cards and Insurance Choice." *Inquiry* 35: 9–22.

Chiswick, B. R. 1976. "The Demand for Nursing Home Care: An Analysis of the Substitution between Institutional and Noninstitutional Care. *Journal of Human Resources* 9: 293–316.

Chollet, D. 2003. "The Medigap Market: Product and Pricing Trends, 1999–2001." *Monitoring Medicare+Choice Operational Insights.* Princeton, NJ: Mathematica Policy Research, Inc.

Chollet, D. J., and A. M. Kirk. 1998. *Understanding Individual Health Insurance Markets.* Menlo Park, CA: Henry J. Kaiser Family Foundation.

Chollet, D. J., A. M. Kirk, and M. E. Chow. 2000. *Mapping State Health Insurance Markets: Structure and Change in the States' Group and Individual Health Insurance Markets, 1995–1997.* Washington, DC: AcademyHealth State Coverage Initiatives.

Claxton, G., J. Gabel, I. Gil, J. Pickreign, H. Whitmore, B. Finder, B. DiJulio, and S. Hawkins. 2006a. "Health Benefits in 2006: Premium Increases Moderate, Enrollment in Consumer-Directed Health Plans Remains Modest." *Health Affairs* Web Exclusive, September 26.

Claxton, G., I. Gil, B. Finder, B. DiJulia, S. Hawkins, J. Pickreign, H. Whitmore, and J. Gabel. 2006b. *Employer Health Benefits 2006 Annual Survey.* Menlo Park, CA: Kaiser Family Foundation and Health Research and Educational Trust.

Colby, D. C., T. Rice, J. Bernstein, and L. Nelson. 1995. "Balance Billing under Medicare: Protecting Beneficiaries and Preserving Physician Participation." *Journal of Health*

Politics, Policy and Law 20 (1): 49–74.

Commonwealth Fund. 2001. "Security Matters: How Instability in Health insurance Puts U.S. Workers at Risk: Findings from the Commonwealth Fund 2001 Survey of Health Insurance—Chart Book." [Online information.] www.cmwf.org/usr_doc/duchon_2001HI_surveycharts.pdf.

Communicating for Agriculture. 2006. "Overview—State High-Risk Health Insurance Pools Today." [Online information.] www.selfemployedcountry.org/riskpools/overview.html.

Congressional Budget Office. 2007. "Fact Sheet for CBO's March 2007 Baseline: Medicare." [Online information.] www.cbo.gov/ftpdocs/78xx/doc7861/m_m_schip.pdf.

———. 2006. "Testimony of Donald B. Marron, Acting Director before the Senate Special Committee on Aging: Medicaid Spending Growth and Options for Controlling Costs." Washington, DC, July 13, 2006.

———. 2004. "An Analysis of the Literature on Disease Management Programs." Washington, DC, October 13th. [Online information.] www.cbo.gov/ftpdocs/59xx/doc5909/10-13-DiseaseMngmnt.pdf.

Congressional Research Service. 2005. *Medicaid/SCHIP Enrollees: Comparison of Counts from Administrative Data and Survey Estimates.* Washington, DC: Congressional Research Service.

Conrad, D. A., D. Grembowski, and P. Milgram. 1987. "Dental Care Demand: Insurance Effects and Plan Design." *Health Services Research* 22: 341–67.

Council for Affordable Health Insurance. 2006. *Health Insurance Mandates in the States 2006.* Alexandria, VA: Council for Affordable Health Insurance.

Crowley, J. 2003. *Medicaid Needy Programs: An Important Source of Medicaid Coverage.* Washington, DC: The Kaiser Commission on Medicaid and the Uninsured.

Cunningham III, R., and R. M. Cunningham, Jr. 1997. *The Blues: A History of the Blue Cross and Blue Shield System.* DeKalb, IL: Northern Illinois University Press.

Currie, J., and J. Fahr. 2004. "Hospitals, Managed Care, and the Charity Caseload in California." *Journal of Health Economics* 23: 421–42.

Cutler, D. M. 2002. "Employee Costs and the Decline in Health Insurance Coverage," National Bureau of Economic Research Working Paper 9036.

Cutler, D. M., and J. Gruber. 1997. "Medicaid and Private Insurance: Evidence and Implications." *Health Affairs* 16 (1): 194–200.

Cutler, D. M., McClellen, M., and J. P. Newhouse. 2000. "How Does Managed Care Do It?" *RAND Journal of Economics* 31: 526–48.

Cutler, D. M., and S. Reber. 1996. "Paying for Health insurance: The Tradeoff between Competition and Adverse Selection." National Bureau of Economic Research Working Paper 5796.

Danzon, P. M. 1983. "Rating Bureaus in U.S. Property-Liability Insurance Markets: Anti or Pro-Competitive?" *Geneva Papers on Risk and Insurance* 8: 371–402.

Daves, A. R., J. E. Ware, Jr., R. H. Brook, J. R. Peterson, and J. P. Newhouse. 1986. "Consumer Acceptance of Prepaid and Fee-for-Service Medical Care: Results from a Randomized Controlled Trial." *Health Services Research* 21 (3): 429–52.

Davidson, G., L. A. Blewett, and K. T. Call. 2004. *Public Program Crowd-Out of Private Coverage: What Are the Issues?* Robert Wood Johnson Foundation Research Synthesis Report No. 5. Princeton, NJ: Robert Wood Johnson Foundation.

Donabedian, A. 1976. *Benefits in Medical Care Programs.* Cambridge, MA: Harvard University Press.

Dor, A., S. M. Koroukian, and M. Grossman. 2004. "Managed Care Discounting: Evidence from the MarketScan Database." *Inquiry* 41: 159–69.

Dowd, B., and R. Feldman. 1994/95. "Premium Elasticities of Health Plan Choice." *Inquiry* 31: 438–44.

Dowd, B., R. Feldman, M. Maciejewski, and M. V. Pauly. 2001. "The Effect of Tax-Exempt Out-of-Pocket Premiums on Health Plan Choice." *National Tax Journal* 54 (4): 741–56.

Dranove, D., M. Shanley, and C. Simon. 1992. "Is Hospital Competition Wasteful?" *RAND Journal of Economics* 23 (2): 247–62.

Dranove, D., C. J. Simon, and W. D. White. 2002. "Is Managed Care Leading to Consolidation in Health Care Markets?" *Health Services Research* 37 (3): 573–94.

Dranove, D., K. E. Spier, and L. Baker. 2000. "Competition among Employers Offering Health Insurance." *Journal of Health Economics* 19 (1): 121–40.

Draper, D. A., R. E. Hurley, and A. C. Short. 2004. "Medicaid Managed Care: The Last Bastion of the HMO?" *Health Affairs* 23 (2): 155–68.

eHealthInsurnace.com. 2005. "Health Savings Accounts: First Year in Review." [Online information.] www.cahi.org/cahi_contents/consumerinfo/pdf/ehealth insuranceHSA0205.pdf.

Ehrlich, I., and G. Becker. 1972. "Market Insurance, Self Insurance and Self Protection." *Journal of Political Economy* 80: 623–48.

Eichhorn, R. L., and L. Aday. 1972. *The Utilization of Health Services: Indices and Correlates; A Research Bibliography.* NTIS No. PB-211 720. Beverly Hills, CA.: Sage.

Ellis, R. J., and T. McGuire. 1993. "Supply Side and Demand Side Cost Sharing in Health Care." *Journal of Economic Perspectives* 7: 135–51.

Ellis, R. P. 1985. "The Effect of Prior-Year Health Expenditures on Health Coverage Plan Choice." In *Advances in Health Economics and Health Services Research*, vol. 6, edited by R. M. Scheffler and L. F. Rossiter, 149–170. Greenwich, CT.: JAI Press.

Escarce, J. J., K. Kapur, G. F. Joyce, and K. A. Van Vorst. 2001. "Medical Care Expenditures under Gatekeeper and Point-of-

Service Arrangements." *Health Services Research* 36 (1, part 1): 1037–57.

Escarce, J. J., D. Polsky, G. D. Woziak, and P. R. Kletke. 2000. "HMO Growth and the Geographical Redistribution of Generalist and Specialist Physicians, 1987–1997." *Health Services Research* 35 (4): 825–48.

Escarce, J. J., D. Polsky, G. D. Woziak, M. V. Pauly, and P. R. Kletke. 1998. "Health Maintenance Organization Penetration and the Practice Location Choices of New Physicians: A Study of Large Metropolitan Areas in the United States." *Medical Care* 36 (11): 1555–66.

Excite. 2005. "EU Drops Plans for Unisex Insurance Premiums." [Online information.] www.excite.co.uk/insurance/special/eu_drops_plan.

Federal Register. 2006. 71, no. 180 (September 18): 54662-4.

Federal Trade Commission. 2005. "Administrative Law Judge Orders Evanston Northwestern Healthcare Corporation to Sell Highland Park Hospital." FTC press release, October 21, 2005. [Online information.] www.ftc.gov/opa/2005/10/evanston.htm.

———. 2004a. "FTC Challenges Hospital Merger That Allegedly Led to Anticompetitive Price Increases." FTC press release, February 10, 2004. [Online information.] www.ftc.gov/opa/2004/02/enh.htm.

———. 2004b. "FTC Staff: Rhode Island Bills Would Raise Prices for Pharmaceuticals." FTC press release and related letter to Rhode Island officials. [Online information.] www.ftc.gov/opa/2004/04/ribills.htm.

———. 2004c. "San Francisco's Brown & Toland Medical Group Settles FTC Price Fixing Charges." FTC press release, February 9, 2004. [Online information.] www.ftc.gov/opa/2004/ 01/browntoland.htm.

Federal Trade Commission and the Department of Justice. 2004. "Improving Health Care: A Dose of Competition." FTC-DOJ joint report, July 2004. [Online information.] www.ftc.gov/reports/healthcare/040723healthcarerpt.pdf.

Feldman, R., and J. W. Begun. 1978. "The Effects of Advertising Restrictions: Lessons from Optometry." *Journal of Human Resources* 13(supplement): 247–62.

Feldman, R., H-C Chan, J. Kralewski, B. Dowd, and J. Shapiro. 1990. "Effects of HMOs on the Creation of Competitive Markets for Hospital Services." *Journal of Health Economics* 9: 207–22.

Feldman, R., and B. Dowd. 1982. "Simulation of a Health Insurance Market with Adverse Selection." *Operations Research* 30(6): 1027–42.

Feldman, R., B. Dowd, S. Leitz, and L. A. Blewett. 1997. "The Effect of Premiums on the Small Firm's Decision to Offer Health Insurance." *Journal of Human Resources* 32 (4): 635–58.

Feldman, R., M. Finch, B. Dowd, and S. Cassou. 1989. "The Demand for Employment-Based Health Insurance Plans." *Journal of Human Resources* 24 (1): 115–42.

Feldman, R., and D. Wholey. 2001. "Do HMOs Have Monopsony

Power?" *International Journal of Health Care Finance and Economics* 1 (1): 7–22.

Feldstein, M. S. 1974. "Econometric Studies of Health Economics." In *Frontiers of Quantitative Economics*, vol. II, edited by D. Kendrick and M. Intrilligator. Amsterdam: North-Holland Press.

Feldstein, M. S., and E. Allison. 1974. "Tax Subsidies of Private Health Insurance: Distribution, Revenue Loss, and Effects." In *The Economics of Federal Subsidy Programs*, 977-94, Washington. DC: U.S. Government Printing Office.

Ferris, T. G., Y. Chang, D. Blumenthal, and S. D. Pearson. 2001. "Leaving Gatekeeping Behind—Effects of Opening Access to Specialists for Adults in a Health Maintenance Organization." *New England Journal of Medicine* 345(18): 1312–17.

Finkelstein, A. 2004. "Minimum Standards, Insurance Regulation, and Adverse Selection: Evidence for the Medigap Market." *Journal of Public Economics* 88 (12): 2515–47.

Finkelstein, A., and K. McGarry. 2003. "Private Information and Its Effect on Market Equilibrium: New Evidence from Long-Term Care Insurance." National Bureau of Economic Research Working Paper 9957, September.

Finkelstein, A. and J. Poterba. 2000. "Adverse Selection in Insurance Markets: Policyholder Evidence from the U.K. Annuity Market." National Bureau of Economic Research Working Paper 8045.

Fishback, P. V., and S. E. Kantor. 2000. *A Prelude to the Welfare State: The Origins of Workers' Compensation*. Chicago:

University of Chicago Press for the National Bureau of Economic Research.

Forrest, C. B., J. P. Weiner, J. Fowles, K. Frick, C. Vogeli, K. Lemke, and B. Starfield. 2001. "Self-Referral in Point-of-Service Health Plans." *Journal of the American Medical Association* 285 (17): 2223–31.

Fowles, J. B., J. P. Weiner, D. Knutson, A. M. Tucker, and M. Ireland. 1996. "Taking Health Status into Account When Setting Capitation Rates." *Journal of the American Medical Association* 276 (16): 1316–21.

Frakt, A. B., S. D. Pizer, and M. V. Wrobel. 2004. "HighRisk Pools for Uninsurable Individuals: Recent Growth, Future Prospects." *Health Care Financing Review* 26 (2): 73–87.

Friedman, M., and L. C. Savage. 1948. "The Utility Analysis of Choices Involving Risk." *Journal of Political Economy* 56: 251–80.

Friedman, M., and A. J. Schwartz. 1963. *A Monetary History of the United States: 1867–1960*. Princeton, NJ: Princeton University Press.

Fronstin, P. 2007. "Employment-Based Health Benefits: Access and Coverage 1988 to 2005." *Employee Benefits Research Institute Issue Brief,* no. 303. Washington, DC: Employee Benefits Research Institute.

———. 2006. "Sources of Health Insurance and Characteristics of the Uninsured: Analysis of the March 2006 Current Population Survey." *Employee Benefits Research Institute Issue Brief,* no. 298. Washington, DC: Employee Benefits Research Institute.

———. 2005. "Sources of Health Insurance and Characteristics of the Uninsured: Analysis of the March 2005 Current Population Survey." *Employee Benefits Research Institute Issue Brief,* no. 287. Washington, DC: Employee Benefit Research Institute.

———. 1999. "Employment-Based Health Insurance: A Look at Tax Issues and Public Opinion." *Employee Benefits Research Institute Issue Brief,* no. 211. Washington, DC: Employee Benefits Research Organization.

Fronstin, P., and S. R. Collins. 2005. "Early Experience with High-Deductible and Consumer-Driven Health Plans: Findings from the EBRI/Commonwealth Fund Consumerism in Health Care Survey." *Employee Benefits Research Institute Issue Brief,* no. 288. Washington, DC: Employee Benefits Research Institute, December.

Gabel, J. R., G. Claxton, I. Gil, J. Pickreign, H. Whitmore, B. Finder, S. Hawkins, and D. Rowland. 2005. "Health Benefits in 2005: Premium Increase Slow Down, Coverage Continues to Erode." *Health Affairs* 24 (5): 1273–80.

Gabel, J. R., G. A. Jensen, and S. Hawkins. 2003. "Self-Insurance in an Era of Growing and Retreating Managed Care." *Health Affairs* 22 (2): 202–10.

Garber, A. M., T. E. McCurdy, and M. B. McClellan. 1999. "Persistence of Medicare Expenditures among Elderly Beneficiaries." *Frontiers of Health Policy Research* (2): 153–80.

Garfinkel, S. A. 1995. "Self-Insuring Employee Health Benefits." *Medical Care Research and Review* 52: 475–91.

Gaskin, D. J., J. J. Escarce, K. Schulman, and J. Hadley. 2002. "The Determinants of HMOs' Contracting with Hospitals for Bypass Surgery." *Health Services Research* 37 (4): 963–84.

Gaskin, D. J. and J. Hadley. 1997. "The Impact of HMO Penetration on the Rate of Hospital Cost Inflation, 1985–1993." *Inquiry* 34 (3): 205–16.

Gentry, W., and E. Peress. 1994. "Taxes and Fringe Benefits Offered by Employers." National Bureau of Economic Research Working Paper 4764.

Gold, M. 2006. *The Growth of Medicare Private Plans in 2006.* Washington, DC: Mathematica Policy Research.

Goldman, D. A., N. Sood and A. A. Leibowitz. 2005. "Wages and Benefit Changes in Response to Rising Health Insurance." *Frontiers in Health Policy Research* 8: 1–15.

Goldman, D. P., J. L. Buchanan, and E. B. Keeler. 2000. "Simulating the Impact of Medical Savings Accounts on Small Business." *Health Services Research* 35 (1): 53–75.

Goldman, D. P., G. F. Joyce, J. J. Escarce, J. E. Pace, M. D. Solomon, M. Laouri, P. B. Landsman, and S. M. Teutsch. 2004. "Pharmacy Benefits and the Use of Drugs by the Chronically Ill." *Journal of the American Medical Association* 291 (19): 2344–50.

Goldstein, G. S., and M. V. Pauly. 1976. "Group Health Insurance as a Local Public Good." In *The Role of Health Insurance in the Health Services Sector,* edited by R. Rosett, 73–109. Cambridge,

MA: National Bureau of Economic Research.

Goodman, J. C., and G. I. Musgrave. 1987. *Freedom of Choice in Health Insurance.* Dallas, TX: National Center for Policy Analysis.

Grembowski, D., and D. Conrad. 1986. "Health Insurance Effects on Group Dental Expenditures." *Medical Care* 22: 501–10.

Grembowski, D., D. A. Conrad, and P. Milgram. 1987. "Dental Care Demand among Children with Dental Insurance." *Health Services Research* 21: 755–77.

Gruber, J. 1994a. "The Effect of Competition Pressure in Medical Markets: Hospital Responses to Price Shopping in California." *Journal of Health Economics* 13: 183–212.

———. 1994b. "The Incidence of Mandated Maternity Benefits." *American Economic Review* 84 (3): 622–41.

Gruber, J., and A. B. Krueger. 1991. "The Incidence of Mandated Employer-Provided Insurance: Lessons from Workers' Compensation." in *Tax Policy and the Economy,* edited by D. Bradford, 111–44. Cambridge, MA: MIT Press.

Gruber, J., and M. Lettau. 2004. "How Elastic Is the Firm's Demand for Health Insurance?" *Journal of Public Economics* 88: 1273–94.

Gruber, J., and R. McKnight. 2003. "Why Did Employee Premium Contributions Rise?" *Journal of Health Economics* 22: 1085–1104.

Gruber, J., and E. Washington. 2005. "Subsidies to Employee Health Insurance Premiums and the Health Insurance Market." *Journal of Health Economics* 24 (1): 253–76.

Hadley, J., and J. M. Mitchell. 1999. "HMO Penetration and Physician Earnings." *Medical Care* 37 (11): 1116–27.

Hadley, J., and J. D. Reschovsky. 2003. "Health and the Cost of Non-group Insurance." *Inquiry* 40 (3): 235–53.

———. 2002. "Small Firms' Demand for Health Insurance: The Decision to Offer Insurance." *Inquiry* 39 (Summer): 118–37.

Hall, M. 1999. "The Structure and Enforcement of Health Insurance Rating Reforms." Working paper, Wake Forest University, Winston-Salem, NC.

Hammermesh, D. S., and S. A. Woodbury. 1990. "Taxes, Fringe Benefits and Faculty." National Bureau of Economic Research Working Paper 3455.

Health Insurance Association of America. 1990. *Source Book of Health Insurance Data 1990.* Washington, DC: Health Insurance Association of America.

Health Research and Educational Trust/Henry J. Kaiser Family Foundation (HRET/Kaiser). 2004. "Employer Health Benefits, 2004 Annual Survey," September. [Online information.] www.kff.org/insurance/7148/ index.cfm.

Helena Independent Record. 2005. "Unisex Premiums Debated." [Online information.] www .helenair.com/articles/2005/ 02/ 09/leg_other_articles/ a06020905 _01.txt.

Hellinger, F. J. 1998. "The Effect of Managed Care on Quality: A Review of Recent Evidence." *Archives of Internal Medicine* 158: 833–41.

Helms, R. B. 2005. "Tax Reform and Health Insurance." *Health Policy Outlook.* Washington, DC:

American Enterprise Institute, January/February.

Helms, W. D., A. K. Gauthier, and D. M. Campion. 1992. "Mending the Flaws in the Small Group Market." *Health Affairs* 11 (2): 8–27.

Hennessy, S., W. B. Bilker, L. Zhou, A. Weber, C. Brensinger, Y. Wang, and B. Strom. 2003. "Retrospective Drug Utilization Review, Prescribing Errors, and Clinical Outcomes." *Journal of the American Medical Association* 290 (2): 1494–99.

Herring, B., and M. V. Pauly. 2001. "Premium Variation in the Individual Health Insurance Market." *International Journal of Health Care Finance and Economics* 1: 43–58.

Hillman, A. L., W. P. Welch, and M. V. Pauly. 1992. "Contractual Arrangements between HMOs and Primary Care Physicians: Three-Tiered HMOs and Risk Pools." *Medical Care* 30 (2): 136–48.

Hing, E., and G. A. Jensen. 1999. "Health Insurance Portability and Accountability Act of 1996: Lessons from the States." *Medical Care* 37 (7): 692–705.

Horgan, C. 1986. "The Demand for Ambulatory Mental Health Services from Specialty Providers." *Health Services Research* 21: 291–320.

Humo, T. 2003. *Employer's Guide to Self-insuring Health Benefits.* Tampa, FL: Thompson Publishing Group.

Hurley, R. E., and S. M. Retchin. 2006. "Medicare and Medicaid Managed Care: A Tale of Two Trajectories." *American Journal of Managed Care* 12 (1): 40–44.

Iglehart, J. 2002. "Medicare's Declining Payments to Physicians." *New England Journal of Medicine* 346 (24): 1924–30.

Ingber, M. J. 2000. "Implementation of Risk Adjustment for Medicare." *Health Care Financing Review* 21 (3): 119–126.

Jackson-Beeck, M., and J. H. Kleinman. 1983. "Evidence of Self-Selection among Health Maintenance Enrollees." *Journal of the American Medical Association* 250 (23): 2826–29.

Jensen, G. A., K. Cotter, and M. A. Morrisey. 1995. "State Insurance Regulation and an Employer's Decision to Self-Insure." *Journal of Risk and Insurance* 62: 185–213.

Jensen, G. A., and J. Gabel. 1992. "State Mandated Benefits and the Small Firm's Decision to Offer Insurance." *Journal of Regulatory Economics* 4 (4): 379–404.

Jensen, G. A., and M. A. Morrisey. 2003. "Self-Insured Employer Sponsored Health Plans and the Regulation of Managed Care." Working paper, Wayne State University, Institute of Gerontology.

———. 2001. "Endogenous Fringe Benefits, Compensating Wage Differentials and Older Workers." *International Journal of Health Care Finance and Economics* 1 (3/4): 203–26.

———. 1999a. "Employer-Sponsored Health Insurance and Mandated Benefit Laws." *Milbank Quarterly* 77: 425–59.

———. 1999b. "Small Group Reform and Insurance Provision by Small

Firms, 1989–1995." *Inquiry* 36: 176–86.

———. 1990. "Group Health Insurance: A Hedonic Approach." *Review of Economics and Statistics* 72 (1): 38–44.

Jensen, G. A., M. A. Morrisey, S. Gaffney, and D. K. Liston. 1997. "The New Dominance of Managed Care: Insurance Trends in the 1990s, *Health Affairs* (January/February) 16 (1): 125–36.

Jensen G. A., K. Rost, R. P. D. Burton, and M. Bulycheva. 1998. "Mental Health Insurance in the 1990s: Are Employers Offering Less to More?" *Health Affairs* 17 (3): 201–8.

Jensen, G. A., C. Roychoudhury, and D. C. Cherkin. 1998. "Employer-Sponsored Health Insurance for Chiropractic Services." *Medical Care* 36 (4): 544–53.

Joyce, G. F., J. J. Escarce, M. D. Solomon, and D. P. Goldman. 2002. "Employer Drug Benefit Plans and Spending on Prescription Drugs." *Journal of the American Medical Association* 288 (14): 1733–39.

Kaiser Family Foundation. 2006a. *The Medicaid Program at a Glance.* Washington, DC: Kaiser Commission on Medicaid and the Uninsured.

———. 2006b. *Retiree Health Benefits Examined: Findings from the Kaiser/Hewitt 2006 Survey of Retiree Health Benefits.* Menlo Park, CA: Kaiser Family Foundation. [Online at www.kff.org/medicare/upload/7587.pdf.]

———. 2005. *Medicare Chartbook*, 3rd edition. Menlo Park, CA:

Kaiser Family Foundation. [Online at www.kff.org/medicare/upload/Medicare-Chart-Book-3rd-Edition-Summer-2005-Report.pdf.]

———. 2002. *National Survey of Small Businesses.* Menlo Park, CA: Kaiser Family Foundation, April.

Kaiser Family Foundation and Health Research and Educational Trust. 2006. *Employer Health Benefits: Summary of 2006 Findings.* Menlo Park, CA: Kaiser Family Foundation.

Kapur, K., C. R. Gresenz, and D. M. Studdert. 2003. "Managing Care: Utilization Review in Action at Two Capitated Medical Groups." *Health Affairs* Web Exclusive, June 18.

Keeler, E. B., J. D. Malkin, D. P. Goldman, and J. L. Buchanan. 1996. "Can Medical Savings Accounts for the Nonelderly Reduce Health Care Costs?" *Journal of the American Medical Association* 275 (21): 1666–71.

Keeler, E. B., K. B. Wells, W. G. Manning, J. D. Rumpel and J. M. Hanley. 1986. *The Demand for Episodes of Mental Health Services.* RAND Report R-3432-NIMH.

Kessel, R. A. 1959. "Price Discrimination in Medicine." *Journal of Law and Economics* 1: 20–53.

Khandker, R. K., and W. G. Manning. 1992. "The Impact of Utilization Review on Costs and Utilization." In *Health Economics Worldwide,* edited by P. Zweifel and H. E. Frech III, 47–62. Amsterdam: Kluwer Academic Publishers.

Khandker, R. K., and L. A. McCormack. 1999.

"Medicare Spending by Beneficiaries with Various Types of Supplemental Insurance." *Medical Care Research and Review* 56 (2): 137–55.

Kotlikoff, L., and D. A. Wise. 1985. "Labor Compensation and the Structure of Private Pension Plans: Evidence for Contractual versus Spot Labor Markets." In *Pensions, Labor, and Individual Choice,* edited by D. A. Wise, 55–85. Chicago: University of Chicago Press.

Kralewski, J. E., E. C. Rich, |R. Feldman, B. E. Dowd, T. Bernhardt, C. Johnson, and W. Gold. 2000. "The Effects of Medical Group Practice and Physician Payment Methods on Costs of Care." *Health Services Research* 35 (3): 591–613.

Kronick, R., and L. C. Olsen. 2006. "A Needle in a Haystack? Uninsured Workers in Small Businesses That Do Not Offer Coverage." Health Services Research 41 (1): 40–57.

Lamers, L. M. 1999. "The Simultaneous Predictive Accuracy for Future Health Care Expenditures of DCGs, PCGs, and Prior Costs." Paper presented at the iHEA Conference, June 6–9, 1999, Rotterdam, Netherlands.

Laugesen, M. J., R. R. Paul, H. S. Luft, W. Aubry, and T. G. Ganiats. 2006. "A Comparative Analysis of Mandated Benefit Laws, 1949–2002." *Health Services Research* 41 (3, part 2): 1081–1103.

Leibowitz, A. 1989. "Substitution between Prescribed and Over-the-Counter Medications." *Medical Care* 27: 85–94.

Leibowitz, A., J. L. Buchanan, and J. Mann. 1992. "A Randomized Trial to Evaluate the Effectiveness of a Medicaid HMO." *Journal of Health Economics* 11 (3): 235–57.

Leibowitz, A., and M. Chernew. 1992. "The Firm's Demand for Health Insurance." In *Health Benefits and the Workplace*, U.S. Department of Labor, Washington, DC: U.S. Government Printing Office.

Leibowitz, A., W. G. Manning and J. P. Newhouse. 1985. "The Demand for Prescription Drugs as a Function of Cost-Sharing." *Social Science and Medicine* 21: 1063–69.

Lessler, D. S., and T. M. Wickizer. 2000. "The Impact of Utilization Management on Readmissions among Patients with Cardiovascular Disease." *Health Services Research* 34 (6): 1315–29.

Levy, H., and R. Feldman. 2001. "Does the Incidence of Group Health Insurance Fall on Individual Workers?" *International Journal of Health Care Finance and Economics* 1 (3/4): 227–48.

Liang, J., X. Liu, E. Tu, and N. Whitelaw. 1996. "Probabilities and Lifetime Durations of Short-Stay Hospital and Nursing Home Utilization in the U.S. 1985." *Medical Care* 34 (10): 1018–36.

Lippe, G. J. 1996. "Operational Underwriting in Managed Care Organizations." In *The Managed Care Handbook*, edited by P. R. Kongstvedt, 679–99. Gaithersburg, MD: Aspen Publishers.

Lohr, K. N., R. Brook, C. Kamberg, G. A Goldberg, and A. Leibowitz. 1986. "Effect of Cost Sharing on Use of Medically Effective and Less Effective Care." *Medical Care* 24: S1–87.

Long, J. E., and F. A. Scott. 1982. "The Income Tax and Nonwage Compensation." *Review of Economics and Statistics* 64: 211–19.

Long, S., M. S. Marquis, and J. Rogers. 1998. "Do People Shift Their Use of Health Services over Time to Take Advantage of Insurance?" *Journal of Health Economics* 17 (1): 105–15.

Long, S. H., R. F. Settle, and C. W. Wrightson. 1988. "Employee Premiums, Availability of Alternative Plans, and HMO Disenrollment." *Medical Care* 26 (10): 927–28.

LoSasso, A. T., and T. C. Buchmueller. 2004. "The Effect of State Children's Health Insurance Program on Health Insurance Coverage." *Journal of Health Economics* 23 (6): 1059–82.

LoSasso, A. T., and I. Z. Lurie. 2003. "The Effect of State Policies on the Market for Private Non-Group Health Insurance." Working paper, Northwestern University Institute for Policy Research.

Lynk, W. J. 2000. "Some Basics about Most Favored Nation Contracts in Health Care Markets." *Antitrust Bulletin* 45 (2): 491–530.

MacIntyre, D. M. 1962. *Voluntary Health Insurance and Rate Making.* Ithica, NY: Cornell University Press.

Manning, W. G., B. Benjamin, H. L. Bailit, and J. P. Newhouse. 1985. "The Demand for Dental Care: Evidence from a Randomized Trial in Health Insurance." *Journal of the American Dental Association* 110: 895–903.

Manning, W. G., J. P. Newhouse, N. Duan, E. B. Keeler, A. Leibowitz, and M. S. Marquis. 1987. "Health Insurance and the Demand for Medical Care: Evidence from a Randomized Experiment." *American Economic Review* 77: 251–77.

Marquis, M. S. 1985. "Cost-Sharing and Provider Choice." *Journal of Health Economics* 4: 137–57.

Marquis, M. S., and M. B. Buntin. 2006. "How Much Risk Pooling Is There in the Individual Insurance Market?" *Health Services Research* 41 (5): 1782–1800.

Marquis, M. S., and S. H. Long. 2001/2002. "Effects of 'Second Generation' Small Group Health Insurance Market Reforms, 1993–1997." *Inquiry* 38 (Winter): 365–80.

Marquis, M. S., J. A. Rogowski, and J. J. Escarce. 2004/05. "The Managed Care Backlash: Did Consumers Vote with Their Feet?" *Inquiry* 47: 376–90.

Marsteller, J. A., R. R. Bovbjerg, L. M. Nichols, and D. K. Verrilli. 1997. "The Resurgence of Selective Contracting Restrictions." *Journal of Health Politics, Policy and Law* 22 (2): 1133–90.

McCaffree, K., and M. E. McCaffree. 2001. *Piecing Together Our Separate Lives.* Seattle, WA: Gorham Printing.

McCormack, L. A., J. R. Gabel, H. Whitmore, W. L. Anderson, and J. Pickreign. 2002. "Trends in Retiree Health Benefits." *Health Affairs* 21 (6): 169–76.

McGuire, T. G. 2000. "Physician Agency." In *Handbook of Health Economics*, vol. 1A, edited by A. J. Culyer and J. P. Newhouse, 461–536, Amsterdam, Netherlands: Elsevier.

———. 1981. "Price and Membership in a Prepaid Group Medical Practice." *Medical Care* 19: 172–83.

McLaughlin, C. G., M. Chernew, and E. F. Taylor. 2002. "Medigap Premiums and Medicare HMO Enrollment." *Health Services Research* 37 (6): 1445–68.

McLaughlin, C. G., W. K. Zellers, and L. D. Brown. 1989. "Health Care Coalitions: Characteristics, Activities and Prospects." *Inquiry* 26 (Spring): 72–83.

Medical Benefits. 2005a. "Average COBRA Claims as Percent of Average Active Worker Claims." *Medical Benefits* (January 30): 5.

———. 2005b. "The MetLife Study of Employee Benefits Trends." *Medical Benefits* 22 (2): 1.

Medicare Payment Advisory Commission. 2006. *Report to Congress: Increasing the Value of Medicare.* Washington, DC: Medicare Payment Advisory Commission, June.

———. 2005. *Issues in a Modernized Medicare Program.* Washington, DC: Medicare Payment Advisory Commission, June.

Melnick, G. A., and J. Zwanziger. 1988. "Hospital Behavior under Competition and Cost-Containment Policies." *Journal of the American Medical Association* 260 (18): 2669–75.

Melnick, G. A., J. Zwanziger, A. Bamezai, and R. Pattison. 1992. "The Effects of Market Structure and Bargaining Position on Hospital Prices." *Journal of Health Economics* 11: 217–33.

Miller. R. D. 2004. "Estimating the Compensating Differential for Employer-Provided Health Insurance." *International Journal of Health Care Finance and Economics* 4 (1): 27–41.

Miller, R. H., and H. S. Luft. 1994. "Managed Care Plan Performance Since 1980." *Journal of the American Medical Association* 271 (19): 1512–19.

Miller, T. 2003. "How the Tax Exclusion Shaped Today's Private Health Insurance Market." Report of the Joint Economic Committee, U.S. Congress, December 17.

Mobley, L. R., and H. E. Frech. 2000. "Managed Care, Distance Traveled, and Hospital Market Definition." *Inquiry* 37 (1): 91–107.

Monheit, A. C., and J. P. Vistnes. 1999. "Health Insurance Availability at the Workplace: How Important Are Worker Preferences? *Journal of Human Resources* 34 (4): 770–85.

Montgomery, E., K. Shaw, and M-E Benedict. 1992. "Pensions and Wages: An Hedonic Price Theory Approach." *International Economic Review* 33 (1): 111–28.

Moore, M. J., and W. K. Viscusi. 1990. *Compensation for Job Risks: Wages, Workers' Compensation and Product Liability.* Princeton, NJ: Princeton University Press.

Moran, J. R., M. E. Chernew, and R. A. Hirth. 2001. "Preference Diversity and the Breadth of Employee Health Insurance Options," *Health Services Research* 36 (5):911–34.

Morrisey, M. A. 2005. *Price Sensitivity in Health Care: Implications for Health Policy*, 2nd ed. Washington, DC: NFIB Research Foundation.

———. 2003. "Health Insurance." *NFIB National Small Business Poll* 3 (4). [Online at www.nfib .com/object/sbPolls?fed StartPos=11&fedEndPos= 20&stateStartPos=1&state EndPos=10.]

———. 2001. "Competition in Hospital and Health Insurance Markets: A Review and Research Agenda." *Health Services Research* 36 (1, part II): 191–221.

———. 1993. "Retiree Health Benefits." *Annual Review of Public Health* 14: 271–92.

Morrisey, M. A., and J. H. Cawley. 2006. "What Health Economists Think about Health Policy Questions." Working paper, UAB Lister Hill Center for Health Policy, Birmingham, AL.

Morrisey, M. A., and G. A. Jensen. 2001. "The Near-Elderly, Early Retirees and Managed Care." *Health Affairs* 20 (6): 197–206.

———. 1997. "Switching to Managed Care in the Small Employer Market." *Inquiry* 34 (Fall): 237–48.

———. 1996. "State Small Group Insurance Reform." In *Health Policy, Federalism and the American States*, edited by R. F. Rich and W. D. White, 71–95. Washington, DC: Urban Institute Press.

———. 1993. "State Mandates, Self-Insurance and Employer Demand for Substance Abuse and Mental Health Insurance Coverage." *Advances in Health Economics and Health Services Research* 14: 209–24.

Morrisey, M. A., G. A. Jensen and J. R. Gabel. 2003. "Managed Care and Employer Premiums." *International Journal of Health Care Finance and Economics* 3 (2): 95–116.

Morrisey, M. A., G. A. Jensen, and R. J. Morlock. 1994. "Small Employers and the Health Insurance Market." *Health Affairs* 13 (5): 149–61.

Morrisey, M. A., and R. L. Ohsfeldt. 2003/2004. "Do 'Any Willing Provider' and 'Freedom of Choice' Laws Affect HMO Market Shares?" *Inquiry* 40: 362–74.

Motheral, B., and K. A. Fairman. 2001. "Effect of a Three-Tier Prescription Copay on Pharmaceutical and Other Medical Utilization." *Medical Care* 39 (12): 1293–1304.

Mukamel, D. B., and W. D. Spector. 2002. "The Competitive Nature of the Nursing Home Industry: Price Mark Ups and Demand Elasticities." *Applied Economics* 34: 413–20.

Muller, C. D., and A. C. Monheit. 1987. "Insurance Coverage and the Demand for Dental Care." *Journal of Health Economics* 7: 59–72.

Muris, Timothy J. 2002. "Everything Old Is New Again: Health Care and Competition in the 21st Century." Paper presented at Seventh Annual Competition in Health Care Forum, Chicago, IL, November 2.

National Committee for Quality Assurance. 1993. Health Plan Employer Data and Information Set (HEDIS) 2.0. Washington, DC.

National Health Policy Forum. 2004. *The Basics: SCHIP.* Washington, DC: George Washington University.

National Highway Traffic Safety Administration. 2003. *Traffic Safety Facts, 2003: A Compilation of Motor Vehicle Crash Data from the Fatality Analysis Reporting System and the General Estimates System.* Washington, DC: National Center for Statistics and Analysis, U.S. Department of Transportation.

Newhouse, J. P. 1996. "Reimbursing Health Plans and Health

Providers: Efficiency in Production Versus Selection." *Journal of Economic Literature* 34: 1236–63.

———. 1978. "Insurance Benefits, Out-of-Pocket Payments, and the Demand for Medical Care." *Health & Medical Care Services Review* 1 (4): 1, 3–15.

Newhouse, J. P., and the Insurance Experiment Group. 1993. *Free for All? Lessons from the RAND Health Insurance Experiment.* Cambridge, MA: Harvard University Press.

Newhouse, J. P., W. G. Manning, E. B. Keeler, and E. M. Sloss. 1989. "Adjusting Capitation Rates Using Objective Health Measures and Prior Utilization." *Health Care Financing Review* 10 (3): 41–54.

Newhouse, J. P., and C. E. Phelps. 1976. "New Estimates of Price and Income Elasticities." In *The Role of Health Insurance in the Health Services Sector*, edited by R. Rosett, 261–312. New York: National Bureau of Economic Research.

Numbers, R. L. 1979. "The Third Party: Health Insurance in America." In *The Therapeutic Revolution: Essays in the History of Medicine*, edited by H. J. Vogal and C. E. Rosenberg, 177–200. Philadelphia: University of Pennsylvania Press.

Nyman, J. A. 1999. "The Value of Health Insurance: The Access Motive." *Journal of Health Economics* 18 (2): 141–52.

Nyman, J. A. 1989. "Analysis of Nursing Home Use and Bed Supply in Wisconsin, 1983." *Health Services Research* 24 (4): 511–38.

Nyman, J. A., M. Finch, R. A. Kane, R. L. Kane and L. H. Illston.

1997. "The Substitutability of Adult Foster Care for Nursing Home Care in Oregon." *Medical Care* 35 (8): 801–13.

O'Grady, K. F., W. G. Manning, J. P. Newhouse, and R. H. Brook. 1985. "The Impact of Cost Sharing on Emergency Department Use." *New England Journal of Medicine* 313: 484–90.

Ohsfeldt, R. L., M. A. Morrisey, V. Johnson, and L. Nelson. 1998. "The Spread of Any Willing Provider Laws." *Health Services Research* 33 (5, part 2): 1537–62.

Ozanne, L. 1996. "How Will Medical Savings Accounts Affect Medical Spending?" *Inquiry* 33 (Fall): 225–36.

Palmer, J. L., and T. R. Saving. 2006. "A Message to the Public." [Online information.] www.ssa .gov/OACT/TRSUM/tr06 summary.pdf.

Parente, S. T., R. Feldman, and J. B. Christianson. 2004a. "Employee Choice of Consumer-Driven Health Insurance in a Multiplan, Multiproduct Setting." *Health Services Research* 39 (4, part II): 1091–1111.

———. 2004b. "Evaluation of the Effect of a Consumer-Driven Health Plan on Medical Care Expenditures and Utilization." *Health Services Research* 39 (4, part II): 1189–1209.

Park, C. 1999. "Prevalence of Employer Self-Insured Health Benefits: National and State Variation." Working paper, National Center for Health Statistics, Hyattsville, MD.

Pati, S., S. Shea, D. Rabinowitz, and O. Carasquillo. 2003. "Does Gatekeeping Control Costs for Privately Insured Children?

Findings from the 1996 Medical Expenditure Survey." *Pediatrics* 111 (3): 456–60.

Pauly, M. V. 1998. "Managed Care, Market Power, and Monopoly." *Health Services Research* 33 (5, Part II): 1439–60.

Pauly, M. V., B. Herring, and D. Song. 2002b. "Tax Credits, the Distribution of Subsidized Health Insurance Premiums, and the Uninsured." *Frontiers in Health Policy Research* 5: 103–22.

———. 2002a. "Health Insurance on the Internet and the Economics of Search." National Bureau of Economic Research working paper 9299. Cambridge, MA: National Bureau of Economic Research.

Pauly, M. V. and L. M. Nichols. 2002. "The Nongroup Health Insurance Market: Short On Facts, Long on Opinions and Policy Disputes." *Health Affairs* Web Exclusive, October 23.

Pauly, M. V., and A. M. Percy. 2000. "Cost and Performance: A Comparison of the Individual and Group Health Insurance Markets." *Journal of Health Politics, Policy and Law* 25 (1): 9–26.

Phelps, C. E. 2000. "Information Diffusion and Best Practice Adoption." In *Handbook of Health Economics*, vol. 1A, edited by A. J. Cuyler and J. P. Newhouse, 223–64. Amsterdam, Netherlands: Elsevier.

———. 1973. *The Demand for Health Insurance: A Theoretical and Empirical Investigation.* Rand Report R-1054-OEO. Santa Monica, CA.

Phelps, C. E., and J. P. Newhouse. 1972. "Effects of Coinsurance: A Multivariate Analysis." *Social Security Bulletin* 35: 20–29.

Physician Payment Review Commission. 1994. "A Comparison of Alternative Approaches to Risk Measurement." Selected External Research Series, no. 1. Washington, DC.

Pope, G. C., K. W. Adamache, R. K. Khandker, and E. G. Walsh. 1998. "Evaluating Alternative Risk Adjusters for Medicare." *Health Care Financing Review* 20 (2): 109–29.

Pope, G. C., J. Kautter, R. P. Ellis, A. S. Ash, J. Z. Avanian, L. I. Iezzoni, M. J. Ingber, J. M. Levy, and J. Robst. 2004. "Risk Adjustment of Medicare Capitation Payments Using the CMS-HCC Model." *Health Care Financing Review* 25 (4): 119–41.

Prospective Payment Assessment Commission. 1996. "Risk Selection and Risk Adjustment in Medicare." *Annual Report to Congress.* Washington, DC: Prospective Payment Assessment Commission.

Rector, T. S., M. D. Finch, P. M. Danzon, M. V. Pauly and G. S. Manda. 2003. "Effect of Tiered Prescription Copayments on the Use of Preferred Brand Medications." *Medical Care* 41 (3): 398–406.

Reischauer, R. D. 1997. "Medicare: Beyond 2002." In *Policy Options for Reforming the Medicare Program,* edited by S. H. Altman, U. E. Reinhardt, and D. Shactman. Princeton, NJ: Robert Wood Johnson Foundation, July.

Reschovsky, J. D. 1998. "The Roles of Medicaid and Economic Factors in the Demand for Nursing Home Care." *Health Services Research* 33 (4): 787–813.

Reynolds, L. G. 1976. *Microeconomics: Analysis and Policy.* Homewood, IL: Richard D. Irwin.

Rice, T., M. L. Graham, and P. D. Fox. 1997. "The Impact of Policy Standardization on the Medigap Market." *Inquiry* 34 (2): 106–16.

Robinson, J. C., and H. S. Luft. 1987. "Competition and the Cost of Hospital Care, 1972 to 1982." *Journal of the American Medical Association* 257 (23): 3241–45.

Robst, J. 2006. "Estimation of a Hedonic Pricing Model for Medigap Insurance." *Health Services Research* 41 (6): 2097–2113.

Roddy, P. C., J. Wallen, and S. M. Meyers. 1986. "Cost Sharing and Use of Health Services: The United Mine Workers of America Health Plan." *Medical Care* 24: 873–77.

Rogowski, J., A. K. Jain, and J .J. Escarce. 2007. "Hospital Competition, Managed Care, and Mortality after Hospitalization for Medical Conditions in California." *Health Services Research* 42 (2): 682–705.

Rothschild, M., and J. E. Stiglitz. 1976. "Equilibrium in Competitive Insurance Markets: An Essay on the Economics of Imperfect Information." *Quarterly Journal of Economics* 90: 629–49.

Royalty, A. B. 1999. "Tax Preferences for Fringe Benefits and Workers' Eligibility for Employer Health Insurance." *Journal of Public Economics* (forthcoming).

Royalty, A. B., and N. Solomon. 1999. "Health Plan Choice: Price Elasticities in a Managed Competition Setting." *Journal of Human Resources* 34 (1): 1–41.

Sari, N. 2002. "Do Competition and Managed Care Improve Quality?" *Health Economics* 11: 571–84.

Saver, B. G., and M. P. Doescher. 2000. "To Buy or Not to Buy: Factors Associated with the Purchase of Nongroup, Private Health Insurance." *Medical Care* 38: 141–51.

Scandlen, G. 2003. *Nothing but HSAs.* The Galen Institute, Consumer Choice Matters no. 41, November 25.

Scanlon, D., M. Chernew, C. McLaughlin, and G. Solon. 2002. "The Impact of Health Plan Report Cards on Managed Care Enrollment." *Journal of Health Economics* 21: 19–41.

Scanlon, W. 1980. "A Theory of the Nursing Home Market." *Inquiry* 17 (1): 25–41.

Scheffler, R. M. 1984. "The United Mine Workers' Health Plan." *Medical Care* 22: 247–54.

Scheffler, R. M., S. D. Sullivan, and T. H. Ko. 1991. "The Impact of Blue Cross and Blue Shield Plan Utilization Management Programs, 1980–1988." *Inquiry* 28: 263–75.

Schelelle, P. G., W. H. Rogers, and J. P. Newhouse. 1996. "The Effect of Cost Sharing on the Use of Chiropractic Services." *Medical Care* 34 (9): 863–72.

Scitovsky, A. A., and N. McCall. 1977. "Coinsurance and the Demand for Physician Services Four Years Later." *Social Security Bulletin* 40: 19–27.

Scitovsky, A. A., and N. M Snyder. 1972. "Effect of Coinsurance on the Use of Physician Services." *Social Security Bulletin* 35: 3–19.

Selby, J. B., B. H. Fireman, and B. E. Swain. 1996. Effect of a Copayment on the Use of the Emergency Department in a Health Maintenance Organization." *New England Journal of Medicine* 334 (10): 635–41.

Seldon, T. M. and B. M. Gray. 2006. "Tax Subsidies for Employment-Related Health Insurance: Estimates for 2006." *Health Affairs* 25 (6): 1568–79.

Sheiner, L. 1999. "Health Care Costs, Wages, and Aging." Working paper, Federal Reserve Board of Governors, Washington, DC.

Short, A., G. Mays, and J. Miller. 2003. "Disease Management: A Leap of Faith to Lower-Cost, Higher Quality Health Care." *Center for Studying Health System Change Issue Brief*, no. 69.

Simon, C. J., D. Dranove, and W. D. White. 1998. "The Effect of Managed Care on the Incomes of Primary Care and Specialty Physicians." *Health Services Research* 33 (3, part 1): 549–70.

Simon, K. I. 2001. "Displaced Workers and Employer-Provided Health Insurance: Evidence of a Wage/Fringe Benefit Tradeoff?" *International Journal of Health Care Finance and Economics* 1 (3/4): 249–72.

Siu, A. L. 1986. "Inappropriate Use of Hospitals in a Randomized Trial of Health Insurance Plans." *New England Journal of Medicine* 315: 1259–66.

Sloan, F. A. 1982. "Effects of Health Insurance on Physician Fees." *Journal of Human Resources* 17: 331–57.

Sloan, F. A., and K. Adamache. 1986. "Taxation and the Growth of Nonwage Benefits." *Public Finance Quarterly* 14: 115–39.

Sloan, F. A., and C. Conover. 1998. "Effects of State Reforms on Health insurance Coverage of Adults." *Inquiry* 35: 280–93.

Sloan, F. A., and M. W. Shayne. 1993. "Long-Term Care, Medicaid, and Impoverishment of the Elderly." *Milbank Quarterly* 71 (4): 575–99.

Starr, P. 1982. "The Triumph of Accommodation." In *The Social Transformation of American Medicine*, Book II, Chapter 2, 290–334. New York: Basic Books.

State of Florida. 2005. "Florida Medicaid Reform Implementation Plan, Tallahassee, FL." [Online information.] http://ahca .myflorida.com/Medicaid/ medicaid_reform/ implementationplan/index.shtml.

Stearns, S. C., and T. A. Mroz. 1995/96. "Premium Increases and Disenrollment from State Risk Pools." *Inquiry* 32 (Winter): 392–406.

Stigler, G. J. 1971. "The Theory of Economic Regulation." *Bell Journal of Economics and Management Science* 2: 1–21.

Stires, D. 2002. "The Coming Crash in Health Care." *Fortune* (October 14).

Taube, C. A., L. G. Kessler, and B. J. Burns. 1986. "Estimating the Probability and Level of Ambulatory Mental Health Services Use." *Health Services Research* 21: 321–40.

Thomasson, M. A. 2003. "The Importance of Group Coverage: How Tax Policy Shaped U.S. Health Insurance." *American Economic Review* 93 (4): 1373–84.

Thorpe, K. E., A. Hendricks, D. Garnick, K. Donelan, and J. P. Newhouse. 1992.

"Reducing the Number of Uninsured by Subsidizing Employment-Based Health Insurance: Results from a Pilot Study." *Journal of the American Medical Association* 267 (7): 945–48.

Thorpe, K. E., E. E. Seiber, and C. S. Florence. 2001. "The Impact of HMOs on Hospital-Based Uncompensated Care." *Journal of Health Politics, Policy and Law* 26 (3): 543–55.

Town, R., D. Wholey, R. Feldman, and L. R. Burns. 2005. "Did the HMO Revolution Cause Hospital Consolidation?" National Bureau of Economic Research working paper 11087. Cambridge, MA.

U.S. Congress, Senate Committee on the Judiciary. 2006. "Hearings June 20, 2006: The McCarran-Ferguson Act: Implications of Repealing the Insurers' Antitrust Exemption." [Online information.] http://judiciary.senate.gov/hearing.cfm?id=1952.

U.S. Department of Health and Human Services. 2006a. "Over 38 Million People with Medicare Now Receiving Prescription Drug Coverage." News release, June 14, 2006. [Online at http://hhs.gov/news/press/2006pres/20060614.html.]

———. 2006b. "The 2006 HHS Poverty Guidelines." [Online information.] http://aspe.hhs.gov/poverty/06poverty.shtml.

U.S. Department of Labor, Employee Benefit Security Administration. 2005. "An Employee's Guide to Health Benefits under COBRA." Washington, DC [Online information.] www.dol.gov/ebsa/pdf/cobraemployee.pdf.

U.S. Department of the Treasury. 2005. "All about HSAs." [Online information.] www.treasury.gov/offices/public-affairs/hsa/pdf/hsa-basics.pdf.

U.S. Government Accountability Office. 2005. *Federal Employees Health Benefit Program: Competition and Other Factors Linked to Wide Variation in Health Care Price.* Report GAO 05-856.

Van de Ven, W. P. M. M., and R. P. Ellis. 2000. "Risk Adjustment in Competitive Health Plan Markets." In *Handbook of Health Economics,* edited by A. J. Culyer and J. P. Newhouse, 755–845. Amsterdam, Netherlands: Elsevier.

Van Vliet, R. C. J. A. 2004. "Deductibles and Health Care Expenditures: Empirical Estimates of Price Sensitivity Based on Administrative Data." *International Journal of Health Care Finance and Economics* 4: 283–305.

Van Vliet, R. C. J. A., and W. P. M. M. van de Ven. 1992. "Towards a Capitation Formula for Competing Health Insurers: An Empirical Analysis." *Social Science and Medicine* 34: 1035–48.

Vistnes, J. P., M. A. Morrisey, and G. A. Jensen. 2006. "Employer Choices of Family Premium Sharing." *International Journal of Health Care Finance and Economics* 6 (1): 25–47.

Vita, M. G. 2001. "Regulatory Restrictions on Selective Contracting: An Empirical Analysis of Any Willing Provider Regulations." *Journal of Health Economics* 20 (6): 955–66.

Wall Street Journal. 2006. "More Employers Try Limited Health Plans." January 17, 2006, Section D, p. 17.

———. 2002. "Is All Fair in Health and Insurance?" July 30, 2002, Section D, p. 3.

———. 1991. "Tough Trade-off: Health Benefits Would Win-Out Over Pensions." December 17, 1991, Section A, p. 1.

———. 1987. "Proposals for Equal insurance Fees for Men and Women Spark Battle." August 27, 1987, Section 2, p. 1.

Wallen, J., P. Roddy, and M. Fahs. 1982. "Cost Sharing, Mental Health Visits and Physical Complaints in Retired Miners and Their Families." Paper presented at the American Public Health Association convention, Montreal.

Webb, D., J. F. Culhane, S. Snyder, and J. Greenspan. 2001. "Pennsylvania's Early Discharge Legislation: Effect on Maternity and Infant Lengths of Stay and Hospital Charges in Philadelphia." *Health Services Research* 36 (6, part 1): 1073–83.

Wedig, G. J., and M. Tai-Seale. 2002. "The Effect of Report Cards on Consumer Choice in the Health Insurance Market." *Journal of Health Economics* 21: 1031–48.

Weinberger, M., E. Z. Oddone, W. G. Henderson. 1996. "Does Increased Access to Primary Care Reduce Hospital Readmissions?" *New England Journal of Medicine* 334 (22): 1441–47.

Welch, W. P. 1986. "The Elasticity of Demand for Health Maintenance Organizations." *Journal of Human Resources* 21 (2): 252–66.

Wells, K. B., K. B. Keeler, and W. G. Manning. 1990. "Patterns of Outpatient Mental Health Care over Time: Some Implications for Estimates of Demand and Benefit Design." *Health Services Research* 24: 773–89.

Wheeler, J. R. C., and T. M. Wickizer. 1990. "Relating Health Care Market Characteristics to the Effectiveness of Utilization Review Programs." *Inquiry* 27: 344–51.

White, W. D., and M. A. Morrisey. 1998. "Are Patients Traveling Further?" *International Journal of the Economics of Business* 5 (2): 203–22.

Wickizer, T. M., J. R. C. Wheeler, and P. J. Feldstein. 1989. "Does Utilization Review Reduce Unnecessary Hospital Care and Contain Costs?" *Medical Care* 27 (6): 632–47.

Wilensky, G. R., and L. F. Rossiter. 1986. "Patient Self-Selection in HMOs." *Health Affairs* 5 (1): 66–80.

Woodbury, S. A. 1983. "Substitution between Wage and Nonwage Benefits." *American Economic Review* 73: 166–82.

Young, G. J., J. F. Burgess, Jr., and D. Valley. 2002. "Competition among Hospitals for HMO Business: Effect of Price and Nonprice Attributes." *Health Services Research* 37 (5): 1267–89.

Zarabozo, C. 2000. "Milestones in Medicare Managed Care." *Health Care Financing Review* 22 (1): 61–67.

Ziller, E. C., A. F. Coburn, R. T. D. McBride, and C. Andrews. 2004. "Patterns of Individual Health Insurance Coverage, 1996–2000." *Health Affairs* 23 (6): 210–21.

Zuckerman, S., and S. Rajan. 1999. "An Alternative Approach to Measuring the Effects of Insurance Market Reforms." *Inquiry* 36: 44–56.

Zwanziger, J. 2002. "Physician Fees and Managed Care Plans." *Inquiry* 39: 184–93.

Zwanziger, J., and A. Meirowitz. 1998. "Strategic Factors in Hospital Selection for HMO and PPO Networks." In *Managed Care and Changing Health Care Markets*, edited by M.A. Morrisey, 77–94. Washington, DC: AEI Press.

Zwanziger, J., and G. A. Melnick. 1988. "The Effects of Hospital Competition and the Medicare PPS Program on Hospital Cost Behavior in California." *Journal of Health Economics* 7: 301–20.

NAME INDEX

SUBJECT INDEX

Page numbers in *italics* identify illustrations. An italic *t* next to a page number (e.g., 241*t*) indicates information that appears in a table.

ABOUT THE AUTHOR

Michael A. Morrisey is a professor in the Department of Health Care Organization and Policy in the School of Public Health at the University of Alabama at Birmingham (UAB), where he has taught health insurance for more than 18 years. He is the director of the UAB Lister Hill Center for Health Policy and holds appointments in several other UAB departments and centers. Prior to coming to UAB, he was senior economist with the American Hospital Association. He is the author of over 140 research papers, many dealing with employee-sponsored health insurance and managed care. He is a fellow of the Employee Benefits Research Institute. His other research interests include hospital economics, organization, finance, and pricing; the role of regulation in health and healthcare markets; and the professional activities of health economists.

Dr. Morrisey was the first recipient of the John Thompson Prize for health services research, awarded by the Association of University Programs in Health Administration, and he serves on the editorial boards of several journals, including *Health Affairs* and *Medical Care Research and Review*. He was an officer of the International Health Economics Association for over ten years. He is a recipient of the UAB President's Award for teaching and the UAB School of Public Health Distinguished Investigator Award. He holds a BA in economics from Northern State University in South Dakota and a Ph.D. in economics from the University of Washington (Seattle).